O'

Democracy's Discontent

America in Search of a Public Philosophy

Michael J. Sandel

THE BELKNAP PRESS OF
HARVARD UNIVERSITY PRESS
Cambridge, Massachusetts
London, England

First Harvard University Press paperback edition, 1998

Library of Congress Cataloging-in-Publication Data

Sandel, Michael J.
Democracy's discontent :
America in search of a public philosophy /
Michael J. Sandel.
p.   cm.
Includes bibliographical references and index.
ISBN 0-674-19744-5 (cloth)
ISBN 0-674-19745-3 (pbk.)
1. Democracy—United States.
2. Liberalism—United States.
3. Citizenship—United States.
I. Title.
JK1726.S325   1996
320.973—dc20   95-46825

For Kiku

Contents

Preface

Political philosophy seems often to reside at a distance from the world. Principles are one thing, politics another, and even our best efforts to live up to our ideals seldom fully succeed. Philosophy may indulge our moral aspirations, but politics deals in recalcitrant facts. Indeed some would say the trouble with American democracy is that we take our ideals too seriously, that our zeal for reform outruns our respect for the gap between theory and practice.

But if political philosophy is unrealizable in one sense, it is unavoidable in another. This is the sense in which philosophy inhabits the world from the start; our practices and institutions are embodiments of theory. We could hardly describe our political life, much less engage in it, without recourse to a language laden with theory—of rights and obligations, citizenship and freedom, democracy and law. Political institutions are not simply instruments that implement ideas independently conceived; they are themselves embodiments of ideas. For all we may resist such ultimate questions as the meaning of justice and the nature of the good life, what we cannot escape is that we live some answer to these questions—we live some *theory*—all the time.

In this book I explore the theory we live now, in contemporary America. My aim is to identify the public philosophy implicit in our practices and institutions and to show how tensions in the philosophy show up in the practice. If theory never keeps its distance but inhabits the world from the start, we may find a clue to our condition in the theory that we live. Attending to the theory implicit in our public life may help us to diagnose our political condition. It may also reveal that the predicament of American democracy resides not only in the gap between our ideals and institutions, but also within the ideals themselves, and within the self-image our public life reflects.

Part I of this book took form as the Julius Rosenthal Foundation Lectures at Northwestern University School of Law in 1989. I am grateful to Dean Robert W. Bennett and the faculty for their warm hospitality and searching questions, and also for their permission to incorporate the lectures into this larger project. I also benefited from opportunities to try out portions of this book on faculty and students at Brown University, the University of California at Berkeley, Indiana University, New York University, Oxford University, Princeton University, the University of Utah, the University of Virginia, the Institute for Human Sciences in Vienna, and at sessions of the American Political Science Association, the Association of American Law Schools, the Society for Ethical and Legal Philosophy, and the Harvard University Law School Faculty Workshop. Portions of Chapters 3 and 4 appeared, in earlier versions, in *Utah Law Review*, 1989, pp. 597–615; and in *California Law Review*, 77 (1989), 521–538, respectively.

For generous support of the research and writing of this book, I am grateful to the Ford Foundation, the American Council of Learned Societies, the National Endowment for the Humanities, and Harvard Law School's Summer Research Program. Colleagues in the Department of Government and the Law School at Harvard provided a constant source of stimulating conversation on the themes of this book. I am especially indebted to the Harvard graduate and law students in my course, "Law and Political Theory: The Liberal and Republican Traditions," who subjected my arguments to vigorous critical scrutiny. I owe special thanks to friends who, at various stages of this project, gave me the benefit of extensive written comments on parts or all of the manuscript: Alan Brinkley, Richard Fallon, Bonnie Honig, George Kateb, Stephen Macedo, Jane Mansbridge, Quentin Skinner, and Judith Jarvis Thomson. John Bauer and Russ Muirhead provided research assistance that went far beyond the gathering of information and did much to inform my thinking. At Harvard University Press, I was fortunate to work with Aida Donald, an exemplary editor and a patient one, and with Ann Hawthorne, who saw the book through its final stages with skill and care. My greatest regret about this book is that my friend and colleague Judith N. Shklar did not live to see it finished. Dita disagreed with much of what I had to say, and yet from my first days at Harvard was a wellspring of encouragement and advice, of buoyant and bracing intellectual camaraderie.

During the time I worked on this book, my sons Adam and Aaron grew from babies to boys. They made these years of writing a season of joy. Finally, this work reflects much that I have learned from my wife, Kiku Adatto, a gifted writer on American culture. She did more than anyone else to improve this book, which I dedicate to her with love.

Democracy's Discontent

I

The Constitution of the Procedural Republic

1

The Public Philosophy of Contemporary Liberalism

Times of trouble prompt us to recall the ideals by which we live. But in America today, this is not an easy thing to do. At a time when democratic ideals seem ascendant abroad, there is reason to wonder whether we have lost possession of them at home. Our public life is rife with discontent. Americans do not believe they have much say in how they are governed and do not trust government to do the right thing.[1] Despite the achievements of American life in the last half-century—victory in World War II, unprecedented affluence, greater social justice for women and minorities, the end of the Cold War—our politics is beset with anxiety and frustration.

The political parties, meanwhile, are unable to make sense of our condition. The main topics of national debate—the proper scope of the welfare state, the extent of rights and entitlements, the proper degree of government regulation—take their shape from the arguments of an earlier day. These are not unimportant topics; but they do not reach the two concerns that lie at the heart of democracy's discontent. One is the fear that, individually and collectively, we are losing control of the forces that govern our lives. The other is the sense that, from family to neighborhood to nation, the moral fabric of community is unraveling around us. These two fears—for the loss of self-government and the erosion of community—together define the anxiety of the age. It is an anxiety that the prevailing political agenda has failed to answer or even address.

Why is American politics ill equipped to allay the discontent that now engulfs it? The answer lies beyond the political arguments of our day, in the public philosophy that animates them. By public philosophy, I mean the political theory implicit in our practice, the assumptions about citizenship and freedom that inform our public life. The inability of contemporary American politics to speak convincingly about self-government and community has something to do with the public philosophy by which we live.

A public philosophy is an elusive thing, for it is constantly before our eyes. It forms the often unreflective background to our political discourse and pursuits. In ordinary times, the public philosophy can easily escape the notice of those who live by it. But anxious times compel a certain clarity. They force first principles to the surface and offer an occasion for critical reflection.

Liberal and Republican Freedom

The political philosophy by which we live is a certain version of liberal political theory. Its central idea is that government should be neutral toward the moral and religious views its citizens espouse. Since people disagree about the best way to live, government should not affirm in law any particular vision of the good life. Instead, it should provide a framework of rights that respects persons as free and independent selves, capable of choosing their own values and ends.[2] Since this liberalism asserts the priority of fair procedures over particular ends, the public life it informs might be called the procedural republic.[3]

In describing the prevailing political philosophy as a version of liberal political theory, it is important to distinguish two different meanings of liberalism. In the common parlance of American politics, liberalism is the opposite of conservatism; it is the outlook of those who favor a more generous welfare state and a greater measure of social and economic equality.[4] In the history of political theory, however, liberalism has a different, broader meaning. In this historical sense, liberalism describes a tradition of thought that emphasizes toleration and respect for individual rights and that runs from John Locke, Immanuel Kant, and John Stuart

Mill to John Rawls. The public philosophy of contemporary American politics is a version of this liberal tradition of thought, and most of our debates proceed within its terms.

The idea that freedom consists in our capacity to choose our ends finds prominent expression in our politics and law. Its province is not limited to those known as liberals rather than conservatives in American politics; it can be found across the political spectrum. Republicans sometimes argue, for example, that taxing the rich to pay for welfare programs is a form of coerced charity that violates people's freedom to choose what to do with their own money. Democrats sometimes argue that government should assure all citizens a decent level of income, housing, and health, on the grounds that those who are crushed by economic necessity are not truly free to exercise choice in other domains. Although the two sides disagree about how government should act to respect individual choice, both assume that freedom consists in the capacity of persons to choose their values and ends.

So familiar is this vision of freedom that it seems a permanent feature of the American political and constitutional tradition. But Americans have not always understood freedom in this way. As a reigning public philosophy, the version of liberalism that informs our present debates is a recent arrival, a development of the last forty or fifty years. Its distinctive character can best be seen by contrast with a rival public philosophy that it gradually displaced. This rival public philosophy is a version of republican political theory.

Central to republican theory is the idea that liberty depends on sharing in self-government. This idea is not by itself inconsistent with liberal freedom. Participating in politics can be one among the ways in which people choose to pursue their ends. According to republican political theory, however, sharing in self-rule involves something more. It means deliberating with fellow citizens about the common good and helping to shape the destiny of the political community. But to deliberate well about the common good requires more than the capacity to choose one's ends and to respect others' rights to do the same. It requires a knowledge of public affairs and also a sense of belonging, a concern for the whole, a moral bond with the community whose fate is at stake. To share in self-rule therefore requires that citizens possess, or come to acquire, certain qualities of character, or civic virtues. But this means that republican politics cannot be neutral toward the values and ends its citizens espouse. The republican conception of freedom, unlike the liberal conception, requires a formative politics, a politics that cultivates in citizens the qualities of character self-government requires.

Both the liberal and republican conceptions of freedom have been present throughout our political experience, but in shifting measure and relative importance. Broadly speaking, republicanism predominated earlier in American history, liberalism later. In recent decades, the civic or formative aspect of our politics has largely given way to the liberalism that conceives persons as free and independent selves, unencumbered by moral or civic ties they have not chosen.

This shift sheds light on our present political predicament. For despite its appeal, the liberal vision of freedom lacks the civic resources to sustain self-government. This defect ill-equips it to address the sense of disempowerment that afflicts our public life. The public philosophy by which we live cannot secure the liberty it promises, because it cannot inspire the sense of community and civic engagement that liberty requires.

How the liberal conception of citizenship and freedom gradually crowded out the republican conception involves two intersecting tales. One traces the advent of the procedural republic from the first stirrings of American constitutionalism to recent debates about religious liberty, free speech, and privacy rights. Another traces the decline of the civic strand of American political discourse from Thomas Jefferson's day to the present.[5]

These stories, taken together, bring to clarity the self-image that animates—and sometimes debilitates—our public life. They do not reveal a golden age when all was right with American democracy. The republican tradition coexisted with slavery, with the exclusion of women from the public realm, with property qualifications for voting, with nativist hostility to immigrants; indeed it sometimes provided the terms within which these practices were defended.

And yet, for all its episodes of darkness, the republican tradition, with its emphasis on community and self-government, may offer a corrective to our impoverished civic life. Recalling the republican conception of freedom as self-rule may prompt us to pose questions we have forgotten how to ask: What economic arrangements are hospitable to self-government? How might our political discourse engage rather than avoid the moral and religious convictions people bring to the public realm? And how might the public life of a pluralist society cultivate in citizens the expansive self-understandings that civic engagement requires? If the public philosophy of our day leaves little room for civic considerations, it may help to recall how earlier generations of Americans debated such questions, before the procedural republic took hold. But in order to identify the relevant strands of the story, we need to specify more fully the version of liberalism that informs our present politics.

The Aspiration to Neutrality

The idea that government should be neutral on the question of the good life is distinctive to modern political thought. Ancient political theory held that the purpose of politics was to cultivate the virtue, or moral excellence, of citizens. All associations aim at some good, Aristotle wrote, and the polis, or political association, aims at the highest, most comprehensive good: "any polis which is truly so called, and is not merely one in name, must devote itself to the end of encouraging goodness. Otherwise, a political association sinks into a mere alliance, which only differs in space from other forms of alliance where the members live at a distance from one another. Otherwise, too, law becomes a mere covenant—or (in the phrase of the Sophist Lycophron) 'a guarantor of men's rights against one another'—instead of being, as it should be, a rule of life such as will make the members of a polis good and just."[6]

According to Aristotle, political community is more than "an association for residence on a common site, or for the sake of preventing mutual injustice and easing exchange." Although these are necessary conditions for political community, they are not its purpose or ultimate justification. "The end and purpose of a polis is the good life, and the institutions of social life are means to that end." It is only as participants in political association that we can realize our nature and fulfill our highest ends.[7]

Unlike the ancient conception, liberal political theory does not see political life as concerned with the highest human ends or with the moral excellence of its citizens. Rather than promote a particular conception of the good life, liberal political theory insists on toleration, fair procedures, and respect for individual rights—values that respect people's freedom to choose their own values. But this raises a difficult question. If liberal ideals cannot be defended in the name of the highest human good, then in what does their moral basis consist?

It is sometimes thought that liberal principles can be justified by a simple version of moral relativism. Government should not "legislate morality," because all morality is merely subjective, a matter of personal preference not open to argument or rational debate. "Who is to say what is literature and what is filth? That is a value judgment, and whose values should decide?" Relativism usually appears less as a claim than as a question: "Who is to judge?" But the same question can be asked of the values that liberals defend. Toleration and freedom and fairness are values too, and they can hardly be defended by the claim that no values can be defended. So it is a mistake to affirm liberal values by arguing that all values are merely subjective. The relativist defense of liberalism is no defense at all.

Utilitarianism versus Kantian Liberalism

What, then, is the case for the neutrality the liberal invokes? Recent political philosophy has offered two main alternatives—one utilitarian, the other Kantian.[8] The utilitarian view, following John Stuart Mill, defends liberal principles in the name of maximizing the general welfare. The state should not impose on its citizens a preferred way of life, even for their own good, because doing so will reduce the sum of human happiness, at least in the long run. It is better that people choose for themselves, even if, on occasion, they get it wrong.

"The only freedom which deserves the name," writes Mill in *On Liberty*, "is that of pursuing our own good in our own way, so long as we do not attempt to deprive others of theirs, or impede their efforts to obtain it." He adds that his argument does not depend on any notion of abstract right, only on the principle of the greatest good for the greatest number. "I regard utility as the ultimate appeal on all ethical questions; but it must be utility in the largest sense, grounded on the permanent interests of man as a progressive being."[9]

Many objections have been raised against utilitarianism as a general doctrine of moral philosophy. Some have questioned the concept of utility and the assumption that all human goods are in principle commensurable. Others have objected that by reducing all values to preferences and desires, utilitarians are unable to admit qualitative distinctions of worth, unable to distinguish noble desires from base ones. But most recent debate has focused on whether utilitarianism offers a convincing basis for liberal principles, including respect for individual rights.[10]

At first glance, utilitarianism seems well suited to liberal purposes. Seeking to maximize overall happiness does not require judging people's values, only aggregating them. And the willingness to aggregate preferences without judging them suggests a tolerant spirit, even a democratic one. When people go to the polls we count their votes, whatever they are.

But the utilitarian calculus is not always as liberal as it first appears. If enough cheering Romans pack the Coliseum to watch the lion devour the Christian, the collective pleasure of the Romans will surely outweigh the pain of the Christian, intense though it be. Or if a big majority abhors a small religion and wants it banned, the balance of preferences will favor suppression, not toleration. Utilitarians sometimes defend individual rights on the grounds that respecting them now will serve utility in the long run. But this calculation is precarious and contingent. It hardly secures the liberal promise not to impose on some the values of others.

The case against utilitarianism was made most powerfully by Immanuel Kant. He argued that empirical principles such as utility were unfit to serve as a basis for morality. A wholly instrumental defense of freedom and rights not only leaves rights vulnerable but fails to respect the inherent dignity of persons. The utilitarian calculus treats people as means to the happiness of others, not as ends in themselves, worthy of respect.[11]

Contemporary liberals extend Kant's argument with the claim that utilitarianism fails to take seriously the distinction between persons. In seeking above all to maximize the general welfare, the utilitarian treats society as a whole as if it were a single person; it conflates our many, diverse desires into a single system of desires. It is indifferent to the distribution of satisfactions among persons, except insofar as this may affect the overall sum. But this fails to respect our plurality and distinctness. It uses some as means to the happiness of all, and so fails to respect each as an end in himself or herself.

In the view of modern-day Kantians, certain rights are so fundamental that even the general welfare cannot override them. As John Rawls writes in *A Theory of Justice*, "Each person possesses an inviolability founded on justice that even the welfare of society as a whole cannot override.... The rights secured by justice are not subject to political bargaining or to the calculus of social interests."[12]

So Kantian liberals need an account of rights that does not depend on utilitarian considerations. More than this, they need an account that does not depend on any particular conception of the good, that does not presuppose the superiority of one way of life over others. Only a justification neutral among ends could preserve the liberal resolve not to favor any particular ends or to impose on its citizens a preferred way of life. But what sort of justification could this be? How is it possible to affirm certain liberties and rights as fundamental without embracing some vision of the good life, without endorsing some ends over others?

The solution proposed by Kantian liberals is to draw a distinction between the "right" and the "good"—between a framework of basic rights and liberties, and the conceptions of the good that people may choose to pursue within the framework. It is one thing for the state to support a fair framework, they argue, something else to affirm some particular ends. For example, it is one thing to defend the right to free speech so that people may be free to form their own opinions and choose their own ends, but something else to support it on grounds that a life of political discussion is inherently worthier than a life unconcerned with public affairs, or on the grounds that free speech will increase the general welfare. Only the first defense is available on the Kantian view, resting as it does on the ideal of a neutral framework.

Now the commitment to a framework neutral with respect to ends can be seen as a kind of value—in this sense the Kantian liberal is no relativist—but its value consists precisely in its refusal to affirm a preferred way of life or conception of the good. For Kantian liberals, then, the right is prior to the good, and in two senses. First, individual rights cannot be sacrificed for the sake of the general good; and second, the principles of justice that specify these rights cannot be premised on any particular vision of the good life. What justifies the rights is not that they maximize the general welfare or otherwise promote the good, but rather that they constitute a fair framework within which individuals and groups can choose their own values and ends, consistent with a similar liberty for others.

The claim for the priority of the right over the good connects the ideal of neutrality with the primacy of individual rights. For Kantian liberals, rights "function as trump cards held by individuals." They protect individuals from policies, even democratically enacted ones, that would impose a preferred conception of the good and so fail to respect people's freedom to choose their own conceptions.[13]

Of course, proponents of the liberal ethic notoriously disagree about what rights are fundamental and what political arrangements the ideal of the neutral framework requires. Egalitarian liberals support the welfare state and favor a scheme of civil liberties together with certain social and economic rights—rights to welfare, education, health care, and so on. They argue that respecting the capacity of persons to pursue their own ends requires government to assure the minimal prerequisites of a dignified life. Libertarian liberals (usually called conservatives in contemporary politics) defend the market economy and claim that redistributive policies violate people's rights. They argue that respect for persons requires assuring to each the fruits of his or her own labor, and so favor a scheme of civil liberties combined with a strict regime of private property rights. Whether egalitarian or libertarian, Kantian liberalism begins with the claim that we are separate, individual persons, each with our own aims, interests, and conceptions of the good life. It seeks a framework of rights that will enable us to realize our capacity as free moral agents, consistent with a similar liberty for others.

The Liberal Self

The Kantian case against utilitarianism derives much of its force from its contrasting conception of the person, its view of what it means to be a moral agent. Where utilitarians conflate our many desires into a single system of desire, Kantian liberals insist on the separateness of persons. Where the utilitarian self is simply defined as the sum of its desires, the

Kantian self is a choosing self, independent of the desires and ends it may have at any moment. Kant expressed this idea by attributing to human beings the capacity to act with an autonomous will. Contemporary liberals rely on the similar notion of a self given prior to and independent of its purposes and ends.

The claim for the priority of the right over the good, and the conception of the person that attends it, oppose Kantian liberalism not only to utilitarianism but also to any view that regards us as obligated to fulfill ends we have not chosen—ends given by nature or God, for example, or by our identities as members of families, peoples, cultures, or traditions. Encumbered identities such as these are at odds with the liberal conception of the person as free and independent selves, unbound by prior moral ties, capable of choosing our ends for ourselves. This is the conception that finds expression in the ideal of the state as a neutral framework. For Kantian liberals, it is precisely because we are freely choosing, independent selves that we need a neutral framework, a framework of rights that refuses to choose among competing values and ends. For the liberal self, what matters above all, what is most essential to our personhood, is not the ends we choose but our capacity to choose them. "It is not our aims that primarily reveal our nature," but rather the framework of rights we would agree to if we could abstract from our aims. "For the self is prior to the ends which are affirmed by it; even a dominant end must be chosen from among numerous possibilities."[14]

The liberal ethic derives much of its moral force from the appeal of the self-image that animates it. This appeal has at least two sources. First, the image of the self as free and independent, unencumbered by aims and attachments it does not choose for itself, offers a powerful liberating vision. Freed from the sanctions of custom and tradition and inherited status, unbound by moral ties antecedent to choice, the liberal self is installed as sovereign, cast as the author of the only obligations that constrain. More than the simple sum of circumstance, we become capable of the dignity that consists in being persons of our "own creating, making, choosing."[15] We are agents and not just instruments of the purposes we pursue. We are "self-originating sources of valid claims."[16]

A second appeal of the liberal self-image consists in the case it implies for equal respect. The idea that there is more to a person than the roles he plays or the customs she keeps or the faith he affirms suggests a basis for respect independent of life's contingencies. Liberal justice is blind to such differences between persons as race, religion, ethnicity, and gender, for in the liberal self-image, these features do not really define our identity in the first place. They are not constituents but merely attributes of the self, the sort of things the state should look beyond. "Our social position and class, our sex and race should not influence deliberations made from a moral point of view."[17] Once these contingencies are seen as products of our situation rather than as aspects of our person, they cease to supply the familiar grounds for prejudice and discrimination.

Nor does it matter, from the standpoint of liberal justice, what virtues we display or what values we espouse. "That we have one conception of the good rather than another is not relevant from a moral standpoint. In acquiring it we are influenced by the same sort of contingencies that lead us to rule out a knowledge of our sex and class."[18] Despite their many differences, libertarian and egalitarian liberals agree that people's entitlements should not be based on their merit or virtue or moral desert, for the qualities that make people virtuous or morally deserving depend on factors "arbitrary from a moral point of view."[19] The liberal state therefore does not discriminate; none of its policies or laws may presuppose that any person or way of life is intrinsically more virtuous than any other. It respects persons as persons, and secures their equal right to live the lives they choose.

Critique of Kantian Liberalism

Kantian liberals thus avoid affirming a conception of the good by affirming instead the priority of the right, which depends in turn on a picture of the self given prior to its ends. But how plausible is this self-conception? Despite its powerful appeal, the image of the unencumbered self is flawed. It cannot make sense of our moral experience, because it cannot account for certain moral and political obligations that we commonly recognize, even prize. These include obligations of solidarity, religious duties, and other moral ties that may claim us for reasons unrelated to a choice. Such obligations are difficult to account for if we understand ourselves as free and independent selves, unbound by moral ties we have not chosen. Unless we think of ourselves as encumbered selves, already claimed by certain projects and commitments, we cannot make sense of these indispensable aspects of our moral and political experience.

Consider the limited scope of obligation on the liberal view. According to Rawls, obligations can arise in only one of two ways, as "natural duties" we owe to human beings as such or as voluntary obligations we incur by consent. The natural duties are those we owe persons *qua* persons—to do justice, to avoid cruelty, and so on. All other obligations, the ones we owe to particular others, are founded in consent and arise only in virtue of agreements we make, be they tacit or explicit.[20]

Conceived as unencumbered selves, we must respect the dignity of all persons, but beyond this, we owe only what we agree to owe. Liberal justice requires that we respect people's rights (as defined by the neutral framework), not that we advance their good. Whether we must concern ourselves with other people's good depends on whether, and with whom, and on what terms, we have agreed to do so.

One striking consequence of this view is that "there is no political obligation, strictly speaking, for citizens generally." Although those who run for office voluntarily incur a political obligation (that is, to serve their country if elected), the ordinary citizen does not. "It is not clear what is the requisite binding action or who has performed it."[21] The average citizen is therefore without any special obligations to his or her fellow citizens, apart from the universal, natural duty not to commit injustice.

The liberal attempt to construe all obligation in terms of duties universally owed or obligations voluntarily incurred makes it difficult to account for civic obligations and other moral and political ties that we commonly recognize. It fails to capture those loyalties and responsibilities whose moral force consists partly in the fact that living by them is inseparable from understanding ourselves as the particular persons we are—as members of this family or city or nation or people, as bearers of that history, as citizens of this republic. Loyalties such as these can be more than values I happen to have, and to hold, at a certain distance. The moral responsibilities they entail may go beyond the obligations I voluntarily incur and the "natural duties" I owe to human beings as such.[22]

Some of the special responsibilities that flow from the particular communities I inhabit I may owe to fellow members, such as obligations of solidarity. Others I may owe to members of those communities with which my own community has some morally relevant history, such as the morally burdened relations of Germans to Jews, of American whites to American blacks, or of England and France to their former colonies.[23] Whether they look inward or outward, obligations of membership presuppose that we are capable of moral ties antecedent to choice. To the extent that we are, the meaning of our membership resists redescription in contractarian terms.

It is sometimes argued, in defense of the liberal view, that loyalties and allegiances not grounded in consent, however psychologically compelling, are matters of sentiment, not of morality, and so do not suggest an obligation unavailable to unencumbered selves. But it is difficult to make sense of certain familiar moral and political dilemmas without acknowledging obligations of solidarity and the thickly constituted, encumbered selves that they imply.

Consider the case of Robert E. Lee on the eve of the Civil War. Lee, then an officer in the Union army, opposed secession, in fact regarded it as treason. And yet when war loomed, Lee concluded that his obligation to Virginia outweighed his obligation to the Union and also his reported opposition to slavery. "With all my devotion to the Union," he wrote, "I have not been able to make up my mind to raise my hand against my relatives, my children, my home. . . . If the Union is dissolved, and the Government disrupted, I shall return to my native State and share the miseries of my people. Save in her defense, I will draw my sword no more."[24]

One can appreciate the poignance of Lee's predicament without necessarily approving of the choice he made. But one cannot make sense of his dilemma as a *moral* dilemma without acknowledging that the call to stand with his people, even to lead them in a cause he opposed, was a claim of moral and not merely sentimental import, capable at least of weighing in the balance against other duties and obligations. Otherwise, Lee's predicament was not really a moral dilemma at all, but simply a conflict between morality on the one hand and mere sentiment or prejudice on the other.

A merely psychological reading of Lee's predicament misses the fact that we not only sympathize with people such as Lee but often admire them, not necessarily for the choices they make but for the quality of character their deliberation reflects. The quality at stake is the disposition to see and bear one's life circumstance as a reflectively situated being— claimed by the history that implicates me in a particular life, but self-conscious of its particularity, and so alive to other ways, wider horizons. But this is precisely the quality that is lacking in those who would think of themselves as unencumbered selves, bound only by the obligations they choose to incur.

As the Lee example illustrates, the liberal conception of the person is too thin to account for the full range of moral and political obligations we commonly recognize, such as obligations of solidarity. This counts against its plausibility generally. But it may even be too weak to support the less strenuous communal obligations expected of citizens in the modern welfare state. Some stronger conception of community may be required, not only to make sense of tragic-heroic dilemmas such as Lee's, but even to sustain the rights that many liberals defend.

While libertarian liberals ask little of citizens, more generous expressions of the liberal ethic support various policies of public provision and redistribution. Egalitarian liberals defend social and economic rights as well as civil and political rights, and so demand of their fellow citizens a high measure of mutual engagement. They insist on the "plurality and distinctness" of individuals but also require that we "share one another's fate" and regard the distribution of natural talents as "a common asset."[25]

Liberalism as an ethic of sharing emphasizes the arbitrariness of fortune and the importance of certain material prerequisites for the meaningful exercise of equal liberties. Since "necessitous men are not free men," and since in any case the distribution of assets and endowments that make for success is "arbitrary from a moral point of view," egalitarian liberals would tax the rich to help the poor secure the prerequisites of a dignified life. Thus the liberal case for the welfare state depends not on a theory of the common good or on some strong notion of communal obligation, but instead on the rights we would agree to respect if we could abstract from our interests and ends.

The liberal case for public provision seems well suited to conditions in which strong communal ties cannot be relied on, and this is one source of its appeal. But it lies vulnerable nonetheless to the libertarian objection that redistributive policies use some people as means to others' ends, and so offend the "plurality and distinctness" of individuals that liberalism seeks above all to secure.[26] In the contractual vision of community alone, it is unclear how the libertarian objection can be met. If those whose fate I am required to share really are, morally speaking, *others,* rather than fellow participants in a way of life with which my identity is bound, then liberalism as an ethic of sharing seems open to the same objections as utilitarianism. Its claim on me is not the claim of a community with which I identify, but rather the claim of an arbitrarily defined collectivity whose aims I may or may not share.

If the egalitarian replies that social and economic rights are required as a matter of equal respect for persons, the question remains why *these* persons, the ones who happen to live in my country, have a claim on my concern that others do not. Tying the mutual responsibilities of citizenship to the idea of respect for persons *qua* persons puts the moral case for welfare on a par with the case for foreign aid—a duty we owe strangers with whom we share a common humanity but possibly little else. Given its conception of the person, it is unclear how liberalism can defend the particular boundaries of concern its own ethic of sharing must presuppose.

What egalitarian liberalism requires, but cannot within its own terms provide, is some way of defining the relevant community of sharing, some way of seeing the participants as mutually indebted and morally engaged to begin with. It needs a way of answering Emerson's challenge to the man who solicited his contribution to the poor—"Are they *my* poor?"[27] Since liberal social and economic rights cannot be justified as expressing or advancing a common life of shared pursuits, the basis and bounds of communal concern become difficult to defend. For as we have seen, the strong notion of community or membership that would save and situate the sharing is precisely the one denied to the liberal self. The moral encumbrances and antecedent obligations it implies would undercut the priority of right.

Minimalist Liberalism

If we are not the freely choosing, unencumbered selves that Kantian liberals imagine us to be, does it follow that government need not be neutral, that politics should cultivate the virtue of its citizens after all? Some political philosophers argue that the case for neutrality can be detached from the Kantian conception of the person. The case for liberalism, they argue, is political, not philosophical or metaphysical, and so does not depend on controversial claims about the nature of the self. The priority of the right over the good is not the application to politics of Kantian moral philosophy, but a practical response to the familiar fact that people in modern democratic societies typically disagree about the good. Since this defense of neutrality does not depend on a Kantian conception of the person but instead "stays on the surface, philosophically speaking," it might be described as minimalist liberalism.[28]

Minimalist liberals acknowledge that we may sometimes be claimed by moral or religious obligations unrelated to a choice. But they insist that we set these obligations aside when we enter the public realm, that we bracket our moral and religious convictions when deliberating about politics and law. In our personal lives, we may regard it as unthinkable to view ourselves "apart from certain religious, philosophical, and moral convictions, or from certain enduring attachments and loyalties." But we should draw a distinction between our personal and our political identities. However encumbered we may be in private, however claimed by moral or religious convictions, we should bracket our encumbrances in public and regard ourselves, *qua* public selves, as independent of any particular loyalties or conceptions of the good.[29]

The insistence that we separate our identity as citizens from our identity as persons gives rise to an obvious challenge. Why should our political identities not express the moral and religious convictions we affirm in our personal lives? Why, in deliberating about justice and rights, must we set aside the moral judgments that inform the rest of our lives? Minimalist liberals reply that separating our identity as citizens from our identity as persons honors an important fact about modern democratic life. In traditional societies, people sought to shape political life in the image of their own moral and religious ideals. But modern democratic societies are marked by a plurality of moral and religious ideals. Moreover, this pluralism is reasonable; it reflects the fact that, even after reasoned reflection, decent, intelligent people will come to different conceptions about the nature of the good life. Given the fact of reasonable pluralism, we should try to decide questions of justice and rights without affirming one conception of the good over others. Only in this way can we affirm the political value of social cooperation based on mutual respect.[30]

Minimalist liberalism seeks to detach liberal principles from political controversy, including debates about the nature of the self. It presents itself "not as a conception of justice that is true," but as one that can serve as a basis for political agreement in a democratic society. It asserts "the priority of democracy over philosophy." It offers a political conception of justice, not a metaphysical or philosophical one.[31]

The minimalist case for liberalism depends on the plausibility of separating politics from philosophy, of bracketing moral and religious questions where politics is concerned. But this raises the question why the practical interest in securing social cooperation and mutual respect is always so compelling as to defeat any competing moral interest that could arise from within a substantive moral or religious view. One way of assuring the priority of the practical is to deny that any of the moral or religious conceptions it brackets could be true. But this is precisely the sort of controversial metaphysical claim the minimalist liberal wants to avoid. If the liberal must therefore allow that some such conceptions might be true, then the question remains: What guarantees that no moral or religious doctrine can generate interests sufficiently compelling to burst the brackets, so to speak, and morally outweigh the practical interest in social cooperation?

Critique of Minimalist Liberalism

Minimalist liberalism lacks a convincing answer to this question. For notwithstanding the importance of political values such as toleration, social cooperation, and mutual respect, it is not always reasonable to set aside competing values that may arise from substantive moral and religious doctrines. At least where grave moral questions are concerned, whether it is reasonable to bracket moral and religious controversies for the sake of political agreement partly depends on which of the contending moral or religious doctrines is true. Minimalist liberalism wants to separate the case for toleration from any judgment about the moral worth of the practices being tolerated. But this separation is not always defensible. We cannot determine whether toleration is justified in any given case without passing moral judgment on the practice in question.

This difficulty is illustrated by two political controversies that bear on grave moral and religious questions. One is the contemporary debate about abortion rights. The other is the famous debate in 1858 between Abraham Lincoln and Stephen Douglas over popular sovereignty and slavery.[32]

The Abortion Debate

Given the intense disagreement over the moral permissibility of abortion, the case for seeking a political solution that brackets the moral and religious issues—that is neutral with respect to them—would seem especially strong. But whether it is reasonable to bracket, for political purposes, the moral and religious doctrines at stake depends largely on which of those doctrines is true. If the doctrine of the Catholic church is true, if human life in the relevant moral sense really does begin at conception, then bracketing the moral-theological question of when human life begins is far less reasonable than it would be on rival moral and religious assumptions. The more confident we are that fetuses are, in the relevant moral sense, *different* from babies, the more confident we can be in affirming a political conception of justice that sets aside the controversy about the moral status of fetuses.

As the contemporary debate over abortion reflects, even a political conception of justice presupposes a certain view of the controversies it would bracket. For the debate about abortion is not only a debate about when human life begins, but also a debate about how reasonable it is to abstract from that question for political purposes. Opponents of abortion resist the translation from moral to political terms because they know that more of their view will be lost in the translation; the neutral territory offered by minimalist liberalism is likely to be less hospitable to their religious convictions than to those of their opponents. For defenders of abortion, little comparable is at stake; there is little difference between believing that abortion is morally permissible and agreeing that, as a political matter, women should be free to decide the moral question for themselves. The moral price of political agreement is far higher if abortion is wrong than if it is permissible. How reasonable it is to bracket the contending moral and religious views depends partly on which of those views is more plausible.

The minimalist liberal might reply that the political values of toleration and equal citizenship for women are sufficient grounds for concluding that women should be free to choose for themselves whether to have an abortion; government should not take sides on the moral and religious controversy over when human life begins. But if the Catholic church is right about the moral status of the fetus, if abortion is morally tantamount to murder, then it is not clear why the political values of toleration and women's equality, important though they are, should prevail. If the Catholic doctrine is true, then the minimalist liberal's case for the priority of political values must become an instance of just-war theory; he or she would have to show why these values should prevail even at the cost of some 1.5 million civilian deaths each year.

Of course, to suggest the impossibility of bracketing the moral-theological question of when human life begins is not to argue against a right to abortion. It is simply to show that the case for abortion rights cannot be neutral with respect to the underlying moral and religious controversy. It must engage rather than avoid the substantive moral and religious doctrines at stake. Liberals often resist this engagement because it violates the priority of the right over the good. But the abortion debate shows that this priority cannot be sustained. The case for respecting a woman's right to decide for herself whether to have an abortion depends on showing that there is a relevant moral difference between aborting a fetus at a relatively early stage of development and killing a child.

The Lincoln-Douglas Debates

Perhaps the most famous case for bracketing a controversial moral question for the sake of political agreement was made by Stephen Douglas in his debates with Abraham Lincoln. Since people were bound to disagree about the morality of slavery, Douglas argued, national policy should be neutral on that question. The doctrine of popular sovereignty he defended did not judge slavery right or wrong but left the people of the territories free to make their own judgments. "To throw the weight of federal power into the scale, either in favor of the free or the slave states," would violate the fundamental principles of the Constitution and run the risk of civil war. The only hope of holding the country together, he argued, was to agree to disagree, to bracket the moral controversy over slavery and respect "the right of each state and each territory to decide these questions for themselves."[33]

Lincoln argued against Douglas' case for a political conception of justice. Policy should express rather than avoid a substantive moral judgment about slavery, he maintained. Although Lincoln was not an abolitionist, he believed that government should treat slavery as the moral wrong it was and prohibit its extension to the territories. "The real issue in this controversy—pressing upon every mind—is the sentiment on the part of one class that looks upon the institution of slavery as a wrong, and of another class that does not look upon it as a wrong." Lincoln and the Republican party viewed slavery as a wrong and insisted that it "be treated as a wrong, and one of the methods of treating it as a wrong is to make provision that it shall grow no larger."[34]

Whatever his personal moral views, Douglas claimed that, for political purposes at least, he was agnostic on the question of slavery; he did not care whether slavery was "voted up or voted down." Lincoln replied that it was reasonable to bracket the question of the morality of slavery only on the assumption that it was not the moral evil he regarded it to be. Any man can advocate political neutrality "who does not see anything wrong in slavery, but no man can logically say it who does see a wrong in it; because no man can logically say he don't care whether a wrong is voted up or voted down."[35]

The debate between Lincoln and Douglas was not primarily about the morality of slavery, but about whether to bracket a moral controversy for the sake of political agreement. In this respect, their debate over popular sovereignty is analogous to the contemporary debate over abortion rights. As some contemporary liberals argue that government should not take a stand one way or another on the morality of abortion, but let each woman decide the question for herself, so Douglas argued that national policy should not take a stand one way or the other on the morality of slavery, but let each territory decide the question for itself. There is of course the difference that in the case of abortion rights, those who would bracket the substantive moral question typically leave the choice to the individual, while in the case of slavery, Douglas' way of bracketing was to leave the choice to the territories.

But Lincoln's argument against Douglas was an argument about bracketing as such, at least where grave moral questions are at stake. Lincoln's point was that the political conception of justice defended by Douglas depended for its plausibility on a particular answer to the substantive moral question it sought to bracket. Even in the face of so dire a threat to social cooperation as the prospect of civil war, it made neither moral nor political sense to aspire to political neutrality. As Lincoln concluded in his final debate with Douglas, "Is it not a false statesmanship that undertakes to build up a system of policy upon the basis of caring nothing about the very thing that every body does care the most about?"[36]

Present-day liberals will surely resist the company of Douglas and want national policy to oppose slavery, presumably on the grounds that slavery violates people's rights. But it is doubtful that liberalism conceived as a political conception of justice can make this claim without violating its own strictures against appeals to comprehensive moral ideals. For example, a Kantian liberal can oppose slavery as a failure to treat persons as ends in themselves, worthy of respect. But this argument, resting as it does on a Kantian conception of the person, is unavailable to minimalist liberalism. So too are the antislavery arguments of many American abolitionists in the 1830s and 1840s, who emphasized the sin of slavery and made their case in religious terms.

The debates over abortion and slavery show that a political conception of justice must sometimes presuppose an answer to the moral and religious questions it purports to bracket. At least where grave moral questions are at stake, it is not possible to detach politics and law from substantive moral judgment. But even in cases where it is possible to conduct political debate without reference to our moral and religious convictions, it may not always be desirable. The effort to banish moral and religious argument from the public realm for the sake of political agreement may end by impoverishing political discourse and eroding the moral and civic resources necessary to self-government.

This tendency can be seen in our present public life. With a few notable exceptions, such as the civil rights movement of the 1950s and 1960s, our political discourse in recent decades has come to reflect the liberal resolve that government be neutral on moral and religious questions, that matters of policy and law be debated and decided without reference to any particular conception of the good life. But we are beginning to find that a politics that brackets morality and religion too completely soon generates its own disenchantment. A procedural republic cannot contain the moral energies of a vital democratic life. It creates a moral void that opens the way for narrow, intolerant moralisms. And it fails to cultivate the qualities of character that equip citizens to share in self-rule.

In the chapters that follow, I try to show that the liberalism of the procedural republic provides the public philosophy by which we live. Despite its philosophical failings, it is the theory most thoroughly embodied in our practices and institutions. Now it might be thought that the very existence of the procedural republic as a sustained practice puts to rest the philosophical objections raised against it. If the neutral state succeeds in securing a scheme of rights without appealing to a sense of community beyond the social contract, if its members can exercise their agency as free citizens without seeing themselves as claimed by civic obligations beyond consent, then abstract worries about community and self-government, toleration and moral judgment, would seem at best beside the point. Either those objections are mistaken, or liberal politics is sufficiently autonomous of theory to proceed unimpaired by philosophical infirmity.

But its prevalence as practice is no proof against its poverty as theory. To the contrary, what goes wrong with the philosophy shows up in the practice. The predicament of liberal democracy in contemporary America recapitulates the tensions that inhabit its ideals. Far from proving the autonomy of liberal politics, its practice confirms what its philosophy foretells: The procedural republic cannot secure the liberty it promises, because it cannot sustain the kind of political community and civic engagement that liberty requires.

2

Rights and the Neutral State

Liberty and Self-Government

Republican political theory contrasts with the liberalism of the procedural republic in at least two respects. The first concerns the relation of the right to the good; the second, the relation of liberty to self-government. Instead of defining rights according to principles that are neutral among conceptions of the good, republican theory interprets rights in the light of a particular conception of the good society—the self-governing republic. In contrast to the liberal claim that the right is prior to the good, republicanism thus affirms a politics of the common good. But the common good it affirms does not correspond to the utilitarian notion of aggregating individual preferences. Unlike utilitarianism, republican theory does not take people's existing preferences, whatever they may be, and try to satisfy them. It seeks instead to cultivate in citizens the qualities of character necessary to the common good of self-government. Insofar as certain dispositions, attachments, and commitments are essential to the realization of self-government, republican politics regards moral character as a public, not merely private, concern. In this sense, it attends to the identity, not just the interests, of its citizens.

The second contrast between the liberal and republican traditions consists in the way they relate liberty to self-government. On the liberal view, liberty is defined in opposition to democracy, as a constraint on self-government. I am free insofar as I am a bearer of rights that guarantee my immunity from certain majority decisions. On the republican view, liberty is understood as a consequence of self-government. I am free insofar as I am a member of a political community that controls its own fate, and a participant in the decisions that govern its affairs.

To put the point another way, the republican sees liberty as internally connected to self-government and the civic virtues that sustain it. Republican freedom requires a certain form of public life, which depends in turn on the cultivation of civic virtue. Some versions of republicanism construe the dependence of liberty on self-government more strongly than others. The strong version of the republican ideal, going back to Aristotle, sees civic virtue and political participation as *intrinsic* to liberty; given our nature as political beings, we are free only insofar as we exercise our capacity to deliberate about the common good, and participate in the public life of a free city or republic.[1] More modest versions of the republican ideal see civic virtue and public service as *instrumental* to liberty; even the liberty to pursue our own ends depends on preserving the freedom of our political community, which depends in turn on the willingness to put the common good above our private interests.[2]

On the liberal conception, by contrast, liberty is not internally but only incidentally related to self-government. Where liberty consists in the opportunity to pursue my own interests and ends, it may or may not coincide with democratic government. "Liberty in this sense is not incompatible with some kinds of autocracy, or at any rate with the absence of self-government," writes Isaiah Berlin, a leading defender of the liberal tradition. A democracy may violate individual rights that an enlightened despot could in principle respect. Freedom is "not logically connected with democracy or self-government. . . . There is no necessary connection between individual liberty and democratic rule."[3]

On similar grounds, Thomas Hobbes, writing in the seventeenth century, rejected the classical view linking liberty and self-government. Hobbes ridicules the ancients for confusing "the liberty of the commonwealth" with the "liberty of particular men." Athens and Rome may have been free commonwealths, but this fact says nothing about the freedom of the individuals who lived there. It cannot be inferred, Hobbes insists, "that a particular man has more liberty" in a republic than in a monarchy. Since liberty consists in "immunity from the service of the commonwealth," it does not depend on any particular form of rule. "Whether a commonwealth be monarchical or popular, the freedom is still the same."[4]

In virtue of their contrasting accounts of liberty, the two traditions assess political institutions by asking different questions. The liberal begins by asking how government should treat its citizens,[5] and seeks principles of justice that treat persons fairly as they pursue their various interests and ends. The republican begins by asking how citizens can be capable of self-government, and seeks the political forms and social conditions that promote its meaningful exercise.

Finally, each tradition highlights a potential deficiency in the other. From the liberal standpoint, the republican emphasis on self-government leaves individual rights vulnerable to the tyranny of the majority. Moreover, the republican claim that freedom depends on civic virtue gives the state a stake in the character of its citizens that may open the way to coercion and oppression. From the republican standpoint, on the other hand, to view citizens first and foremost as objects of treatment, however fair, rather than as agents of self-rule is to concede from the start a certain disempowerment, or loss of agency. If liberty requires citizens whose identity is defined in part by civic responsibilities, then the public life of the neutral state may erode rather than secure our agency as free persons.

The procedural republic represents the triumph of a liberal public philosophy over a republican one, and accordingly reverses the terms of relation between liberty and self-government. In the early republic, liberty was understood as a function of democratic institutions and dispersed power. The relation of the individual to the nation was not direct but mediated by decentralized forms of political association and participation. The Bill of Rights did not apply to the states and was not understood to create individual immunities from all government action. Liberty was secured "largely through the preservation of boundaries between and among institutions."[6] Tocqueville describes the link between liberty and democracy in his account of the New England township: "Town meetings are to liberty what primary schools are to science; they bring it within the people's reach, they teach men how to use and how to enjoy it. A nation may establish a free government, but without municipal institutions it cannot have the spirit of liberty."[7]

By contrast, liberty in the procedural republic is defined in opposition to democracy, as an individual's guarantee against what the majority might will. Federalism fades as a constitutional concern, and freedom comes to depend on rights that enable persons to choose and pursue their own ends.[8] Given its reliance on rights secured by the government, the liberal conception of freedom does not depend on dispersed power. This is one source of liberalism's appeal under modern conditions; it may also shed light on the difficulty the procedural republic confronts in answering the aspiration for self-government.

The Emergence of American Constitutionalism

The version of liberalism that puts the right before the good finds its clearest expression in constitutional law. More explicitly than any other institution, the Supreme Court presides over the priority of right, in both senses of that priority. First, it defines the rights that constrain majority rule. Second, it tries to identify these rights in a way that does not presuppose any particular conception of the good life. Rather than read the Constitution as endorsing a particular moral or religious or economic doctrine, the Court has come in recent decades to view the Constitution as a neutral framework of rights within which persons can pursue their own ends, consistent with a similar liberty for others. Finally, the Court increasingly interprets the requirement of neutrality as expressing or advancing a conception of persons as free and independent selves.

The priority of individual rights, the ideal of neutrality, and the conception of persons as freely choosing, unencumbered selves, taken together form the public philosophy of the procedural republic. These three connected notions inform our present constitutional practice. They do not, however, characterize our tradition as a whole.

Of the three, the first goes back the farthest. The idea that certain rights are prior to government, and so limit what government may do, has figured in American political experience since before the Revolution. Its first stirrings can be found in the emergence of American constitutionalism in the decade before independence. It was then, in the course of the imperial debate with England, that the colonists arrived at the idea of a constitution as a fundamental law given prior to government and superior to ordinary law.[9] So familiar is this notion of a constitution, and so decisive for American government, that it is difficult to recall the rival understanding against which it arose.

When the Revolutionary controversy began, the colonists, like their English contemporaries, did not conceive the constitution as a thing distinct from government and law; rather, it *was* the law, or "that assemblage of laws, customs, and institutions which form the general system" of government. For Blackstone, there was no distinction between the "constitution or frame of government" and the "system of laws." Given the sovereignty of Parliament, every law formed a part of the constitution, and so no law could be unconstitutional.[10]

But if no law were unconstitutional, then how could the colonists describe what was wrong with the laws Parliament imposed on them in the 1760s and 1770s? How could they explain their belief that the laws enacted to tax and regulate colonial trade denied them their rights as Englishmen and violated the liberty that made the English constitution so worthy of admiration and allegiance? In order to articulate their protest, the colonists were compelled to abstract the fundamental principles of justice and right from the institutions and traditions in which they were embodied, and to give these principles priority. To identify the animating principles of the constitution, to set them apart, and to place them above the body of statutory and customary law—these were the impulses that led away from English constitutionalism and toward the distinctive American version. Under the pressure of events leading up to the Revolution, the colonists came to insist on the kind of constitution that even Parliament could not infringe, "a set of fixed principles and rules distinguishable from, antecedent to, more fundamental than, and controlling the operating institutions of government."[11]

James Otis took the first step in this direction in a famous case in 1761. He argued that the writs of assistance, search warrants issued to enforce the navigation laws, were unconstitutional. Both the navigation acts and the writs themselves were "against the fundamental principles of law" and therefore void. For "an act against the constitution is void: an act against natural equity is void," and the "courts must pass such acts into disuse."[12]

In *The Rights of the British Colonies,* a pamphlet he published three years later, Otis continued to argue that the power of Parliament was subject to certain limits. The imposition of taxes on the colonies was "absolutely irreconcilable with the rights of the colonists as British subjects and as men." Taking property without consent violated the law of nature, and "no law of society can make it just." Parliament could no more repeal God's natural laws than it can "make 2 and 2, 5." Any act of Parliament in violation of natural law "would be contrary to eternal truth, equity, and justice, and consequently void."[13]

At this point, however, Otis' bold thought took a conservative turn. Instead of inventing the doctrine of judicial review, Otis concluded that it was for Parliament itself to determine when it had erred, and so to "repeal such acts as soon as they find they have been mistaken." In the meantime, the colonists had to submit. "The power of Parliament is uncontrollable but by themselves, and we must obey. They only can repeal their own acts. . . . Therefore let the Parliament lay what burdens they please on us, we must, it is our duty to submit and patiently bear them till they will be pleased to relieve us."[14]

Otis' conclusion reflected the traditional assumption that Parliament was the supreme judicial as well as legislative body, and that its legislative function consisted in declaring the law rather than in willing or creating it. But by the time Otis wrote, this assumption was an anachronism. Parliament was no longer a court but a sovereign lawmaking body. In the face of its power, the colonists sought to define its limits in a constitution conceived as fundamental law. In the Massachusetts Circular Letter of 1768, opposing the Townshend Acts, Samuel Adams wrote: "In all free states the Constitution is fixed; and as the supreme legislative derives its power and authority from the Constitution, it cannot overleap the Bounds of it without destroying its own foundation."[15] By the 1770s, the distinction between constitution and government had begun to take hold. "A Constitution, and a form of government," wrote a Pennsylvania author in 1776, "are frequently confounded together, and spoken of as synonimous things; whereas they are not only different, but are established for different purposes: All countries have some form of government, but few, or perhaps none, have truly a Constitution."[16]

Along with shifting understandings of constitutionalism came a new understanding of rights. When the Revolutionary controversy began, the distinction between the rights of Englishmen and the rights of man was not sharply drawn. The English "constitution" was understood to embody the natural, inalienable rights given by God. But the emergence of American constitutionalism brought a "steadily increasing emphasis on the universal, inherent, indefeasible qualities of rights."[17] As the colonists abstracted fundamental principles from the body of statutory and customary law, they also abstracted human rights from the charters and laws that secured them. The rights essential to happiness "are not annexed to us by parchments and seals," wrote John Dickinson. "They are created in us by the decrees of Providence, which establish the laws of our nature. They are born with us; exist with us; and cannot be taken from us by any human power without taking our lives. In short, they are founded on the immutable maxims of reason and justice."[18]

For the colonists, the related ideas of a fixed constitution limiting government and of natural rights antecedent to law took shape in the struggle to secure liberty against the encroachments of imperial power. When it came time to establish constitutions of their own, the Americans groped for ways to apply their new understandings in practice. As the early efforts at state constitution-making revealed, the fundamental character of constitutional law had yet to find unambiguous expression.

Six weeks before adopting the Declaration of Independence, the Continental Congress called upon the thirteen colonies to form new governments based on the "authority of the people." From 1776 to 1780, eleven of the thirteen states adopted new constitutions. (Connecticut and Rhode Island continued to rely on their colonial charters.) Neither the constitutions themselves nor the means of their enactment fully realized the distinction between a constitution of entrenched rights and ordinary legislation. Although most contained "declarations of rights," these typically took the form of general admonitions rather than explicit restrictions on legislative power, leaving their legal status in question.[19] Moreover, most of the early constitutions were enacted by ordinary legislatures and adopted without ratification by the people. Some assemblies proceeded without even holding new elections to authorize their constitution-writing role.[20]

Some questioned how fundamental law could be constituted by ordinary legislation, and sought means of enactment capable of conferring the higher authority that constitutions required. For how can a constitution constrain the very body that creates it? Thomas Jefferson was troubled by this problem of authority and considered it a "capital defect" of Virginia's constitution "that the ordinary legislature may alter the constitution itself." Those who enacted it "could not pass an act transcendant to the powers of other legislatures," for no legislature can bind its successors. "If the present assembly pass any act, and declare it shall be irrevocable by subsequent assemblies, the declaration is merely void, and the act repealable, as other acts are."[21]

Various states struggled with devices to confer on constitutions a higher authority, beyond the reach of ordinary legislation. The New Jersey constitution required elected officials to take an oath not to repeal those sections of the constitution providing for annual elections, trial by jury, and religious freedom and prohibited the legislature from passing laws "repugnant to the rights and privileges contained in this Charter."[22] The constitutions of Delaware, Pennsylvania, and North Carolina provided that their declarations of rights "ought never to be violated on any pretence whatever." Pennsylvania's declared that the legislature "shall have no power to add to, alter, abolish, or infringe any part of this constitution," and provided for an amendment process supervised by an independent "Council of Censors."[23]

By the 1780s, Americans had developed institutions more adequate to the distinction between fundamental and ordinary law. Massachusetts' constitution of 1780 was the first to be drafted by a constitutional convention elected specially for the purpose, and adopted by popular ratification. Four years later, New Hampshire adopted its constitution by a similar process. In 1784 Thomas Tudor Tucker of South Carolina urged his state to elevate its constitution beyond merely legislative status in terms that captured the new understanding: "The constitution should be the avowed act of the people at large. It should be the first and fundamental law of the State, and should prescribe the limits of all delegated power. It should be declared to be paramount to all acts of the Legislature, and irrepealable and unalterable by any authority but the express consent of a majority of the citizens collected by such regular mode as may be therein provided."[24]

The Bill of Rights in the Early Republic

The idea of a framework of government given prior to government, distinctive to American constitutionalism, gestures toward the liberalism of the procedural republic, but only from a distance. The limited role of constitutional rights in the first century of the republic suggests that Americans have not always understood liberty to consist in the right to choose our values and ends. From the standpoint of twentieth-century constitutional law, so consumed by debates about individual rights, it is striking to recall that the federal Constitution of 1787 contained no Bill of Rights. In their almost four months of deliberation at Philadelphia, the Framers scarcely even discussed the question of whether to include one. Only in the final week of the convention, as the proposed constitution was being prepared for submission to Congress, did George Mason of Virginia rise to say he "wished the plan had been prefaced with a Bill of Rights." It would "give great quiet to the people," he thought, and would not take long to write. "With the aid of the state declarations, a bill might be prepared in a few hours." Elbridge Gerry of Massachusetts agreed, and moved for a committee to draft one.[25]

The only recorded discussion on the motion was Roger Sherman's comment that although he was in favor of securing the rights of the people where required, "the state declarations of rights are not repealed by this Constitution," and so nothing further was necessary. Mason replied that the laws of the United States would be paramount to the state bills of rights. But the motion lost, ten states to none, and the delegates turned to a discussion of whether states could levy duties on exports to defray storage and inspection costs.[26] As James Wilson would explain in the heat of the ratification debate, the question of a bill of rights, "which has since occasioned so much clamor and debate, never struck the mind" of the delegates until just before adjournment, "and even then of so little account was the idea that it passed off in a short conversation."[27]

The Anti-Federalists found in the absence of a bill of rights their most compelling argument against the Constitution. But the controversy that surrounded the issue throughout the ratification debates had less to do with individual rights as such than with the respective roles of the state and federal governments. "Why did the Constitution include no bill of rights?" the Anti-Federalists constantly asked. The defenders of the Constitution offered two answers—one legalistic, the other more broadly political. The legalistic explanation was that no bill of rights was necessary because all rights not granted to the federal government were reserved by the people.[28] The political argument invoked the bold but unconvincing claim that a bill of rights is inappropriate to popular government. As Hamilton wrote in *Federalist* no. 84, "bills of rights are in their origin, stipulations between kings and their subjects, abridgements of prerogative in favor of privilege, reservations of rights not surrendered to the prince. . . . they have no application to constitutions professedly founded upon the power of the people, and executed by their immediate representatives and servants." A constitution founded on the consent of "We the people" is "better recognition of popular rights than volumes of those aphorisms" which appeared in state bills of rights "and which would sound much better in a treatise of ethics than in a constitution of government."[29]

Benjamin Rush told the Pennsylvania convention he considered it "an honor to the late convention, that this system has not been disgraced with a bill of rights." The new federal government would not, after all, be "administered by foreigners—strangers to our habits and opinions, and unconnected with our interests and prosperity." Apprehensions about rights were more appropriate to the dispute with Great Britain than to the institutions of self-government established by the Constitution. According to Rush, liberty depended less on bills of rights than on "a pure and adequate representation" in the legislature.[30]

It was this broader argument of political theory that evoked from the most sophisticated Anti-Federalists a case for individual rights against even popular government, with its potential to impose a tyranny of the majority. "There are certain unalienable and fundamental rights," wrote "The Federal Farmer," "which in forming the social compact, ought to be explicitly ascertained and fixed." A free and enlightened people "will not resign all their rights to those who govern, and they will fix limits to their legislators and rulers."[31] "Agrippa" argued that even in a government by the people, a bill of rights was needed "to secure the minority against the usurpation and tyranny of the majority." History showed that power could threaten freedom whether vested in a king or in a mob. "It is therefore as necessary to defend an individual against the majority in a republic as against the king in a monarchy."[32] Thomas Jefferson, writing to James Madison from Paris, also insisted that popular government did not remove the need for a bill of rights. "A bill of rights is what the people are entitled to against every government on earth, general or particular, and what no just government should refuse, or rest on inferences."[33]

Seen from the standpoint of current constitutional debates, the Anti-Federalist case for a bill of rights might appear to provide an early example of "rights-based political morality."[34] But the Anti-Federalists were no harbingers of the procedural republic. Although they sometimes argued in the name of individual rights, their primary objection to the Constitution was that it threatened the independence of the states. They were concerned above all with the power of the national government, which they feared would annihilate the states. In opposing the Constitution, they sought to limit national power, and they found in the bill of rights the most popular, though not necessarily the most effective, way of doing so.

Throughout the ratification debates, the Anti-Federalist case for individual rights was bound up with, and often derivative from, concern for the prerogatives of the states. For most Anti-Federalists, the need for a bill of rights arose only in light of the threat to state sovereignty. "There would be no need of a bill of rights, were the states properly confederated."[35] The Anti-Federalist case for a national bill of rights cannot wholly be explained as an attempt to protect from the federal government rights already guaranteed by the states. Six of the states had no bill of rights, and the ones that existed were far from comprehensive. Even Virginia's famous Declaration of Rights, drafted by Anti-Federalist George Mason, contained no rights to freedom of speech, assembly, or petition, to habeas corpus, grand jury proceedings, counsel, or separation of church and state, or any protection against double jeopardy or bills of attainder or ex post facto laws. The only right secured by all twelve states that had constitutions was trial by jury in criminal cases. Only two guaranteed freedom of speech, and five permitted establishments of religion.[36] A national bill of rights was not simply a way of assuring continued protection for rights the states already protected, but primarily a way of restraining the power of a national government that threatened the independence of the states. As one Anti-Federalist argued, "A bill of rights should either be inserted, *or* a declaration made, that whatever is not decreed to Congress is reserved to the several states for their own disposal."[37]

Some Anti-Federalists acknowledged that a bill of rights would be inadequate to their larger purpose of restraining national power. "A declaration of rights alone will be of no essential service," wrote Samuel Chase. "Some of the powers must be abridged, or public liberty will be endangered, and, in time, destroyed."[38] Nevertheless, the Anti-Federalists had made the bill of rights their primary issue, and several states voted ratification only on the promise that a bill of rights would be added by amendment.

Although enumerating rights would not achieve the Anti-Federalist aim of reducing national power vis-à-vis the states, it would remove the one popular source of opposition to the Constitution. No one grasped this more keenly than James Madison. A leading defender of the Constitution, he did not think a bill of rights was needed. He worried about the tyranny of the majority but saw the greatest threat to liberty residing within the states themselves. "An elective despotism was not the government we fought for,"[39] but a bill of rights was not the way to avoid it. The experience of the states convinced him that bills of rights were least effective when most needed. "Repeated violations of these parchment barriers have been committed by overbearing majorities in every State." In Virginia, he had seen the bill of rights "violated in every instance where it has been opposed to a popular current."[40]

Madison took rights seriously—more seriously than the Anti-Federalists—but thought that structures of government, not "parchment barriers," would best protect them. In the *Federalist* he emphasized three such structures. First, representative government would "refine and enlarge the public views, by passing them through the medium of a chosen body of citizens." Second, an extended republic would "make it less probable that a majority of the whole will have a common motive to invade the rights of other citizens," or at least make it difficult to carry out the invasion. And finally, the separation and balance of powers would ensure that no part of government could transcend its legal limits, "without being effectually checked and restrained by the others."[41]

To these three safeguards Madison had sought unsuccessfully to add a fourth. In the Federal Convention he proposed to give Congress a "negative," or veto power, over the laws of the states. Such a negative would enable the national government to act directly to protect individual rights, to control "the internal vicissitudes of state policy, and the aggressions of interested majorities on the rights of minorities and of individuals." The proposal failed, but its underlying impulse would later find life in the hands of the judiciary.[42]

Despite his earlier doubts, it was Madison who led the effort in the First Congress to amend the Constitution by adding a bill of rights. This reversal reflected shrewd political strategy and astute political science. Madison realized that a bill of rights would reassure the people and undercut such opposition to the Constitution as remained. He also saw that guaranteeing individual rights was not inconsistent with the strong national government he favored. In fact one of the amendments he proposed would have gone beyond anything the Anti-Federalists had sought, and constrained the conduct of the states. In addition to the restraints on Congress ultimately adopted, Madison proposed an amendment to protect certain individual rights from infringement by state governments: "No State shall infringe the equal rights of conscience, nor the freedom of speech, or of the press, nor of the right of trial by jury in criminal cases."[43]

Madison's proposal clarified a choice that the ratification debate had blurred—between the primacy of individual rights and the prerogatives of the states. Once stated, the choice would reverberate in constitutional debate for a century and a half. For Madison the case was clear. "It is proper that every Government should be disarmed of powers which trench upon those particular rights. I know, in some of the state constitutions, the power of the government is controlled by such a declaration; but others are not. I cannot see any reason against obtaining even a double security on those points." Here too would be the test of the Anti-Federalists' civil libertarian convictions. "Nothing can give a more sincere proof of the attachment of those who opposed this Constitution to these great and important rights than to see them join in obtaining the security I have now proposed, because it must be admitted on all hands that the state governments are as liable to attack these invaluable privileges as the general government is, and therefore ought to be as cautiously guarded against."[44]

The House of Representatives adopted Madison's proposal, but the Senate voted it down and sent to the state legislatures for ratification a Bill of Rights that restrained the federal government alone. It was adopted in 1791, despite the opposition of many Anti-Federalists who had clamored for it in the first place.[45]

Madison's attempt to protect certain individual rights against infringement by the states would not find constitutional expression until the adoption of the Fourteenth Amendment seventy-nine years later. In the meantime, the Bill of Rights would not apply to the states, as the Supreme Court confirmed in *Barron v. Baltimore* (1833). When the City of Baltimore ruined a privately owned wharf while paving its streets, the owner of the wharf claimed the city had violated the Fifth Amendment by taking his property for public use without just compensation. A unanimous Supreme Court ruled otherwise. As Chief Justice John Marshall wrote, "the Fifth Amendment must be understood as restraining the power of the general government, not as applicable to the States." Restrictions on state governments were a matter for the various state constitutions to determine. The Bill of Rights, he recalled, had been enacted to quiet fears about the encroachment of federal power, not to protect individuals against state and local governments.[46]

Nor, for the first century of its existence, did the Bill of Rights play an important role in protecting individual liberties against federal infringement. Liberty in the early republic had less to do with individual guarantees against government action than with the dispersion of power among branches and levels of government. The Bill of Rights was not importantly implicated in federal activities, and "seemed hardly to matter during our first century."[47] Despite the prominence of First Amendment rights in our contemporary understanding of liberty, the Supreme Court did not strike down a law of Congress for violating the First Amendment until 1965.[48]

Before the Civil War, the Supreme Court enforced the Bill of Rights against an act of Congress only once. That was in 1857, when it ruled that the property rights of Dred Scott's master trumped the Missouri Compromise. Scott, a slave, was not a citizen and so could not sue for his freedom on grounds that his master had taken him into free territory. Moreover, when Congress prohibited slavery in certain territories, it deprived Scott's master of his property rights under the Fifth Amendment. "An act of Congress which deprives a citizen of the United States of his liberty or property, without due process of law, merely because he . . . brought his property into a particular territory of the United States . . . could hardly be dignified with the name of due process of law."[49]

After the Fourteenth Amendment: Rights as Trumps

The Civil War resolved what the Constitution had not, and established the supremacy of the national government over the states. During Reconstruction the Thirteenth through Fifteenth Amendments abolished slavery, overruled *Dred Scott* by defining as citizens "all persons born or naturalized in the United States," and guaranteed the newly emancipated slaves the right to vote. The Fourteenth Amendment also imposed on the states certain restrictions that would transform the role of the Supreme Court in protecting individual rights. It established that no state may "abridge the privileges or immunities of citizens of the United States" or "deprive any person of life, liberty, or property, without due process of law" or deny to any person "the equal protection of the laws."

How to interpret such terms as "due process" and "equal protection" would fuel constitutional controversy for a century. But these debates found their occasion only because the Fourteenth Amendment empowered the Supreme Court to protect individual rights from state infringement as never before. In this respect, it realized Madison's attempt in the First Congress to guarantee certain rights against violation by any government. And as Madison had glimpsed, national power and individual rights would expand together, at the expense of the sovereignty of the states.

At first the Supreme Court refused to take up its new career. The first test of the Fourteenth Amendment, the *Slaughter-House Cases* (1873), was brought not by former slaves, but by some butchers from New Orleans. They claimed that a Louisiana law granting a monopoly on the slaughtering business violated their rights under the Fourteenth Amendment. In a five–four decision, the Supreme Court rejected their claim. To invalidate the law in the name of individual rights would be radically to transform the federal system, to "fetter and degrade the State governments . . . in the exercise of powers heretofore universally conceded to them." Justice Samuel F. Miller, writing for the Court, was convinced that

Congress could not have intended "so serious, so far-reaching and pervading, so great a departure from the structure and spirit of our institutions." While deploring the consequences of such a departure, Miller aptly described its constitutional significance. Such a construction "would constitute this court a perpetual censor upon all legislation of the States, on the civil rights of their own citizens, with authority to nullify such as it did not approve as consistent with those rights."[50]

Justice Stephen J. Field, writing in dissent, agreed that the case posed a constitutional question of "the gravest importance." At stake was "nothing less than the question whether the recent amendments to the Federal Constitution protect the citizens of the United States against the deprivation of their common rights by State legislation." Field answered in the affirmative. "The amendment was adopted . . . to place the common rights of American citizens under the protection of the National government." It "was intended to give practical effect to the declaration of 1776 of inalienable rights, rights which are the gift of the Creator, which the law does not confer, but only recognizes."[51] Among these rights was the right to pursue the lawful occupation of one's choice, butchering included. Louisiana's slaughterhouse monopoly violated this right, the dissenters argued, a right now protected against infringement by the states.

By the turn of the century, American constitutional law began to unfold as Field had hoped and Miller feared. In the landmark case of *Allgeyer v. Louisiana* (1897), the Supreme Court interpreted the Fourteenth Amendment broadly and struck down a law restricting out-of-state insurance contracts as a denial of liberty without due process of law. The liberty protected by that amendment included "the right of the citizen to be free in the enjoyment of all his faculties; to be free to use them in all lawful ways; to live and work where he will; to earn his livelihood by any lawful calling; to pursue any livelihood or avocation, and for that purpose to enter into all contracts" necessary to do so.[52] All these liberties would now count as fundamental rights not subject to legislative infringement.

For the next four decades the Supreme Court scrutinized state and federal laws for their compliance with this expansive reading of the Fourteenth Amendment, emphasizing the rights to property and contract. During this period the Court invalidated close to two hundred laws, including attempts by state and federal governments to regulate the industrial economy through laws governing prices, wages and hours, and labor union activities.[53] Many of these laws fell victim to "substantive due process" review by the Court, on grounds of infringing the liberty of contract.

In the most famous of these cases, *Lochner v. New York* (1905), the Court struck down a law prohibiting the employment of bakery employees for more than sixty hours per week. "The general right to make a contract in relation to his business is part of the liberty of the individual protected by the Fourteenth Amendment," the Court held. New York's statute was "an illegal interference with the rights of individuals, both employers and employees, to make contracts regarding labor upon such terms as they may think best." Laws "limiting the hours in which grown and intelligent men may labor to earn their living are mere meddlesome interferences with the rights of the individual," and so beyond the power of the legislature.[54]

In other cases, the Court struck down laws setting minimum wages for women[55] and laws prohibiting "yellow dog" contracts—contracts providing that workers could be fired for joining a union.[56] Although a worker had a right to join a union, the Court ruled, his employer had a right to fire him if he did. The bargaining power of workers and employers might be unequal, but it was "impossible to uphold freedom of contract and the right of private property without at the same time recognizing as legitimate those inequalities of fortune that are the necessary result of the exercise of those rights." Since the Fourteenth Amendment recognized liberty and property as "co-existent human rights," no state could interfere with them, even for the sake of redressing the inequalities of bargaining power that were the "normal and inevitable result of their exercise."[57]

Not all the laws that fell victim to substantive due process review involved economic regulations.[58] For the most part, however, the *Lochner* Court protected property rights and the freedom to make a contract on whatever terms the market would bear. Such economic and constitutional views led the Court to strike down New Deal legislation in the 1930s and brought mounting political resistance. A few months after the Court invalidated New York's minimum-wage law,[59] Franklin Roosevelt, fresh from his 1936 electoral mandate, announced his plan to pack the Court. Although the actual effect of this threat is subject to dispute, the Court reversed course in 1937, and upheld a minimum wage law for women. In *West Coast Hotel Co. v. Parrish,* a decision that marked the end of the *Lochner* era, a five–four majority rejected the familiar argument that the law deprived women and their employers of freedom of contract. "What is this freedom?" wrote Chief Justice Charles Evans Hughes. "The Constitution does not speak of freedom of contract. It speaks of liberty and prohibits the deprivation of liberty without due process of law." The legislature was clearly entitled to address the evil of sweatshops and to consider that women's "bargaining power is relatively weak, and that they are the ready victims of those who would take advantage of their necessitous circumstances."[60]

Given its hostility to humane reforms, the *Lochner* Court's service to contemporary liberalism may not be readily apparent. Armed with the doctrine of substantive due process, it had defended the excesses of industrial capitalism and frustrated progressive reforms. In the process, it discredited both the economic theory it favored and the constitutional doctrine it used to enforce it. Later liberals would enforce different rights, but not without the worry that they, like the *Lochner* justices, were failing to let the majority rule.

After 1937, laissez-faire economics lost its privileged constitutional place; no economic legislation has fallen to substantive due process since.[61] But despite its legacy of reaction, it cannot be said that the *Lochner* Court failed to take rights seriously. To the contrary, its rights-based jurisprudence put in place the constitutional structure that present-day liberals take for granted. The constitutional transformation that cast the Court, in the name of rights, as "a perpetual censor upon all legislation of the states"[62] would outlive the economic orthodoxy that provided its first occasion.

For the first time in American history, rights functioned as trumps. Liberty no longer depended on dispersed power alone, but found direct protection from the courts. Where fundamental rights were seen to be at stake, even the principles of federalism and state sovereignty no longer impeded judicial intervention. The *Lochner* Court thus offered the first sustained constitutional expression of the priority of the right over the good, at least in the sense that certain individual rights prevailed against legislative policies enacted in the name of the public good.

Justice Holmes in Dissent: Intimations of Neutrality

While the *Lochner* Court established the priority of right in the sense of rights as trumps, it would remain for later courts to install the priority of right in the further sense of the Constitution as a framework of rights that is neutral among ends. This second aspect of the priority of right, the one characteristic of the procedural republic, would not emerge fully in constitutional law until after World War II. But during the first third of the century, it found early expression in the dissents of Justices Oliver Wendell Holmes, Louis D. Brandeis, and, later, Harlan F. Stone.

The dissenters offered two main objections to the judicial decisions of the *Lochner* majority. First, they resisted the notion that the Constitution affirms any particular social or economic philosophy, and argued instead for judicial deference to democratic institutions. Second, they championed judicial protection for civil liberties such as freedom of speech, as a check on the tyranny of the majority. These two positions would together give shape to modern judicial liberalism. The deferential strand would support the idea that the Constitution does not endorse but rather brackets controversial moral and political beliefs. And the libertarian strand would issue in the modern liberal's special concern for personal liberties and civil rights.

But it was not obvious at first—or, for that matter, later—how these two strands hung together. The deferential argument seemed to endorse virtually unqualified majoritarianism, while the civil libertarian argument would restrain majorities for the sake of certain individual rights. But how could any case for rights survive the general objection to judicial interference with democracy?

The answer would have been easy had Holmes simply accepted the doctrine of substantive due process and argued in dissent that the Court enforced the wrong rights, that his conception of liberty was better, or truer to the Constitution, than theirs. But Holmes's disagreement with the Court was more thoroughgoing than that. Time and again he insisted that the wisdom of the law was not for him, as judge, to judge. "There is nothing that I more deprecate than the use of the Fourteenth Amendment beyond the absolute compulsion of its words to prevent the making of social experiments that an important part of the community desires . . .

even though the experiments may seem futile or even noxious to me and to those whose judgment I most respect."[63] In a letter to Harold Laski, Holmes stated his judicial philosophy even more succinctly: "if my fellow citizens want to go to Hell I will help them. It's my job."[64]

And yet for all his insistence on judicial deference, it was Holmes, along with Brandeis, who pioneered the cause of judicial protection for freedom of speech. In *Schenck v. United States* (1919), he enunciated the "clear and present danger" test to uphold censorship provisions of the wartime Espionage Act.[65] But less than a year later, dissenting in *Abrams v. United States* (1919), Holmes defended the right of radical protesters to distribute a leaflet urging a general strike. "The surreptitious publishing of a silly leaflet by an unknown man" posed no real threat and so was protected by the Constitution.[66]

After *Abrams,* Holmes and Brandeis sought to protect free speech against infringement by the states. Despite their reluctance to embrace an expansive view of the Fourteenth Amendment, they argued in effect that if any rights were protected under that amendment, then surely freedom of speech and press must be among them. "I cannot believe that the liberty guaranteed by the Fourteenth Amendment includes only liberty to acquire and to enjoy property," Brandeis dissented in *Gilbert v. Minnesota* (1920).[67] Later he went further: "Despite arguments to the contrary which had seemed to me persuasive, it is settled that the due process clause of the Fourteenth Amendment applies to matters of substantive law as well as to matters of procedure. Thus all fundamental rights comprised within the term liberty are protected by the Federal Constitution from invasion by the States."[68]

Dissenting in *Gitlow v. California* (1924), Holmes wrote: "The general principle of free speech, it seems to me, must be taken to be included in the Fourteenth Amendment, in view of the scope that has been given to the word 'liberty' as there used." As if to ease the tension between his commitments to civil liberties and to majority rule, Holmes went on to defend free speech with the same moral relativism he elsewhere invoked on behalf of majority rule. "If in the long run the beliefs expressed in proletarian dictatorship are destined to be accepted by the dominant forces of the community, the only meaning of free speech is that they should be given their chance and have their way."[69]

But this relativist argument does not succeed in reconciling civil liberties with majority rule. To the contrary, it puts in question the grounds for restraining majorities in the first place, for the sake of free speech or anything else. If "the dominant forces of the community" should prevail, why not sooner rather than later? If Holmes would help the people go to Hell, why not let them silence subversives on the way?

Despite his relativist moments, Holmes's argument with the *Lochner* Court was based on more than simple majoritarianism. Although Holmes's dissents are often read as arguments about the role of the judge, they also contain a larger claim about the nature of the Constitution. Implicit in his dissents is not only an argument for judicial deference to majorities but also a certain reading of the Constitution, a reading that says the Constitution does not embody any particular conception of the good. His point was not only that judges should refrain from imposing *their* morality on the Constitution, but also that the Constitution itself refuses to endorse any particular morality.

As early as his first Supreme Court opinion, Holmes's case for judicial restraint appears in connection with the idea of the Constitution as framework of rights that is neutral among ends. "While the courts must exercise a judgment of their own," he wrote, "it by no means is true that every law is void which may seem to the judges who pass upon it excessive, unsuited to its ostensible end, or based upon conceptions of morality with which they disagree." And then: "Considerable latitude must be allowed for differences of view. . . . Otherwise a constitution, instead of embodying only relatively fundamental rules of right . . . would become the partisan of a particular set of ethical or economical opinions, which by no means are held *semper ubique et ab omnibus.*"[70]

In interpreting the Constitution, judges should neither be partisans themselves nor construe the Constitution as itself the partisan of a particular ethical or economic philosophy. Not only should judges bracket their own moral and political opinions when reading the Constitution; they should read the Constitution as itself bracketing such questions.

These two different claims can also be found in Holmes's *Lochner* dissent. He begins by arguing that judges should not decide the constitutionality of a law by imposing their own values: "This case is decided upon an economic theory which a large part of the country does not entertain. If it were a question whether I agreed with that theory, I should desire to study it further and long before making up my mind. But I do not conceive that to be my duty, because I strongly believe that my agreement or disagreement has nothing to do with the right of a majority to embody their opinions in law." But he goes on to make the further claim that the Constitution does not affirm any particular economic theory, that it is neutral among competing doctrines: "The Fourteenth Amendment does not enact Mr. Herbert Spencer's Social Statics . . . a constitution is not intended to embody a particular economic theory, whether of paternalism and the organic relation of the citizen to the State or of laissez faire. It is made for people of fundamentally differing views."[71]

The idea that a constitution is neutral among ends is central to the liberalism of the procedural republic. By affirming this idea, Holmes's dissents gave early expression to the procedural liberalism that has since come to inform American constitutional law. But there are two ways of interpreting the idea that the Constitution is neutral among ends, and Holmes did not distinguish them. On the first interpretation, constitutional neutrality simply means that the Constitution does not favor any particular economic or ethical doctrine, and so states are free to enact whatever such doctrines they choose. On the second interpretation, constitutional neutrality means that the Constitution requires states to be neutral among the ends its citizens espouse. The second interpretation is the one that asserts the priority of the right over the good and defines rights according to the requirement that government be neutral among conceptions of the good life.

Although Holmes himself did not explicitly embrace the second interpretation, the idea that the Constitution mandates neutrality toward competing conceptions of the good suggests a way of reconciling his general majoritarianism with his seeming exception for civil liberties, a way of connecting his dissents in *Lochner* and in *Abrams*. In *Lochner*, the Court wrongly read the Constitution as enacting a particular economic doctrine, and so intervened where it should have deferred. In *Abrams*, the Court deferred where it should have intervened to uphold the requirement that government not enforce any particular doctrine or creed. That the government suppressed speech *absent* a clear and present danger implied it had passed judgment on the merits of the speech, and so wrongly imposed values the Constitution means to bracket. The defendants were made to suffer not for hindering the war effort, "but for the creed that they avow—a creed [that] no one has a right even to consider in dealing with the charges before the Court."[72] Read in this way, Holmes's dissent in *Abrams* offers the first example of what would later be known as the "content neutrality" doctrine of the First Amendment.[73]

It is clear in any case that the second strand in his dissents (about constitutional neutrality), more profoundly than the first (about judicial self-restraint), connects Holmes's jurisprudence with the subsequent course of American liberalism. More immediately, it set the challenge that confronted the Supreme Court after 1937. No longer would New Deal reforms fall victim to the "countermajoritarian" veto of an ideologically hostile Court. But then what role remained for judicial review? Only a theory of constitutional rights that did not presuppose any particular conception of the good could avoid imposing values on the majority, as the *Lochner* Court had done. But how would it be possible to find a basis for constitutional rights without attributing to the Constitution a particular conception of the good, without ranking rights according to the intrinsic value of the interests they protect? The ideal of neutrality implicit in Holmes's dissents offered a hint that the Court would soon pursue.

Democracy and Rights in the Neutral State

In *United States v. Carolene Products Co.* (1938), the Supreme Court offered two possible answers to the challenge it faced. Upholding a federal law banning interstate commerce in adulterated milk, Justice Stone declared that "regulatory legislation affecting ordinary commercial transactions" would be presumed constitutional so long as it had "some rational basis." But in a famous footnote, he suggested two possible grounds for heightened judicial review in other areas, two ways of defining constitutional rights under the Fourteenth Amendment without imposing a particular conception of the good.[74]

The first was to seek refuge in a kind of positivist solution—to interpret the Fourteenth Amendment as protecting those rights already specified in the Bill of Rights. "There may be narrower scope for operation of the presumption of constitutionality when legislation appears on its face to be within a specific prohibition of the Constitution, such as those of the first ten amendments, which are deemed equally specific when held to be embraced within the Fourteenth."[75] If the "liberty" protected by the Fourteenth Amendment could be interpreted as simply incorporating the Bill of Rights and applying them to the states, then the Court could avoid the task of ranking rights according to controversial conceptions of their value or importance.

This view, which came to be known as the "total incorporation" position, found its most vigorous advocate in Justice Hugo L. Black. Dissenting in *Adamson v. California* (1947), he argued that the framers of the Fourteenth Amendment had intended to apply the Bill of Rights to the states, and furthermore, that any other reading of the amendment put the Court in the position of "substituting its own concepts of decency and fundamental justice for the language of the Bill of Rights." Such an ill-defined approach had been used before, and could be used again, to license the Court "to roam at large in the broad expanses of policy and morals and to trespass, all too freely, on the legislative domain of the States as well as the Federal Government." While Black acknowledged the need for interpretation, he thought it was one thing to do so by "looking to the particular standards enumerated in the Bill of Rights," and quite another to invalidate statutes on the basis of standards "undefined" by the Constitution itself.[76]

Black's view neither prevailed as constitutional doctrine nor provided an adequate answer to the problem of defining rights without relying on a conception of the good. As a matter of doctrine, the Court opted not for "total" but for "selective" incorporation, an approach expounded by Justice Benjamin N. Cardozo in *Palko v. Connecticut* (1937). The Fourteenth Amendment did not absorb the Bill of Rights as a whole, but only those rights "of the very essence of a scheme of ordered liberty" or required by "principle[s] of justice so rooted in the traditions and conscience of our people as to be ranked as fundamental."[77] While proceeding "selectively," the Court eventually enforced against the states virtually all the rights contained in the Bill of Rights, and then some.[78] But the fact that the Court never read the due process clause of the Fourteenth Amendment as simple shorthand for a nationalized Bill of Rights makes clear its reliance on principles of selection independent of the "specific prohibitions" of the Constitution itself.

In any event, Black's quasi-positivist proposal did not offer the Court an adequate solution to the problem it faced. Despite their relative "specificity," the guarantees contained in the Bill of Rights scarcely admit less controversial interpretation than the Fourteenth Amendment itself. Like the "selective" incorporation the Court pursued, Black's "total" incorporation would require a further interpretive principle that positivism could not supply. To find such a principle without presupposing a particular conception of the good is a challenge that Black's approach postpones rather than resolves.

Stone's second suggestion in *Carolene Products* was subtler and more far-reaching. It proposed, in effect, that the Court enforce those rights necessary to realize the ideals implicit in the democratic process itself. This proposal had two parts. One was to assure access to the political process. "Legislation which restricts those political processes which can ordinarily be expected to bring about repeal of undesirable legislation" might be subject to "more exacting judicial scrutiny." The other was to prevent prejudice from infecting the political process. Since "prejudice against discrete and insular minorities may seriously curtail the operation of those political processes ordinarily to be relied upon to protect minorities," laws directed against "particular religious, or national, or racial minorities" might also warrant "more searching judicial inquiry."[79]

Stone's suggestion answered the challenge the Court confronted in several ways. First, it defined a role for judicial review that addressed the "countermajoritarian" objection. Rather than impose controversial values on democratic institutions, judges could act instead in the name of the very values that give democracy its moral force in the first place. The exercise of judicial review would not frustrate democracy but perfect it. Second, Stone's suggestion offered a basis for rights consistent with the idea of the Constitution as neutral among ends. While arguments would continue about which rights this conception required, the arguments would not be about the intrinsic value of the interests the rights protect, but rather about the constraints appropriate to an open political process, free of prejudice, within which people can choose their values for themselves.

Finally, Stone's footnote contained a hint of the conception of the person that would emerge more explicitly in later constitutional decisions, and complete the vision of contemporary liberalism. This conception was implicit in his distinction between civil rights and liberties on the one hand, and economic liberties on the other. Subsequent Courts would follow Stone's suggestion that the first sort of liberties warrants judicial protection that the second does not. But Stone did not explain the grounds for this distinction, and some have called it a constitutional "double standard."[80] Once fully realized, the conception of the person implicit in Stone's footnote would help clarify and justify the distinction itself. Although Stone did not elaborate the political theory underlying his footnote—it was, after all, only a footnote—the justification for his distinction, and its connection with the liberal conception of the person, might be reconstructed along the following lines:

The priority of civil liberties over economic liberties, of personal rights over property rights, is sometimes defended on the grounds that the first are intrinsically more important than the second, that freedom of speech is more essential to human flourishing, or to a good society, than liberty of contract.[81] But this defense is at odds with the idea of the Constitution as a framework of rights that is neutral among ends. How then can the idea of constitutional neutrality support the priority of civil liberties and rights? What sort of rights does the ideal of neutrality require? The answer to this question depends on what it means to be a free and independent moral agent, capable of choosing one's ends for oneself.

The idea that the Constitution is a framework of rights neutral among ends does not, by itself, argue for judicial protection of civil liberties rather than economic liberties. What counts as neutrality is often controversial, and admits competing interpretations. Some claim that the best way for government to be neutral among ends is to respect above all the liberty of contract, and to leave in place the distribution of power and resources that results from the workings of the market economy. Underlying this view is a particular conception of what free moral agency consists in, a conception characteristic of laissez-faire assumptions. The railroad employee required by his employer to choose between his union membership and his job is thus "a free agent . . . at liberty to choose what was best from the standpoint of his own interests . . . free to exercise a voluntary choice."[82]

On this view, government intervention, democratically sanctioned though it be, violates individual freedom. By constraining people's choices, it also fails to be neutral. It overrules the valuations that parties to various agreements would themselves place on the things they exchange, and so imposes on some the values of others. The right to make contracts exchanging labor for wages is "as essential to the laborer as to the capitalist, to the poor as to the rich." Any interference with this right is "a substantial impairment of liberty."[83]

Progressive critics of laissez-faire capitalism met this argument not by rejecting but by perfecting the ideal of free agency the contractarian ethic invoked. Under conditions of industrial capitalism, they argued, inequalities of bargaining power effectively undercut the freedom that gives contracts their moral force in the first place. Contracts compelled by the scourge of economic necessity are not truly voluntary, but a kind of coercion. Nor are they neutral. Instead of revealing people's different valuations of the goods they exchange, such agreements also reflect differences of market power associated with various natural and social contingencies. The results they produce are only as legitimate as the initial distribution of endowments they reflect.

Progressive legislation of the early twentieth century sought to remedy this defect by establishing the "equality of position between the parties in which liberty of contract begins."[84] While labor laws such as those contested in *Adair* and *Coppage* restricted the liberty of contract, they did so for the sake of realizing more completely the ideal of freedom implicit but imperfect in contractual liberty as practiced at the time. The welfare state itself was sometimes defended in similar terms. Proposing an "economic bill of rights" in 1944, Franklin Roosevelt argued that "true individual freedom cannot exist without economic security and independence. 'Necessitous men are not free men.'"[85]

The modern welfare state can be understood as answering the advocates of unbridled capitalism in the following way: A market economy constrained by a democratic process in which citizens are represented as equals comes closer to realizing the conception of persons as free moral agents than does a scheme of contracts unconstrained. Understood in this light, government intervention in the economy does not violate but rather vindicates individual freedom. Nor is it at odds with neutrality. It imposes constraints on individual choice not for the sake of some particular theory of value—as in an intrinsically "just wage," for example—but rather for the sake of a structure of choice less likely to reflect unequal market power. Far from imposing a particular end, such a structure more fully respects the capacity of persons to choose their ends for themselves.

Given this picture, it is not obvious what role remains for judicial review. In principle at least, the democratic process is well suited to constraining the market economy in a way consistent with the liberal aspiration to neutrality. Like the market, the democratic process aggregates people's preferences without judging them, without assessing their intrinsic merit or worth. And unlike the market, it reflects an initial situation of equality. Ideally at least, democratic consent is unimpaired by those contingencies that make for unequal market power. From the standpoint of liberal political theory, democracy can be justified, not for the virtues it cultivates or the way of life it promotes, but "because it enforces the right of each person to respect and concern as an individual," capable of choosing his or her own ends.[86]

In practice, however, the democratic process may violate that right in at least two ways. First, it may fail to be fully inclusive, and so fail to give equal weight to the interests and preferences of all. Second, even where all have equal access and the preferences of each have equal weight, some may vote preferences that are themselves at odds with the ideal of equal respect. Some may, in other words, vote intolerant or prejudiced preferences. But then the democratic process may produce policies at odds with neutrality—policies that presuppose that certain sorts of persons, or ways of life, are intrinsically less worthy than others.

These two ways in which democracy may betray its underlying ideal of equal respect for persons as free moral agents suggests a role for rights of the sort that Stone proposed. If democracy depends for its moral force on the sense in which it expresses respect for persons as free and independent selves, then it too must be subject to certain constraints. Stone proposed that the Court supply those constraints in the name of a constitution that is neutral among ends. Just as the legislatures constrained the market to redress the unequal bargaining position of employers and workers, so the Constitution would now constrain the legislatures to assure equal access to the political process, and to prevent people's prejudices from finding their way into public policy. The Court would overcome its "counterma-joritarian" difficulty much as the democracy overcame its "countercon-tractarian" difficulty—by perfecting the vision of freedom implicit but unrealized in the practices it regulated.

Stone's distinction thus drew its justification from the conception of the person it implicitly affirmed, a conception that emerged more explicitly in subsequent constitutional law. In the decades to follow, the courts would protect civil liberties in the name of the priority of the right over the good. And they would interpret this priority according to a conception of persons as free and independent agents, capable of choosing their ends for themselves.

Affirming the Priority of the Right

The transition to new constitutional assumptions found vivid illustration in two cases about pledging allegiance to the flag. The case of *Minersville School District v. Gobitis* (1940) involved two children of Jehovah's Witnesses who were expelled from public school for refusing to salute the flag. Their parents claimed the flag salute violated their religious beliefs. Justice Felix Frankfurter, writing for the Court, upheld the law as a legitimate way of cultivating the communal identity of its citizens. "The ultimate foundation of a free society is the binding tie of cohesive senti-ment. Such a sentiment is fostered by all those agencies of the mind and spirit which may serve to gather up the traditions of a people, transmit them from generation to generation, and thereby create the continuity of a treasured common life which constitutes a civilization." The Constitu-tion should not be understood to prevent states and school districts from "evok[ing] that unifying sentiment without which there can ultimately be no liberties, civil or religious," or from "inculcating those almost uncon-scious feelings which bind men together in a comprehending loyalty."[87] Only Justice Stone dissented.

Three years later, in *West Virginia State Board of Education v. Barnette*, the Court reversed course and struck down a compulsory flag salute. Justice Robert H. Jackson's opinion for the Court was an eloquent statement of the liberal political theory that the U.S. Constitution had come to embody: "The very purpose of a Bill of Rights was to withdraw certain subjects from the vicissitudes of political controversy, to place them beyond the reach of majorities and officials and to establish them as legal principles to be applied by the courts. One's right to life, liberty, and property, to free speech, a free press, freedom of worship and assembly, and other fundamental rights may not be submitted to vote; they depend on the outcome of no elections."[88]

Not only does the Bill of Rights put fundamental liberties beyond the reach of majorities (the first sense of the priority of right); underlying these rights is the idea that the Constitution is neutral among ends, that government may not impose a particular conception of the good life (the second sense of the priority of right): "Free public education, if faithful to the ideal of secular instruction and political neutrality, will not be partisan or enemy of any class, creed, party, or faction. . . . If there is any fixed star in our constitutional constellation, it is that no official, high or petty, can prescribe what shall be orthodox in politics, nationalism, religion, or other matters of opinion . . ."[89]

If not by compulsory flag salutes, how may the state cultivate a common citizenship? The answer came in a concurring opinion by Justices Black and Douglas, who had changed their minds in the years since *Gobitis*. Patriotism would be a matter of choice, not of inculcation, a voluntary act by free and independent selves. A sense of community would flow from a sense of justice rather than the other way around: "Love of country must spring from willing hearts and free minds, inspired by a fair administration of wise laws enacted by the people's elected representatives within the bounds of express constitutional prohibitions."[90]

With *West Virginia v. Barnette*, the procedural republic had arrived.

3

Religious Liberty and Freedom of Speech

After World War II, the Supreme Court assumed as its primary role the protection of individual rights against government infringement. Increasingly, it defined these rights according to the requirement that government be neutral on the question of the good life, and defended neutrality as essential to respecting persons as free and independent selves, unencumbered by moral ties antecedent to choice. The modern Supreme Court thus gives clear expression to the public philosophy of the procedural republic. In its hands, American constitutional law has come to embody the priority of the right over the good. The areas of religion and speech illustrate the influence of this liberalism in our constitutional practice; they also display the difficulties it confronts.

Seeking Neutrality toward Religion

The principle of government neutrality found its first sustained application in cases involving religion. Time and again the Supreme Court has held that "in the relationship between man and religion, the State is firmly committed to a position of neutrality."[1] "Government in our democracy, state and national, must be neutral in matters of religious theory, doctrine, and practice. . . . The First Amendment mandates governmental neutrality between religion and religion, and between religion and nonreligion."[2] Whether described as "a strict and lofty neutrality,"[3] a "wholesome neutrality,"[4] or a "benevolent neutrality,"[5] the principle "that the Government must pursue a course of complete neutrality toward religion"[6] is well established in American constitutional law.

In liberal political thought, religion offers the paradigmatic case for bracketing controversial conceptions of the good.[7] The Supreme Court has conveyed its insistence on bracketing religion by invoking Jefferson's metaphor of a "wall of separation between church and state."[8] While some have complained that "a rule of law should not be drawn from a figure of speech,"[9] most see the wall as a symbol of resolve to keep religion from bursting the constitutional brackets that contain it. Since "the breach of neutrality that is today a trickling stream may all too soon become a raging torrent,"[10] the "wall between Church and State . . . must be kept high and impregnable."[11]

For all its familiarity, the requirement that government be neutral on matters of religion is not a long-standing principle of constitutional law, but a development of the last fifty years. Not until 1947 did the Supreme Court hold that government must be neutral toward religion.[12] The American tradition of religious liberty goes back further, of course. The Constitution forbids religious tests for federal office (Article VI), and the first words of the First Amendment declare that "Congress shall make no law respecting an establishment of religion, or prohibiting the free exercise thereof." But the Bill of Rights did not apply to the states, and at the time of its adoption, six of the thirteen states maintained religious establishments.[13] Far from prohibiting these arrangements, the First Amendment was enacted in part to protect state religious establishments from federal interference.[14]

Within the states, the most eventful struggle for the separation of church and state occurred in Virginia, where it was waged by Jefferson and Madison. In 1776 the legislature disestablished the Anglican church but left open the possibility of a "general assessment," or tax for the support of religion. Jefferson argued for complete separation of church and state, and in "A Bill for Establishing Religious Freedom" (1779) he proposed that "no man shall be compelled to frequent or support any religious worship, place, or ministry whatsoever."[15]

After several years of inconclusive debate, Patrick Henry introduced a general assessment bill to support "teachers of the Christian Religion." Under Henry's proposal, each taxpayer could designate which Christian church would receive his tax. Henry defended his plan on the nonsectarian grounds that the diffusion of Christian knowledge would help "correct the morals of men, restrain their vices, and preserve the peace of society." Madison led the opposition and wrote a pamphlet, *Memorial and Remonstrance against Religious Assessments* (1785), that helped turn opinion against the bill. After defeating the general assessment, Madison won passage of Jefferson's bill guaranteeing separation of church and state.[16]

Some states did not disestablish religion until well into the nineteenth century. Connecticut continued tax support for religion until 1818, Massachusetts until 1833. New Jersey restricted full civil rights to Protestants until 1844, and Maryland required belief in God as a condition of public office until the U.S. Supreme Court struck it down in 1961.[17] Even in states without establishments, some nineteenth-century courts held Christianity to be part of the common law. In a New York case in 1811, Chancellor James Kent upheld a conviction for blasphemy on the ground that "we are a Christian people, and the morality of the country is deeply ingrafted upon Christianity."[18]

In 1845 the U.S. Supreme Court confirmed that the Bill of Rights did not prevent the states from infringing religious freedom: "The Constitution makes no provision for protecting the citizens of the respective states in their religious liberties; this is left to the state constitutions and laws."[19] As far as the U.S. Constitution was concerned, the states were free to establish a church or even "to recreate the Inquisition," at least until the adoption of the Fourteenth Amendment.[20]

Even after the adoption of the Fourteenth Amendment, attempts to assert government neutrality toward religion confronted difficulty. In 1876 President Grant spoke out against public support for sectarian schools, and fellow Republican James G. Blaine introduced in Congress a constitutional amendment to that end: "No State shall make any law respecting an establishment of religion or prohibiting the free exercise thereof; and no money raised by taxation in any state for the support of public schools . . . shall ever be under the control of any religious sect or denomination." The amendment passed the House but was defeated in the Senate, partly because of Catholic opposition, partly because of a belief that existing constitutional protections were adequate.[21]

Two years later the Supreme Court upheld a federal law banning polygamy, a practice the Mormons regarded a religious duty. In *Reynolds v. United States* (1878), a Mormon convicted under the statute complained it denied him the free exercise of religion guaranteed in the First Amendment. After citing Madison's *Memorial and Remonstrance* and Jefferson's "wall of separation," the Court nonetheless upheld the conviction, arguing that the First Amendment protected religious belief but not practice. "Polygamy has always been odious" among Western nations, the Court declared, adding that polygamy was less conducive than monogamy to democratic government.[22]

Not until the 1940s did the Court apply the First Amendment's religion clauses to the states and declare the separation of church and state a principle of constitutional law. In *Cantwell v. Connecticut* (1940), the Court held that the Fourteenth Amendment incorporated both the establishment and free exercise clauses of the Bill of Rights and "rendered the legislatures of the states as incompetent as Congress to enact such laws."[23] In *Everson v. Board of Education of Ewing Township* (1947), the Court gave the establishment clause a broad interpretation and enforced, for the first time, Jefferson's "wall of separation between church and state."[24]

Writing for the Court, Justice Black gave forceful expression to the principle of government neutrality. "Neither a state nor the Federal Government can set up a church. Neither can pass laws which aid one religion, aid all religions, or prefer one religion over another. . . . No tax in any amount, large or small, can be levied to support any religious activities or institutions." The First Amendment "requires the state to be a neutral in its relations with groups of religious believers and non-believers."[25]

Since *Everson*, religion has generated much constitutional controversy, but the principle that government must be neutral toward religion has rarely been questioned.[26] For the most part, the justices have cast their disagreements as arguments about the proper application of neutrality, not about the principle itself. In fact Black's landmark opinion in *Everson* came in the course of upholding a state subsidy for bus transportation of parochial school students. The dissenters applauded the Court's insistence on "complete and uncompromising separation" but found it "utterly discordant" with the result in the case.[27]

In 1963 the Court ruled that Bible reading in the public schools was a religious exercise at odds with the requirement "that the Government maintain strict neutrality, neither aiding nor opposing religion." Justice Potter Stewart dissented, but in the name of neutrality. Permission of religious exercises is necessary, he argued, "if the schools are truly to be neutral in the matter of religion. A refusal to permit religious exercises thus is seen, not as the realization of state neutrality, but rather as the establishment of a religion of secularism, or at the least, as government support of the beliefs of those who think that religious exercises should be conducted only in private."[28]

In 1968 the Court struck down an Arkansas law that banned the teaching of evolution. "Government must be neutral in matters of religious theory, doctrine, and practice," wrote Justice Abe Fortas. "It may not be hostile to any religion." In a concurring opinion, Justice Black agreed with the result but doubted that the principle of neutrality supported it. If Darwinism contradicts some people's religious convictions, then it is hardly neutral to teach it in the public schools: "If the theory is considered anti-religious, how can the State be bound by the Federal Constitution to permit its teachers to advocate such an 'anti-religious' doctrine to schoolchildren?"[29]

Black pointed out that the Court might simply take the view that fundamentalists who regard evolution as antireligious are wrong. But that would be taking sides in the controversy the Court purports to bracket. "Unless this Court is prepared simply to write off as pure nonsense the views of those who consider evolution an anti-religious doctrine," Black argued, the issue was more difficult than the Court acknowledged. A better way to bracket, he suggested, might be to remove the controversial subject from the schools altogether, as Arkansas arguably did. So long as the biblical account of creation was not taught instead, "does not the removal of the subject of evolution leave the State in a neutral position toward these supposedly competing religious and anti-religious doctrines?"[30]

The contest for the mantle of neutrality continued in 1985, when the Court struck down a moment-of-silence statute permitting voluntary prayer in Alabama schools. The Court held that since the purpose of the law was to restore prayer to the schools, it violated "the established principle that the Government must pursue a course of complete neutrality toward religion." Chief Justice Warren Burger dissented, arguing that the prohibition "manifests not neutrality but hostility toward religion."[31]

Even in cases in which the Supreme Court has upheld government involvement in arguably religious practices, it has taken pains to maintain that the religious aspect is only incidental, that the involvement does not endorse or advance or prefer religion. In *McGowan v. Maryland* (1961), the Court upheld Sunday closing laws on the grounds that they no longer retained their religious character. Notwithstanding their religious origins, wrote Chief Justice Warren, laws prohibiting business and commercial activity on Sundays now served the secular purpose of "providing a Sunday atmosphere of recreation, cheerfulness, repose and enjoyment. . . . The air of the day is one of relaxation rather than one of religion."[32]

In 1984 the Burger Court upheld on similar grounds a city-sponsored Christmas display including a creche, or nativity scene. The purpose of the display was to celebrate the holiday and to depict its origins, the Court held. "These are legitimate secular purposes." Any benefit it brought to religion was "indirect, remote and incidental." Display of the creche was no more an advancement or endorsement of religion than the exhibition of religious paintings in governmentally supported museums.[33]

In both cases, dissenters criticized the Court for failing to take seriously the religious character of the practices they upheld. "No matter what is said, the parentage of [the Sunday closing] laws is the Fourth Commandment," wrote Justice William O. Douglas. "They serve and satisfy the religious predispositions of our Christian communities."[34] Dissenting in the creche case, Justice Harry A. Blackmun complained that the majority had done "an injustice to the creche and the message it manifests." In the hands of the Court, "The creche has been relegated to the role of a neutral harbinger of the holiday season, useful for commercial purposes, but devoid of any inherent meaning and incapable of enhancing the religious tenor of a display of which it is an integral part. . . . Surely, this is a misuse of a sacred symbol."[35]

Justifying Neutrality toward Religion

In order to assess the Court's conflicting applications of neutrality, it is necessary to consider the reasons for neutrality. What counts as neutrality depends partly on what justifies neutrality, and the Court has offered two different sorts of justification for insisting that government be neutral toward religion. The first has to do with protecting the interests of religion on the one hand and those of the state on the other. "The First Amendment rests on the premise that both religion and government can best work to achieve their lofty aims if each is left free from the other within its respective sphere."[36] "We have staked the very existence of our country on the fact that complete separation between the state and religion is best for the state and best for religion."[37] "In the long view the independence of both church and state in their respective spheres will be better served by close adherence to the neutrality principle."[38]

The religious interest served by separation is in avoiding the corruption that comes with dependence on civil authority. A century and a half before Jefferson stated the secular case for a "wall of separation" between church and state, Roger Williams gave the metaphor a theological meaning. "When they have opened a gap in the hedge or wall of separation between the garden of the church and the wilderness of the world," he wrote, "God hath ever broke down the wall itself, removed the candlestick, and made His garden a wilderness, as at this day."[39]

The Court has invoked the theological argument for separation only occasionally, and usually in combination with other arguments. In striking down school prayer, for example, Justice Black argued that the establishment clause "rested on the belief that a union of government and religion tends to destroy government and to degrade religion." The history of established religion "showed that many people lost their respect for any religion that had relied upon the support of government to spread its faith." The Founders sought by the Establishment clause to avoid the "unhallowed perversion" of religion by a civil magistrate.[40] And Justice William J. Brennan emphasized that separation is important not only for the sake of the nonbeliever but also for "the devout believer who fears the secularization of a creed which becomes too deeply involved with and dependent upon the government."[41]

The political interest served by separation is in avoiding the civil strife that has historically attended church-state entanglements. Providing public funds for religion brings "the struggle of sect against sect. . . . It is only by observing the prohibition rigidly that the state can maintain its neutrality and avoid partisanship in the dissensions inevitable when sect opposes sect over demands for public moneys."[42] Opposing public school involvement in a "released time" program for religious instruction, Justice Frankfurter wrote that "the public school must be kept scrupulously free from entanglement in the strife of sects."[43] In a similar case, Justice Black vividly recalled the danger of sectarian strife that separation was meant to prevent. "Colonial history had already shown that, here as elsewhere zealous sectarians entrusted with governmental power to further their causes would sometimes torture, maim and kill those they branded 'heretics,' 'atheists' or 'agnostics.'"[44]

Existing alongside the argument that neutrality is best for both religion and the state is an argument in the name of individual freedom. On this justification, the state must be neutral not only to avoid compromising religion and provoking sectarian strife, but also to avoid the danger of coercion. This argument goes back to the eighteenth-century concern for freedom of conscience, and in its modern form emphasizes respect for persons' freedom to choose their religious convictions for themselves. It thus connects the case for neutrality with the liberal conception of the person.

In its modern, or voluntarist, version, this argument for religious liberty first appears in *Cantwell,* the case that announced the incorporation of the religion clauses. "Freedom of conscience and freedom to adhere to such religious organization or form of worship as the individual may choose cannot be restricted by law." The First Amendment "safeguards the free exercise of the chosen form of religion."[45] In banning Bible reading in the public schools, the Court found justification for neutrality in "the right of every person to freely choose his own course" with reference to religion, "free of any compulsion from the state." Justice Stewart dissented from the result but endorsed the view that neutrality is required for the sake of respect for individual choice, "a refusal on the part of the state to weight the scales of private choice."[46]

Contemporary commentators have identified the voluntarist argument for neutrality as the primary justification for the separation of church and state. "[T]he fundamental principle underlying both religion clauses is the protection of individual choice in matters of religion—whether pro or con."[47] "[S]ince freedom of religious choice, not neutrality per se, is the fundamental establishment value, the neutrality tool is useful only insofar as it promotes that choice."[48] "[T]he moral basis of the antiestablishment clause is . . . equal respect," not for religious beliefs themselves, but "for the processes of forming and changing such conceptions."[49]

By the 1980s and 1990s, the freedom of choice assumed to be at stake in religion cases was not only the right to choose a form of worship that expresses one's religious beliefs but also the right to choose the beliefs themselves. In a case involving a city-sponsored display of a menorah alongside a Christmas tree, Justice Sandra Day O'Connor approved the arrangement on the grounds that it did not endorse religion but conveyed "a message of pluralism and freedom to choose one's own beliefs."[50] Concurring in a case that banned prayers led by clergy at public school graduation ceremonies, Justice Blackmun wrote: "Even subtle pressure diminishes the right of each individual to choose voluntarily what to believe."[51]

Perhaps the most explicit statement of the voluntarist conception of religious liberty is the one that appears in Justice John Paul Stevens' opinion for the Court in a 1985 case striking down Alabama's moment of silence for voluntary prayer in public schools. "[T]he individual's freedom to choose his own creed is the counterpart of his right to refrain from accepting the creed established by the majority," Stevens wrote; "the Court has unambiguously concluded that the individual freedom of conscience protected by the First Amendment embraces the right to select any religious faith or none at all. This conclusion derives support not only from the interest in respecting the individual's freedom of conscience, but also from the conviction that *religious beliefs worthy of respect are the product of free and voluntary choice* by the faithful."[52]

Stevens' opinion illustrates the connection between the voluntarist justification of neutrality and the liberal conception of the person. It holds that government should be neutral toward religion in order to respect persons as free and independent selves, capable of choosing their religious convictions for themselves. The respect this neutrality commands is not, strictly speaking, respect for religion, but respect for the self whose religion it is, or respect for the dignity that consists in the capacity to choose one's religion freely. Religious beliefs are "worthy of respect," not in virtue of what they are beliefs *in,* but rather in virtue of being "the product of free and voluntary choice," in virtue of being beliefs of a self unencumbered by convictions antecedent to choice.

By invoking the voluntarist conception of neutrality, the Court gives constitutional expression to the version of liberalism that conceives the right as prior to the good and the self as prior to its ends, at least where religion is concerned. We are now in a position to see how both the promise and the problems of the theory make themselves felt in the practice the theory informs.

The voluntarist case for neutrality, insisting as it does on respect for persons, seems to secure for religious liberty a firm foundation. Unlike Roger Williams' case for separation of church and state, it does not depend on any particular religious doctrine. And unlike the political case for separation, it does not leave religious liberty hostage to uncertain calculations about how best to avoid civil strife. Under present conditions, such calculations may or may not support the separation of church and state. As Justice Lewis Powell has observed, the risk "of deep political division along religious lines" is by now "remote."[53] We do not live on the brink of the wars of religion that made the case for separation so pressing. Even granting the importance of avoiding sectarian strife, a strict separation of church and state may at times provoke more strife than it prevents. The school prayer decisions of the early 1960s, for example, set off a storm of political controversy that has persisted over three decades.[54] A Court concerned above all to avoid social discord might reasonably have decided those cases the other way.

The voluntarist case for neutrality, by contrast, does not tie religious liberty to such contingencies. In affirming a notion of respect for persons, it recalls the ideal of freedom of conscience. By emphasizing the individual's right to choose his or her beliefs, it points beyond religion to "the broader perspective" of autonomy rights in general, including "the rights of privacy and personhood."[55] It thus casts religious liberty as a particular case of the liberal claim for the priority of the right over the good and the self-image that attends it. Respecting persons as selves defined prior to the religious convictions they affirm becomes a particular case of the general principle of respect for selves defined prior to their aims and attachments.

But as we have seen, the image of the unencumbered self, despite its appeal, is inadequate to the liberty it promises. In the case of religion, the liberal conception of the person ill equips the Court to secure religious liberty for those who regard themselves as claimed by religious commitments they have not chosen. Not all religious beliefs can be redescribed without loss as "the product of free and voluntary choice by the faithful."

Freedom of Conscience versus Freedom of Choice

This difficulty can be seen by contrasting the voluntarist account of religious liberty with freedom of conscience as traditionally conceived. For Madison and Jefferson, freedom of conscience meant the freedom to exercise religious liberty—to worship or not, to support a church or not, to profess belief or disbelief—without suffering civil penalties or incapacities. It had nothing to do with a right to choose one's beliefs. Madison's *Memorial and Remonstrance* consists of fifteen arguments for the separation of church and state, and not one makes any mention of "autonomy" or "choice."[56] The only choice referred to in Jefferson's "Bill for Establishing Religious Freedom" is attributed to God, not man.[57]

Madison and Jefferson understood religious liberty as the right to exercise religious duties according to the dictates of conscience, not the right to choose religious beliefs. In fact their argument for religious liberty relies heavily on the assumption that beliefs are not a matter of choice. The first sentence of Jefferson's Bill states this assumption clearly: "the opinions and beliefs of men depend not on their own will, but follow involuntarily the evidence proposed to their own minds."[58] Since I can believe only what I am persuaded is true, belief is not the sort of thing that coercion can compel. Coercion can produce hypocrisy but not conviction. In this assumption Jefferson echoed the view of John Locke, who wrote in *A Letter concerning Toleration* (1689), "it is absurd that things should be enjoined by laws which are not in men's power to perform. And to believe this or that to be true, does not depend upon our will."[59]

It is precisely because belief is not governed by the will that freedom of conscience is inalienable. Even if he would, a person could not give it up. This was Madison's argument in *Memorial and Remonstrance*. "The Religion then of every man must be left to the conviction and conscience of every man; and it is the right of every man to exercise it as these may dictate. This right is in its nature an unalienable right. It is unalienable, because the opinions of men, depending only on the evidence contemplated by their own minds cannot follow the dictates of other men: It is unalienable also, because what is here a right towards men, is a duty towards the Creator."[60]

Oddly enough, Justice Stevens cited this passage from Madison in support of the voluntarist view. But freedom of conscience and freedom of choice are not the same; where conscience dictates, choice decides. Where freedom of conscience is at stake, the relevant right is to perform a duty, not to make a choice. This was the issue for Madison and Jefferson. Religious liberty addressed the problem of encumbered selves, claimed by duties they cannot renounce, even in the face of civil obligations that may conflict.

To question the voluntarist justification of religious liberty is not necessarily to agree with Locke that people never choose their religious beliefs. It is simply to dispute what the voluntarist view asserts, that religious beliefs worthy of respect are the products of free and voluntary choice. What makes a religious belief worthy of respect is not its mode of acquisition—whether by choice, revelation, persuasion, or habituation—but its place in a good life or, from a political point of view, its tendency to promote the habits and dispositions that make good citizens.[61] Insofar as the case for religious liberty rests on respect for religion, it must assume that, generally speaking, religious beliefs and practices are of sufficient moral or civic importance to warrant special constitutional protection.

For procedural liberalism, however, the case for religious liberty derives not from the moral importance of religion but from the need to protect individual autonomy; government should be neutral toward religion for the same reason it should be neutral toward competing conceptions of the good life generally—to respect people's capacity to choose their own values and ends. But despite its liberating promise, or perhaps because of it, this broader mission depreciates the claims of those for whom religion is not an expression of autonomy but a matter of conviction unrelated to a choice. Protecting religion as a life-style, as one among the values that an independent self may have, may miss the role that religion plays in the lives of those for whom the observance of religious duties is a constitutive end, essential to their good and indispensable to their identity. Treating persons as "self-originating sources of valid claims"[62] may thus fail to respect persons bound by duties derived from sources other than themselves.

The case of *Thornton v. Caldor, Inc.* (1985) shows how voluntarist assumptions can crowd out religious liberty for encumbered selves. In an eight-to-one decision, the Supreme Court struck down a Connecticut statute guaranteeing sabbath observers a right not to work on their sabbath.[63] Although the law gave all workers the right to one day off each week, it gave to sabbath observers alone the right to designate their day. In this lack of neutrality the Court found constitutional infirmity.

Chief Justice Burger, writing for the Court, noted that sabbath observers would typically take a weekend day, "widely prized as a day off." But "other employees who have strong and legitimate, but non-religious reasons for wanting a weekend day off have no rights under the statute." They "must take a back seat to the Sabbath observers." Justice O'Connor echoed this worry in a concurring opinion: "All employees, regardless of their religious orientation, would value the benefit which the statute bestows on Sabbath observers—the right to select the day of the week in which to refrain from labor."[64]

But this objection confuses the right to perform a duty with the right to make a choice. Sabbath observers, by definition, do not *select* the day of the week they rest; they rest on the day their religion requires. The benefit the statute confers is not the right to choose a day of rest, but the right to perform the duty of sabbath observance on the only day it can be carried out.

Considered together with earlier decisions upholding Sunday closing Laws, *Thornton v. Caldor* yields a curious constitutional conclusion: A state may require everyone to rest on Sunday, the day of the Christian sabbath, so long as the aim is not to accommodate observance of the sabbath. But it may not give sabbath observers the right to rest on the day of the week their religion requires. Perverse though this result may seem from the standpoint of respecting religious liberty, it aptly reflects the constitutional consequences of seeing ourselves as unencumbered selves.

The Court has on occasion accorded greater respect to the claims of encumbered selves. When a Seventh-Day Adventist was fired from her job for refusing to work on Saturday, her sabbath, she was denied unemployment compensation under a rule requiring applicants to accept available work. The Supreme Court decided in her favor, holding that the state could not force a worker to choose between her religious convictions and means of support. According to the Court, requiring the state to take account of sabbath observance in the administration of its unemployment program did not prefer religion in violation of neutrality. Rather, it enforced "the governmental obligation of neutrality in the face of religious differences." In this case at least, the Constitution was not blind to religion but alive to its imperatives.[65]

In cases involving conscientious objection to military service, the Court has interpreted federal law broadly and refused to restrict exemptions to those with theistic beliefs. The relevant test is "whether a given belief that is sincere and meaningful occupies a place in the life of its possessor parallel to that filled by the orthodox belief in God."[66] What matters is not "conventional piety" but an imperative of conscience rising above the level of a policy preference.[67] The point of the exemption, according to the Court, is to prevent persons bound by moral duties they cannot renounce from having to violate either those duties or the law. This aim is consistent with Madison's and Jefferson's concern for the predicament of persons claimed by dictates of conscience they are not at liberty to choose. As the Court wrote, "the painful dilemma of the sincere conscientious objector arises precisely because he feels himself bound in conscience not to compromise his beliefs or affiliations."[68]

In *Wisconsin v. Yoder* (1972), the Court upheld the right of the Old Order Amish not to send their children to school beyond the eighth grade, despite a state law requiring school attendance until age sixteen. Higher education would expose Amish children to worldly and competitive values contrary to the insular, agrarian way of life that sustains Amish community and religious practice. The Court emphasized that the Amish claim was "not merely a matter of personal preference, but one of deep religious conviction" that pervades their way of life. Though "neutral on its face," Wisconsin's school attendance law unduly burdened the free exercise of religion, and so offended "the constitutional requirement for governmental neutrality."[69]

The Court's occasional hospitality to the claims of encumbered selves did not extend to Captain Simcha Goldman, an Orthodox Jew whom the Air Force prohibited from wearing a yarmulke while on duty in the health clinic where he served. Justice William H. Rehnquist, writing for the Court, held for the Air Force on grounds of judicial deference to the "professional judgment of military authorities" on the importance of uniform dress. Of the precedents he cited in support of deference to the military, all involved interests other than religious duties or conscientious imperatives. "The essence of military service 'is the subordination of the desires and interests of the individual to the needs of the service.'" Standardized uniforms encourage "the subordination of personal preferences and identities in favor of the overall mission." Having compared the wearing of a yarmulke to "desires," "interests," and "personal preferences" unrelated to religion, Rehnquist did not require the Air Force to show that an exception for yarmulkes would impair its disciplinary objectives. Nor even did he acknowledge that a religious duty was at stake, allowing only that, given the dress code, "military life may be more objectionable for petitioner."[70]

The Court's lack of concern for persons encumbered by religious convictions found its most decisive expression in a 1990 case that involved the sacramental use of the drug peyote by members of the Native American Church. Two members of the church were fired from their jobs at a private drug rehabilitation center because they ingested peyote, a drug prohibited by state law, as part of a religious ceremony. The workers were denied unemployment compensation on the grounds that they had been dismissed for violating a law. The Supreme Court upheld the denial. Writing for the Court, Justice Antonin Scalia maintained that the right of free exercise protects persons only from laws directed against their religion, not from neutral laws of general applicability that happen to burden their religious practice. Provided it did not target a particular religion, a state could pass laws that burdened certain religious practices even without having to show a "compelling state interest," or special justification.[71]

It might seem that Court rulings refusing special protection for sacramental peyote, the wearing of yarmulkes, or the accommodation of sabbath observance are decisions that depart from liberal principles; since they fail to vindicate the rights of individuals against the prerogatives of the majority, such decisions might seem at odds with the liberalism that asserts the priority of the right over the good. But these cases illustrate two features of procedural liberalism that, ironically, lead to illiberal consequences where religion is concerned. First, the conception of persons as freely choosing selves, unencumbered by antecedent moral ties, supports the notion that religious beliefs should be regarded, for constitutional purposes at least, as products of "free and voluntary choice." If all religious beliefs are matters of choice, however, it is difficult to distinguish between claims of conscience on the one hand and personal preferences and desires on the other. Once this distinction is lost, the right to demand of the state a special justification for laws that burden religious beliefs is bound to appear as nothing more than "a private right to ignore generally applicable laws." So indiscriminate a right would allow each person "to become a law unto himself" and create a society "courting anarchy."[72]

Second, the procedural liberal's insistence on neutrality fits uneasily with the notion that the Constitution singles out religion for special protection. If religious beliefs must be accorded constitutional protection that other interests do not enjoy, then judges must discriminate, at least to the extent of assessing the moral weight of the governmental interest at stake and the nature of the burden that interest may impose on certain religious practices. The attempt to avoid substantive moral judgments of this kind leads some to insist on neutrality even at the cost of leaving religious liberty subject to the vagaries of democratic politics. For example, Scalia concedes that leaving religious accommodation to the political process will place religious minorities at a disadvantage, but he maintains that this "unavoidable consequence of democratic government must be preferred to a system in which each conscience is a law unto itself or in which judges weigh the social importance of all laws against the centrality of all religious beliefs."[73]

Outrage from religious organizations and civil liberties groups at the weakening of religious liberty in the peyote case prompted Congress to enact the Religious Freedom Restoration Act (1993), a statute barring government from substantially burdening the exercise of religion without demonstrating a compelling governmental interest.[74] But the way the constitutional law of religion has unfolded over the past half-century sheds light on the liberal political theory it came to express. The Court's tendency to assimilate religious liberty to liberty in general reflects the aspiration to neutrality; people should be free to pursue their own interests and ends, whatever they are, consistent with a similar liberty for others. But this generalizing tendency does not always serve religious liberty well. It confuses the pursuit of preferences with the exercise of duties, and so forgets the special concern of religious liberty with the claims of conscientiously encumbered selves.

This confusion has led the Court to restrict religious practices it should permit, such as yarmulkes in the military, and also to permit practices it should probably restrict, such as nativity scenes in the public square. In different ways, both decisions fail to take religion seriously. Permitting Pawtucket's creche might seem to be a ruling sympathetic to religion. But as Justice Blackmun rightly protested, the Court's permission came at the price of denying the sacred meaning of the symbol it protected.

Freedom of Speech: The Advent of Neutrality

In American constitutional law, the principle that government must be neutral among competing conceptions of the good goes beyond the case of religion. It also applies to freedom of speech. Just as government may not favor one religious belief over others, so it must be neutral in its treatment of the various views its citizens may advocate. Although government may impose "content-neutral" restrictions on the time, place, and manner of speech in public places, such regulations "may not be affected by sympathy or hostility for the point of view being expressed."[75] The Supreme Court has repeatedly ruled that the First Amendment "bars the state from imposing on its citizens an authoritative vision of the truth"[76] or a preferred conception of the good life. "Above all else, the First Amendment means that government has no power to restrict expression because of its message, its ideas, its subject matter, or its content."[77]

As with religion, so with speech, the requirement of neutrality is a recent development, a product of the last few decades. For all the prominence of freedom of speech in recent constitutional debates—free speech issues consume more than one-quarter of a leading constitutional law casebook[78]—the Supreme Court scarcely dealt with the subject until after World War I.[79] The First Amendment provided that "Congress shall make no law . . . abridging the freedom of speech, or of the press," but did not protect individual rights against government as such. Its framers cared less about protecting individual expression "than they cared for states' rights and the federal principle." They intended the clause "to reserve to the *states* an exclusive legislative authority in the field of speech and press."[80]

The Sedition Act of 1798, enacted by the Federalists to make libel against the government a federal crime, was never challenged to the Supreme Court. In the Kentucky and Virginia Resolutions, Jefferson and Madison attacked the law as unconstitutional, not for infringing individual rights, but for usurping the prerogatives of the states to punish seditious libel. As Jefferson later wrote, the power to restrain the "overwhelming torrent of slander which is confounding all vice and virtue, all truth and falsehood in the US . . . is fully possessed by the several state legislatures. . . . While we deny that Congress have a right to controul the freedom of the press, we have ever asserted the right of the states, and their exclusive right to do so."[81]

It was more than a century before the Supreme Court gave serious attention to free speech claims. Not until the passage of the Espionage and Sedition Acts of 1917 did civil liberties become a significant issue in American political debate.[82] In a number of early cases, the Court refused to uphold the free speech claims of radical advocates, citing the "clear and present danger" of subversive speech.[83] Holmes and Brandeis soon began to champion free speech in dissent,[84] but it was not until the late 1920s and early 1930s that the Court began to reverse convictions for subversive advocacy.[85]

Even when the Court began to protect freedom of speech, it did not insist that government had to treat all speech neutrally, without regard to its value. Throughout the 1940s and 1950s, the Court routinely distinguished speech the First Amendment protected from speech it did not, "high-value" versus "low-value" speech. This "two-level theory of free speech"[86] found its clearest expression in *Chaplinsky v. New Hampshire* (1942), where a unanimous court ruled that certain classes of speech are not protected by the First Amendment. "These include the lewd and obscene, the profane, the libelous, and the insulting or 'fighting' words—those which by their very utterance inflict injury or tend to incite an immediate breach of the peace." Such utterances, the Court held, "are no essential part of any exposition of ideas, and are of such slight social value" as to be outweighed by "the social interest in order and morality."[87]

Through the 1940s and 1950s, the Court continued to rule certain speech outside the bounds of the First Amendment. In 1942 it added commercial advertising to the categories of unprotected speech.[88] In *Beauharnais v. Illinois* (1952), it upheld a group libel law prohibiting racial defamation, holding that libelous utterances are not "within the area of constitutionally protected speech."[89] And in *Roth v. United States* (1957), the Court continued to distinguish among categories of speech, ruling that obscenity, being "utterly without redeeming social importance," is "not within the area of constitutionally protected speech or press."[90]

According to its advocates, the two-level theory enabled the Court to protect high-value speech more absolutely than an indiscriminate approach would allow.[91] On the other hand, critics object that discriminating among categories of speech compelled the Court to make "value judgments concerned with the content of expression, a role foreclosed to it by the basic theory of the First Amendment."[92] In the 1960s and 1970s, the Court gradually adopted the view of the critics and largely abandoned the *Chaplinsky* approach. In *New York Times Co. v. Sullivan* (1964), the Court rejected the two-level theory where libel was concerned, stating that laws against libel "can claim no talismanic immunity from constitutional limitations."[93] In *Stanley v. Georgia* (1969), it protected the private possession of obscene materials, holding that the "right to receive information and ideas, regardless of their social worth, is fundamental to our free society."[94] A series of decisions in the early 1970s narrowed the "fighting words" exception to virtual extinction,[95] and in 1976 the Court ruled that commercial speech was no longer outside the protection of the First Amendment.[96]

The erosion of the two-level theory relieves the Court of the task of assigning values to various categories of speech, and so signals the rise of neutrality as a principle of First Amendment jurisprudence. Meanwhile, the principle that government must be neutral toward speech found more explicit statement in the content neutrality doctrine of the 1970s and 1980s. This doctrine recognizes that government may have legitimate reasons to regulate speech, but insists that no restriction may be based on approval or disapproval of the speech in question.

While glimmers of the content neutrality doctrine can be found as early as Holmes's dissent in *Abrams*,[97] it found its first clear statement in *Police Department of the City of Chicago v. Mosley* (1972). The City of Chicago had banned picketing in front of schools except in connection with labor disputes, but the Supreme Court ruled that the ordinance wrongly discriminated on the basis of the content of speech. "Above all else, the First Amendment means that government has no power to restrict expression because of its message, its ideas, its subject matter, or its content." Government may not favor some views over others or "select which issues are worth discussing or debating in public facilities. There is an 'equality of status in the field of ideas,' and government must afford all points of view an equal opportunity to be heard."[98]

Since *Mosley*, the content neutrality doctrine has found wide application, and by the 1980s it had become "the most pervasively employed doctrine in the jurisprudence of free expression."[99] When the City of Jacksonville, Florida, prohibited drive-in movie theaters from showing films containing nudity on screens visible from public streets, the Court overturned the law for "discriminat[ing] among movies solely on the basis of content." The city had argued, somewhat paradoxically, that the ordinance was needed both to protect people from seeing things they did not want to see and to avoid distracting motorists and slowing traffic. The Court replied that "the Constitution does not permit government to decide which types of otherwise protected speech are sufficiently offensive to require protection for the unwilling listener or viewer." Moreover, other movies could also distract passing motorists, and "even a traffic regulation cannot discriminate on the basis of content unless there are clear reasons for the distinctions."[100]

When the New York Public Service Commission tried to prevent Consolidated Edison Company from inserting statements in its billing envelopes advocating nuclear power, the Court ruled that the restriction violated the utility's freedom of speech: "Governmental action that regulates speech on the basis of its subject matter 'slip[s] from the neutrality of time, place, and circumstance into a concern about content.'" The commission allowed inserts giving consumer information but banned those giving political views. According to the Court, this distinction failed the test of content neutrality, because restrictions "may not be based upon either the content or the subject matter of speech."[101]

The Court also invoked the content neutrality doctrine in striking down a law against burning the American flag.[102] And when the city of St. Paul, Minnesota, sought to convict a youth for burning a cross on a black family's lawn, the Court struck down St. Paul's ordinance against bias-motivated crimes on the grounds that it was not neutral. The ordinance prohibited cross-burnings and other symbols and graffiti targeting persons "on the basis of race, color, creed, religion, or gender." Since the law proscribed only those symbols "that communicate messages of racial, gender, or religious intolerance," it amounted to illegitimate content-based discrimination. "Selectivity of this sort," Justice Scalia wrote for the Court, "creates the possibility that the city is seeking to handicap the expression of particular ideas," a purpose the city readily acknowledged. Although the justices disagreed whether the law was objectionable because it covered too many categories of speech or too few, none dissented in the outcome.[103]

Obscenity and Neutrality

The assumption that government must be neutral among conceptions of the good generally appears in cases in which the Court protects speech that government would restrict. But the force of this assumption can also be seen where the Court has upheld restrictions on speech, most notably in obscenity cases. Although the Court has been reluctant to protect obscenity under the First Amendment, its reasoning in recent obscenity cases displays the powerful influence of neutrality assumptions on constitutional law.

Obscenity laws are sometimes justified on the grounds that obscenity leads to increased crime or other harmful consequences. But more often than not, they also reflect the view that obscenity is immoral as such: "Communities believe, and act on the belief, that obscenity is immoral, is wrong for the individual, and has no place in a decent society." Conceived in this way, obscenity laws are "based on traditional notions, rooted in this country's religious antecedents, of governmental responsibility for communal and individual 'decency' and 'morality.'"[104]

Insofar as they are justified on moral grounds, restrictions on obscenity violate the liberal principle that law should not embody any particular conception of the good. On the liberal view, it is illegitimate to base laws on judgments about morality and immorality, because to do so violates the principle that government should be neutral among ends. It violates people's "right to moral independence" by embodying in law a particular theory of the good life and the decent society. Laws restricting obscenity cannot be justified except insofar as it is possible "to winnow out those [reasons] that express moral condemnation." Obscenity laws reflecting "adverse moral convictions" about obscenity are "corrupted by such convictions," and so unjustifiable.[105]

In the years since *Roth* (1957), the Supreme Court has continued to uphold restrictions on the commercial publication and display of obscenity. But despite this continuity, the Court's arguments for upholding obscenity laws subtly changed from the 1950s to the 1970s, and changed in a way that came to acknowledge the principle of government neutrality. In *Roth*, the Court based its decision on traditional moral grounds; obscenity was "utterly without redeeming social importance," and so wholly outside constitutional protection.[106] In the 1970s, by contrast, the Court began to examine the state interests underlying obscenity laws. It upheld most of the laws, but only after attributing to them a purpose that did not involve a substantive moral judgment against obscenity as such. Consistent with the liberal commitment to neutrality, the Court strained, sometimes implausibly, to winnow out the reasons that expressed moral condemnation.

In *Paris Adult Theatre I v. Slaton* (1973), the Court upheld a law against the commercial exhibition of hard-core pornographic films. But the Court's opinion reflects its unease with the moral grounds that traditionally underlie such restrictions. Writing for the Court, Chief Justice Burger held that the "legitimate state interests at stake in stemming the tide of commercialized obscenity" include "the quality of life and the total community environment, the tone of commerce in the great city centers, and, possibly, the public safety itself."[107] Quite apart from any possible correlation between obscenity and crime, he added, "what is commonly read and seen and heard and done intrudes upon us all, want it or not."[108] As if reluctant to admit that his argument allowed states to affirm a particular conception of the good, however, Burger went on to deny that the obscenity law in question implies a moral judgment. "The issue . . . goes beyond whether someone, or even the majority, considers the conduct depicted as 'wrong' or 'sinful.' The States have the power to make a *morally neutral judgment* that public exhibition of obscene material, or commerce in such material, has a tendency to injure the community as a whole, to endanger the public safety, or to jeopardize . . . the States' 'right to maintain a decent society.'"[109]

Even in defending the right of states to regulate obscenity, Burger wrote as if embarrassed to acknowledge the moral objection to obscenity as such. But this flight from moral judgment undercuts the coherence of Burger's argument. Allowing the states to decide that commerce in obscenity may "injure the community as a whole" begs the question whether communal injury can consist in an offense against shared moral standards. If communal injury may not include moral corruption, then why speak of "the tone of society" rather than crime rates and public safety alone? If communal well-being does include a moral dimension, then why pretend it can be protected by a "morally neutral judgment"? Burger's opinion in *Paris* is revealing not just for its confusion but for the way its confusion reflects the pressure to bracket moral judgments.

In subsequent cases the Court continued to insist that government not discriminate against sexually explicit films on grounds of moral disapproval. Sometimes this insistence on neutrality took the form of striking down a restriction, as in *Erznoznik v. City of Jacksonville*.[110] In other cases, it meant upholding restrictions while insisting, however implausibly, that they did not presuppose any adverse moral judgment of the movies they regulated.

In *Young v. American Mini Theatres, Inc.* (1976), for example, the Court upheld a Detroit "Anti–Skid Row Ordinance" as wholly consistent with "government's paramount obligation of neutrality in its regulation

of protected communication." Regulating the places where sexually explicit films may be exhibited is "unaffected by whatever social, political,
or philosophical message a film may be intended to communicate," wrote
Justice Stevens. "Whether a motion picture ridicules or characterizes one
point of view or another, the effect of the ordinances is exactly the
same."[111] The ordinance was justified by the city's interest in "preserving
the character of its neighborhoods," not in suppressing unworthy depictions. According to Stevens, the city's interest was in avoiding crime and
deterioration of the neighborhood, not moral offense. This rendered its
interest morally neutral, and hence legitimate. "It is this secondary effect
which the zoning ordinances attempt to avoid, not the dissemination of
'offensive' speech."[112]

In 1986 the Court upheld another zoning ordinance on similar
grounds. According to Justice Rehnquist, a Renton, Washington, city
ordinance restricting the location of "adult" film theaters "aimed not at
the *content* of the films shown at 'adult motion picture theaters,' but
rather at the *secondary effects* of such theaters on the surrounding community." Among these secondary effects were preventing crime, protecting the city's retail trade, maintaining property values, and generally
"protecting and preserving the quality of the city's neighborhoods, commercial districts, and the quality of urban life," where the quality of life
presumably did not include its moral tone or character. The law was thus
"unrelated to the suppression of free expression," and so consistent with
requirement that regulations be "justified without reference to the content
of the regulated speech."[113]

Writing in dissent, Justice Brennan disputed the Court's claim that the
zoning laws were "unrelated to the suppression of free expression," and
argued that the Court allowed the city of Renton "to conceal its illicit
motives." He pointed out that the city council's stated reasons for its
ordinance included the claims that adult entertainment on main commercial thoroughfares "gives an impression of legitimacy to, and causes a loss
of sensitivity to the adverse effect of pornography upon children, established family relations, respect for marital relationship and for the sanctity
of marriage relations of others," and that locating such entertainment in
close proximity to homes, churches, parks, and schools "will cause a
degradation of the community standard of morality." Only later, indeed

only after the lawsuit began, did the city argue that the purpose of the law was to address the "secondary effects" of adult movie theaters.[114]

As these cases show, it is difficult to justify laws restricting obscenity and pornography by relying on "morally neutral judgments" about "secondary effects" alone. What is striking is how hard the Court tries nonetheless to bracket these moral considerations even as it upholds the laws. Although the principle of neutrality has taken hold of First Amendment law only in recent decades, its presence can now be seen in decisions permissive and restrictive alike. And with speech as with religion, the ideal of neutrality has emerged alongside a certain conception of the self.

From Self-Government to Self-Expression

With the advent of neutrality as a First Amendment principle came a shift in the underlying justification for free speech, a shift that gestures toward the liberal conception of the self. Traditional justifications of free speech emphasize its importance for the pursuit of truth or for the exercise of self-government. Thus Holmes wrote that "time has upset many fighting faiths," and "the best test of truth is the power of the thought to get itself accepted in the competition of the market."[115] Brandeis, meanwhile, defended free speech as essential to republican government: The founders believed that in "government the deliberative forces should prevail over the arbitrary. . . . that the greatest menace to freedom is an inert people; that public discussion is a political duty; and that this should be a fundamental principle of the American government."[116] According to Alexander Meiklejohn, a leading commentator of the 1940s and 1950s, the primary purpose of the First Amendment "is to give to every voting member of the body politic the fullest possible participation in the understanding of those problems with which the citizens of a self-governing society must deal." Free speech is concerned primarily with "the public freedom which is required for the purposes of self-government," not with "the private freedom of this or that individual" as he plies his wares in the marketplace of ideas.[117]

Although the courts continue to acknowledge the importance of free speech to the exercise of self-government,[118] courts and constitutional commentators alike increasingly defend free speech in the name of individual fulfillment and self-expression. The shift from self-government to self-expression, most evident in the 1970s and 1980s, casts freedom of speech as a particular case of a more general principle of respect for persons as independent selves, capable of choosing their values for themselves. It thus connects the case for content neutrality with the liberal conception of the person. According to the self-expression rationale for free speech, government must be neutral toward the views its citizens espouse in order to respect "the ultimate moral sovereignty of persons."[119] The focus on *self*-fulfillment emphasizes "the source of the speech in the self, and make[s] the choice of the speech by the self the crucial factor in justifying protection."[120]

By the 1970s the Supreme Court made frequent appeal to the ideal of self-expression, and the conception of the person it reflects. In *Cohen v. California* (1971), the Court reversed the conviction of a man who wore a jacket reading "Fuck the Draft" in a Los Angeles courthouse. "[N]o other approach would comport with the premise of individual dignity and choice upon which our political system rests," Justice Harlan wrote for the Court. Although many find the four-letter word distasteful, he added, "it is nevertheless often true that one man's vulgarity is another's lyric."[121]

Opinions in subsequent cases found in the First Amendment the need "to assure self-fulfillment for each individual"[122] and the right to "autonomous control over the development and expression of one's intellect, interests, tastes, and personalities."[123] Justice Brennan found freedom of speech "intrinsic to individual dignity," especially so "in a democracy like our own, in which the autonomy of each individual is accorded equal and incommensurate respect."[124] And Justice Byron R. White gave striking expression to the voluntarist aspect of the liberal conception by arguing that "ideas which are not a product of individual choice are entitled to less First Amendment protection."[125]

Group Defamation and Conceptions of the Person

Beyond these explicit judicial statements, two recent controversies suggest a second, subtler sense in which the unencumbered self finds expression in contemporary constitutional law. In both cases, federal courts upheld the claims of free speech against attempts to prevent the harm of group defamation. The first was an attempt by the residents of Skokie, Illinois, with a large population of Jewish survivors of the Holocaust, to prevent a group of neo-Nazis from marching in their town. The second was an attempt by feminists and others in Indianapolis to restrict the sale of pornography. Both attempts failed, for reasons that reveal the power of assumptions drawn from the liberal conception of the person.

In both cases, the courts ruled the laws invalid for failing to be neutral with respect to the content of speech; the First Amendment requires a community to "bracket" its disapproval of the content of speech, however odious the speech may be. Skokie and Indianapolis argued that it was unreasonable to bracket their disapproval of the speech they would restrict, on two grounds. First, they claimed that some speech not only leads to various harms, such as violence or crime, but constitutes an injury in and of itself. Second, they claimed that speech-inflicted injury can be public as well as personal; it can injure persons not only as individuals (as in private libel cases) but also as members of groups to which they belong.

In striking down the laws, the courts rejected both claims. Before turning to the cases, it may be helpful to consider how these two theses—of speech-intrinsic injury, and of group-based or communal harm—are at odds with the assumptions of the unencumbered self, and so difficult to reconcile with liberal jurisprudence.

The notion of speech-intrinsic injury finds its most familiar role in the area of defamation law, which seeks to prevent unjust harm to persons' reputations. But on the liberal conception of the person, it is not obvious what injury to reputation can consist in. Traditional understandings of reputation presuppose notions of honor that define a person's identity in relation to social roles: "The concept of honor implies that identity is essentially, or at least importantly, linked to institutional roles. . . . In a world of honor, the individual discovers his true identity in his roles, and to turn away from the roles is to turn away from himself."[126] Reputation as honor thus presupposes thickly constituted selves, whose basis of respect is tied to social institutions. As it developed in preindustrial England, the common law of defamation protected reputation in this sense. It dealt with speech-inflicted injuries, such as insults, that injured by dishonoring, by denying persons the esteem they were due in virtue of their place in the social order.[127]

Where the self is conceived as prior to its ends, independent of the roles it may occupy at any given time, reputation cannot be a matter of honor in the traditional sense. For the unencumbered self, not honor but dignity is the basis of respect—the dignity that consists in the capacity of persons as autonomous agents to choose their ends for themselves. Unlike honor, which ties respect for persons to the roles they inhabit, dignity resides in a self antecedent to social institutions, and so is invulnerable to injury by insult alone. For selves such as these, reputation matters, not intrinsically, as a matter of honor, but only instrumentally, as a business asset for example. In order for defamation to injure an unencumbered self, some "actual" harm must be shown, some harm, that is, independent of the speech itself.

This contrast is borne out by the different roles of libel law in Europe and the United States. "In Europe, where pre-capitalist concepts of honor, family, and privacy survive, reputation is a weighty matter" that fuels not only duels but also much slander litigation. In the United States, by contrast, "where tradition is capitalistic rather than feudalistic, reputation is only an asset, 'good will,' not an attribute to be sought after for its intrinsic value. . . . The law of libel is consequently unimportant."[128]

If the liberal conception of the person cannot support speech-intrinsic notions of the cause of injury, neither is it hospitable to communal conceptions of the object of injury. It resists the idea that libel can apply to groups or communities as such. If a face-to-face insult can scarcely count as injury, it is all the more difficult to count racial or religious slurs as punishable harms. This is so because, on the liberal conception of the person, the highest respect is the self-respect of a self independent of its aims and attachments. However much I might prize the esteem of others, the respect that counts cannot conceivably be injured by a slur against the racial or religious groups to which I happen to belong. For the unencumbered self, the grounds of self-respect are antecedent to any particular ties or attachments, and so beyond the reach of an insult to "my people."

Here too the cultural contrast is revealing. Unlike England, which has a group libel statute,[129] the United States, with its more individualistic political culture, has generally been reluctant to recognize group defamation: "our law of defamation, such as it is, is conceived of only as a protection against individual injury, as the law of assault and battery is a protection for individual life and limb. Hence, defamatory attacks upon social groups are pretty much outside the scope of existing law."[130]

Despite the general reluctance of American law to recognize group defamation, it is only in recent decades that the federal courts have rejected in principle the notions of speech-intrinsic injury and group-based harm. In two notable cases of the 1940s and 1950s, the Supreme Court accepted both. That the courts have eroded these precedents over the last forty years is yet another measure of the advent of the procedural republic.

Chaplinsky *and* Beauharnais

In 1942 the Supreme Court considered the case of a Jehovah's Witness named Chaplinsky who had been convicted for calling a city marshall a "damned Fascist" and a "damned racketeer." In a unanimous decision, the Court upheld the conviction on the grounds that "there are certain well-defined and narrowly limited classes of speech, the prevention and punishment of which have never been thought to raise any Constitutional problem." In addition to obscenity, profanity, and libel, these included what the Court called "insulting or 'fighting' words—*those which by their very utterance inflict injury* or tend to incite an immediate breach of the peace." In an opinion unconstrained by latter-day scruples of content neutrality, the Court reasoned that such utterances "are of such slight social value as a step to truth that any benefit that may be derived from them is clearly outweighed by the social interest in order and morality."[131] By allowing that words can inflict injury "by their very utterance," the Court acknowledged that "fighting" words not only lead to fights but sometimes fight on their own.

Ten years later, the Supreme Court considered its first and only case of group libel. Joseph Beauharnais, the president of the white supremacist White Circle League of America, had been convicted and fined $200 under an Illinois statute prohibiting any publication portraying "depravity, criminality, unchastity, or lack of virtue of a class of citizens" that "exposes the citizens of any race, color, creed or religion to contempt, derision, or obloquy." Justice Frankfurter, writing for a five–four majority, upheld the law.[132]

Frankfurter began by citing *Chaplinsky* and by observing that every American state punished libels directed at individuals. The question was not whether libel could be outlawed but whether the Constitution prevented a state from punishing libels "directed against designated collectivities." He answered that it did not: "if an utterance directed at an individual may be the object of criminal sanctions, we cannot deny to a State power to punish the same utterance directed at a defined group," provided the restriction is not without a purpose related to the well-being of the state. Given its history of racial and religious strife, the state of Illinois was not without reason "in seeking ways to curb false or malicious defamation of racial and religious groups, made in public places and by means calculated to have a powerful emotional impact on those to whom it was presented."[133]

Although it was not for the Court to say whether group libel laws were the best way of dealing with racial and religious tensions, Frankfurter held that the Constitution did not prevent states from treating their citizens as situated selves—as selves defined, for purposes of life prospects and social esteem, by the groups to which they belonged: "a man's job and his educational opportunities and the dignity accorded him *may depend as much on the reputation of the racial and religious group to which he willy-nilly belongs, as on his own merits.* This being so, we are precluded from saying that speech concededly punishable when immediately directed at individuals cannot be outlawed if directed at *groups with whose position and esteem in society the affiliated individual may be inextricably involved.*"[134]

Frankfurter's view that respect for persons may require treating them as situated selves was at odds with the assumptions of the procedural republic, and would not survive to support the claims of Skokie and Indianapolis. Indeed, the objections to his view appeared in the dissenting opinions to *Beauharnais* itself. Justice Black rejected the extension of libel law from individuals to groups. As constitutionally recognized, the crime of libel "has provided for the punishment of false, malicious, scurrilous charges against individuals," he wrote, "not against huge groups." As such, it has applied to "nothing more than purely private feuds." Black did not deny that words can injure, but he emphasized that the "fighting" words in *Chaplinsky* were directed at an individual on a public street, "face-to-face." The insults in Beauharnais's leaflet, by contrast, were not directed against particular individuals, but were part of an argument for racial segregation, and therefore worthy of constitutional protection.[135]

Justice Jackson did not challenge the analogy between individual and group libel, but he rejected the idea that speech can inflict a punishable injury independent of the physical harm it may cause. If the leaflet resulted in a riot or caused individual blacks to be denied housing or employment, the state could impose liability for these "actual results." But the racist leaflet could not be held punishable "as criminal libel *per se* irrespective of its actual or probable consequences. . . . *Words on their own account* are not to be punished in such cases but are reachable only as the root of punishable evils."[136] The dissents of Black and Jackson, taken together, anticipated the grounds on which the courts would reject the legal challenges to the Nazis in Skokie and to pornography in Indianapolis.

The Nazis in Skokie

Skokie offered an inviting target for the Nazis' provocative purposes, since it contained a large population of Jewish concentration camp survivors. The initial impulse of town officials and Jewish groups such as the Anti-Defamation League was to ignore the Nazis and thus deny them the publicity a confrontation would bring. But the survivor community was unwilling to bracket its abhorrence. Indeed, given their shared memory and resolve to bear witness, the survivors could not bracket their view of the Nazis without destroying something essential to their identity. After much debate, they persuaded their fellow citizens that a Nazi demonstration in their community would be more than mere offense, a kind of invasion.[137] The Skokie village government responded by seeking an injunction to prevent the demonstration, and passed three ordinances prohibiting demonstrations by hate groups. Meanwhile, the Nazis found a defender in the American Civil Liberties Union, which challenged the restrictions in state and federal courts. "Free speech exists in the most extreme cases," an ACLU official declared, "or it doesn't exist at all."[138]

The courts struck down all the restrictions as violations of the First Amendment. Repeatedly citing the Supreme Court in *Mosley,* they insisted that government must treat all speech with neutrality, however reprehensible the speech might be.[139] Content-based restrictions could be justified only "on the basis of imminent danger of a grave substantive evil."[140]

But the evil that Skokie sought to prevent presupposed a theory about the moral import of speech that the courts refused to accept. The central issue was posed by the "racial slur" ordinance, which prohibited the dissemination of materials promoting "hatred against persons by reason of their race, national origin, or religion." Skokie did not defend the ordinance on grounds of averting violence or breach of the peace. Citing *Chaplinsky* and *Beauharnais,* it argued instead that racial slurs are "speech-inflicted harms," and offered evidence of the psychological and communal trauma such slurs inflict. But the district court concluded that *Beauharnais* was no longer good law, at least in the two respects the Skokie law required. Although "government may punish speech which defames individual reputation, or which incites a breach of the peace," it may not punish defamation against groups, nor may it prevent speech-inflicted injuries that do not cause some further, physical harm.[141]

The Feminist Case against Pornography

A similar dispute about personhood and speech underlay the controversy over Indianapolis' antipornography law. Unlike traditional obscenity laws, the 1984 Indianapolis ordinance sought to restrict pornography on the grounds that it degrades women and undermines civic equality. The law was premised on the view that "pornography is central in creating and maintaining sex as a basis for discrimination." The "bigotry and contempt it promotes, with the acts of aggression it fosters," harm women's opportunities for equal rights in employment, education, and other areas and "contribute significantly to restricting women in particular from full exercise of citizenship and participation in public life, including in neighborhoods."[142]

The ordinance defined pornography as "the graphic sexually explicit subordination of women, whether in pictures or in words." It made trafficking in pornography subject to civil action, which could be brought by "any woman . . . as a woman acting against the subordination of women."[143]

The law depended for its justification on both a speech-intrinsic conception of injury—that pornography harms women independently of the sex crimes it may cause—and a communal description of the injured party—that women as women are the victims of the harm pornography inflicts. In these respects, it resembled the group libel law in *Beauharnais* and Skokie's "racial slur" ordinance.

Catharine MacKinnon, a leading feminist and one of the authors of the ordinance, argued that pornography is an intrinsic harm because it shapes the understandings that constitute relations between the sexes. "Men treat women as who they see women as being. Pornography constructs who that is. Men's power over women means that the way men see women defines who women can be. Pornography is that way."[144] Although earlier debates centered on a search for causal links between exposure to pornography and the propensity to commit crimes,[145] they overlooked the way commercial pornography on a vast scale constitutes a social world inhospitable to the equality of women. Although narrow notions of causality "privatize the injury pornography does to women," the idea that speech constitutes social practices suggests the possibility of communal notions of injury. According to MacKinnon, the "individuated, atomistic" conception of injury misses the way pornography harms women, "not as individuals in a one-at-a-time sense, but as members of the group 'women.'"[146] In this way, the feminist case against pornography connects the speech-intrinsic notion of injury and the communal description of the injured party.

U.S. District Court judge Sarah Barker rejected both of these assumptions and invalidated the law. She dismissed as "a certain sleight of hand" the city's contention that pornography "*is* the subordination of women and not an expression of ideas deserving of First Amendment protection." The city sought to "redefine offensive speech as harmful action," Judge Barker held, but "the clear wording of the Ordinance discloses that they seek to control speech." The "fighting words" doctrine of *Chaplinsky* did not support the notion of pornography as intrinsic injury, despite its recognition of words that "by their very utterance inflict injury."[147]

Judge Barker also objected to the claim that the harm of pornography is to women as a group. "The Ordinance does not presume or require specifically defined, identifiable victims" It sought instead "to protect adult women, as a group, from the diminution of their legal and sociological status as women, that is, from the discriminatory stigma which befalls women *as women* as a result of 'pornography.'" If the court were to accept this argument, she reasoned, what would prevent other city councils "from enacting protections for other equally compelling claims against exploitation and discrimination"? As if to suggest a litany of unjustified restrictions, she observed that other legislative bodies might prohibit racist publications or ethnic and religious slurs. Citing *Collin v. Smith,* Judge Barker concluded that upholding restrictions such as these "would signal so great a potential encroachment upon First Amendment freedoms that the precious liberties reposed within those guarantees would not survive."[148]

Unlike Judge Barker, the U.S. Court of Appeals accepted the city's claim that "pornography is the injury," that "pornography is what pornography does." Nevertheless, it affirmed her decision. Whatever its harm, pornography is a viewpoint, the court maintained, and so the Indianapolis ordinance, contrary to the First Amendment, "is not neutral with respect to viewpoint." Because the law affirmed a particular conception of the good society, at least to the extent of condemning the sexual subordination of women, it violated the principle that government must be neutral among visions of the good. "It establishes an 'approved' view of women, of how they may react to sexual encounters, of how the sexes may relate to each other." But "the state may not ordain preferred viewpoints in this way. The Constitution forbids the state to declare one perspective right and silence opponents."[149]

The three decades from *Beauharnais* to Skokie and Indianapolis measure the triumph of the procedural republic. With speech as with religion, the notion of the unencumbered self has accompanied, even animated, the growing insistence that government be neutral among conceptions of the good. Although the result is a judiciary more permissive of speech than at any time in American history, these developments raise questions about the liberalism they embody.

First, how reasonable it is to bracket disapproval of speech depends, as we have seen, on competing theories about the relation of speech to social practices, and about the relation of individual to communal identity. The liberal case for protecting speech by bracketing moral judgments is therefore not neutral after all, but presupposes a controversial theory of personhood and speech, a theory open to at least two objections: (1) protecting racists or Nazis or violent pornographic depictions in the name of neutrality may fail to respect persons as members of the particular communities to which they belong, and on whose status their social esteem may largely depend; (2) enforcing the theory that speech only advocates and never constitutes social practices fails to acknowledge the injuries that speech can inflict independent of the physical harm it may cause. Paradoxically, the procedural republic tolerates speech more by respecting it less, by failing to take seriously its power to inflict injury on its own.

Second, protecting speech by insisting that local communities bracket moral judgments carries costs for self-government. Not only does it underestimate the good of respect for persons as situated selves; it also prevents political communities from acting democratically to realize this good. Although the Holocaust survivors had most at stake in preventing the Nazis from marching, it was the citizens of Skokie who agreed to the ordinance the courts overturned; although feminists were the most vigorous critics of pornography, it was the Indianapolis city council that passed the law the courts struck down. Not only the good of communal respect but also the good of self-governing communities acting to secure this end is frustrated by the strictures of the procedural republic.

The liberal may reply at this point that restraining majorities—and hence restricting self-government—is precisely the point of rights as trumps. The principle that government must be neutral among ends prevents majorities from imposing their will to suppress speech they happen to deplore. This, the liberal insists, is its great advantage. Consider, for example, the civil rights movement of the 1960s. Segregationist whites did not want Martin Luther King to march in their communities any more than the Jews wanted the Nazis in Skokie. If all speech need not be tolerated, asks the liberal, then what is to distinguish the case of the Nazis in Skokie from civil rights marches in the South?

The answer may be simpler than liberal political theory permits: the Nazis promote genocide and hate, while Martin Luther King sought civil rights for blacks. The difference consists in the content of the speech, in the nature of the cause.[150] Given their responsibility to interpret the law, judges are rightly reluctant to make substantive moral distinctions of this kind in defining freedom of speech or other rights. But the difficulty they confront in trying to bracket moral judgment illustrates a broader problem with the liberalism that informs the procedural republic. In a notable case of the 1960s, Judge Frank Johnson concluded that it was not always possible to adjudicate rights without passing judgment on the morality of the cause they would advance.

When Martin Luther King sought to lead a march from Selma to Montgomery in 1965, Alabama Governor George Wallace tried to stop him. The case quickly made its way to the U.S. District Court, where it confronted Judge Johnson with a dilemma. The courts had upheld the rights of speech and assembly, but the states have the right to regulate the use of their highways for the safety and convenience of the public. As Judge Johnson acknowledged, a mass march along a public highway reached "to the outer limits of what is constitutionally allowed." Nevertheless, he ordered the state to permit the march, on grounds of the justice of its cause: "the extent of the right to assemble, demonstrate and march peaceably along the highways . . . should be commensurate with the enormity of the wrongs that are being protested and petitioned against. In this case, the wrongs are enormous. The extent of the right to demonstrate against these wrongs should be determined accordingly."[151]

Judge Johnson's decision was not content neutral; it would not have helped the Nazis in Skokie. It was, in this sense, an illiberal decision. But it did not lead to a slippery slope of relativism or repression. The march it made possible prodded the moral imagination of the nation and helped pass the Voting Rights Act of 1965.[152]

4

Privacy Rights and Family Law

The principle that government must be neutral among conceptions of the good life finds further constitutional expression in the area of privacy rights. The constitutional history of the right to privacy is far shorter than that of religious liberty or free speech. Although the Third Amendment prohibits quartering soldiers in houses without consent, and the Fourth Amendment protects persons against unreasonable search and seizure, the Bill of Rights makes no mention of privacy as such. Nevertheless, the Supreme Court has in recent years found implicit in the Constitution a right of privacy that protects from governmental interference such personal activities as marriage, procreation, contraception, and abortion.

These decisions have occasioned voluminous scholarly debate about methods of judicial interpretation, and of course much political debate about abortion itself. Rather than address these controversies, however, I propose to explore the political theory and conception of the person the privacy cases reveal. These cases, together with recent developments in family law, connect the ideal of the neutral state with the image of the unencumbered self. They also display the flaws in the theory they embody.

Intimacy and Autonomy

In the constitutional right of privacy, the neutral state and the unencumbered self are often joined. In the case of abortion, for example, no state may, "by adopting one theory of life," override a woman's right to decide whether or not to terminate her pregnancy.[1] Government may not enforce a particular moral view, however widely held, for "no individual should be compelled to surrender the freedom to make that decision for herself simply because her 'value preferences' are not shared by the majority."[2]

As with religious liberty and freedom of speech, so with privacy, the ideal of neutrality often reflects a voluntarist conception of human agency. Government must be neutral among conceptions of the good life in order to respect the capacity of persons to choose their values and relationships for themselves. So close is the connection between privacy rights and the voluntarist conception of the self that commentators frequently assimilate the values of privacy and autonomy: Privacy rights are said to be "grounded in notions of individual autonomy," because "the human dignity protected by constitutional guarantees would be seriously diminished if people were not free to choose and adopt a lifestyle which allows expression of their uniqueness and individuality."[3] In "recognizing a constitutional right to privacy," the Court has given effect to the view "that persons have the capacity to live autonomously and the right to exercise that capacity."[4] Supreme Court decisions voiding laws against contraceptives "not only protect the individual who chooses not to procreate, but also the autonomy of a couple's association." They protect men and women "against an unchosen commitment" to unwanted children and "against a compelled identification with the social role of parent."[5]

In Supreme Court decisions and dissents alike, the justices have often tied privacy rights to voluntarist assumptions. The Court thus held that laws banning contraceptives violate "the constitutional protection of individual autonomy in matters of childbearing."[6] It defended the right to an abortion on the grounds that few decisions are "more properly private, or more basic to individual dignity and autonomy, than a woman's decision . . . whether to end her pregnancy."[7] Concurring in an abortion case, Justice Douglas held the right of privacy to protect such liberties as "the autonomous control over the development and expression of one's intellect, interests, tastes, and personality," and "freedom of choice in the basic decisions of one's life respecting marriage, divorce, procreation, contraception, and the education and upbringing of children."[8] Writing in dissent, Justice Thurgood Marshall would have struck down a regulation limiting the hair length of policemen as "inconsistent with the values of privacy, self-identity, autonomy, and personal integrity" he believed the Constitution was designed to protect.[9] And four members of the Court would have extended privacy protection to consensual homosexual activity, on the grounds that "much of the richness of a relationship will come from the freedom an individual has to *choose* the form and nature of these intensely personal bonds."[10]

Although the link between privacy and autonomy is now so familiar as to seem natural, even necessary, the right of privacy need not presuppose a voluntarist conception of the person. In fact, through most of its history in American law, the right of privacy has implied neither the ideal of the neutral state nor the ideal of a self freely choosing its aims and attachments. That the meaning of privacy has in recent years come to carry these assumptions reflects their growing prominence in our moral and political culture.

Where the contemporary right of privacy is the right to engage in certain conduct without government restraint, the traditional version is the right to keep certain personal facts from public view. The new privacy protects a person's "independence in making certain kinds of important decisions," whereas the old privacy protects a person's interest "in avoiding disclosure of personal matters."[11]

The tendency to identify privacy with autonomy not only obscures these shifting understandings of privacy; it also restricts the range of reasons for protecting it. Although the new privacy typically relies on voluntarist justifications, it can also be justified in other ways. A right to be free of governmental interference in matters of marriage, for example, can be defended not only in the name of individual choice but also in the name of the intrinsic value or social importance of the practice it protects. As the Court has sometimes acknowledged, "certain kinds of personal bonds have played a critical role in the culture and traditions of the Nation by cultivating and transmitting shared ideals and beliefs; they thereby foster diversity and act as critical buffers between the individual and the power of the State."[12] The Court's greater tendency, however, has been to view privacy in voluntarist terms, as protecting "the ability independently to define one's identity."[13] This tendency offers further evidence of the triumph of the procedural republic.

From the Old Privacy to the New

The right to privacy first gained legal recognition in the United States as a doctrine of tort law, not of constitutional law. In an influential article in 1890, Louis Brandeis, then a Boston lawyer, and his onetime law partner Samuel Warren argued that the civil law should protect "the right to privacy."[14] Far from latter-day concerns with sexual freedoms, Brandeis' and Warren's notion of privacy was quaint by comparison, concerned with the publication of high-society gossip by the sensationalist press or the unauthorized use of people's portraits in advertising. In fact their joint article was inspired by Warren's annoyance at press coverage of the lavish entertainment he conducted at his home in Boston's elite Back Bay.[15]

"The press is overstepping in every direction the obvious bounds of propriety and of decency," they wrote. "Gossip is no longer the resource of the idle and of the vicious, but has become a trade, which is pursued with industry as well as effrontery. To satisfy a prurient taste the details of sexual relations are spread broadcast in the columns of the daily papers. To occupy the indolent column upon column is filled with idle gossip, which can only be procured by intrusion upon the domestic circle." According to Warren and Brandeis, such indiscretions brought "a lowering of social standards and of morality" and also infringed the "right of the individual to be let alone."[16]

Gradually at first, then more frequently in the 1930s, the right to privacy gained recognition in the civil law of most states.[17] Before the 1960s, however, privacy received scant attention in constitutional law. Two *Lochner* era cases held the Fourteenth Amendment to protect the right "to marry, establish a home and bring up children," and "to direct the upbringing and education of children," but did not mention privacy as such.[18] When in 1927 the Supreme Court refused to count wiretapping as a search and seizure limited by the Fourth Amendment, Brandeis wrote a memorable dissent, extending his earlier privacy concerns to a constitutional setting. The guarantee against unreasonable search and seizure "conferred, as against the Government, the right to be let alone," he argued. "To protect that right, every unjustifiable intrusion by the Government upon the privacy of the individual, whatever the means employed, must be deemed a violation of the Fourth Amendment."[19] And in 1942 the Court invalidated an Oklahoma law providing for compulsory sterilization after a third conviction for a felony involving "moral turpitude," holding that the law touched "one of the basic civil rights of man."[20]

The Supreme Court first addressed the right of privacy as such when Connecticut's ban on contraceptives came under challenge in *Poe v. Ullman* (1961). Although the majority dismissed the case on technical grounds, Justices Douglas and Harlan dissented, arguing that the law violated the right of privacy. The privacy they defended was privacy in the traditional sense. The right at stake was not the right to use contraceptives but the right to be free of the surveillance that enforcement would require. "If we imagine a regime of full enforcement of the law," wrote Douglas, "we would reach the point where search warrants issued and officers appeared in bedrooms to find out what went on. . . . If [the State] can make this law, it can enforce it. And proof of its violation necessarily involves an inquiry into the relations between man and wife."[21]

Banning the sale of contraceptives would be different from banning their use, Douglas observed. Banning the sale would restrict access to contraceptives, but without exposing intimate relations to public inspection. Enforcement would take police to the drugstore, not to the bedroom, and so would not offend privacy in the traditional sense.[22]

Justice Harlan also objected to the law on grounds that distinguish the old privacy from the new. He did not object that the law against contraceptives failed to be neutral among competing moral conceptions. To the contrary, he acknowledged that the law was based on the belief that contraception is immoral in itself and encourages such "dissolute action" as fornication and adultery by minimizing their "disastrous consequence."[23] But Harlan did not find this failure of neutrality contrary to the Constitution.

In a statement clearly opposed to the assumptions of the procedural republic, Harlan argued that morality is a legitimate concern of government: "society is not limited in its objects only to the physical well-being of the community, but has traditionally concerned itself with the moral soundness of its people as well. Indeed to attempt a line between public behavior and that which is purely consensual or solitary would be to withdraw from community concern a range of subjects with which every society in civilized times has found it necessary to deal."[24]

Although he rejected the ideal of the neutral state, Harlan did not conclude that Connecticut had a right to prohibit married couples from using contraceptives. Like Douglas, he reasoned that enforcing the law would intrude on the privacy essential to the prized institution of marriage. His objection was to the violation of privacy in the traditional sense, to "the intrusion of the whole machinery of the criminal law into the very heart of marital privacy, requiring husband and wife to render account before a criminal tribunal of their uses of that intimacy." According to Harlan, the state was entitled to embody in law the belief that contraception is immoral, but not to implement "the obnoxiously intrusive means it has chosen to effectuate that policy."[25]

Four years later, in *Griswold v. Connecticut*, the dissenters prevailed. The Supreme Court invalidated Connecticut's law against contraceptives and for the first time gave explicit constitutional recognition to the right of privacy. The right the Court upheld remained tied to the traditional notion of privacy as the interest in keeping intimate affairs from public view. The violation of privacy consisted in the intrusion required to enforce the law, not in the restriction on the freedom to use contraceptives. "Would we allow the police to search the sacred precincts of marital bedrooms for telltale signs of the use of contraceptives?," wrote Justice Douglas for the Court. "The very idea is repulsive to the notions of privacy surrounding the marriage relationship."[26]

The justification for the right was not voluntarist but based on a substantive moral judgment; the Court vindicated privacy not for the sake of letting people lead their sexual lives as they choose, but rather for the sake of affirming and protecting the social institution of marriage. "Marriage is a coming together for better or for worse, hopefully enduring, and intimate to the degree of being sacred. It is an association that promotes a way of life . . . a harmony in living . . . a bilateral loyalty . . . it is an association for as noble a purpose as any involved in our prior decisions."[27]

Although *Griswold* is often viewed as a dramatic constitutional departure, the privacy right it proclaimed is consistent with traditional notions of privacy going back to the turn of the century. From the standpoint of shifting privacy conceptions, the more decisive turn came seven years later in *Eisenstadt v. Baird* (1972), a seemingly similar case.[28] Like *Griswold*, it involved a state law restricting contraceptives. But in *Eisenstadt*, the challenged law restricted the distribution of contraceptives, not their use. While it therefore limited access to contraceptives, its enforcement could not be said to require governmental surveillance of intimate activities. It did not violate privacy in the traditional sense. (In fact the case arose when a man was convicted for giving away a contraceptive device at a public lecture on contraception.) Furthermore, the law prohibited the distribution of contraceptives only to unmarried persons, and so did not burden the institution of marriage as the Connecticut law did.

Despite these differences, the Supreme Court struck down the law, with only a single dissent. Its decision involved two innovations, one explicit, the other unacknowledged. The explicit change was to redescribe the bearers of privacy rights from persons *qua* participants in the social institution of marriage to persons *qua* individuals, independent of their roles or attachments. "It is true that in *Griswold* the right of privacy in question inhered in the marital relationship. Yet the marital couple is not an independent entity with a mind and heart of its own, but an association of two individuals each with a separate intellectual and emotional makeup."[29]

The subtler though no less fateful change was in the shift from the old privacy to the new. More than freedom from surveillance or disclosure of intimate affairs, the right to privacy would now protect the freedom to engage in certain activities without governmental restriction. Whereas privacy in *Griswold* prevented intrusion into "the sacred precincts of marital bedrooms," privacy in *Eisenstadt* prevented intrusion into *decisions* of certain kinds. Moreover, as the meaning of privacy changed, so did its justification. The Court protected privacy in *Eisenstadt*, not for the social practices it promotes but for the individual choice it secures. "If the right of privacy means anything, it is the right of the *individual*, married or single, to be free from unwarranted governmental intrusion into matters so fundamentally affecting a person as the decision whether to bear or beget a child."[30]

One year later, in *Roe v. Wade*, the Supreme Court gave the new privacy its most controversial application, striking down a Texas law against abortion. "This right of privacy . . . founded in the Fourteenth Amendment's concept of personal liberty and restrictions upon state action . . . is broad enough to encompass a woman's decision whether or not to terminate her pregnancy."[31] First with contraception, then with abortion, the right of privacy had become the right to make certain sorts of choices, free of interference by the state. The choice had also to be free of interference by husbands or parents. A few years after *Roe*, the Court struck down a law requiring a husband's consent as a condition for an abortion, or parental consent in the case of unmarried minors. Since the state could not prevent even minors from having abortions in the first trimester, it could not delegate to "a third party" such as a husband or parent the authority to do so.[32] More recently, the Court upheld a parental consent requirement but invalidated a spousal notification provision as imposing an undue burden on the woman's right to choose.[33]

The voluntarist grounds of the new privacy found explicit statement in a 1977 case invalidating a New York law prohibiting the sale of contraceptives to minors under age sixteen. For the first time, the Court used the language of autonomy to describe the interest privacy protects, and argued openly for the shift from the old privacy to the new. Writing for the Court in *Carey v. Population Services International*, Justice Brennan admitted that *Griswold* focused on the fact that a law forbidding the *use* of contraceptives can bring the police into marital bedrooms. "But subsequent decisions have made clear that the constitutional protection of individual autonomy in matters of childbearing is not dependent on that element." *Eisenstadt* protected the "*decision* whether to bear or beget a child," he emphasized. *Roe* protected "a woman's *decision* whether or not to terminate her pregnancy." "Read in the light of its progeny, the teaching of *Griswold* is that the Constitution protects individual decisions in matters of childbearing from unjustified intrusion by the State."[34]

Given the voluntarist construal of privacy, restricting the *sale* of contraceptives violates privacy as harshly as banning their *use*; the one limits choice as surely as the other. "Indeed, in practice," Brennan observed, "a prohibition against all sales, since more easily and less offensively enforced, might have an even more devastating effect upon the freedom to choose contraception."[35] Ironically, the very fact that a ban on sales does *not* threaten the old privacy makes it a greater threat to the new.

Later decisions upholding abortion rights also used the language of autonomy to describe the privacy interest at stake. "Few decisions are . . . more properly private, or more basic to individual dignity and autonomy," held the Court in one such case, "than a woman's decision . . . whether to end her pregnancy. A woman's right to make that choice freely is surely fundamental."[36] The notion of privacy as autonomy found perhaps its fullest expression in a 1992 abortion rights opinion authored jointly by Justices Sandra Day O'Connor, Anthony Kennedy, and David Souter. Privacy rights protect "the most intimate and personal choices a person may make in a lifetime, choices central to personal dignity and autonomy." The justices went on to draw an explicit connection between privacy as autonomy and the voluntarist conception of the person: "At the heart of liberty is the right to define one's own concept of existence, of meaning, of the universe, and of the mystery of human life. Beliefs about these matters could not define the attributes of personhood were they formed under compulsion of the State."[37]

Despite its increasing tendency to identify privacy with autonomy, the Court refused, in a five–four decision, to extend privacy protection to consensual homosexual activity. Writing for the majority, Justice White emphasized that the Court's previous privacy cases protected choice only with respect to childrearing and education, family relationship, procreation, marriage, contraception, and abortion. "We think it evident," he held, "that none of the rights announced in those cases bears any resemblance to the claimed constitutional right of homosexuals to engage in acts of sodomy." He also rejected the claim that the citizens of Georgia could not embody in law their belief "that homosexual sodomy is immoral and unacceptable." Neutrality to the contrary, "the law . . . is constantly based on notions of morality, and if all laws representing essentially moral choices are to be invalidated under the Due Process Clause, the courts will be very busy indeed."[38]

Writing for the four dissenters, Justice Blackmun argued that the Court's previous privacy rights decisions did not depend on the virtue of the practices they protected but on the principle of free individual choice in intimate matters. Since the right of privacy in sexual relationships protects "the freedom an individual has to *choose* the form and nature of these intensely personal bonds," it protects homosexual activity no less than other intimate choices. Blackmun also invoked the ideal of the neutral state. That certain religions abhor homosexuality "gives the State no license to impose their judgments on the entire citizenry." Law may not depend for its justification on religious conviction. To the contrary, the state's appeal to religious teachings against homosexuality undermines its claim that the law "represents a legitimate use of secular coercive power."[39]

Despite the Court's reluctance to extend privacy rights to homosexuals, the privacy cases of recent decades offer ample evidence of assumptions drawn from the liberal conception of the person. They also raise two questions about the liberalism they reflect. One concerns the case for bracketing controversial moral issues; the other concerns the way the voluntarist conception of privacy tends to limit the range of reasons for protecting privacy.

Abortion and the Minimalist Case for Toleration

As we have seen, minimalist liberalism seeks a conception of justice that is political not philosophical, that does not presuppose any particular conception of the person, Kantian or otherwise. It proposes bracketing controversial moral and religious issues for political purposes, not for the sake of such "comprehensive" liberal ideals as autonomy or individuality, but rather for the sake of securing social cooperation in the face of disagreement about ends.[40] One objection to this version of liberalism is that the case for bracketing a particular moral or religious controversy may depend on an implicit answer to the controversy it purports to bracket. In the case of abortion, for example, the more confident we are that fetuses are, in the relevant moral sense, different from babies, the more confident we can be in bracketing the question about the moral status of fetuses for the political purposes.

The Court's argument in *Roe v. Wade* illustrates the difficulty of deciding constitutional cases by bracketing controversial moral and religious issues. While the Court claimed to be neutral on the question of when life begins, its decision presupposed a particular answer to that question. The Court began by observing that Texas' law against abortion presupposes a particular theory of when life begins: "Texas urges that . . . life begins at conception and is present throughout pregnancy, and that, therefore, the State has a compelling interest in protecting that life from and after conception."[41]

The Court then claimed to be neutral on that question: "We need not resolve the difficult question of when life begins. When those trained in the respective disciplines of medicine, philosophy, and theology are unable to arrive at any consensus, the judiciary . . . is not in a position to speculate as to the answer." It then noted "the wide divergence of thinking on this most sensitive and difficult question," throughout the Western tradition and in the law of various American states.[42]

From its summary of diverging views, the Court concluded that "the unborn have never been recognized in the law as persons in the whole sense." And from this conclusion it argued that Texas was wrong to embody in law a particular theory of life: "In view of all this, we do not agree that, by adopting one theory of life, Texas may override the rights of the pregnant woman that are at stake."[43]

The Court claimed to be neutral on the question of when life begins, and struck down Texas' law for failing to be neutral, for embodying in law "one theory of life." But contrary to its professions of neutrality, the Court's decision presupposed a particular answer to the question it claimed to bracket. "With respect to the State's important and legitimate interest in potential life, the 'compelling' point is at viability. This is so because the fetus then presumably has the capability of meaningful life outside the mother's womb. State regulation protective of fetal life after viability thus has both logical and biological justifications."[44]

That the Court's decision in *Roe* presupposed a particular answer to the question it purported to bracket is no argument against its decision, only an argument against its claim to have bracketed the controversial question of when life begins. It did not replace Texas' theory of life with a neutral stance, but with a different theory of its own.

The minimalist liberal's case for neutrality is also subject to a further difficulty: Even given an agreement to bracket controversial moral and religious issues for the sake of social cooperation, what counts as bracketing may remain controversial; and this controversy may require for its solution either a substantive evaluation of the interests at stake or at least a conception of the self that minimalist liberalism resolves to avoid. An abortion case upholding *Roe* offers an example of this difficulty.

Dissenting in *Thornburgh v. American College of Obstetricians* (1986), Justice White urged the Court to overrule *Roe v. Wade* and "return the issue to the people." He agreed that abortion was a controversial moral issue, but argued that the best way for the Court to bracket this controversy was to let each state decide the question for itself. He proposed, in effect, to bracket the intractable controversy over abortion as Stephen Douglas proposed to bracket the intractable controversy over slavery—by refusing to impose a single answer on the country as a whole. "Abortion is a hotly contested moral and political issue," White wrote. "Such issues, in our society, are to be resolved by the will of the people, either as expressed through legislation or through the general principles they have already incorporated into the Constitution they have adopted." For the Court to do otherwise was not to be neutral but to "impose its own controversial choices of value upon the people."[45]

Responding to White, Justice Stevens advocated a different way of bracketing. He argued that, given the controversial moral issues at stake, not the legislatures but rather individual women should decide the question for themselves. For the Court to insist that women be free to choose for themselves was not to impose the *Court's* values, but simply to prevent local majorities from imposing *their* values on individuals: "no individual should be compelled to surrender the freedom to make that decision for herself simply because her 'value preferences' are not shared by the majority." For Stevens, the basic question was not which theory of life is true, but "whether the 'abortion decision' should be made by the individual or by the majority 'in the unrestrained imposition of its own, extra-constitutional value preferences.'"[46]

Both ways of bracketing are in principle consistent with minimalist liberalism; the practical interest in social cooperation under conditions of disagreement about the good offers no grounds for choosing one over the other. Even given agreement to bracket an intractable moral or religious controversy for the sake of social cooperation, it may still be unclear what counts as bracketing. And resolving that question—deciding between White's position and Stevens'—requires either a substantive view about the moral and religious interests at stake or a conception of the person such as Kantian liberalism affirms. But both solutions would deny minimalist liberalism its minimalism; each would implicate its putatively political conception of justice in moral and philosophical commitments it seeks to avoid.

The minimalist liberal might reply that the conception of the person required to resolve the dispute need not be derived from a comprehensive moral conception such as Kant's, but can be drawn instead from an interpretation of our political culture. Stevens' view that neutrality requires respect for individual choice can be justified by appeal to the conception of the person "implicit in the public culture of a democratic society."[47] It need not resort to moral philosophy, not even to the ideals of autonomy and individuality as Kant and Mill conceived them.

But as we have seen, the liberal conception of the person on which Stevens' view relies is not characteristic of our political and constitutional tradition as such. The image of the person as a freely choosing, unencumbered self has only recently come to inform our constitutional practice. Whatever its appeal, it does not underlie the American political tradition as a whole, much less "the public culture of a democratic society" as such. Any role it may play in the justification of liberalism must therefore depend on moral argument, not cultural interpretation or appeals to tradition alone. If liberals want to bracket controversial moral questions in a way that assures individual choice (Stevens' way over White's), they must affirm after all a conception of the person on which the self is prior to its ends. They cannot avoid confronting the difficulties that this conception of the person entails.

Homosexuality and the Voluntarist Case for Toleration

As the abortion case poses problems for minimalist liberalism, the homosexual case raises problems for the version of liberalism that ties toleration to autonomy rights alone. This can be seen in the argument for toleration advanced by the dissenters in *Bowers v. Hardwick* (1986).[48]

In refusing to extend the right of privacy to homosexuals, the Court declared that none of the rights announced in earlier privacy cases "bears any resemblance" to the rights homosexuals seek: "No connection between family, marriage, or procreation on the one hand and homosexual activity on the other has been demonstrated."[49] Any reply to the Court's position would have to show some connection between the practices already subject to privacy protection and the homosexual practices not yet protected. What then is the resemblance between heterosexual intimacies on the one hand, and homosexual intimacies on the other, such that both are entitled to a constitutional right of privacy?

This question might be answered in at least two different ways—one voluntarist, the other substantive. The first argues from the autonomy the practices reflect, whereas the second appeals to the human goods the practices realize. The voluntarist answer holds that people should be free to choose their intimate associations for themselves, regardless of the virtue or popularity of the practices they choose, so long as they do not harm others. On this view, homosexual relationships resemble the heterosexual relationships the Court has already protected in that all reflect the choices of autonomous selves.

By contrast, the substantive answer claims that much that is valuable in conventional marriage is also present in homosexual unions. On this view, the connection between heterosexual and homosexual relations is not that both are the products of individual choice but that both realize important human goods. Instead of relying on autonomy alone, this second line of reply articulates the virtues that homosexual intimacy may share with heterosexual intimacy, as well as any distinctive virtues of its own. It defends homosexual privacy in the way *Griswold* defended marital privacy, by arguing that like marriage, homosexual union may also be "intimate to the degree of being sacred . . . a harmony in living . . . a bilateral loyalty," an association for a "noble purpose."[50]

Of these two possible replies, the dissenters in *Bowers* relied wholly on the first. Instead of defending homosexual intimacies in terms of the human goods they share with intimacies already protected by the Court, Justice Blackmun cast the Court's earlier cases in individualist terms, and found their connection with the homosexual case in the idea that "much of the richness of a relationship will come from the freedom an individual has to *choose* the form and nature of these intensely personal bonds." At issue in the case was not homosexuality as such but respect for the fact that "different individuals will make different choices" in deciding how to conduct their lives.[51]

Justice Stevens, in a separate dissent, also avoided reference to the values homosexual intimacy may share with heterosexual love. Instead, he wrote broadly of "the individual's right to make certain unusually important decisions" and "respect for the dignity of individual choice," rejecting the notion that such liberty belongs to heterosexuals alone: "From the standpoint of the individual, the homosexual and the heterosexual have the same interest in deciding how he will live his own life, and, more narrowly, how he will conduct himself in his personal and voluntary associations with his companions."[52]

The voluntarist argument so dominates the dissents that it seems difficult to imagine a judicial rendering of the substantive view. But a glimmer of this view can be found in a lower court's opinion in the same case. The U.S. Court of Appeals had ruled in Hardwick's favor and struck down the law under which he was convicted.[53] Like Blackmun and Stevens, it argued for an analogy between privacy in marriage and privacy in homosexual relations. But unlike the Supreme Court dissenters, it did not rest the analogy on voluntarist grounds alone. It argued instead that both practices may realize important human goods.

The marital relationship is significant, wrote the court of appeals, not only because of its procreative purpose but also "because of the unsurpassed opportunity for mutual support and self-expression that it provides." It recalled the Supreme Court's observation in *Griswold* that "[m]arriage is a coming together for better or for worse, hopefully enduring, and intimate to the degree of being sacred." And it went on to suggest that the qualities the Court so prized in *Griswold* can sometimes be present in homosexual unions as well. "For some, the sexual activity in question here serves the same purpose as the intimacy of marriage."[54]

Ironically, this way of extending privacy rights to homosexuals depends on an "old-fashioned" reading of *Griswold,* a reading the Court has long since renounced in favor of an individualist reading.[55] By drawing on the aspect of *Griswold* that affirms certain values and ends, the substantive case for homosexual privacy offends the liberalism that informs the procedural republic. It grounds the right of privacy on the good of the practice it would protect, and so fails to be neutral among conceptions of the good.

The more frequently employed precedent for homosexual rights is not *Griswold* but *Stanley v. Georgia* (1969), which upheld the right to possess obscene materials in the privacy of one's home. *Stanley* did not hold that the obscene films found in the defendant's bedroom served a "noble purpose," only that he had a right to view them in private. True to the assumptions of the procedural republic, the toleration it defended was wholly independent of the value or importance of the thing being tolerated.[56]

A New York State court vindicated privacy rights for homosexuals on precisely these grounds. If, following *Stanley*, there is a right to the "satisfaction of sexual desires by resort to material condemned as obscene," there should also be a right "to seek sexual gratification from what at least once was commonly regarded as 'deviant' conduct," so long as it is private and consensual. The court emphasized its neutrality toward the conduct it protected: "We express no view as to any theological, moral or psychological evaluation of consensual sodomy. These are aspects of the issue on which informed, competent authorities and individuals may and do differ." The court's role was simply to assure that the state bracketed these competing moral views rather than embodying any one of them in law: "it is not the function of the Penal Law in our governmental policy to provide either a medium for the articulation or the apparatus for the intended enforcement of moral or theological values."[57]

The case for toleration that brackets the morality of homosexuality has a familiar appeal. In the face of deep disagreement about values, it seems to ask least of the contending parties. It offers social peace and respect for rights without the need for moral conversion. Those who view sodomy as sin need not be persuaded to change their minds, only to tolerate those who practice it in private. By insisting only that each respect the freedom of others to live the lives they choose, this toleration promises a basis for political agreement that does not await shared conceptions of the good.

But despite its promise, the neutral case for toleration is subject to two related difficulties. First, as a practical matter, it is by no means clear that social cooperation can be secured on the strength of autonomy rights alone, absent some measure of agreement on the moral permissibility of the practices at issue. It may not be accidental that the practices now subject to the right of privacy were first accorded constitutional protection in cases that spoke of the sanctity of marriage and procreation. Only later were privacy rights abstracted from these practices, and protected without reference to the goods they were once thought to make possible. This would suggest that the voluntarist justification of privacy rights is parasitic—politically as well as philosophically—on some measure of agreement that the practices protected are morally permissible.

A second difficulty with the voluntarist case for toleration concerns the quality of respect it secures. As the New York case suggests, the analogy with *Stanley* tolerates homosexuality at the price of demeaning it; it puts homosexual intimacy on a par with obscenity—a base thing that should nonetheless be tolerated so long as it takes place in private. If *Stanley* rather than *Griswold* is the relevant analogy, the interest at stake is bound to be reduced, as the New York court reduced it, to "sexual gratification." (The only intimate relationship at stake in *Stanley* was between a man and his pornography.)

The majority in *Bowers* exploited this assumption by ridiculing the notion of a "fundamental right to engage in homosexual sodomy."[58] The obvious reply is that *Bowers* is no more about a right to homosexual sodomy than *Griswold* was about a right to heterosexual intercourse. But by refusing to articulate the human goods that homosexual intimacy may share with heterosexual unions, the voluntarist case for toleration forfeits the analogy with *Griswold* and makes the ridicule difficult to refute.

The problem with the neutral case for toleration is the opposite side of its appeal; it leaves wholly unchallenged the adverse views of homosexuality itself. But unless those views can be plausibly addressed, even a court ruling in their favor is unlikely to win for homosexuals more than a thin and fragile toleration. A fuller respect would require, if not admiration, at least some appreciation of the lives homosexuals live. But such appreciation is unlikely to be cultivated by a legal and political discourse conducted in terms of autonomy rights alone.

The liberal may reply that autonomy arguments in court need not foreclose more substantive, affirmative arguments elsewhere; bracketing moral argument for constitutional purposes does not require bracketing moral argument in all domains. Once their freedom of choice in sexual practice is secured, homosexuals can seek, by argument and example, to win from their fellow citizens a deeper respect than autonomy can supply.

But this reply underestimates the extent to which constitutional discourse has come to define the terms of political discourse in American public life. Though most at home in constitutional law, the main motifs of contemporary liberalism—rights as trumps, the neutral state, and the unencumbered self—figure with increasing prominence in our moral and political culture. This is what it means to have become a procedural republic. Assumptions drawn from constitutional discourse increasingly set the terms of moral and political debate in general.

Admittedly, these very developments pose an obstacle to those who would argue for toleration by appealing to the moral worth of the practices it would protect. Even the institutions of marriage and the family are increasingly conceived in voluntarist terms, prized less for the human goods they make possible than for the autonomous choices they express. As we shall see, the ideal of neutrality and the self-image that attends it do not reside in constitutional law alone. They also reflect more general changes in American moral culture, as the recent transformation of family law attests.

No-Fault Family Law

Recent decades have brought "a diminution of the law's discourse in moral terms about the relations between family members, and the transfer of many moral decisions from the law to the people the law once regulated."[59] At the same time, the law increasingly treats persons as individual selves independent of their family roles. These changes have affected the law's treatment of divorce, alimony, marital property, child custody, and family support requirements in virtually every state in the country.[60]

The law of divorce offers the most telling example. For over a century, divorce law reflected and enforced a particular ideal of marriage and "of the proper moral relations between husband and wife."[61] This ideal included duties of lifelong mutual responsibility and fidelity, tied to traditional gender-based roles. The husband had the duty of economic support; the wife, the duty of domestic service. The mutual responsibilities of marriage constituted "a unity that transcended the parties' individual interests." Only a serious breach of moral duties, such as adultery, cruelty, or desertion, provided grounds for divorce. And the obligations of marriage could persist long after divorce, in the form of alimony payments by the husband to his former wife.[62]

In 1970 the state of California enacted the first "no-fault" divorce law in the country. Its effect was to bracket the moral considerations that had traditionally governed the law of divorce. The new law removed all reference to guilt and innocence and provided for divorce upon either party's claim that "irreconcilable differences" had caused the marriage to break down. Moral grounds were no longer required, neither spouse had to prove fault or guilt, nor did the spouses have to agree to end their marriage. Either could decide unilaterally to get a divorce, without the consent of the other. Whereas the old law implied "'a right' to remain married if one adhered to one's marriage contract, the new law elevates one's 'right' to divorce by permitting divorce at either party's request."[63]

Like the divorce itself, financial awards were also detached from moral considerations of guilt and innocence, punishment and reward. Alimony payments and property settlements are now based on financial need, not marital behavior. "Under the old law the adulterous husband or wife typically had to pay for his or her infidelity with a disadvantageous property or alimony award. Today, in contrast, there are no penalties for adultery and no rewards for fidelity."[64] Instead of concerning themselves with guilt or innocence, the courts now employ such "nonjudgmental" criteria as the economic needs and resources of the parties.

The new law brackets marital roles as well as fault. The gender-based responsibilities of the old law give way to gender neutrality in the new. Husbands are no longer held responsible for the financial support of their former wives, and women are expected to become self-sufficient after divorce. The law now views alimony as a temporary, not a lifelong, obligation, whose purpose is to ease the wife's transition from economic dependence to self-sufficiency. In the wake of the reform, permanent alimony dropped from 62 to 32 percent of alimony awarded. By 1972 "two-thirds of the spousal support awards were transitional awards for a limited and specified duration," about two years on average. By 1978 only 17 percent of divorced women were awarded any alimony at all.[65]

The California law also rejects traditional role-based responsibilities in child custody and support. It replaces the old preference for maternal custody with a gender-neutral standard, although in practice most children continue to live with their mothers. It also makes both parents responsible for child support.[66]

California's revolution in family law quickly spread across the country. By 1985 every state in the nation had adopted some version of no-fault divorce. Some, like California, rejected moral grounds for divorce altogether, while others added "no-fault" as an option, alongside traditional versions. A few even provided for divorce by mail.[67]

Most states have also banned fault as a factor in alimony awards. Even the language of spousal support has changed in ways that reflect the rejection of desert-based considerations. For example, a Colorado court recently distinguished between "alimony," which presupposes fault, and "maintenance," which seeks simply to ensure that "the basic (economic) needs of a disadvantaged spouse are met." Such maintenance is sometimes called "rehabilitative alimony," as if to suggest that the role of homemaker and mother is a kind of infirmity from which entry into the labor market constitutes recovery. An Indiana law goes further and restricts alimony to "physically or mentally handicapped spouses."[68]

Child support obligations continue in law but often go unenforced in practice. In 1975 only one-fourth of divorced, separated, or single women with children received any child support payments.[69] Court-ordered child support and alimony combined rarely amount to even one-third of the husband's income, and fewer than half of child support awards are ever actually paid.[70] A Wisconsin law sought to enforce payment by preventing fathers in arrears on child support from getting a marriage license, but the U.S. Supreme Court struck it down for infringing the right to marry.[71]

The law also reflects the decline of obligations beyond the conjugal family. "Filial responsibility" statutes requiring adults to support indigent parents or grandparents are gradually disappearing, and those that remain are rarely enforced. Meanwhile, interest groups have formed to press for the recognition of "grandparents' visiting rights."[72]

The new family law has proven at best a mixed success. The removal of fault as grounds for divorce has spared couples the pain and humiliation of airing their disputes in public, and spared the courts the sordid task of assessing guilt in broken marriages. The advent of gender neutrality does away with outmoded assumptions about the roles of husbands and wives and gives legal recognition to the ideal of sexual equality.

On the other hand, reform has brought economic hardship for women and children that its proponents did not foresee. Treating men and women equally in the division of marital property and in expectations of self-sufficiency overlooks the inequality of earning capacity, especially for women who devoted their lives to child rearing while their husbands pursued careers. And since women continue to retain custody of children in most cases, they must meet greater responsibilities with fewer economic resources. Few mothers are awarded alimony (only 13 percent of mothers with preschool children), and child support payments average only $2,200 per year, often for the support of two or more children. For men, divorce brings a 42 percent increase in standard of living, while divorced women and their children suffer a 73 percent decline.[73] As a result, "divorce now constitutes a major cause of poverty among women and their children."[74]

Further reforms giving greater attention to the economic conditions of women and children after divorce might alleviate the hardships while preserving some of the gains of the new family law. In the 1990s, efforts in this direction included national legislation to strengthen enforcement of child support obligations.[75] While some such efforts can be defended in terms consistent with procedural liberalism, the new family law that unfolded in the 1970s and 1980s nonetheless offered a striking expression of assumptions drawn from the liberal conception of the person and displayed some of the difficulties to which it gives rise.

Marriage, Divorce, and the Unencumbered Self

First, the rejection of fault as grounds for divorce and property settlements reflects the liberal resolve to bracket moral judgments, to make law neutral among competing conceptions of the good. As in liberal theories of distributive justice, so now in divorce settlements, distributive shares are not intended to reward virtue but simply to meet the economic needs of the parties. Under the new law, unlike the old, the principles that determine the distribution of marital assets upon divorce "do not mention moral desert, and there is no tendency for distributive shares to correspond to it."[76]

Second, the provision for divorce as a unilateral decision without mutual consent, the rejection of marital roles tied to lifelong obligations, and the emphasis on self-sufficiency after divorce all reflect the liberal conception of persons as unencumbered selves independent of their roles and unbound by moral ties they choose to reject. The old law treated persons as situated selves, whose identity as legal persons was tied to their roles as husbands, wives, and parents. The new law loosens the relation between the self and its roles; it makes family roles easier to shed and relaxes the obligations that attach to them.

More than a reflection of law alone, the image of the unencumbered self is consistent with actual developments in American family life in recent decades. Divorce rates more than doubled from the 1960s to the late 1970s, to the point where half of all marriages are expected to end in divorce.[77] With the rise in divorce came a growing tendency to cast off the obligations of parenthood. A leading demographer observes that "since 1960 the conjugal family has begun to divest itself of care for children in much the same way that it did earlier for the elderly," and that this phenomenon is due mainly to "a disappearing act by fathers." The percentage of births out of wedlock rose from 5.3 percent in 1960 to 18.4 percent in 1980, reaching 30.1 percent by 1992. Of children born in wedlock, as many as half are expected to experience the breakup of their parents' marriage before they reach age seventeen, up from 22 percent in the mid-1960s. Most children of divorced parents live with their mothers, and over half of these children have not seen their fathers in the past year. Only about 40 percent receive any child support payments from their father. Not surprisingly, 56 percent of children in single female-headed households live in poverty.[78]

Quite apart from the social pathology of broken families and missing fathers, national surveys conducted in the 1950s and 1970s found a growing tendency among Americans to conceive their identities as independent of familial or parental roles.[79] One indication of this shift was a growing view of children as encumbrances, as obstacles to parents' freedom. Asked in 1976 how having children changes one's life, 45 percent of adults mentioned only the restrictions parenthood imposes, such as the added responsibility, the need to think of someone else, the lost freedom. In 1957 only 30 percent responded by citing restrictions alone.[80]

The same survey found that married persons in the 1950s tended to describe their family life in terms of their duties as husbands, wives, and parents. By the 1970s people described family life less as an arrangement of roles and more as a relationship of persons behind the roles. In the 1950s, for example, parents were concerned largely with such role-based responsibilities as the physical care and financial support of their children. In the 1970s parents were more concerned with their personal relationships with their children—how much time they spent together, how well they got along. "While earlier generations stressed role aspects of parenthood," concluded the authors of the survey, "later generations adopted [a] more psychological, interpersonal orientation." Especially among men, the 1970s brought "a very large shift toward seeing parental inadequacies in terms of affiliative relationships with children."[81]

As these attitudes suggest, the liberal self-image has had beneficial consequences as well as destructive ones. For better and for worse, however, the new views of family life support the conclusion that Americans increasingly conceive of themselves as bearers of selves independent of their roles. As a popular inspirational book called *Personhood* proclaims, "We have a right to choose our own selves, even if that self is different from the selves of others."[82] In family life as in family law, "role and status designations have become objects of suspicion, as though they were different from—and even contradictory to—the core self, the essential person."[83] In the procedural republic the unencumbered self not only governs public life but penetrates the precincts of family life as well.

The new law of divorce illustrates two difficulties with the liberal assumptions it embodies. One concerns the notion of respect for persons; the other, the claim to be neutral among conceptions of the good.

First, by treating all persons as bearers of a self independent of its roles, the new law fails to respect mothers and homemakers of traditional marriages whose identity is constituted by their roles, who have lived their married lives as situated selves. By insisting on self-sufficiency after divorce, it penalizes women whose economic reliance on their husbands expressed the mutual dependence of traditional marital roles. Her care for children and home enabled him to pursue a career. But when the marriage dissolves, he has the career, with its income and status, while she has the children and a sudden requirement to enter a labor market that rewards the skills she has forgone while making his career possible.

Since the law now brackets the roles that defined her identity and made sense of her dependence, she is typically left with half the marital property (less than $10,000 on average), no alimony, minimal child support that may never be paid, and responsibility for the care of children. Although courts supposedly consider the earning capacity of the parties, in the majority of cases even women married fifteen years or longer receive no alimony.[84]

For the woman whose identity is tied to family rather than to career, the injury goes beyond the risk of economic hardship should her marriage end in divorce. By failing to reward women's unpaid contributions to child rearing, homemaking, and husband's career, the new law of divorce devalues those contributions and erodes the significance of the roles they reflect. It strengthens the assumption that the work that counts is work for pay outside the home. Even those whose marriages remain intact suffer the loss of social status that goes with this assumption. Among professional classes, for example, the woman's reply to the proverbial question "What do you do?" sadly reflects the loss of esteem accorded those whose work is in the home: "I'm just a mother."

Second, the new divorce law calls into question the liberal assumption that treating persons as independent selves expands rather than constrains their choice of lives, and so is neutral among conceptions of the good. For as we have seen, the ideals of independence and self-sufficiency embodied in the new law do not simply enlarge the range of possible lives; they also make some ways of life more difficult, especially those like traditional marriage that involve a high degree of mutual dependence and obligation.

Although couples are free in principle to divide the roles of breadwinner and homemaker and to tie their identities to family roles and obligations, the new law poses a powerful obstacle to such arrangements. It gives married persons, and especially women, a harsh incentive not to devote themselves too completely to the care of children and family, but to pursue a career as a hedge against the day when they may have to fend for themselves. As sociologist Lenore Weitzman has observed, the clear message of current divorce settlements is that "women had better not forgo any of their own education, training, and career development to devote themselves fully or even partially to their families. The law assures that they will not be rewarded for their devotion, either in court or in the job market, and they will suffer greatly if their marriage dissolves."[85]

Liberals often argue that the good of community can be fully accounted for "by a conception of justice that in its theoretical basis is individualistic."[86] Given a neutral framework of individual rights, people are free to join in voluntary association on whatever terms they choose, whether to pursue their private ends or to enjoy the communal sentiments that such cooperation often inspires. "[W]ithin this framework communitarian aims may be pursued, and quite possibly by the vast majority of persons."[87]

But the new law of divorce offers a counterexample to this claim. By making dependence a dangerous thing, it burdens the practice of marriage as a community in the constitutive sense. By bracketing moral judgments, celebrating self-sufficiency, and loosening the relation between the self and its roles, the law is not neutral among competing visions of married life, but recasts the institution of marriage in the image of the unencumbered self.

Some see in this conception a long-term threat to family life as such. As growing numbers of women understand that they cannot count on the economic stability of marriage, they seek to assure their economic security by committing themselves to a career. As men and women find that greater benefits derive from holding a job, family life will diminish in relative importance to the world of work, and people will invest less in the family than in their individual lives and careers.[88] That careers have come to matter more and families less in modern life may explain why the law now makes it easier to divorce a spouse than to fire an employee. While much of the labor force can only be fired for "good cause," no-fault divorce makes marriage a relationship that can be "terminated at will."[89]

Whether or not these worries are well-founded, whatever the merits or drawbacks of the new arrangements, it is clear in any case that the new family law, for all its liberating promise, does not simply free people to arrange their marital roles as they choose. It is not neutral among conceptions of the good, but favorable to certain visions of family life, inhospitable to others.

Toleration, Self-Government, and Community

We have seen how the key features of contemporary liberalism—rights as trumps, the neutral state, and the unencumbered self—have come to inform the theory and practice of constitutional law and of family law in recent decades.

We have also seen how problems in the theory show up in the practice. First, attempts to be neutral among competing conceptions of morality or religion often rely on implicit answers to the controversies they purport to bracket, as the abortion example illustrates. Second, treating persons as freely choosing, independent selves may fail to respect persons encumbered by convictions or life circumstances that do not admit the independence the liberal self-image requires. In different ways, the sabbath observers in Connecticut, the victims of racial defamation in Chicago, the Holocaust survivors in Skokie, the feminists against pornography in Indianapolis, the homosexuals denied privacy in Georgia, and the traditional mothers and homemakers impoverished by divorce are all situated selves with good reason to resist the demand to bracket their identities for the sake of political agreement; their concerns cannot be translated without loss into the voluntarist, individuated terms on which the procedural republic insists.

The difficulties we have considered so far bear primarily on the kind of toleration the procedural republic provides. Given its aspiration to neutrality, it brackets the value of the practices it tolerates. Given its conception of the self, it seeks respect for persons without winning respect for the convictions they hold or the lives they live. The toleration that results does not cultivate appreciation for the ways of life it permits, only respect for the selves whose lives they are. This reflects the priority of the right to the good, and of the self to its ends. But the cases we have considered illustrate the limits of toleration based on this conception. Respecting persons as unencumbered selves may afford a kind of social peace, but it is unlikely to realize the higher pluralism of persons and communities who appreciate and affirm the distinctive goods their different lives express.

In seeking the public philosophy implicit in our practice, we have focused so far on constitutional law, for it is here that the assumptions of the procedural republic most vividly appear. Beyond the issue of toleration, these assumptions raise a further question for American politics: Is the liberal self-image that has emerged in recent decades adequate to self-government in the modern welfare state? There are at least two reasons to doubt that it is—one old, the other relatively new.

The old reason to doubt whether unencumbered selves are suited to self-government derives from the republican tradition. According to that tradition, liberty depends on self-government, and self-government depends on the members of a political community's identifying with the role of citizen and acknowledging the obligations that citizenship entails. But in the procedural republic, "role designations have become objects of suspicion."[90] When the self is conceived as prior to its ends, the role of citizen becomes a convention like the rest, an obstacle to autonomy.

Moreover, the republican tradition emphasizes the need to cultivate citizenship through particular ties and attachments. More than a legal condition, citizenship requires certain habits and dispositions, a concern for the whole, an orientation to the common good. But these qualities cannot be taken as given. They require constant cultivation. Family, neighborhood, religion, trade unions, reform movements, and local government all offer examples of practices that have at times served to educate people in the exercise of citizenship by cultivating the habits of membership and orienting people to common goods beyond their private ends.[91] A public life that fails to nurture these practices or is indifferent to their fate fails to cultivate the virtues essential to self-government as the republican tradition conceives it.

But as we have seen, the procedural republic is often inhospitable to claims premised on self-definitions such as these. It brackets the constitutive ties that the republican tradition sees as essential to political education. The thin pluralism the procedural republic provides is not only a problem for its own sake; it also erodes the resources of self-government. A pluralism that nurtures the distinctive expressions of community is better suited to citizenship, and so to self-government, than one that merely tolerates them.

The second reason for wondering whether the unencumbered self is adequate to self-government in contemporary America concerns the nature of the modern welfare state. In sharp contrast to the voluntarist conception of human agency, the modern state consists of a vast network of dependencies and expectations largely ungoverned by voluntary agreements or acts of consent. Even as it flourishes in contemporary liberalism, the notion of contract has little to do with the actual organization of modern economic and political life.

In fact, legal commentators write of "the death of contract" as a distinct body of law.[92] Social legislation of the twentieth century, responding to the unequal bargaining power of large corporations in a "free market," has "systematically robbed contract of its subject-matter" in such areas as labor law, antitrust law, insurance law, business regulation, and social welfare legislation.[93] Statutory rules now govern the terms of almost every type of ordinary contract, from employment to rent to consumer credit. In addition to the expansion of government, the dominance of large-scale corporations has further displaced the role of individual contracts in organizing economic activity. "What we now have is a relatively small number of large organizations, who exercise more or less control over their own members, and who enter into relationships, whether commercial or otherwise, with other similar organizations. The role of the individual as the center of a network of relationships has largely disappeared."[94] As a result, the classical law of contract that predominated in the nineteenth century has been reduced to a residual category, of little practical importance. As the nineteenth century saw the shift from status to contract as the basis of rights and duties, the twentieth century has witnessed the shift from contract to administration.[95]

Ironically, the freely choosing, autonomous self has come to prevail in constitutional law just at the time it has faded as a plausible self-image in contract law, and in economic life generally. Confronted with the complex scheme of mutual dependence that has arisen in the years since World War II, we seek an independence in our personal lives that eludes us in our public life. It is as if the triumph of autonomy in matters of religion, speech, and sexual morality were a kind of consolation for the loss of agency in an economic and political order increasingly governed by vast structures of power.

Whatever the explanation, there is reason to wonder whether the unencumbered self is suited to the dependencies and obligations the modern welfare state requires. On the one hand, the welfare state holds out a powerful promise of individual rights, including social and economic entitlements that go beyond legal and civil rights alone. This rights orientation fits well with the public philosophy of contemporary liberalism. On the other hand, the public provision of these rights and entitlements would seem to demand of fellow citizens a strong sense of mutual responsibility and moral engagement. Unless persons regard their identities as claimed to some extent by their role as participants in a common life, it is not obvious on what grounds they can affirm the obligations the modern welfare state expects them to fulfill. But it is just this strong notion of membership that the unencumbered self resists.

In this respect, the case for public provision in the procedural republic and the case for toleration seem to suffer a similar minimalism. Both try to avoid relying on a conception of the good life. But just as we have found reason to question the kind of toleration that fails to cultivate a pluralism of mutual appreciation, so there may be reason to worry about the legitimacy of a welfare state that fails to cultivate community in the constitutive sense.

The chapters that follow explore the consequences for self-government of the public philosophy we have identified with the procedural republic. The emphasis thus shifts from constitutional to political debates. As I shall try to show, the version of liberalism that asserts the priority of the right over the good cannot secure the part of liberty bound up with self-government.

II

The Political Economy of Citizenship

5

Economics and Virtue in the Early Republic

As we have seen, the public philosophy of the procedural republic finds powerful expression in contemporary constitutional law. In the decades since World War II, the Supreme Court has come to insist that government be neutral among competing conceptions of the good life. But what about American public life beyond its constitutional aspect? Does the version of liberalism that conceives the right as prior to the good describe our political practice beyond the judicial realm, or is it characteristic of legal and constitutional discourse alone?

It might seem that the Court's tendency to bracket competing conceptions of the good life simply reflects its distinctive role in a constitutional democracy. While democratic politics is free to traffic in conceptions of the good—whether in aggregating individual interests or in deliberating about the good of the whole—courts must constrain what majorities can decide, and so insist on the priority of right. Given this institutional division of labor, we might expect our political discourse to partake of the moral arguments that constitutional discourse seeks to bracket.

The increased role of government since World War II offers a further reason to expect our national political life to address rather than avoid our conflicting moral conceptions. The state's active intervention in the market economy would seem to defy the aspiration to neutrality, and require government unavoidably to confront the competing purposes and ends its citizens espouse.

But these appearances are misleading. The version of liberalism that has recently emerged in constitutional law also finds expression in American political discourse generally. Despite the prominent role of government in the modern economy, there is an important sense in which this role reflects the version of liberalism that holds that government should be neutral among competing conceptions of the good life, in order to respect persons as free and independent selves, capable of choosing their ends for themselves. Not only is the public philosophy of the procedural republic consistent with the activist state; it illuminates the distinctive way this state has developed in the United States since the New Deal, and provides the terms of its justification.

Prosperity, Fairness, and Civic Virtue

Consider the way we think and argue about economics today, by contrast with the way Americans debated economic policy through much of our history. In contemporary American politics, most of our economic arguments revolve around two considerations: prosperity and fairness. Whatever tax policies or budget proposals or regulatory schemes people may favor, they usually defend them on the grounds that they will contribute to economic growth or improve the distribution of income; they claim that their policy will increase the size of the economic pie, or distribute the pieces of the pie more fairly, or both.

So familiar are these ways of justifying economic policy that they might seem to exhaust the possibilities. But our debates about economic policy have not always focused solely on the size and distribution of the national product. Throughout much of American history they have also addressed a different question, namely, what economic arrangements are most hospitable to self-government? Along with prosperity and fairness, the civic consequences of economic policy have often loomed large in American political discourse.

Thomas Jefferson gave classic expression to the civic strand of economic argument. In his *Notes on the State of Virginia* (1787), he argued against developing large-scale domestic manufactures on the grounds that the agrarian way of life makes for virtuous citizens, well suited to self-government. "Those who labour in the earth are the chosen people of God," the embodiments of "genuine virtue." The political economists of Europe may claim that every nation should manufacture for itself, but large-scale manufacturing undermines the independence that republican citizenship requires. "Dependance begets subservience and venality, suffocates the germ of virtue, and prepares fit tools for the designs of ambition." Jefferson thought it better to "let our work-shops remain in Europe" and avoid the moral corruption they bring; better to import manufactured goods than the manners and habits that attend their production. "The mobs of great cities add just so much to the support of pure government, as sores do to the strength of the human body. It is the manners and spirit of a people which preserve a republic in vigour. A degeneracy in these is a canker which soon eats to the heart of its laws and constitution."[1]

Whether to encourage domestic manufactures or retain the nation's agrarian character was the subject of intense debate in the early decades of the republic. In the end, Jefferson's agrarian vision did not prevail. But the republican assumption underlying his economics—that public policy should cultivate the qualities of character self-government requires—found broader support and a longer career. From the Revolution to the Civil War, the political economy of citizenship played a prominent role in American national debate.

In 1784 the Virginia legislature passed a law known as the "Port Bill," designed to centralize commerce by restricting all foreign trade to five coastal towns. The bill's advocates, including James Madison, sought to break Britain's monopoly on trade and to improve the collection of duties. By the time of the Revolution, British merchants had come to dominate the scattered wharves of Virginia's waterways. Madison hoped that a centralized system would promote economic independence by giving other nations equal access to Virginia's commerce.[2]

The Port Bill met with strong opposition, not least from the counties that lost trade under the law. Urging repeal, the opponents offered three different arguments—one about fairness, one about prosperity, and one about civic virtue. The argument from fairness denounced the bill as "unjust and unequal," since it failed to divide wealth and power equally among the various districts and towns. The argument from prosperity held that any gains from centralized commerce would be outweighed by the costs of transporting goods to and from the central ports.[3]

George Mason, the leading opponent of the bill, offered a further consideration. He argued that large commercial cities would undermine the civic virtue that republican government requires. "If virtue is the vital principle of a republic, and it cannot long exist, without frugality, probity and strictness of morals," Mason asked, "will the manners of populous commercial cities be favorable to the principles of our free government? Or will not the vice, the depravity of morals, the luxury, venality, and corruption, which invariably prevail in great commercial cities, be utterly subversive of them?" Virginia's Port Bill narrowly survived the repeal efforts, but it was soon overridden by a new Constitution that transferred to the federal government the regulation of foreign trade.[4]

Mason's case against the Port Bill, like Jefferson's argument against large-scale manufactures, reflected a way of thinking about politics that had its roots in the classical republican tradition. Central to republican theory is the idea that liberty requires self-government, which depends in turn on civic virtue. This idea figured prominently in the political outlook of the founding generation. "[P]ublic virtue is the only foundation of republics," wrote John Adams on the eve of independence. "There must be a positive passion for the public good, the public interest, honour, power and glory, established in the minds of the people, or there can be no republican government, nor any real liberty."[5] Benjamin Franklin agreed: "Only a virtuous people are capable of freedom. As nations become corrupt and vicious, they have more need of masters."[6]

The founders also learned from the republican tradition that they could not take civic virtue for granted. To the contrary, public spirit was a fragile thing, susceptible of erosion by such corrupting forces as luxury, wealth, and power. Anxiety over the loss of civic virtue was a persistent republican theme. "Virtue and simplicity of manners are indispensably necessary in a republic among all orders and degrees of men," wrote John Adams. "But there is so much rascality, so much venality and corruption, so much avarice and ambition, such a rage for profit and commerce among all ranks and degrees of men even in America, that I sometimes doubt whether there is public virtue enough to support a republic."[7]

If liberty cannot survive without virtue, and if virtue tends always to corruption, then the challenge for republican politics is to form or reform the moral character of citizens, to strengthen their attachment to the common good. The public life of a republic must serve a formative role, aimed at cultivating citizens of a certain kind. "[I]t is the part of a great politician to make the character of his people," Adams declared, "to extinguish among them the follies and vices that he sees, and to create in them the virtues and abilities which he sees wanting."[8] Republican government cannot be neutral toward the moral character of its citizens or the ends they pursue. Rather, it must undertake to form their character and ends in order to foster the public concerns on which liberty depends.

The Revolution was itself born of anxiety about the loss of civic virtue, as a desperate attempt to stave off corruption and to realize republican ideals.[9] In the 1760s and 1770s the American colonists viewed their struggle with England in republican terms. The English constitution was imperiled by ministerial manipulation of Parliament, and, worse, the English people had become "too corrupted, too enfeebled, to restore their constitution to its first principles and rejuvenate their country."[10] In the decade following the Stamp Act, attempts by Parliament to exercise sovereignty in America appeared to the colonists a "conspiracy of power against liberty," a small part of a larger assault on the English constitution itself. It was this belief "above all else that in the end propelled [the colonists] into Revolution."[11]

Republican assumptions did more than animate colonial fears; they also defined the Revolution's aims. "The sacrifice of individual interests to the greater good of the whole formed the essence of republicanism and comprehended for Americans the idealistic goal of their Revolution. . . . No phrase except 'liberty' was invoked more often by the Revolutionaries than 'the public good,'" which for them meant more than the sum of individual interests. The point of politics was not to broker competing interests but to transcend them, to seek the good of the community as a whole. More than a break with England, independence would be a source of moral regeneration; it would stave off corruption and renew the moral spirit that suited Americans to republican government.[12]

Such ambitious hopes were bound to meet with disappointment, as they did in the years immediately following independence. When the

Revolution failed to produce the moral reformation its leaders had hoped for, new fears arose for the fate of republican government. During the "critical period" of the 1780s, leading politicians and writers worried that the public spirit inspired by the struggle with Britain had given way to the rampant pursuit of luxury and self-interest. "What astonishing changes a few years are capable of producing," said George Washington in 1786. "From the high ground we stood upon, from the plain path which invited our footsteps, to be so fallen, so lost! It is really mortifying."[13]

Civic Virtue and the Constitution

What troubled the revolutionary leaders most of all was the popular politics increasingly practiced in the state legislatures. They had assumed that under republican government, a "natural aristocracy" of merit and virtue would replace an artificial aristocracy of heredity and patronage. But in the postrevolutionary state legislatures, the best did not necessarily rule. Ordinary, uneducated citizens—small-town shopkeepers, artisans, subsistence farmers—passed laws confiscating property, granting debtor relief, and enacting paper money schemes. For republican leaders such as Madison, this form of politics amounted to an excess of democracy, a perversion of republican ideals. Rather than governing in a disinterested spirit on behalf of the public good, these representatives of the people were all too representative—parochial, small-minded, and eager to serve the private interests of their constituents.[14]

By the standards of a later day, the politics of the 1780s might simply appear as the emergence of a now familiar interest-group pluralism. To the founding generation, however, it was a kind of corruption, a falling away from civic virtue. The Revolution "had unleashed acquisitive and commercial forces" the founders had not anticipated: "in states up and down the continent, various narrow factional interests, especially economic, were flourishing as never before" and gaining protection from the democratically elected state legislatures.[15] Madison despaired at the "mutability" and "injustice" of state laws, which he attributed to the interest-ridden character of local politics: "Is it to be imagined that an ordinary citizen or even Assemblyman of Rhode Island in estimating the policy of paper money, ever considered or cared, in what light the measure would be viewed in France or Holland; or even in Massachusetts or Connecticut? It was a sufficient temptation to both that it was for their interest."[16]

Growing doubts about the prospect of civic virtue in the 1780s prompted two kinds of response—one formative, the other procedural. The first sought, through education and other means, to inculcate virtue more strenuously. The second sought, through constitutional change, to render virtue less necessary.

Benjamin Rush gave stark expression to the formative impulse in his proposal for public schools in Pennsylvania. Writing in 1786, he declared that the mode of education proper to a republic was one that inculcated an overriding allegiance to the common good: "Let our pupil be taught that he does not belong to himself, but that he is public property. Let him be taught to love his family, but let him be taught at the same time that he must forsake and even forget them when the welfare of his country requires it." With a proper system of public education, Rush maintained, it would be "possible to convert men into republican machines. This must be done if we expect them to perform their parts properly in the great machine of the government of the state."[17]

The most eventful procedural response to republican worries about the dearth of civic virtue was the Constitution of 1787. More than mere remedy to the defects of the Articles of Confederation, the Constitution had as its larger ambition "to save American republicanism from the deadly effects of [the] private pursuits of happiness," from the acquisitive preoccupations that so absorbed Americans and distracted them from the public good.[18]

Prompted though it was by fear for the loss of civic virtue, the Constitution did not seek to elevate the moral character of the people, at least not directly. Instead, it sought institutional devices that would save republican government by making it less dependent on the virtue of the people.

By the time they assembled in Philadelphia, the framers had concluded that civic virtue was too much to expect of most of the people most of the time. Several years earlier, Alexander Hamilton had ridiculed the republican hope that virtue could prevail over self-interest among ordinary citizens: "We may preach till we are tired of the theme, the necessity of disinterestedness in republics, without making a single proselyte. The virtuous declaimer will neither persuade himself nor any other person to be content with a double mess of porridge, instead of a reasonable stipend for his services. We might as soon reconcile ourselves to the Spartan community of goods and wives, to their iron coin, their long beards, or their black broth." The republican models of Greece and Rome were no more appropriate to America, Hamilton thought, than the examples of the Hottentots and Laplanders. Noah Webster, a leading defender of the Constitution, agreed: "Virtue, patriotism, or love of country, never was and never will be, till men's natures are changed, a fixed, permanent principle and support of government."[19]

In *Federalist* no. 51 Madison explained how, contrary to classical teachings, republican government could make its peace with interest and ambition after all. Liberty would depend not on civic virtue but instead on a scheme of mechanisms and procedures by which competing interests would check and balance one another: "Ambition must be made to counteract ambition. The interest of the man must be connected with the constitutional rights of the place. It may be a reflection on human nature, that such devices should be necessary to control the abuses of government. But what is government itself but the greatest of all reflections on human nature? If men were angels, no government would be necessary. If angels were to govern men, neither external nor internal controls on government would be necessary."[20] According to Madison, the Constitution would compensate for "the defect of better motives" by institutional devices that would counterpose "opposite and rival interests." The separation of powers among the executive, legislative, and judicial branches, the division of power between federal and state governments, the division of Congress into two bodies with different terms and constituencies, and the indirect election of the Senate were among the "inventions of prudence" designed to secure liberty without relying too heavily on the virtue of citizens. "A dependence on the people is no doubt the primary control on the government," Madison allowed, "but experience has taught mankind the necessity of auxiliary precautions."[21]

Despite their revision of classical republican assumptions, the framers of the Constitution adhered to republican ideals in two important respects. First, they continued to believe that the virtuous should govern, and that government should aim at a public good beyond the sum of private interests. Second, they did not abandon the formative ambition of republican politics, the notion that government has a stake in cultivating citizens of a certain kind.

The framers rejected the notion that the people possessed sufficient virtue to govern directly. But they retained the hope that the national government they had designed would be led by enlightened statesmen like themselves, who would possess the virtue and wisdom that ordinary citizens and local representatives lacked.[22] Such "individuals of extended views, and of national pride" would not cater to parochial interests but would govern with the disinterest of classical republican legislators, "with a sole regard to justice and the public good."[23]

The point of the system of representation they invented was to identify such people and to place them in positions of power and trust. The aim was to design a system that would, in Madison's words, "extract from the mass of the society the purest and noblest characters which it contains," people "whose enlightened views and virtuous sentiments [would] render them superior to local prejudices, and to schemes of injustice."[24]

This aim distances Madison from modern-day interest-group pluralists who invoke his name. For Madison, the reason for admitting interests into the system was not to govern by them but to disempower them, to play them to a draw, so that disinterested statesmen might govern unhindered by them. The reason for taking in, through an extended republic, "a greater variety of parties and interests" was not to better approximate the will of the people; it was to increase the likelihood that these various interests would cancel each other out, and so enable enlightened statesmen to rise above them.[25]

For Madison, the point of republican government was not to give the people what they want, but to do the right thing. This meant placing government in the hands of "a chosen body of citizens, whose wisdom may best discern the true interest of the country, and whose patriotism and love of justice, will be least likely to sacrifice it to temporary or partial considerations." The result, he thought, would be better than could be achieved by consulting the people directly. If the virtuous govern, "it may well happen that the public voice pronounced by the representatives of the people, will be more consonant to the public good, than if pronounced by the people themselves convened for the purpose."[26]

Even Hamilton, who expected little virtue from the people at large, was no apologist for a politics of self-interest. In line with the classical republican tradition, he considered civic life a nobler calling than commercial pursuits, and celebrated the ideal of the legislator motivated not by material gain but by honor and glory. "The station of a member of Congress," Hamilton wrote, "is the most illustrious and important of any I am able to conceive. He is to be regarded not only as a legislator, but as the founder of an empire. A man of virtue and ability, dignified with so precious a trust ... would esteem it not more the duty, than the privilege and ornament of his office, to do good to mankind; from this commanding eminence, he would look down with contempt upon every mean or interested pursuit."[27] Ordinary men were moved by self-interest, but the "love of fame" was "the ruling passion of the noblest minds." This higher motive, "which would prompt a man to plan and undertake extensive and arduous enterprises for the public benefit," was the passion of founders.[28]

The second strand of the republican tradition the framers retained was its formative ambition. Although the Constitution limited the role of ordinary citizens in governing, it did not abandon the notion that government should shape the moral character of its citizens. If republican government aimed at something higher than the sum of private interests, then no democratic republic, however carefully designed to limit popular participation, could afford to ignore the character of its people.

Even Madison, the principal architect of the mechanisms designed to "refine and enlarge the public views,"[29] affirmed that virtue among the people was indispensable to self-government. At the very least, he told the Virginia ratifying convention, the people need the virtue and intelligence to elect virtuous representatives. "Is there no virtue among us? If there be not, we are in a wretched situation. No theoretical checks, no form of government, can render us secure. To suppose that any form of government will secure liberty or happiness without any virtue in the people, is a chimerical idea."[30] In his Farewell Address, George Washington echoed the familiar republican view: "Virtue or morality is a necessary spring of popular government."[31]

Hamilton also assigned government a formative role, although the quality he hoped to cultivate was not traditional civic virtue but attachment to the nation. In *Federalist* no. 27 he argued that the new national government would establish its authority only if it came to infuse the lives and sentiments of the people: "the more the citizens are accustomed to meet with it in the common occurrences of their political life; the more it is familiarised to their sight and to their feelings; the further it enters into those objects which touch the most sensible cords, and put in motion the most active springs of the human heart; the greater will be the probability that it will conciliate the respect and attachment of the community." For Hamilton, the national government depended for its success on its capacity to shape the habits of the people, to interest their sensations, to win their affection, to "[circulate] through those channels and currents, in which the passions of mankind naturally flow."[32]

Although the framers believed that republican government required a certain kind of citizen, they did not view the Constitution as the primary instrument of moral or civic improvement. For the formative dimension of public life, they looked elsewhere—to education, to religion, and, more broadly, to the social and economic arrangements that would define the character of the new nation.

Federalists versus Jeffersonians

After ratification, American political debate turned from constitutional questions to economic ones. But the economic debate that unfolded was not only about national wealth and distributive justice; it was also about the civic consequences of economic arrangements—about the kind of society America should become and the kind of citizens it should cultivate.[33]

Two major issues illustrate the prominence of civic considerations in the political discourse of the early republic. One was the debate over Hamilton's treasury system, the debate that gave rise to the division between Federalists and Republicans. The second was the debate over whether to encourage domestic manufactures, a debate that cut across party lines.

Hamilton's Treasury System

As the first secretary of the Treasury, Hamilton made proposals to Congress on public credit, a national bank, a mint, and manufacturing.

Though all but the last were adopted, the proposals sparked much controversy and, taken as a whole, led opponents to conclude that Hamilton sought to undermine republican government. His program for government finance proved especially contentious, and raised fears that Hamilton planned to create in America a political economy like Britain's, based on patronage, influence, and connections. In his *Report on Public Credit* (1790) he proposed that the federal government assume the revolutionary debts of the states and combine them with existing federal debts. Rather than pay off the consolidated debt, Hamilton proposed to fund it through the sale of securities to investors, using revenues from duties and excise taxes to pay regular interest.[34]

Hamilton offered various economic arguments in support of his funding plan—that it would establish the nation's credit, create a money supply, provide a source for investment, and so create the basis for prosperity and wealth. But beyond these economic considerations, Hamilton sought an equally important political aim—to build support for the new national government by giving a wealthy and influential class of investors a financial stake in it.

Fearful that local sentiments would erode national authority and doubtful that disinterested virtue could inspire allegiance to the nation, Hamilton saw in public finance an instrument of nation-building: "If all the public creditors receive their dues from one source, their interest will be the same. And having the same interests, they will unite in support of the fiscal arrangements of the government." If state and federal debts were financed separately, he argued, "there will be distinct interests, drawing different ways. That union and concert of views, among the creditors . . . will be likely to give place to mutual jealousy and opposition."[35]

By regular payments on a national debt, the national government would "interweave itself into the monied interest of every state" and "insinuate itself into every branch of industry," thereby winning the support of an important class of society.[36] The political purpose of Hamilton's funding plan was no hidden agenda, but an explicit rationale for the policy. As a sympathetic newspaper commented at the time, "a national debt attaches many citizens to the government who, by their numbers, wealth, and influence, contribute more perhaps to its preservation than a body of soldiers."[37]

It was the political ambition of Hamilton's policy that sparked the most heated controversy. What Hamilton considered nation-building, others considered a kind of bribery and corruption. To a generation of Americans acutely suspicious of executive power, Hamilton's funding plan seemed an assault on republican government. It recalled the practice of the eighteenth century British prime minister Robert Walpole, who placed paid government agents in Parliament to support government policies. Although Hamilton did not propose to hire members of Congress, the fact that creditors of the government sat in Congress and supported Hamilton's financial program struck opponents as similarly corrupt. Such creditors would not be disinterested seekers of the public good, but interested partisans of the administration and the policy that secured their investments.[38]

Republican fears of a conspiracy of power against liberty had fueled the Revolution. Now Hamilton seemed to be recreating in America the English system of government finance so despised by republicans for its reliance on patronage, connections, and speculation. Hamilton acknowledged what his opponents feared, that his model was Britain. In an after-dinner conversation with Adams and Jefferson, he even defended its reliance on patronage and corruption. Adams observed that, purged of its corruption, the British constitution would be the most perfect devised by the wit of man. Hamilton replied, "purge it of its corruption, and give to its popular branch equality of representation, and it would become an *impracticable* government. As it stands at present, with all its supposed defects, it is the most perfect government which ever existed." Jefferson, appalled, concluded that "Hamilton was not only a monarchist, but for a monarchy bottomed on corruption."[39]

The opponents of Hamiltonian finance advanced two different arguments against it. One concerned its distributive consequences, the other its civic consequences. The distributive argument objected to the fact that, under Hamilton's plan, the wealthy would gain at the expense of ordinary Americans. Speculators who had bought revolutionary bonds from their original owners at a fraction of their value now stood to reap huge profits, with interest to be paid from excise taxes borne by ordinary citizens.

As it figured in political debate of the 1790s, however, this distributive worry was secondary to a broader political objection. The argument that brought the Republican party into being was that Hamilton's political economy would corrupt the morality of citizens and undermine the social conditions essential to republican government. When Republicans objected that Hamilton's system would deepen inequality in American society, they were less concerned with distributive justice as such than with the need to avoid the wide disparities of wealth that threatened republican government. Civic virtue required the capacity for independent, disinterested judgment. But poverty bred dependence, and great wealth traditionally bred luxury and distraction from public concerns.[40]

Writing to President Washington in 1792, Jefferson emphasized these moral and civic considerations. Hamilton's financial system, he complained, encouraged paper speculation and "nourishes in our citizens habits of vice and idleness instead of industry and morality." It created a "corrupt squadron" in the legislature, the ultimate object of which "is to prepare the way for a change, from the present republican form of government, to that of a monarchy, of which the English constitution is to be the model."[41]

By the mid-1790s, Republican writers joined the attack. Hamilton's program created a moneyed aristocracy, corrupted the legislature, and "promoted a general depravity of morals and a great decline of republican virtue."[42] Stockholders in Congress, subservient to the Treasury, formed "a vast and formidable body united in a close phalanx by a tie of mutual interest distinct from the general interest."[43] The Republican publicist John Taylor later summarized the moral and civic critique of Federalist finance: "The manners and principles of government are objects of imitation, and influence national character . . . but what virtues for imitation appear in the aristocracy of the present age? Avarice and ambition being its whole soul, what private morals will it infuse, and what national character will it create?"[44]

Republicans in Congress opposed Hamilton's "treasury system" and its attendant corruption. They offered measures to divide the Treasury Department, abolish the national bank, repeal the excise tax, and to exclude public debtholders from Congress.[45] But they were not without an affirmative vision of their own. Even before the first party division arose, Jefferson, Madison, and other republicans had sought "to form a national political economy capable of permitting and encouraging Americans to engage industriously in virtue-sustaining occupations."[46] If liberty depended on a virtuous, independent, property-owning citizenry, which depended in turn on a predominantly agricultural economy, the question was how to preserve the agrarian character of American society.

Republican Political Economy

In the 1780s Madison and others worried that the republican character of the American people was in danger of decay. The agrarian way of life they considered indispensable to virtue was threatened by restrictions on free trade imposed by the British mercantile system and by the growth of a propertyless class in crowded urban centers. Staving off the corruption that they feared would attend an advanced commercial and manufacturing society would require policies of two kinds: open markets for American agricultural surplus abroad, and westward expansion to preserve access to land.[47]

The states, however, could not enact these policies on their own. Only a strong national government would have sufficient power to force the dismantling of the mercantile system and confront foreign powers such as Spain that posed obstacles to westward expansion. Madison hoped that the new Constitution would create a national government capable of implementing policies he deemed necessary to securing a republican political economy.

For Madison, then, the new Constitution promised more than a procedural response to the erosion of civic virtue. For all its filtering mechanisms, checks and balances, and "auxiliary precautions," it did not abandon the formative ambition of republican government after all. In Madison's view, the Constitution would make its contribution to moral and civic improvement indirectly, by empowering the national government to shape a political economy hospitable to republican virtue.

Madison's and Hamilton's contrasting visions of civic virtue explain why these allies in defense of the Constitution parted company on matters of political economy. As soon became clear, they had different ends in mind for the national government they helped create, and for the kind of citizens they hoped to cultivate. Madison sought national power to preserve the agrarian way of life he believed republican government required.

Hamilton rejected the ideal of a virtuous agrarian republic. He sought national power to create the conditions for the advanced commercial and manufacturing economy that Jefferson and Madison considered inimical to republican government. Hamilton did not despair at the prospect of a modern commercial society, with its social inequalities and rampant pursuit of self-interest. To the contrary, he regarded these developments as inevitable conditions of the powerful and prosperous nation he hoped to build.[48]

From the standpoint of twentieth-century politics, the issue between Hamilton and his republican opponents might appear a familiar contest between economic growth on the one hand and fairness on the other. But these were not the primary terms of the debate. The arguments for and against Hamiltonian finance had less to do with prosperity and fairness than with the meaning of republican government and the kind of citizen it required.

Hamilton did believe his plan would lay the basis for economic growth, but his primary purpose was not to maximize the gross national product. For Hamilton, as for Jefferson and Madison, economics was the hand-maiden of politics, not the other way around. The political vision that animated Hamilton's economics was a vision of republican glory and greatness. In the modern world, such greatness depended, he believed, on an advanced economy of commerce, manufacturing, sound currency, and public finance.

Skeptical of inspiring disinterested patriotism or virtue among the people, Hamilton sought to turn self-interest to a public good beyond mere interests, to build what he called "the future grandeur and glory of America."[49] In Hamilton's view, the classical ideal of republican glory could now only be achieved by modern expedients: "Our prevailing passions are ambition and interest; and it will ever be the duty of a wise government to avail itself of those passions, in order to make them subservient to the public good."[50] Given the prevalence of avarice and interest, the challenge for the founder of a great republic was to use those passions for higher things. Not self-interest or even the quest for power, but "the love of fame" was "the ruling passion of the noblest minds."[51]

For their part, Hamilton's opponents did complain that his policies favored the wealthy. But this distributional worry was secondary to the more fundamental objection that Hamilton's "vision of a great republic—a commercial, manufacturing country dependent on public credit, British investment, and a sound system of public finance—necessarily threatened their contrasting ideal of a virtuous American state."[52]

These rival political economies found expression in the early debates between Federalists and Republicans. To achieve free trade for America's agriculture, Madison advocated "commercial discrimination," a policy of retaliatory duties aimed at coercing Britain to remove restrictions on American commerce. Hamilton opposed it on the grounds that coercion would not work and that America needed British commerce, credit, and capital to fund the national debt and fuel economic development, even at the price of submitting to British domination.[53] Federalists favored a national bankruptcy law to promote an advanced commercialized economy; Jeffersonians opposed it as promoting a spirit of reckless speculation and eroding the moral character of the people.[54]

When Jefferson was elected president in 1800, his goal was to reverse the "Anglicization" of American government and society. In order to purge the national government of the corruption of Hamilton's system, he sought to retire the national debt, reduce government expenditures, and repeal internal taxes. Beyond restoring republican simplicity and virtue to government, Jefferson and Madison sought, through the sixteen years of their presidencies, to secure the two conditions for a republican political economy—westward expansion and free trade. The Louisiana Purchase of 1803 achieved the first; the Embargo of 1807–1809 attempted, unsuccessfully, to achieve the second. Both policies aroused debates that illustrated the civic strand of economic argument in the early republic.[55]

The Louisiana Purchase served certain economic ends that Republicans and Federalists could agree on, such as access to the Mississippi River and control of New Orleans. The issue between Republicans and Federalists concerned the vast tract of land west of the Mississippi, and the civic consequences of settling it.[56]

For Republicans, the open land promised to preserve the agricultural way of life that fostered virtuous citizens, and forestall the day when America would become a crowded, dependent, unequal society, inconsistent with republican government. "By enlarging the empire of liberty," Jefferson observed, "we multiply its auxiliaries, and provide new sources of renovation, should its principles, at any time, degenerate, in those portions of our country which gave them birth."[57] John Taylor praised the Louisiana Purchase for its moral and civic consequences. The new territory, he wrote, would encourage "plain and regular manners," a "love of virtue and independence," and would preserve the "equality of possessions" republicanism requires.[58] For Republicans fearful of the centralizing tendency of military establishments, removing the French from Louisiana had the further advantage of distancing America from the wars and intrigues of Europe, and so avoiding the need for the armies, navies, taxes, and debt that concentrate power and threaten republican liberty.[59]

For Federalists, by contrast, the vast wilderness would "prove worse than useless."[60] Settlement of the new territory would disperse the population, increase the scourge of localism, and undermine the Federalist attempt to consolidate national power and assert its influence and control. Rapid westward emigration, Hamilton feared, "must hasten the dismemberment of a large portion of our country, or a dissolution of the Government."[61]

The Republicans were less successful in their attempt to secure the second condition of a republican political economy, a removal of restrictions on foreign trade. When in 1807 Britain prohibited all American trade with Europe that did not first pass through England, Jefferson imposed an embargo on foreign trade that lasted fourteen months. He hoped through "peaceable coercion" to force the European powers to allow free trade for American commerce. Beyond seeking independence for American trade, the embargo sought to assert and encourage the superior virtue of American republican life. The corrupt societies of Europe would not survive without American produce, while Americans could do without the luxuries and fineries of the decadent Old World. Federalist critics, whose New England merchant economies suffered most from the embargo, charged that Jefferson's true aim was to destroy American commerce and impose a primitive, precommercial social order. Some added pointedly that the ancient republic of Sparta, Jefferson's supposed ideal, depended on slaves.[62] In the end, the embargo failed to liberate American commerce, and "the Jeffersonians had to accept war as the dangerous but necessary means of furthering the Revolutionary vision of free trade."[63]

With the War of 1812, Republicans overcame their aversion to war in order to vindicate America's economic independence from Europe. Some Republicans offered a further civic consideration in support of the War of 1812: Rather than undermining republican liberty, the rigors of war might revitalize the waning civic virtue of Americans and recall them to a common good that a rapidly advancing commercial society threatened to obscure.[64]

For their part, the Federalists, now relegated to opposition, voiced their own anxieties about the moral and civic character of the people. The virtues they prized were the conservative virtues of order, deference, and restraint. In Jefferson's America, they saw these virtues slipping away.[65]

What would save America from the "turbulence and inconstancy" that brought the demise of the Roman and Athenian commonwealths? one Federalist asked; "Nothing, nothing but the virtue of our citizens can afford us a bulwark or a barrier." Federalism had depended "on the supposed existence of sufficient political virtue, and on the permanency and authority of the public morals," according to Fisher Ames. But now, Federalists were not optimistic. "We are in fact a much altered people," a Federalist lamented in 1798, "and are no more like what we were some twenty years ago, than . . . the Italians are like the Romans."[66]

The Federalists, ever uneasy about democracy, believed that popular government depended for its order and stability on the restraints imposed by religion and morality: "good laws [are those] tending to the promotion of religion, patriotism, and virtue, without which the happiness of no people can be durable." They blamed Jefferson for the democratization of American society, and especially for the weakening of established relig- ion. "The federalists are dissatisfied," wrote Timothy Pickering, "because they see the public morals debased, by the corrupt and corrupt[ing] system of our rulers. Men are tempted to become apostates, not to federalism merely, but to virtue, and to religion, and to good govern- ment." Another Federalist charged that the effect of Jefferson's presidency was "to corrupt and demoralize the public mind. By corruption, I do not mean that he has bribed the people with money; by demoralization, I do not mean that he has made them thieves or robbers; I mean to say that he has suffered to evaporate that manly pride and spirit of independence which conducted us through the revolutionary war. . . . The people have become impatient of governmental restraint, and have lost all reverence for established usages and the settled order of things."[67]

For all they rejected in the republican tradition, the Federalists in dissent, like the Jeffersonians they opposed, carried its formative ambition into the nineteenth century.

The Debate over Domestic Manufactures

History sometimes resolves a question so completely that it is difficult to recall the taking of sides. So it is with the question whether America should be a manufacturing nation. In the early decades of the republic, many Americans thought it should not. The arguments they advanced for remaining an agricultural nation make little sense within the now familiar terms of prosperity and distributive justice. Jefferson and his followers argued against large-scale manufactures primarily on moral and civic grounds; the agrarian way of life was most likely to produce the kind of citizens self-government requires. Like the debate over Hamilton's treasury system, the debate over whether to encourage domestic manufactures illustrates the prominence of civic considerations in the political discourse of the early republic.

The early advocates of American manufactures, like the early opponents, made their case in the name of liberty and virtue, not economic growth. When Britain sought to tax the colonies during the 1760s and 1770s, the colonists responded by refusing to import or consume British goods. By their boycotts, the colonists hoped not only to retaliate against Britain but also to affirm republican virtue, to assert economic independence, and to save themselves from the corruption of imported luxuries. The nonimportation and nonconsumption movements, with their appeal to republican simplicity and frugality, provided the first spur to domestic manufactures. "[I]f we mean still to be free," a newspaper exhorted in 1767, "let us unanimously lay aside foreign superfluities, and encourage our own manufacture."[68]

The manufactures inspired by the nonimportation movement were for the most part coarse, household commodities, such as homespun, produced to supply essential needs. The manufacture of simple household necessities posed no threat to republican citizenship, and few Americans questioned them. Such small-scale production took place either in the home or in the workshops of artisans and craftsmen. Unlike European factory workers, these artisans controlled their skill, labor, and tools. "[L]ike the yeomen of the countryside, they had direct access to the means of production, which conferred upon them the independence that supported republican virtue." Moreover, those who produced basic necessities were not dependent on the whims of fashion for their employment, as were European workers in luxury trades.[69]

Even those who argued for manufacturing on a larger scale cast their arguments in republican terms. Benjamin Rush was the president of the short-lived United Company of Philadelphia for Promoting American Manufactures, the first large-scale attempt at textile manufacturing in the colonies. Speaking at its founding in 1775, Rush argued that domestic manufactures would promote prosperity, employ the poor, and also "erect an additional barrier against the encroachments of tyranny," by reducing America's dependence on foreigners for necessities such as food and clothing. A continuing reliance on British manufactured goods would promote luxury and vice and induce an economic dependence tantamount to slavery. "By becoming slaves, we shall lose every principle of virtue. We shall transfer unlimited obedience from our Master to a corrupted majority in the British House of Commons, and shall esteem their crimes the certificates of their divine commission to govern us."[70]

The 1780s brought the first sustained debate about domestic manufactures. After the Revolution, Americans found to their distress that political independence did not necessarily bring economic independence. Britain resumed its domination of American commerce, and foreign markets for America's agricultural surplus remained restricted. With the commercial crisis came economic depression and new calls for domestic manufactures.[71]

Many Americans objected that encouraging large-scale manufactures would make for a political economy inhospitable to republican citizenship. They feared that manufactures on a scale beyond that of the household or small workshop would create a propertyless class of impoverished workers, crowded into cities, incapable of exercising the independent judgment citizenship requires. As Jefferson wrote in his *Notes on the State of Virginia,* "Dependance begets subservience and venality, suffocates the germ of virtue, and prepares fit tools for the designs of ambition." Factory life breeds a "corruption of morals" not found among farmers. "While we have land to labour then, let us never wish to see our citizens occupied at a work-bench, or twirling a distaff."[72]

In a letter to John Jay, Jefferson's civic argument was even more explicit. "Cultivators of the earth are the most valuable citizens. They are the most vigorous, the most independent, the most virtuous, and they are tied to their country and wedded to its liberty and interest by the most lasting bonds." If ever the day came when there were too many farmers, Jefferson would rather Americans become sailors than manufacturers. "I consider the class of artificers as the panders of vice and the instruments by which the liberties of a country are generally overturned."[73]

Jefferson's objection was not to manufacturing as such, but to enterprises that would concentrate men and machines in cities and erode the political economy of citizenship. He drew a sharp distinction between household manufactures, which he favored, and extensive manufactures, which he opposed. Household manufactures did not pose a threat to the political economy of citizenship, for two reasons. First, dispersed in the country, they did not create the concentrated wealth and power of highly capitalized factory production in large commercial cities. Second, household manufactures did not for the most part draw on the labor of citizens, but on the labor of women and children. It left able-bodied yeomen to work the land, their independence unimpaired. Jefferson's own household manufacturing at Monticello reflected this stark distinction between citizens and those consigned to dependent status. His nail factory was operated by slave boys, his textile manufactory by women and girls.[74]

For the opponents of domestic manufactures, the importance of agrarian life to republican government was not simply the negative virtue of avoiding the degradation of crowded cities. As Noah Webster observed, it also had the positive effect of fostering distinctive civic capacities: "where people live principally by agriculture, as in America, every man is in some measure an artist—he makes a variety of utensils, rough indeed, but such as will answer his purpose—he is a husbandman in summer and a mechanic in winter—he travels about the country—he converses with a variety of professions—he reads public papers—he has access to a parish library and thus becomes acquainted with history and politics. . . . Knowledge is diffused and genius roused by the very situation of America."[75]

Not all Americans of the 1780s shared Jefferson's hostility to domestic manufactures. Such was the prominence of republican assumptions, however, that even the proponents of manufactures argued within their terms. Those who favored tariffs and other measures to encourage more extensive domestic manufacturing made their case on civic grounds, not only economic ones. They argued that a balanced economy of agriculture and manufactures would better foster virtuous, independent citizens than an agrarian economy tied to foreign commerce.

Like agrarian republicans, the proponents of domestic manufactures worried about the consequences for self-government of luxury and dependence. But they believed that foreign commerce, not domestic manufactures, was the greatest source of these dangers. For America to rely wholly on foreign trade for its manufactured goods, they argued, was to erode republican virtue in two respects. First, such reliance diminished America's independence by leaving its economy hostage to the restrictions of foreign powers. Second, the flood of British finery and luxury goods was corrupting the moral character of Americans, eroding the spirit of industry, frugality, and self-denial that had sustained the colonists in their struggle for independence. As one Fourth of July orator proclaimed in 1787, America's foreign trade "is in its very nature subversive of the spirit of pure liberty and independence, as it destroys that simplicity of manners, native manliness of soul, and equality of station, which is the spring and peculiar excellence of a free government."[76]

In the same year, Tench Coxe, a young Philadelphia businessman and leading advocate of domestic manufactures, gave the inaugural address to Pennsylvania's Society for the Encouragement of Manufactures and the Useful Arts. One reason he offered for encouraging domestic manufactures was economic, to promote "private wealth and national prosperity." Another was civic, to secure republican government by employing the idle and by weaning Americans from their corrupt dependence on European luxuries. Coxe worried about poverty less for its injustice than for its tendency to undermine civic virtue: "Extreme poverty and idleness in the citizens of a free government will ever produce vicious habits and disobedience to the laws, and must render the people fit instruments for the dangerous purposes of ambitious men. In this light the employment of our poor in manufactures, who cannot find other honest means of a subsistence, is of the utmost consequence."[77]

Beyond cultivating habits of obedience and industry among the poor, Coxe claimed for domestic manufactures the salutary effect of reducing American's wanton consumption of foreign goods: "It behoves us to consider our untimely passion for European luxuries as a malignant and alarming symptom, threatening convulsions and dissolution to the political body." Domestic manufacture of clothing, furniture, and the like would simplify American habits and reduce the corrupting influence of foreign fashion and luxury. The ultimate benefit of domestic manufactures, Coxe concluded, was not only economic but political. They would "lead us once more into the paths of virtue by restoring frugality and industry, those potent antidotes to the vices of mankind and will give us real independence by rescuing us from the tyranny of foreign fashions, and the destructive torrent of luxury."[78]

Hamilton's *Report on Manufactures,* presented to Congress in 1791, paid less heed to republican sensibilities. It began by conceding that "the cultivation of the earth" provided a "state most favourable to the freedom and independence of the human mind," and thus had a claim to preeminence over other kinds of industry.[79] But it went on to propose, in the name of national prosperity and independence, an ambitious program of American industrial development. Unlike republican advocates of manufactures, Hamilton favored public rather than household manufactures, to be encouraged by government bounties, or subsidies. Since Hamilton envisaged production for export as well as domestic use, his program implied the production of advanced, luxury manufactures rather than the crude, simple necessities favored by republicans.

Taken together with his proposals for public finance, Hamilton's *Report on Manufactures* seemed to his opponents yet another assault on the social conditions republican government required. The notion of government subsidies for industry raised the specter of privilege, connections, and corruption that Americans had renounced in breaking with Britain.

In a newspaper article following Hamilton's *Report,* Madison restated the civic argument against large-scale manufactures: "The class of citizens who provide at once their own food and their own raiment, may be viewed as the most truly independent and happy. They are more; they are the best basis of public liberty and the strongest bulwark of public safety. It follows, that the greater the proportion of this class to the whole society, the more free, the more independent, and the more happy must be the society itself."[80]

Hamilton's *Report on Manufactures* was never adopted, in part because of increased European demand for American produce in the 1790s. As American commerce prospered, the debate over manufactures was postponed, to be renewed during the presidencies of Jefferson and Madison.

In the early decades of the nineteenth century, many Jeffersonians dropped their opposition to domestic manufactures. But even as they revised their economic policy, they retained the formative ambition of the republican tradition and continued to argue within its terms. The Jeffersonians' growing sympathy to manufactures in the early 1800s was prompted by frustration with foreign obstacles to American commerce and by worry about the spirit of avarice and speculation they associated with the merchant class of the Northeast. These tendencies threatened to undermine the conditions that suited Americans to self-government, and led many republicans to conclude that domestic manufactures and home markets would better serve the political economy of citizenship.

George Logan, a friend and ally of Jefferson, urged the promotion of American manufactures in hopes of reducing the importation of foreign luxuries and improving the character of citizens. Unlike foreign luxuries, simple domestic manufactures would foster "those plain and simple manners, and that frugal mode of living . . . best suited to our Republican form of Government."[81]

Tench Coxe, Jeffersonian though he was, went further. An advocate of more advanced, factory production, Coxe argued for a protective tariff to encourage manufactures and an expanded home market for American goods. What was the point of exporting raw materials, he asked, only "to be plundered, rejected, restricted or excluded, according to their criminal will, by foreign markets?"[82] America could move to a "new and more exalted stage of industry, and consequent refinement," Coxe maintained, without the damage to self-government that agrarian republicans feared:

"the republican system is equally adapted to every species of industry that the citizens can be honestly employed in."[83]

Jefferson himself, writing in 1805, qualified his case against manufactures of two decades earlier. His opposition had been formed with the great manufacturing cities of Europe in mind, fearing the "depravity of morals, [the] dependence and corruption" they fostered. Fortunately, American manufactures had not yet approached that debased condition. "As yet our manufacturers are as much at their ease, as independent and moral as our agricultural inhabitants, and they will continue so as long as there are vacant lands for them to resort to." The abundance of land had preserved the independence of workers by giving them the option of quitting the factory and working the earth.[84]

In 1810 Henry Clay, then a young Senator from Kentucky, offered a defense of domestic manufactures characteristic of the emerging Republican view. A manufacturing system limited to supplying domestic needs would not bring the evils of Manchester and Birmingham but would, on the contrary, have favorable effects on the moral character of Americans. It would employ those who would otherwise "be either unproductive, or exposed to indolence and immorality." It would save Americans from the corrupting influence of foreign luxuries. "Dame commerce," Clay declared, "is a flirting, flippant, noisy jade, and if we are governed by her fantasies we shall never put off the muslins of India and the cloths of Europe." Finally, it would bring economic independence and national pride. "The nation that imports its clothing from abroad is but little less dependent than if it imported its bread." Domestic manufacturing, if supported by bounties and protective duties, could supply every necessary article of clothing and redeem America from reliance on foreign countries.[85]

The American Society for the Encouragement of Domestic Manufactures, a New York–based organization, issued a pamphlet urging the importance of manufactures on civic as well as economic grounds. Its 1817 *Address . . . to the People of the United States* argued that in America manufacturing would elevate rather than erode the moral character of the people. American factories would not be situated in choking cities, "but rather on chosen sites, by the fall of waters and the running stream, the seats of health and cheerfulness, where good instruction will secure the morals of the young, and good regulations will promote, in all, order, cleanliness, and the exercise of the civil duties."[86]

Late in life, after the failed embargo and the War of 1812 convinced him of the difficulty of achieving free trade, Jefferson allowed that manufacturing had become necessary to national independence. "We must now place the manufacturer by the side of the agriculturist," he concluded in 1816. Given persistent restrictions on American commerce, those who would oppose domestic manufactures "must be for reducing us either to dependence on that foreign nation, or to be clothed in skins, and to live like wild beasts in dens and caverns. I am not one of these; experience has taught me that manufactures are now as necessary to our independence as to our comfort."[87]

The early 1800s thus brought a shift in Jeffersonian political economy, away from an agrarian economy linked to foreign commerce, and toward the development of domestic manufactures and a home market. This shift was inspired partly by frustration with persistent obstacles to foreign trade, and partly by fear that excessive foreign imports were corrupting republican virtue by making Americans dependent on foreign luxuries and fashion. This shift in economic outlook was embraced most enthusiastically by a younger, more entrepreneurial generation of republicans.

Even as republican political economy eased and then abandoned its opposition to domestic manufactures, however, it retained its civic concerns. The debate over domestic manufactures in the early nineteenth century was not only about prosperity, but also about what economic arrangements were most suitable to self-government. The republican advocates of manufactures in the early 1800s did not renounce the political economy of citizenship that had informed Jefferson's agrarian vision; they argued instead that republican citizenship would now best be advanced by a political economy in which domestic manufactures would free the nation from excessive dependence on foreign luxuries and promote the industry, frugality, and independence self-government requires.

The very events that prompted growing republican support for domestic manufactures—notably the embargo of 1807–1809 and the War of 1812—led some Federalists to fear the destruction of American commerce and to denounce the prospect of large-scale manufacturing. They too employed the language of civic virtue. Some paradoxically accused

Jefferson and Madison of promoting an advanced manufacturing society that republicans had long opposed. A Connecticut Federalist complained that Jefferson's policies would exchange a simple society of agriculture and commerce "for the dissipated and effeminate manners and habits, which extensive establishments of manufactures, never fail to bring in their train."[88] A Boston writer asked, "Would the existence of our present form of government be compatible with such a populace as exists in Lyons, Manchester, or Birmingham?"[89] The Maryland Federalist Philip Barton Key praised the superior civic virtue that agrarian life fostered: "You would never look at men and boys in workshops for that virtue and spirit in defense that you would justly expect from the yeomanry of the country."[90]

In 1814 Daniel Webster, a New Hampshire congressman who would later move to Boston and become a leading defender of manufacturing, argued in moral and civic terms against tariffs that encouraged extensive manufactures: "Habits favorable to good morals and free Governments, are not usually most successfully cultivated in populous manufacturing cities." The extensive division of labor imposed by large factories "render[s] the laborer altogether dependent on his employer." In a fervid paean to pastoral life, the young Webster warned of the day when most Americans would have to "immerse themselves in close and unwhole-some work-shops; when they shall be obliged to shut their ears to the bleatings of their own flocks, upon their own hills, and to the voice of the lark that cheers them at the plough, that they may open them in dust, and smoke, and steam, to the perpetual whirl of spools and spindles, and the grating of rasps and saws."[91]

Factory Life and Republican Ideals

More than a matter of political debate, the moral and civic consequences of manufactures also figured in the design of the first manufacturing towns. The entrepreneurs who established the nation's early factories were keenly aware of republican fears. They were determined to show that American manufacturing could avoid the evils of European factory life. Rather than breed poverty and vice, it could foster the virtues republican citizenship required.

Lowell, Massachusetts, the leading industrial town of the Jacksonian era, was widely seen as a practical test of the republican case for large-scale manufacturing. As Henry Clay observed, "Lowell will tell whether the manufacturing system is compatible with the social virtues."[92] Founded by a group of Boston merchants led by Francis Cabot Lowell, the textile factory at Lowell was carefully designed to protect the moral character of its workers. As one of Lowell's associates explained, "The operatives in the manufacturing cities of Europe, were notoriously of the lowest character, for intelligence and morals. The question therefore arose, and was deeply considered, whether this degradation was the result of the peculiar occupation, or of other and distinct causes."[93]

Lowell's founders concluded that factory work was not intrinsically inimical to moral character, and undertook several measures to assure that Lowell's workers would not suffer the moral and civic degradation of their European counterparts. First, like other American factories, the one at Lowell was operated by water power rather than steam, allowing it to be located in the country rather than in a crowded city. Second, to avoid creating an entrenched proletariat, the Lowell work force would be drawn from a rotating, not a permanent population. Ideal for this purpose were unmarried young women from the New England countryside, for whom factory work would be an interlude in life, not a career.

Finally, in an effort to prove that factory life need not be corrupting, the founders of Lowell undertook to uplift the moral character of their workers. In doing so, they displayed the paternalist tendencies to which some versions of the formative project are prone. Lowell's "factory girls" lived in company boardinghouses supervised by matrons who enforced a strict code of moral and religious conduct. In the few hours remaining to them after a seventy-hour work week, they attended religious services, borrowed books from a lending library, attended lectures, organized "improvement circles," and produced literary magazines such as the *Lowell Offering*, whose writers "offered impressive support for the Lowell system as a model republican community."[94]

The formative aspect of Lowell factory life addressed the republican worry that manufacturing workers would lack the moral character of those who worked the land. From the standpoint of the owners, it had the further advantage of aiding recruitment by assuring workers—and their parents—of a wholesome moral environment. It also enabled the owners to instill and enforce the rigorous discipline the new factory system required.[95]

Lowell's promoters hailed their town as a model republican community. Henry Miles, a Lowell minister, praised its "strict system of moral police."[96] Edward Everett, Lowell's congressman, proclaimed manufacturing towns like Lowell "a peculiar triumph of our political independence," the "complement of the revolution." Even more important than its economic achievement, Everett maintained, Lowell stood as proof against the prejudice that factories must breed degradation and vice: "for physical comfort, moral conduct, general intelligence, and all the qualities of social character which make up an enlightened New England community, Lowell might safely enter into a comparison with any town or city in the land."[97] According to Amos Lawrence, one of the owners, Lowell proved there was no reason to believe "that the character of our people will degenerate, or their true happiness be diminished, while the wealth of our country is increased."[98]

Lowell's reputation as a moral and technological marvel brought a steady stream of visitors. When President Andrew Jackson arrived in 1833, he was greeted with a procession of twenty-five hundred factory girls clad in white dresses with blue sashes, carrying parasols and bearing banners calling for "Protection to American Industry." Other visitors included Davy Crockett, President Polk, and a parade of foreigners, including Charles Dickens. Most came away impressed with Lowell's apparent reconciliation of large-scale manufactures and republican ideals.[99]

But even as Lowell was lauded at home and abroad, its vaunted republican character was breaking down. Wage cuts, industrial growth, urbanization, and the transformation of the labor market soon undermined the harmonious vision of Lowell's founders. One ingredient of that vision was the assumption that relatively high wages would attract intelligent, respectable workers from the countryside and prevent their degradation. If wages fell or conditions deteriorated, workers could retain their independence by returning to the farm.

But in 1834 Lowell's directors responded to an economic downturn with a 25 percent wage cut. The workers "turned out," or struck, without success. The strikers protested not only the wage cuts but also the paternalistic scheme of supervision and discipline. "[I]t was not the reduction of wages alone which caused the excitement," said one of the protesters, "but that haughty, overbearing disposition, that purse-proud insolence, which was becoming more and more apparent."[100] With the depression of 1837, owners were able to impose further wage cuts and still retain sufficient workers to operate the mills. A labor newspaper of the 1840s complained that "American workingmen and women will not long suffer this gradual system of republican encroachment, which is fast reducing them to dependence, vassalage and slavery."[101] But the growing protest had little effect; not until 1853 did the Lowell corporation shorten the work day to eleven hours.[102]

As working conditions deteriorated and discontent grew, the textile mills became less attractive to young New England women. But the massive Irish immigration of the late 1840s relieved company owners of any pressure to meet workers' demands. The new immigrants offered a cheap and abundant labor supply and soon replaced the daughters of Yankee farmers in the mills. In 1845 Irish workers comprised 7 percent of Lowell's textile operatives; by the early 1850s they constituted half the labor force, and grew in subsequent years. The temporary work force that in the beginning was meant to avoid a dependent, impoverished proletariat gave way to permanent factory population. "In less than a decade Lowell lost its prized population of well-educated and temporary New England women and with it the factory system's very rationale."[103]

Meanwhile, American manufacturing was changing in ways that would soon abandon even the gesture to republican ideals. In hopes of increasing productivity, textile manufacturers turned from water power to steam, which could power larger mills. Larger factories increased the attraction of urban settings. The republican promise of small factories dispersed throughout the countryside gave way in the face of the economic advantages of cities. Industrial managers of the 1840s pointed out that America's large commercial cities offered a population willing to work at low wages, and without the housing the Lowell mills had to build to recruit workers. After 1850, "[t]he concerns that had motivated the founding of Lowell were largely abandoned," and "earlier American reservations about the moral and political consequences of manufacturing cities" were forgotten.[104]

Economic Argument in the Jacksonian Era

Seen through the lens of present-day political argument, the underlying concerns of Jacksonian-era politics seem similar to our own. In their rancorous debates over banking, tariffs, and economic development, the Democrats and Whigs of the 1830s and 1840s made frequent appeal to arguments of economic growth and distributive justice. Whigs such as Henry Clay and Daniel Webster argued that their program of a national bank, a protective tariff, and government-sponsored internal improvements would increase national wealth. Democrats led by Jackson objected that such policies would enrich the powerful at the expense of the common man and lead to an unjust distribution of wealth. In a pattern of argument familiar in our time, Whigs replied that economic growth would benefit farmers and laborers as well as businessmen and bankers, that a rising tide would lift all boats.[105]

Jacksonians were troubled above all by the unequal distribution of wealth between producers and those they considered nonproducers, such as merchants, capitalists, and bankers. They complained that the market society emerging around them gave its greatest rewards to those who contributed least. "[T]he workingman is poor and depressed," wrote Democratic radical Orestes Brownson, "while a large portion of the non-workingmen, in the sense we use the term, are wealthy. It may be laid down as a general rule, with but few exceptions, that men are rewarded in an inverse ratio to the amount of actual service they perform."[106] The New York *Evening Post* voiced the same protest more vividly: "Who is it that rolls in his carriage with gilded harness; revels in all the luxuries of the earth; builds palaces and outdoes princes in his entertainments? Is it the man who labours all day and every day? Is it the possessor of houses and lands or anything real? No—it is the minion of paper money."[107]

Leading Whigs and their supporters replied that accumulated wealth and the credit system worked to the benefit of ordinary Americans by increasing the national wealth. They argued that economic growth would do more for the poor than attempts to distribute existing wealth more equally. "Whatever objections may be made to the existing distribution of riches," wrote journalist and sometime Whig Richard Hildreth, "this at least must be conceded, that no mere redistribution of the existing mass of wealth could effectually answer the proposed purpose of elevating the people. Any such redistribution . . . would still leave everybody poor, at the same time that it cut up by the roots a great mass of industrious occupations. . . . Above and beyond any of these schemes of redistribution, in order to redeem the mass of the people from poverty and its incidents, a great increase in the amount both of accumulated wealth and of annual products is absolutely essential."[108]

Whig Congressman Edward Everett, speaking in praise of "accumulation, property, capital, [and] credit," argued that the vast fortune of a leading capitalist served the community well: "What better use could have been made of it? Will it be said, divide it equally among the community; give each individual in the United States a share? It would have amounted to half a dollar each for man, woman, and child; and, of course, might as well have been sunk in the middle of the sea. Such a distribution would have been another name for annihilation. How many ships would have furled their sails, how many warehouses would have closed their shutters, how many wheels, heavily laden with the products of industry, would have stood still, how many families would have been reduced to want, and without any advantage resulting from the distribution?"[109]

Despite this surface similarity, however, the terms of debate in the age of Jackson map uneasily onto our own. In recent decades, those most concerned with distributive justice have argued for a more activist government—a progressive tax system, social welfare programs, laws regulating the health and safety of workers; those most concerned with economic growth have typically argued for less government intervention—lower tax rates, less government regulation. In the Jacksonian era, these sides were reversed. Then it was the Democrats, the party of farmers, mechanics, and laborers, who argued for limited government, while the Whigs, the party of business and banking and industry, favored a more activist government, even including an industrial policy to guide national economic development.

Jacksonian Political Economy

Jacksonian Democrats favored a laissez-faire philosophy of government that finds its present-day expression in "antigovernment" politicians such as Ronald Reagan and libertarian economists such as Milton Friedman. "The best government is that which governs least," declared the Jacksonian *Democratic Review*. "A strong and active democratic government, in the common sense of the term, is an evil, differing only in degree and mode of operation, and not in nature, from a strong despotism. . . . Government should have as little as possible to do with the general business and interests of the people. . . . Its domestic action should be confined to the administration of justice, for the protection of the natural equal rights of the citizen and the preservation of social order."[110] The Jacksonian editorialist William Leggett condemned even such minimal government functions as running the post office, maintaining an insane asylum for the poor, or inspecting bakeries and butcheries.[111]

Unlike Democrats since the time of the New Deal, Andrew Jackson considered government the enemy, not the instrument of justice for the common man. This conviction stemmed partly from his view of government, and partly from his conception of justice. When government intervened in the economy, Jackson maintained, it was bound to favor the rich and the powerful. In any case, justice did not require that government redress the unequal talents and abilities by which some get more and others less. "Distinctions in society will always exist under every just government. Equality of talents, of education, or of wealth can not be produced by human institutions. In the full enjoyment of the gifts of Heaven and the fruits of superior industry, economy, and virtue, every man is equally entitled to protection by law."[112]

According to Jackson, the problem was not how to use government to promote an equality of condition, but how to prevent the rich and the powerful from using government to secure privileges, subsidies, and special advantages. "It is to be regretted that the rich and powerful too often bend the acts of government to their selfish purposes. . . . If [government] would confine itself to equal protection, and, as Heaven does its rains, shower its favors alike on the high and the low, the rich and the poor, it would be an unqualified blessing."[113]

The economic debates of the Jacksonian era differ from our own in ways that go beyond the parties' stance toward government and display the persistence of republican themes in the 1830s and 1840s. Although Jacksonians and Whigs did invoke arguments of economic growth and distributive justice, these considerations figured less as ends in themselves than as means to competing visions of a self-governing republic. The Jacksonian objection to the growing inequality of wealth had less to do with fairness than with the threat to self-government posed by large concentrations of wealth and power. The Whig case for promoting economic development had less to do with increasing the standard of living or maximizing consumption than with cultivating national community and strengthening the bonds of the union. Underlying the debates between Democrats and Whigs were competing visions of a political economy of citizenship.

In different ways, both parties shared Jefferson's conviction that the economic life of the nation should be judged for its capacity to cultivate in citizens the qualities of character that self-government requires. By the 1830s few assumed, as Jefferson once did, that the agrarian life was the only way to civic competence.[114] But even as the parties turned their attention to the national bank, protective tariffs, land policy, and internal improvements, both Democrats and Whigs retained contact with the formative ambition of the republican tradition.

Jackson's policies and rhetoric reflected republican hopes and fears in two respects. First, his stand against the Bank of the United States, and against federal support for commerce and industry, reflected the traditional republican fear that powerful, self-interested forces would dominate government, secure special privileges, and deprive the people of their right to rule. Second, his hostility to large-scale business, banking, and speculation sprang from the conviction that only industrious producers such as farmers, mechanics, and laborers possessed the virtue and independence necessary to self-government. The concentration of power represented by a national bank and a paper currency would corrupt republican government directly, by giving subsidies and privileges to a favored few; meanwhile, the spirit of speculation those institutions encouraged would corrupt republican government indirectly, by undermining the moral qualities republican citizenship requires.[115]

According to its defenders, the Bank of the United States promoted economic stability by regulating the money supply through control of its widely accepted notes. According to its opponents, this power over the nation's currency rivaled the power of the government itself and unjustly enriched the bank's private investors. To Jackson, the bank was a "monster," a "hydra of corruption," and he resolved to destroy it. His war against the bank was the defining issue of his presidency and illustrated both aspects of the Jacksonian political economy of citizenship.

At one level, the struggle over the bank demonstrated the danger of concentrated power. "The result of the ill-advised legislation which established this great monopoly," declared Jackson, "was to concentrate the whole moneyed power of the Union, with its boundless means of corruption and its numerous dependents, under the direction and command of one acknowledged head . . . enabling it to bring forward upon any occasion its entire and undivided strength to support or defeat any measure of the Government." Had the bank not been destroyed, "the Government would have passed from the hands of the many to the hands of the few, and this organized money power from its secret conclave would have dictated the choice of your highest officers and compelled you to make peace or war, as best suited their own wishes. The forms of your Government might for a time have remained, but its living spirit would have departed from it."[116]

At another level, beyond even the evils of concentrated power, an economy dominated by commerce, banking, and business threatened to corrupt republican government by eroding the moral habits that sustain it. The fluctuations of paper currency "engender a spirit of speculation injurious to the habits and character of the people." Wild speculation in land and stock "threatened to pervade all classes of society and to withdraw their attention from the sober pursuits of honest industry. It is not by encouraging this spirit that we shall best preserve public virtue." Paper money fostered an "eager desire to amass wealth without labor" that would "inevitably lead to corruption" and destroy republican government.[117]

In its libertarian moments, Jacksonian politics gestured toward the procedural republic and the notion that government should play no part in forming the character or cultivating the virtue of its citizens. For example, Orestes Brownson claimed, contrary to the republican tradition, that liberty "is not the power to choose our own form of government, to elect our own rulers, and through them to make and administer our own laws," but simply the ability to exercise individual rights without government interference. "So long as the individual trespasses upon none of the rights of others, or throws no obstacle in the way of their free and full exercise, government, law, public opinion even, must leave him free to take his own course."[118]

But unlike modern libertarians, who defend individual rights while insisting that government be neutral among competing conceptions of the good life, Jacksonians explicitly affirmed a certain way of life and sought to cultivate a certain kind of citizen. Like Jefferson and Madison, Jackson frequently justified his economic policies on formative grounds, citing their consequences for the moral character of citizens. Removing public deposits from the Bank of the United States was "necessary to preserve the morals of the people."[119] Restoring gold and silver specie as the medium of exchange would "revive and perpetuate those habits of economy and simplicity which are so congenial to the character of republicans."[120] Refusing federal support for internal improvements and mass markets would preserve an economy of independent producers and make the world safe for the virtue-sustaining occupations that suited Americans to self-government. "The planter, the farmer, the mechanic, and the laborer all know that their success depends upon their own industry and economy, and that they must not expect to become suddenly rich by the fruits of their toil." Such citizens were "the bone and sinew of the country—men who love liberty and desire nothing but equal rights and equal laws."[121]

In the twentieth century, laissez-faire doctrines would celebrate the market economy and the freedom of choice the market supposedly secured. In the age of Jackson, however, laissez-faire notions served a different role, embedded as they were in a vision of "the good republican life." This was the vision, as Marvin Meyers describes it, "of independent producers, secure in their modest competence, proud in their natural dignity, confirmed in their yeoman character, responsible masters of their fate—the order of the Old Republic." Jacksonians assumed that "when government governed least, society—made of the right republican materials—would realize its own natural moral discipline."[122]

No champion of capitalist enterprise, Jackson sought to limit government not to give greater scope to market relations but to slow their advance. Without the "artificial" support of government subsidies and protective tariffs, Jackson believed, large-scale manufacturing, banking, and capitalist enterprise would not soon overrun the economy of small, independent producers. This explains the otherwise strange coexistence in a single political outlook of laissez-faire individualism and the republican concern with the moral character of the people. "Americans of the Jacksonian persuasion took their doctrines of liberty and laissez faire . . . not as a stimulant to enterprise but as a purgative to bring the Old Republic . . . back to moral health."[123] Government would promote virtue not directly, through legislation, but indirectly, by holding off the economic forces that threatened to undermine it.

Whig Political Economy

Although the Whigs welcomed the economic changes Jacksonians opposed, they too advanced a political economy of citizenship and attended to the moral consequences of economic arrangements. "Beginning with the same body of republican tradition as the Democrats, the Whigs chose to emphasize different themes within it and offered a dramatically different assessment of economic changes promised by the Market Revolution."[124] Jacksonians and Whigs shared the republican notions that centralized power is the enemy of liberty and that government should concern itself with the moral character of its citizens. But they applied these teachings differently to the circumstances of nineteenth-century American life.

While Jacksonians feared centralized economic power, the Whigs feared centralized executive power. As Whigs saw it, the threat that power posed to liberty was not to be found in the forces of industry, banking, and commerce, but instead in Jackson's conception of the presidency. When Jackson vetoed the recharter of the Bank of the United States, removed its public deposits, and transferred them to state banks, opponents accused him of "Caesarism," "executive usurpation," and dictatorial designs. Previous presidents had used the veto power infrequently, applying it only to laws they deemed unconstitutional, not laws they simply disagreed with.[125] Confronted with the "Monster," Jackson observed no such restraint. "We are in the midst of a revolution," Henry Clay declared, "hitherto bloodless, but rapidly descending towards a total change of the pure republican character of the government, and to the concentration of all power in the hands of one man."[126]

In 1834 Clay and his followers among National Republicans adopted the name "Whig," after the English opposition party that had drawn on republican themes to resist the arbitrary power of the Crown. Like their English namesakes, Clay and the American Whigs saw the greatest threat to republican government in the abuse of executive power. Invoking the memory of the Revolution, Clay hailed the British Whigs as champions of liberty and opponents of royal executive power. "And what is the present but the same contest in another form? . . . The whigs of the present day are opposing executive encroachment, and a most alarming extension of executive power and prerogative. They are ferreting out the abuses and corruptions of an administration, under a chief magistrate who is endeavoring to concentrate in his own person the whole powers of government."[127] Whig political cartoons portrayed Jackson as "King Andrew I." The first successful Whig presidential candidate, William Henry Harrison, won the White House in 1840 on a platform of executive restraint, promising to use the veto sparingly, to poll his cabinet on decisions, and not to seek a second term.[128]

The Whigs' emphasis on balanced government and fear of executive tyranny fit firmly within the republican tradition that echoed from classical and Renaissance thought to the "country party" opposition of eighteenth-century English politics. Their enthusiasm for commerce, industry, and economic development, however, set them apart. The classical republican tradition had seen commerce as antithetical to virtue, a source of luxury and corruption that distracted citizens from the public good. From the time of the Revolution, American republicans had worried about the civic consequences of large-scale commercial and manufacturing enterprises. The early Jefferson had seen civic virtue as dependent on a simple agrarian economy. And although Jacksonians enlarged the range of virtue-sustaining occupations to include independent laborers and mechanics as well as farmers, they feared that the market revolution unfolding in their day would erode the moral qualities self-government required.[129]

Even as Whigs advocated economic development, however, they retained the formative ambition of the republican tradition. They accepted the republican assumptions that self-government requires certain moral and civic qualities among citizens, and that economic arrangements should be assessed for their tendency to promote those qualities. Their argument with Jacksonians was about what virtues self-government required of nineteenth-century Americans, and how best to promote them.

The Whigs' formative project had two aspects. One was to deepen the bonds of union and cultivate a shared national identity. The other was to elevate the morality of the people, to strengthen their respect for order and their capacity for self-control. Whigs sought to realize these aims through a policy of national economic development and through various public institutions, from schools to reformatories to asylums, designed to improve the moral character of the people.

The centerpiece of Whig economic policy was Henry Clay's "American System." Unlike the British system of laissez-faire economic development, Clay's proposal sought to foster economic development by giving explicit government encouragement to national economic growth. High tariffs would encourage American manufacturing by protecting it from foreign competition. High prices for federal lands would slow westward expansion and generate revenues to support an ambitious program of internal improvements such as roads, canals, and railroads. And a national bank would ease tax collection, commercial transactions, and public spending by establishing a strong currency.[130]

Whigs justified their program of economic development on grounds of prosperity but also on grounds of national integration. The internal "improvements" they sought to foster were moral as well as material. The "idea of progress" was "to bring out the material resources of America" and also "to improve the mind and heart of America."[131] National transportation and communication facilities would promote national harmony as well as commerce and morally uplift remote regions of the country. A railroad from New England to Georgia would "harmonize the feelings of the whole country."[132] Linking the uncivilized West to the East would, according to a Christian Whig journal, promote morality and salvation: "The sooner we have railroads and telegraphs spinning into the wilderness, and setting the remotest hamlets in connexion and close proximity with the east, the more certain it is that light, good manners, and christian refinement will become universally diffused."[133] A Richmond newspaper concluded, "Truly are rail roads bonds of union, of social, of national union."[134]

Clay proposed to fund internal improvements by distributing to the states revenue derived from the sale of public lands. Such a policy would do more than provide resources for important public projects. It would also create "a new and powerful bond of affection and of interest" between the states and the federal government. The states would be grateful for the federal largesse, and the federal government would enjoy "the benefits of moral and intellectual improvement of the people, of great facility in social and commercial intercourse, and of the purification of the population of our country, themselves the best parental sources of national character, national union, and national greatness."[135]

Given their ambition to deepen the bonds of union, Whigs lacked the Jacksonian appetite for territorial expansion. In opposing the annexation of Texas, Daniel Webster revived the classical argument that a republic cannot extend across an unlimited space. An arbitrary regime could be as vast as its army's reach, but republics must cohere "by the assimilation of interests and feelings; by a sense of common country, common political family, common character, fortune and destiny." Such commonality would be difficult to cultivate if the nation expanded too quickly: "there must be some boundary, or some limits to a republic which is to have a common centre . . . political attraction, like other attractions, is less and less powerful, as the parts become more and more distant."[136]

It was on these grounds that Webster opposed the Mexican War and the subsequent acquisition of New Mexico and California. His public life had been dedicated to making Americans "one people, one in interest, one in character, and one in political feeling," Webster declared in 1848. But "what sympathy can there be between the people of Mexico and California" and the rest of the United States? None at all, Webster concluded. "Arbitrary governments may have territories and distant possessions, because arbitrary governments may rule them by different laws and different systems. . . . We can do no such thing. They must be of us, *part* of us, or else strangers."[137]

The Whigs' case for industry, technology, even prosperity itself was closely tied to the moral and civic benefits these developments would bring. "They never employed the argument later apologists for American business would sometimes use, that profitability itself is an indicator of social utility." As Daniel Walker Howe observes, Whig political economy did not assume that prosperity was its own justification; the republican tradition had taught otherwise. Whigs "had to overcome the idea that 'commerce' was opposed to 'virtue' and constituted a threat to it. This had been a major convention of classical-Renaissance-commonwealth thought, and it remained powerful in Jacksonian rhetoric. . . . The Whigs were resolving an age-old polarity in the country-party tradition by arguing that commerce could nourish virtue."[138]

Beyond a political economy of national integration and moral improvement, the Whigs pursued their formative aims through a range of public institutions and benevolent societies designed to build character and inculcate self-control. These efforts included insane asylums, penitentiaries, almshouses, juvenile reformatories, Sunday schools, the temperance movement, and factory communities such as the one at Lowell. Whigs were prominent among the founders and leaders of these institutions and movements, which reflected the religious impulses of evangelical Protestantism and the reformist, paternalist aspect of Whig political thought. Although Whigs welcomed the economic changes of their day, they worried about the social changes, such as the decline of deference, the rise of immmigration, and the general breakdown of the moral order of small-town, rural life.[139]

The blend of religious and civic concerns characteristic of Whig reform can be found in Daniel Webster's praise for the Sunday school movement. "The Sabbath School is one of the great institutions of the day," he wrote. "It leads our youth in the path of truth and morality, and makes them good and useful citizens. As a school of religious instruction it is of inestimable value; as a civil institution it is priceless, and has done more to preserve our liberties than grave statesmen and armed soldiers."[140]

In a democratic age teeming with disorder, Whigs emphasized obedience, discipline, and self-control as the qualities essential to self-government. "The present is a period of great restlessness and agitation among the popular elements of the world," warned Whig congressman Daniel

Barnard. "The established order of things is almost every where being questioned, disturbed, and, in many cases, subverted." This condition posed a challenge to republican government. "Perhaps the severest trial to which the virtue of any people can be subjected, is when every man has a share in the government; for when every one governs, few indeed are willing to submit to be governed; when every one commands, nobody likes to obey. Yet the habit and practice of obedience is indispensable to the moral health of every people."[141]

Of all the Whig projects of moral and civic improvement, their most ambitious instrument of republican soulcraft was the public school. As Horace Mann, the first secretary of the Board of Education of Massachusetts, explained, if all were to share in governing, then true to the republican tradition, all would have to be equipped with the requisite moral and intellectual resources: "with universal suffrage, there must be universal elevation of character, intellectual and moral, or there will be universal mismanagement and calamity." The question whether human beings are capable of self-government admits only a conditional answer; they are capable insofar as they possess the intelligence and goodness and breadth of view to govern on behalf of the public good. "But men are not *born* in the full possession of such an ability," nor do they necessarily develop it as they grow to adulthood.[142]

The role of the public schools, therefore, is to cultivate in citizens the qualities of character republican government requires: "As each citizen is to participate in the power of governing others, it is an essential preliminary that he should be imbued with a feeling for the wants, and a sense of the rights, of those whom he is to govern; because the power of governing others, if guided by no higher motive than our own gratification, is the distinctive attribute of oppression; an attribute whose nature and whose wickedness are the same, whether exercised by one who calls himself a republican, or by one born an irresponsible despot."[143]

The curriculum of the schools should reflect their purpose, said Mann, and give ample attention to civic and moral education: "principles of morality should [be] copiously intermingled with the principles of science"; the Golden Rule should become as familiar as the multiplication table. As for the controversy that inevitably attends instruction in politics, morals, and religion, Mann urged that the public schools aim at a broad middle ground. In politics, they should teach "those articles in the creed of republicanism which are accepted by all," but avoid partisan disputes. In morals and religion, they should convey the teachings, in effect, of nondenominational Protestantism, including "all the practical and preceptive parts of the Gospel" but excluding "all dogmatical theology and sectarianism." If such teaching could be widely diffused, Mann had boundless hopes for the redemptive possibilities: "if all the children in the community, from the age of four years to that of sixteen, could be brought within the reformatory and elevating influences of good schools, the dark host of private vices and public crimes which now imbitter domestic peace, and stain the civilization of the age, might, in ninety-nine cases in every hundred, be banished from the world."[144]

The Public Good

In addition to sharing the formative ambition of republican politics, Jacksonians and Whigs retained the related assumption that the public good is more than the sum of individual preferences or interests. Madison had sought this good in the deliberation of an elite group of enlightened statesmen acting at some distance from popular passions, "a chosen body of citizens, whose wisdom may best discern the true interest of the country."[145] The parties in the age of Jackson did not think democracy could be filtered so finely. They sought a public good beyond the play of interests on terms consistent with the heightened democratic expectations of their day.

"No free government can stand without virtue in the people and a lofty spirit of patriotism," Jackson declared, echoing a traditional republican view; "if the sordid feelings of mere selfishness shall usurp the place which ought to be filled by public spirit, the legislation of Congress will soon be converted into a scramble for personal and sectional advantages." But for Jackson, governing in accordance with the public good did not require an enlightened elite of disinterested statesmen; it simply required preventing the powerful few from dominating government and turning it to their selfish ends. The threat of interested politics came wholly from the moneyed interest. Those engaged in productive labor, "the great body of the people," had neither the inclination nor the capacity to form factions to seek special favors from government; "from their habits and the nature of their pursuits they are incapable of forming extensive combinations to act together with united force." They "desire nothing but equal rights and equal laws" and are therefore, by definition, "uncorrupted and incorruptible."[146]

The Whigs were no less hostile to a politics of self-interest, but they doubted that any class of people possessed by nature the wisdom or virtue to identify the public good. Republicans were made, not born, and although it "may be an easy thing to make a republic . . . it is a very laborious thing to make republicans." Under conditions of universal suffrage, the laborious task of moral and political education would have to be extended to all.[147]

In a passage that stands, despite its hyperbole, as an enduring reproach to interest-based theories of democracy, Horace Mann warned of the consequences for the public good if citizens voted out of base or selfish motives: "In a republican government the ballot-box is the urn of fate; yet no god shakes the bowl or presides over the lot. If the ballot-box is open to wisdom and patriotism and humanity, it is equally open to ignorance and treachery, to pride and envy, to contempt for the poor or hostility towards the rich. It is the loosest filter ever devised to strain out impurities. . . . The criteria of a right to vote respect citizenship, age, residence, tax, and, in a few cases, property; but no inquiry can be put whether the applicant is a Cato or a Catiline . . . if the votes, which fall so copiously into the ballot-box on our days of election, emanate from wise counsels and a loyalty to truth, they will descend, like benedictions from Heaven, to bless the land and fill it with song and gladness . . . but if, on the other hand, these votes come from ignorance and crime, the fire and brimstone that were rained on Sodom and Gomorrah would be more tolerable."[148]

6

Free Labor versus Wage Labor

The debate between Jacksonians and Whigs displays the persistence of republican themes in the first half of the nineteenth century. Their emphasis on the civic consequences of economic arrangements separates their political discourse from our own. In some cases, republican assumptions provided different justifications for positions we now defend in terms of prosperity and fairness—higher or lower tax rates, more or less government spending, more or less economic regulation.

In other cases, however, republican ideals led nineteenth-century Americans to address issues now lost from view. One such issue was whether America should be a manufacturing nation. By the mid-nineteenth century that question had been decided, and the case for domestic manufactures no longer had to be made. But the emergence of factory life raised a related question, no less fundamental, that would reverberate in American politics to the end of the century. This is the question whether working for a wage is consistent with freedom.

Civic and Voluntarist Conceptions

From the distance of our time, it is difficult to make sense of this question, much less to conceive it as a vexing political issue. When we argue about wage-earning, we argue about the minimum wage or access to jobs, about comparable worth or the safety of the workplace. Few if any would now challenge the notion of wage labor as such. But in the nineteenth century, many Americans did. For according to the republican conception of freedom, it is by no means clear that a person who works for wages is truly free.

Of course, exchanging my labor for a wage may be free in the sense that I voluntarily agree to do so. Absent unfair pressure or coercion, wage labor is free labor in the voluntarist, or contractual, sense. But even a voluntary agreement to exchange work for a wage does not fulfill the republican conception of free labor. On the republican view, I am free only to the extent that I participate in self-government, which requires in turn that I possess certain habits and dispositions, certain qualities of character. Free labor is thus labor carried out under conditions likely to cultivate the qualities of character that suit citizens to self-government. Jacksonians and Whigs disagreed to some extent about what those qualities were and what economic arrangements were most likely to foster them. But they shared the long-standing republican conviction that economic independence is essential to citizenship. Those, like the propertyless European proletariat, who must subsist on wages paid by employers were likely to lack the moral and political independence to judge for themselves as free citizens.

Jefferson once thought that only yeoman farmers possessed the virtue and independence that made sturdy republican citizens. By the first decades of the nineteenth century, however, most republicans believed that these qualities could be fostered in the workshop as well as on the farm. The artisans, craftsmen, and mechanics who carried out most manufacturing in the early nineteenth century were typically small producers who owned their means of production and were beholden to no boss, at least not as a permanent condition. Their labor was free not only in the sense that they agreed to perform it but also in the sense that it equipped them to think and act as independent citizens, capable of sharing in self-government. The journeymen and apprentices who labored for wages in the workshops of artisan masters did so with the hope of acquiring the skills and savings that would one day enable them to launch out on their own. Wage-earning was for them not a permanent condition but a temporary stage on the way to independence, and so consistent, at least in principle, with the system of free labor.[1]

Artisans of the Jacksonian era affirmed the republican vision of free labor in public festivals, speeches, and parades, celebrating the connections between the artisan order and civic ideals. As Sean Wilentz explains, these public displays, in which workers marched under the banners of their trades, "announced the artisans' determination to be part of the body politic—no longer 'meer mechanicks,' no longer part of the vague lower and middling sort of the revolutionary mobs, but proud craftsmen, appearing for all to see on important civic occasions, marching in orderly formation up and down lower Broadway with the regalia and the tools of their crafts." Speakers at the rallies and demonstrations depicted the artisan order not as an interest group but as "the very axis of society," in whose hands "the palladium of our liberty" must rest. Distrustful of the mercantile elite on the one hand and the propertyless poor on the other, the artisans portrayed themselves as the embodiment of republican independence and virtue. "In sum, an urban variation of the Jeffersonian social theme of the virtuous husbandman emerged, one that fused craft pride and resentment of deference and fear of dependence into a republican celebration of the trades."[2]

But even as the artisans marched, the free labor system they celebrated was beginning to unravel. Even before the emergence of large-scale industrial production, the growth of the market economy transformed traditional craft production. The competitive pressures of national markets and the growing supply of unskilled labor gave merchant capitalists and master craftsmen incentives to cut costs by dividing tasks and assigning unskilled assembly jobs to outworkers and sweatshop contractors. The new arrangement of work eroded the role of skilled artisans, turning journeymen and apprentices into wage laborers with little control over production and reduced prospects of rising to own their own shops. Masters became more like employers, their artisans more like employees.[3]

Workers protested these developments within the terms of a radicalized artisan republicanism. Leaders of the General Trades' Union of the 1830s complained that prosperous masters had joined with aristocratic merchants and bankers to deprive workers of the product of their labor, making it impossible for the worker to maintain "the independent character of an American citizen."[4] A factory worker involved in the early labor movement deplored the factory system as "subversive of liberty—

calculated to change the character of a people from . . . bold and free, to enervated, dependent, and slavish."[5]

At first the employers defended the new order in republican terms as well, offering "an alternative entrepreneurial vision of the artisan republic." True to the republican tradition, they invoked the ideals of commonwealth, virtue, and independence. The virtues they emphasized included industriousness, temperance, social harmony, and individual initiative, qualities they claimed the new political economy would encourage and reward. Higher profits, the masters argued, would enable them to pay higher wages, which would better prepare their workers for independence.[6]

Ultimately, however, the debate over the meaning of free labor would carry American political argument beyond the terms of republican thought; in time, the defense of industrial capitalism would depart from republican assumptions and take new forms. After the Civil War, defenders of the system of wage labor would abandon the attempt to reconcile capitalist production with the civic conception of free labor, and take up the voluntarist conception instead. Wage labor is consistent with freedom, they would argue, not because it forms virtuous, independent citizens but simply because it is voluntary, the product of an agreement between employer and employee. It is this conception of freedom that the Supreme Court of the *Lochner* era would attribute to the Constitution itself. Although the labor movement retained the civic conception of free labor through the late nineteenth century, it too eventually abandoned the civic conception, conceded the permanence of wage labor, and turned its efforts to increasing wages, reducing hours, and improving conditions of work.

The shift to the voluntarist understanding of free labor did not wholly extinguish the civic strand of economic argument in American politics. But it did mark a decisive moment in America's journey from a political economy of citizenship to a political economy of economic growth and distributive justice, from a republican public philosophy to the version of liberalism that informs the procedural republic.

Fateful though it was, the story of the transition from the civic to the voluntarist conception of free labor is no simple morality tale, no unambiguous fall from grace. It is rather a tale fraught with moral complexity, replete with strange ideological bedfellows. More than a matter of labor relations alone, the contest over the meaning of free labor was shaped in large part by America's confrontation with the two great issues of the nineteenth century: the advent of industrial capitalism, and the conflict over slavery.

Wage Labor and Slavery

The debate over wage labor was sharpened and complicated by the struggle over slavery. The labor movement and the abolitionist movement emerged at roughly the same time. Both raised fundamental questions about work and freedom, yet neither movement displayed much sympathy for the other. Labor leaders dramatized their case against wage labor by equating it with Southern slavery—"wage slavery," as they called it. Working for wages was tantamount to slavery not only in the sense that it left workers impoverished but also in the sense that it denied them the economic and political independence essential to republican citizenship.[7]

"Wages is a cunning device of the devil for the benefit of tender consciences who would retain all the advantages of the slave system without the expense, trouble, and odium of being slaveholders," wrote Orestes Brownson. The wage laborer suffered more than the southern slave and, given the unlikelihood of rising to own his own productive property, was scarcely more free. The only way to make wage labor compatible with freedom, Brownson argued, would be to make it a temporary condition on the way to independence: "There must be no class of our fellow men doomed to toil through life as mere workmen at wages. If wages are tolerated it must be, in the case of the individual operative, only under such conditions that, by the time he is of a proper age to settle in life, he shall have accumulated enough to be an independent laborer on his own capital, on his own farm or in his own shop."[8]

The abolitionists, for their part, disputed the analogy between wage labor and slavery. The grievances of northern workers were hardly comparable, they thought, to the evil of southern slavery. In 1831, when William Lloyd Garrison began publishing *The Liberator,* he criticized attempts by northern labor reformers to "inflame the minds of our working classes against the more opulent" and to persuade them that they were "oppressed by a wealthy aristocracy." In a republican government, where the avenues of wealth were open to all, Garrison argued, inequalities were bound to arise. But such inequalities were no proof of oppression, only the product of an open society in which some achieved more and others less.[9]

What set the abolitionists and the labor movement apart was not only a different assessment of wage-earners' prospects for social and economic advancement. Nor was it simply that abolitionists, drawn largely from ranks of the middle class, lacked sympathy for the impoverished condition of northern laborers. Abolitionists were unable to take seriously the notion of "wage slavery" because, unlike the labor advocates, they held a voluntarist not a civic understanding of freedom. In their view, the moral wrong of slavery was not that the slave lacked economic or political independence but simply that he was forced to work against his will.

The New York abolitionist William Jay, writing in 1835, made explicit the voluntarist conception of freedom underlying the abolitionist position. Immediate and unqualified emancipation, Jay argued, would "[remove] from the slave all cause for discontent. He is free, and his own master, and he can ask for no more." Jay acknowledged that the freed slave would, for a time, be "absolutely dependent on his late owner. He can look to no other person for food to eat, clothes to put on, or house to shelter him." His first wish would therefore be to labor for his former master. But even this wholly dependent condition was consistent with freedom, for "labor is no longer the badge of his servitude, and the consummation of his misery: it is the evidence of his liberty, for it is *voluntary*. For the first time in his life, he is a party to a contract." The transition from slave to free labor could thus be carried out instantaneously, Jay concluded, "and with scarcely any perceptible interruption of the ordinary pursuits of life. In the course of time, the value of negro labor, like all other vendible commodities, will be regulated by the supply and demand."[10]

For Jay, wage labor was the embodiment of free labor, a voluntary exchange between employer and employee. For the labor movement, wage labor was the opposite of free labor, a form of dependence incompatible with full citizenship. For Jay, the transition from slavery to free labor consisted in making labor a commodity the worker could sell; the key to freedom was self-ownership, the ability to sell one's labor for a wage. For the labor movement, the commodification of labor was the mark of wage slavery; the key to freedom was not the right to sell one's labor but the independence that came with owning productive property. What Jay considered emancipation was precisely the condition of dependence the labor movement protested.[11]

Through the 1830s and 1840s, labor advocates urged abolitionists to broaden their conception of freedom, to "include in their movement, a reform of the present wretched organization of labor, called the wage system." As the socialist journalist Albert Brisbane argued, such a stand would win abolitionists support among workers and also "prepare a better state for the slaves when emancipated, than the servitude to capital, to which they now seem destined."[12]

George Henry Evans, an advocate of land reform, also tried to persuade abolitionists to broaden their vision of reform. Since wage slavery, with the poverty, disease, crime, and prostitution it brought, was "even more destructive of life, health, and happiness than chattel slavery, as it exists in our Southern States, the efforts of those who are endeavoring to substitute wages for chattel slavery are greatly misdirected." As a solution to both forms of slavery, Evans urged the free distribution of homesteads to settlers on public lands. Free land would alleviate not only the poverty but also the dependence the wage system created. It "would not merely substitute one form of slavery for another, but would replace every form of slavery by entire freedom."[13]

Another land reformer, William West, also equated the dependence and degradation of the northern laboring classes with the condition of southern slaves. But he emphasized that the analogy implied no indifference to the plight of the slave. Land reformers "do not hate chattel slavery less, but they hate wages slavery more. Their rallying cry is 'Down with all slavery, both chattel and wages.'"[14]

Given their voluntarist conception of freedom, abolitionists could make no sense of the analogy between wage labor and slavery. Garrison deemed it "an abuse of language to talk of the slavery of wages." It was one thing to press for higher wages, quite another to denounce the wage system as such. "The evil in society is not that labor receives wages, but that the wages given are not generally in proportion to the value of the labor performed. We cannot see that it is wrong to give or receive wages; or that money, which is in itself harmless, is the source of almost every human woe."[15]

The abolitionist Wendell Phillips, who later became a strong advocate of labor, at first had little sympathy with the protest against "wage slavery." Writing in the 1840s, he claimed that Northern workers possessed the means to solve their problems for themselves. "Does legislation bear hard upon them?—their votes can alter it. Does capital wrong them?—economy will make them capitalists. Does the crowded competition of cities reduce their wages?—they have only to stay home, devoted to other pursuits, and soon diminished supply will bring the remedy." As for its general condition, the laboring class, like every other class in the country, "must owe its elevation and improvement . . . to economy, self-denial, temperance, education, and moral and religious character."[16]

Labor advocates and land reformers were not the only Americans who equated wage labor with slavery. A similar attack on the northern wage system came from southern defenders of slavery. Before the 1830s, few southerners offered a systematic defense of slavery; most considered it a necessary evil. Only the advent of abolitionism provoked them to defend slavery on moral grounds, as a "positive good," in the words of John C. Calhoun.[17]

Central to the proslavery argument was an attack on capitalist labor relations. "No successful defence of slavery can be made," wrote George Fitzhugh, the leading ideologist of southern slavery, "till we succeed in refuting or invalidating the principles on which free society rests for support or defence." Like northern labor leaders, Fitzhugh argued that the wage-earners of the North were no more free than the slaves of the South: "Capital commands labor, as the master does the slave." The only difference was that southern masters took responsibility for their slaves, supporting them in sickness and old age, while northern capitalists took none for theirs: "You, with the command over labor which your capital gives you, are a slave owner—a master, without the obligations of a master. They who work for you, who create your income, are slaves, without the rights of slaves."[18]

According to Fitzhugh, northern wage laborers, who lived in constant poverty and insecurity, were actually less free than southern slaves, who at least had masters obligated to sustain them in sickness and old age: "The free laborer must work or starve. He is more of a slave than the negro, because he works longer and harder for less allowance than the slave, and has no holiday, because the cares of life with him begin when its labors end. . . . Capital exercises a more perfect compulsion over free laborers than human masters over slaves; for free laborers must at all times work or starve, and slaves are supported whether they work or not. . . . Though each free laborer has no particular master, his wants and other men's capital make him a slave without a master, or with too many masters, which is as bad as none."[19]

Echoing the arguments of northern land reformers, Fitzhugh charged that the monopoly of property in the hands of capitalists deprived northern laborers of true freedom: "What is falsely called Free Society is a very recent invention. It proposes to make the weak, ignorant, and poor, free, by turning them loose in a world owned exclusively by the few." But "[t]he man without property is theoretically, and, too often, practically, without a single right." Left "to inhale the close and putrid air of small rooms, damp cellars and crowded factories," he has nowhere to lay his head. "Private property has monopolized the earth, and destroyed both his liberty and equality. He has no security for his life, for he cannot live without employment and adequate wages, and none are bound to employ him." Were he a slave, he would be no less dependent, but at least he would have the assurance of food, clothing, and shelter. In a defiant challenge to abolitionists, Fitzhugh invoked, in effect, the labor movement's conception of freedom: "Set your miscalled free laborers actually free, by giving them enough property or capital to live on, and then call on us at the South to free our negroes." Until then, he insisted, northern wage laborers would be less free than southern slaves.[20]

Other southerners defended slavery in similar terms. Senator James Henry Hammond of South Carolina disputed the claim that, except for the South, the whole world had abolished slavery. "Aye, the *name*, but not the *thing*," Hammond declared; "the man who lives by daily labor, and scarcely lives at that, and who has to put out his labor in the market, and take the best he can get for it; in short, your whole hireling class of manual laborers and 'operatives,' as you call them, are essentially slaves. The difference between us is, that our slaves are hired for life and well compensated; there is no starvation, no begging. . . . Yours are hired by the day, not cared for, and scantily compensated," as evidenced by the beggars in the streets of northern cities.[21]

Free Labor and Republican Politics

The voluntarist conception of free labor animated the abolitionist movement and, later in the century, offered the terms from which industrial capitalism would draw its justification. But before the Civil War it remained a minor strand in American political discourse; the civic conception of free labor predominated. "The Jeffersonian conviction that political liberty was safe only where no man was economically beholden to any other died hard in America," Daniel Rodgers has observed, "and in the nineteenth century it still had considerable force. In the minds of most Northerners of the Civil War generation, democracy demanded independence, not only political but economic." It also demanded that the distance between rich and poor not be so great as to breed corruption or dependence.[22]

The prevalence of the civic understanding of free labor explains the nineteenth-century conviction that "[w]age working violated the canons of a free society. . . . In the North of 1850, work was still, on the whole, something one did for oneself, a test of one's initiative that gave its direct economic reward. What masters a man had—the weather, prices, the web of commerce—were impersonal and distant. This was the moral norm, the bedrock meaning of free labor. Even as they built an economic structure that undercut it, Northerners found it hard to let go of that ideal upon which so much of their belief in work rested."[23]

When, in the late 1840s and the 1850s, antislavery became a mass movement in the North, it did so under the auspices of the civic, not the voluntarist, conception of freedom. The abolitionist movement, with its roots in evangelical Protestantism, had succeeded in the 1830s "in shattering the conspiracy of silence surrounding the question of slavery." But because of its radicalism, its moralism, and its lack of affinity with the laboring classes, evangelical abolitionism never commanded broad political support. As slavery became the central issue in American politics, political antislavery displaced abolitionism as the dominant movement.[24]

Political antislavery, as represented by the Free Soilers and ultimately the Republican party, differed from the abolitionist movement of the 1830s in both its aims and its arguments. Where the abolitionists sought to emancipate the slaves, the Free Soilers and the Republicans sought to contain slavery, to prevent its expansion into the territories. And where the abolitionists emphasized the sin of slavery and the suffering of the slave, the antislavery parties focused on the effects of slavery on free institutions, especially the system of free labor.[25]

The political antislavery movement offered two main arguments for opposing the spread of slavery, both of which drew on republican themes. One was the notion that the slaveholders of the South constituted a "slave power" that threatened to dominate the federal government, subvert the Constitution, and undermine republican institutions. According to this argument, the founders had sought to restrict slavery, but the southern slaveholders had conspired to control the federal government in order to extend slavery into the territories. The idea that slavery was not just an odious practice restricted to the South but an aggressive power bent on expansion mobilized northern opposition to slavery in a way that abolitionism had not. Events of the 1850s, especially the Kansas-Nebraska Act opening new territories to slavery, and the *Dred Scott* decision, lent growing plausibility to the fear. The *New York Times* called the Kansas-Nebraska bill "part of this great scheme for extending and perpetuating the supremacy of the Slave Power."[26]

Beyond its apparent fit with events, the slave power argument drew strength from its resonance with long-standing republican sensibilities. From the time of the Revolution, Americans had seen concentrated power, whether political or economic, as the enemy of liberty and had feared the tendency of the powerful to corrupt the public good on behalf of special interests. The colonists had viewed British taxation as part of a conspiracy of power against liberty; Jeffersonians had feared that Hamilton's fiscal policy would create a financial aristocracy antithetical to republican government; Jacksonians had railed against the "money power" embodied in the Bank of the United States. Now, antislavery parties spoke of the "slaveocracy" and cast southern slaveholders as a power poised to undermine republican institutions. Jacksonian Democrats who joined the antislavery cause drew explicit analogies between the slave power of the South and the banking power of the North, viewing both as forces that threatened to dominate the national government and destroy liberty.[27]

Why would the expansion of slavery into the territories constitute a threat to the liberty of northerners? The answer to this question formed the second tenet of political antislavery. Extending slavery to the territories would undermine northern liberty because it would destroy the system of free labor. And if the free labor system were lost, so too would be the economic independence that equipped citizens for self-government. Free labor needed free soil in order to prevent wage labor from becoming a permanent career. What saved the northern wage laborer from remaining a hireling for life was the possibility of saving enough to move West and start a farm or a shop of his own. But if slavery spread to the territories, this outlet would be closed.[28]

The defense of free labor was central to the ideology of the Republican party. "The Republicans stand before the country," a spokesman declared, "not only as the anti-slavery party, but emphatically as the party of free labor." For the Republicans as for the labor movement of the 1830s, free labor referred not to permanent wage labor but to labor that issued ultimately in economic independence. The dignity of labor consisted in the opportunity to rise above wage-earning status to work for oneself. Republicans praised northern society for making such mobility possible: "A young man goes out to service—to labor, if you please to call it so—for compensation until he acquires money enough to buy a farm . . . and soon he becomes himself the employer of labor."[29]

But if slavery spread to the territories, then free labor could not. This was the assumption, widely held throughout the North, that linked the slave power argument with the free labor argument. Free labor could not exist alongside slavery, because the presence of slavery undermined the dignity of all labor. When northerners looked south, they were struck not only by the misery of the slaves, but also by the poverty and degradation of nonslaveholding white laborers. The presence of slavery deprived even nonslaves of the qualities of character, such as industriousness and initiative, that the free labor system encouraged. Should slavery spread to the territories, its effects would spill beyond its borders to transform the institutions of northern society and corrupt the character of its people.[30]

The conviction that slavery was not an isolated wrong but a threat to the political economy of citizenship led northerners to conclude, as William Seward stated in 1858, that there was "an irrepressible conflict" between North and South, that "the United States must and will, sooner or later, become either entirely a slave-holding nation, or entirely a free-labor nation." As Republican Theodore Sedgwick asserted on the eve of the Civil War, "The policy and aims of slavery, its institutions and civilization, and the character of its people, are all at variance with the policy, aims, institutions, education, and character of the North. There is an irreconcilable difference in our interests, institutions, and pursuits; in our sentiments and feelings."[31]

The argument that slavery in the territories would render them unfit for free labor commanded broad agreement. But not all was admirable in the antislavery politics of the 1850s. As Eric Foner has pointed out, "the whole free labor argument against the extension of slavery contained a crucial ambiguity. Was it the institution of slavery, or the presence of the Negro, which degraded the white laborer?" Some antislavery politicians argued against the spread of slavery in explicitly racist terms and took pains to show that their opposition to slavery implied no fondness for blacks.[32]

This was especially true of the Barnburner Democrats, a faction of the New York Democratic party instrumental in founding the Free Soil party. "I speak not of the condition of the slave," said one Barnburner congressman. "I do not pretend to know, nor is it necessary that I should express an opinion in this place, whether the effect of slavery is beneficial or injurious to him. I am looking to its effect upon the white man, the free white man of this country." David Wilmot, author of the "Wilmot Proviso" of 1846, which banned slavery from the territories won in the Mexican War, insisted that his bill reflected "no squeamish sensitiveness upon the subject of slavery, no morbid sympathy for the slave." It was, he said, a "White Man's Proviso," whose aim was to preserve the territories for "the sons of toil, of my own race and own color."[33]

This feature of political antislavery was not lost on the black abolitionist Frederick Douglass, who observed: "The cry of Free Men was raised, not for the extension of liberty to the black man, but for the protection of the liberty of the white."[34] George Fitzhugh, the defender of slavery, made a similar point in his perverse complaint that hostility to slavery reflected northern racism: "The aversion to negroes, the antipathy of race, is much greater at the North than at the South; and it is very probable that this antipathy to the person of the negro, is confounded with or generates hatred of the institution with which he is usually connected. Hatred to slavery is very generally little more than hatred of negroes."[35] It is clear in any case that many who opposed the spread of slavery to the territories made no distinction between keeping out slavery and keeping out blacks.

The free labor argument found nobler expression in Abraham Lincoln. Like the abolitionists, Lincoln insisted that slavery was a moral wrong that should not be left open to popular sovereignty in the territories. He opposed, on practical and constitutional grounds, interfering with slavery in the states where it existed, but hoped the containment of slavery would bring its ultimate extinction. Although he opposed social and political equality for blacks, including the suffrage, he argued in his debates with Stephen Douglas that "there is no reason in the world why the negro is not entitled to all the natural rights enumerated in the Declaration of Independence, the right to life, liberty and the pursuit of happiness. I hold that he is as much entitled to these as the white man."[36]

Although he shared the abolitionists' moral condemnation of slavery, Lincoln did not share their voluntarist conception of freedom. Lincoln's main argument against the expansion of slavery rested on the free labor ideal, and unlike the abolitionists, he did not equate free labor with wage labor. The superiority of free labor to slave labor did not consist in the fact that free laborers consent to exchange their work for a wage, whereas slaves do not consent. The difference was rather that the northern wage laborer could hope one day to escape from his condition, whereas the slave could not. It was not consent that distinguished free labor from slavery, but rather the prospect of independence, the chance to rise to own productive property and to work for oneself. According to Lincoln, it was this feature of the free labor system that the southern critics of wage labor overlooked: "They insist that their slaves are far better off than Northern freemen. What a mistaken view do these men have of Northern laborers! They think that men are always to remain laborers here—but there is no such class. The man who labored for another last year, this year labors for himself, and next year he will hire others to labor for him."[37]

Lincoln did not challenge the notion that those who spend their entire lives as wage laborers are comparable to slaves. He held that both forms of work wrongly subordinate labor to capital. Those who debated "whether it is best that capital shall *hire* laborers, and thus induce them to work by their own consent, or *buy* them, and drive them to it without consent," considered too narrow a range of possibilities. Free labor is labor carried out under conditions of independence from employers and masters alike. Lincoln insisted that, at least in the North, most Americans were independent in this sense: "Men, with their families—wives, sons and daughters—work for themselves, on their farms, in their houses and in their shops, taking the whole product to themselves, and asking no favors of capital on the one hand, nor of hirelings or slaves on the other."[38]

Wage labor as a temporary condition on the way to independence was compatible with freedom, and wholly unobjectionable. Lincoln offered himself as an example, reminding audiences that he too had once been a hired laborer splitting rails. What made free labor free was not the worker's consent to work for a wage but his opportunity to rise above wage-earning status to self-employment and independence. "The prudent, penniless beginner in the world, labors for wages awhile, saves a surplus with which to buy tools or land for himself; then labors on his own account another while, and at length hires another new beginner to help him." This was the true meaning of free labor, "the just and generous and prosperous system, which opens the way to all." So confident was Lincoln in the openness of the free labor system that those who failed to rise could only be victims of "a dependent nature" or of "improvidence, folly, or singular misfortune." Those who succeeded in working their way up from poverty, on the other hand, were as worthy as any men living of trust and political power.[39]

In Lincoln's hands, the conception of freedom deriving from the artisan republican tradition became the rallying point for the northern cause in the Civil War. In the 1830s and 1840s, labor leaders had invoked this conception in criticizing northern society; wage labor, they feared, was supplanting free labor. In the late 1850s, Lincoln and the Republicans invoked the same conception in defending northern society; the superiority of the North to the slaveholding South consisted in the independence the free labor system made possible. "The Republicans therefore identified themselves with the aspirations of northern labor in a way abolitionists never did, but at the same time, helped turn those aspirations into a critique of the South, not an attack on the northern social order."[40]

The Union victory in the Civil War put to rest the threat to free labor posed by the slave power, only to revive and intensify the threat posed by the wage system and industrial capitalism. Lincoln had led the North to war in the name of free labor and the small, independent producer, but the war itself accelerated the growth of capitalist enterprise and factory production.[41] In the years after the war, northerners faced with renewed anguish the lack of fit between the free labor ideal and the growing reality of economic dependence. "The rhetoric of the slavery contest had promised independence; mid-nineteenth-century work ideals had assumed it. As the drift of the economy set in in the opposite direction, tugging against ideals, the result was a nagging, anxious sense of betrayal."[42]

In 1869 the *New York Times* reported on the decline of the free labor system and the advance of wage labor. Small workshops had become "far less common than they were before the war," and "the small manufacturers thus swallowed up have become workmen on wages in the greater establishments, whose larger purses, labor-saving machines, etc., refused to allow the small manufacturers a separate existence." The article criticized the trend it described in terms reminiscent of the labor movement of the 1830s and 1840s. The fall of the independent mechanic to wage-earner status amounted to "a system of slavery as absolute if not as degrading as that which lately prevailed at the South."[43]

The 1870 census, the first to record detailed information about Americans' occupations, confirmed what many workers already knew. Notwithstanding a free labor ideology that tied liberty to ownership of productive property, America had become a nation of employees. Two-thirds of productively engaged Americans were wage-earners by 1870, dependent for their livelihood on someone else. In a nation that prized independence and self-employment, only one in three any longer worked his own farm or ran his own shop.[44]

Faced with an economy increasingly at odds with the civic conception of freedom, Americans responded, in the decades after the Civil War, in two different ways. Some continued to insist that wage labor was inconsistent with freedom, and sought to reform the economy along lines hospitable to republican ideals. Others accepted as inevitable (or embraced as desirable) the arrangements of industrial capitalism, and sought to reconcile wage labor with freedom by revising the ideal; wage labor was consistent with freedom, they argued, insofar as it reflected the consent of the parties, a voluntary agreement between employer and employee.

Those who adopted the voluntarist conception of freedom often disagreed about what genuine freedom of contract required. Doctrinaire defenders of industrial capitalism held that any agreement to exchange work for a wage was free, regardless of the economic pressures operating on the worker. Trade unionists and liberal reformers argued, on the other hand, that true freedom of contract required various measures to create a more nearly equal bargaining situation between labor and capital. The question of what social and economic conditions are necessary for individuals to exercise free choice would fuel much controversy in American politics and law throughout the twentieth century. But the argument over the necessary conditions of genuinely free choice is a debate within the terms of the voluntarist conception of freedom. The prominence of this debate in twentieth century legal and political discourse signifies the extent to which the voluntarist conception of freedom has come to inform American public life.

From the 1860s to the 1890s, however, the voluntarist conception of freedom, not yet predominant, coexisted and competed with a rival republican conception that linked freedom to economic independence. In the decades following the Civil War, the civic conception of freedom still figured prominently in American political debate. For the labor movement of the day, it inspired the last sustained resistance to the system of wage labor and informed the search for alternatives.

Labor Republicanism in the Gilded Age

The leading labor organizations of the Gilded Age were the National Labor Union (NLU; 1866–1872) and the Knights of Labor (1869–1902). Their primary aim was "to abolish the wage system," on the grounds that "there is an inevitable and irresistible conflict between the wage-system of labor and the republican system of government."[45] The labor movement emphasized two ways in which the wage system of industrial capitalism threatened republican government—directly, by concentrating unaccountable power in large corporations, and indirectly, by destroying the qualities of character that equip citizens for self-government.

The platform of the Knights of Labor protested "the alarming development and aggressiveness of great capitalists and corporations" and sought "to check unjust accumulation and the power for evil of aggregated wealth." To this end, it called for the purchase and control by the government of the railroads, telegraph, and telephones, lest their monopoly power overwhelm republican institutions. "[T]he power of these corporations over the government, and over their employees, [is] equalled only by the power of the Czar," warned George McNeill, a leader of the Knights; "the question will soon force itself upon the republican citizens in this form: 'Shall these great corporations control the government, or shall they be controlled by the government?'"[46]

Beyond the direct danger posed by monopoly power to republican government lay the damaging effects of the wage system on the moral and civic character of workers. In attacking wage labor, leaders of the NLU and the Knights frequently stressed its formative consequences. "What would it profit us, as a nation," asked William H. Sylvis, the leading labor figure of the 1860s, "were we to preserve our institutions and destroy the morals of the people; save our Constitution, and sink the masses into hopeless ignorance, poverty, and crime; all the forms of our republican institutions to remain on the statute books, and the great body of the people sunk so low as to be incapable of comprehending their most simple and essential principles . . .?"[47]

Speaking in 1865 before the iron molders, in the largest labor convention that had ever assembled, Sylvis reasserted the republican principle that "popular governments must depend for their stability and success upon the virtue and intelligence of the masses." Under existing conditions of work, however, the relations between employers and employees "are, for the most part, that of master and slave, and are totally at variance with the spirit of the institutions of a free people." History has taught that low wages bring not only poverty and suffering, but also the corruption of civic virtue. Where wages are low, the laboring class is "sunk into the depths of political and social degradation, incapable of raising itself to that lofty elevation attained by a free and enlightened people capable of governing their own affairs." When the price of labor declines, it "carries with it not only wages, but all the high and noble qualities which fit us for self-government."[48]

If the wage labor system undermined civic virtue, what alternative economic arrangements would cultivate virtuous and independent citizens? Faced with the conditions of industrial capitalism, the labor movement no longer had faith in the individual mobility central to Lincoln's free labor solution. Nor could it hope to restore an earlier economy of small farms and workshops scattered across the countryside. It called instead for the creation of a cooperative commonwealth, in which producers and consumers would organize cooperative factories, mines, banks, farms, and stores, combining their resources and sharing the profits. Such a system would do more than give workers a fair share of the fruits of their labor; it would also restore to workers the independence the wage system destroyed.

Sylvis hailed cooperation as "the true remedy for the evils of society; this is the great idea that is destined to break down the present system of centralization, monopoly, and extortion. By co-operation, we will become a nation of employers—the employers of our own labor." Terence Powderly, the head of the Knights, declared the cooperative system the way "to forever banish that curse of modern civilization—wage slavery." Cooperation would "eventually make every man his own master—every man his own employer." McNeill looked forward to the day when "the cooperative system will supersede the wage-system." Together with other reforms, it would produce a dignified and independent worker-citizen, "a well-built, fully equipped manhood, using the morning hours in the duties and pleasures of the sunlit-home; taking his morning bath before his morning work, reading his morning paper in the well-equipped reading-room of the manufactory . . . a man upon whom the honors and duties of civilization can safely rest."[49]

The cooperative ideal was as much an ethic as an institutional scheme. Its advocates stressed that the cooperative system was not a program for government to enact, but rather a project for workers acting collectively to bring into being. This emphasis on collective self-help was essential to the formative, edifying, character-building aspiration of the movement. Although most of the reforms advocated by the Knights of Labor required political action, Powderly explained, "it was felt that everything should not be left to the state or the nation." Even while seeking legislative reforms, "the worker should bestir himself in another way." Sylvis urged that workers "not forget that success depends upon our own efforts. It is not what is done for people, but what people do for themselves, that acts upon their character and condition." The labor movement's quest for moral and civic improvement also found expression in an ambitious array of reading rooms and traveling lecturers, dramatics societies and sporting clubs, journals and pamphlets, rituals and parades. "We must get our people to read and think," said a local labor leader, "and to look for something higher and more noble in life than working along in that wretched way from day to day and from week to week and from year to year."[50]

For a time, the labor movement's call to replace the wage system with the cooperative system drew support from middle class reformers, among them E. L. Godkin, an influential Radical Republican journalist. Godkin assailed the wage system for its failure to cultivate virtuous citizens. It was widely recognized, Godkin observed, that "when a man agrees to sell his labor, he agrees by implication to surrender his moral and social independence."[51]

Echoing the arguments of Jefferson and Jackson, Godkin maintained that industrial wage laborers were deprived of the dignity, independence, and public spirit essential to the success of democratic government: "no man whose bread and that of his children are dependent on the will of any other man, or who has no interest in his work except to please an employer, fulfills these conditions; a farmer of his own land does fulfill them. He is the only man, as society is at present constituted in almost all civilized countries, who can be said to be really master of himself." The wage laborer, by contrast, was consigned to a condition of "political and social dependence."[52]

Godkin condemned the "accumulation of capital in the hands of comparatively few individuals and corporations," not on grounds of fairness but rather because it undermined the political economy of citizenship and endangered republican government. The problem with wage labor was not only the poverty it bred but the damage it did to the civic capacities of workers, "the servile tone and servile way of thinking" it produced. For Godkin as for the labor movement, the solution was not to restore an agrarian past, but to recast industrial capitalism by replacing the wage system with a scheme of cooperatives in which workers would share in the profits of their labor and govern themselves. He urged that the labor movement "never cease agitating and combining until the regime of wages, or, as we might perhaps better call it, the servile regime, has passed away as completely as slavery or serfdom, and until in no free country shall any men be found in the condition of mere hirelings," except those few too vicious or unstable to govern themselves.[53]

Like the labor leaders of the Gilded Age, Godkin drew on a republican conception of free labor to criticize the wage system. But Godkin's view also contained elements of a voluntarist conception of freedom that was gaining currency among liberal reformers of the day. This conception, which identified free labor with freedom of contract, recalled the abolitionists' notion that free labor was work voluntarily undertaken in exchange for a wage. In the years before the Civil War, the abolitionists' equation of free labor with wage labor was a minority view. Most Americans, from northern labor leaders to proslavery southerners to Free Soilers to the Republican party of Lincoln, agreed for all their differences that wage labor was a career incompatible with freedom.

By the late nineteenth century, however, the voluntarist conception of free labor found growing expression in American politics and law. Its most conspicuous expression was in the laissez-faire doctrine advanced by conservative economists and judges who insisted that employers and employees should be free to agree to whatever terms of employment they chose, unfettered by legislative interference. But laissez-faire conservatives were not the only ones whose arguments presupposed the voluntarist conception of free labor. Social reformers also invoked the ideal of freedom of contract, but they argued that such freedom could not be realized where the parties to the contract bargained under conditions of severe inequality. By the end of the century, American political debate focused less on what economic conditions were necessary for the formation of virtuous citizens, and more on what economic conditions were necessary for the exercise of genuinely free choice. The passage from the civic to the voluntarist understanding of free labor can be seen most clearly in the response of liberal reformers and the courts to labor's attempt to legislate the eight-hour day.

The Eight-Hour Day

Among liberal reformers, Godkin embodied the moment of transition. Even as he attacked the wage system as "hostile to free government" and damaging to the moral and civic character of workers, he opposed legislation to establish the eight-hour day as a "tyrannical interference of the Government with the freedom of industry and the sanctity of contracts." Like many laissez-faire defenders of industrial capitalism, Godkin condemned the eight-hour movement as "a disgraceful farce," a violation of freedom of contract, and a hopeless attempt to nullify the laws of nature. "No legislature can permanently change or affect these laws any more than it could change the hour of the ebb and flow of the tide." Unlike the orthodox political economists of his day, however, Godkin denied that agreements between workers and employers under the unequal conditions of industrial capitalism were genuinely voluntary.[54]

In explaining why existing labor relations were not truly free, Godkin accepted the voluntarist, or contractual, conception of freedom advanced by laissez-faire conservatives. But he rejected the conservatives' complacent assumption that the practice of wage labor lived up to the ideal of freedom of contract. Living at the margin of existence in degrading conditions, the worker was in no position to make a truly voluntary exchange of his labor for a wage. He simply had to accept whatever the capitalist was willing to pay. "What I agree to do in order to escape from starvation, or to save my wife and children from starvation, or through ignorance of my ability to do anything else, I agree to do under compulsion, just as much as if I agreed to do it with a pistol at my head."[55]

Godkin had no quarrel with the voluntarist assumption that labor is a commodity to be bought and sold like any other. In principle at least, "the hiring of a laborer by a capitalist should simply mean the sale of a commodity in open market by one free agent to another." Under existing conditions, however, the wage system failed to realize the voluntarist ideal. The worker could not approach the ideal of freedom of contract "unless he were by some means raised, in making his bargain, to the master's level,—unless he were enabled to treat with the capitalist on a footing of equality."[56]

Godkin endorsed a number of measures to create the bargaining conditions that would enable workers to exercise genuine consent. The primary one was for workers to combine in unions to balance the market power of capital, to place the worker "on an equality with his master in the matter of contracts, so as to enable him to contract freely." For the long term, Godkin endorsed the cooperative system, in which workers would become capitalists, and share in the profits of their labor. For the short term, however, strikes and trade unions would remain "the only means by which the contract between the laborer and the capitalist . . . can be made really free, and by which the laborer can be enabled to treat on equal terms."[57]

Godkin's arguments displayed both the civic and the voluntarist conceptions of free labor, sometimes in harmony, sometimes in tension. He supported the cooperative movement on the grounds that it would improve the moral and civic character of workers and also on the grounds that it would remedy the unfair bargaining position that prevented labor relations from being truly voluntary. At the same time, he opposed the eight-hour movement on the grounds that it would violate the sanctity of freedom of contract. Although existing conditions prevented freedom of contract from being realized, legislating a shorter workday would not level the playing field; it would simply constitute a further violation of the voluntarist ideal.

The labor movement, by contrast, did not rely heavily on voluntarist arguments. Its case for the eight-hour day, like its case for the cooperative system, drew primarily on civic and formative considerations. When labor leaders of the Gilded Age spoke of freedom of contract, it was to reply to laissez-faire critics. For example, George McNeill of the Knights of Labor derided the notion that legislating the eight-hour day "would destroy the great right of freedom of contract." Under the existing wage system, he argued, there was no genuine freedom of contract between employer and employee. "The contract, so-called, is an agreement that the employer or corporation shall name all of the conditions to the bargain." The only conditions approaching a true freedom of contract arose when powerful labor organizations were able to bargain on behalf of their members.[58]

The labor leaders' main argument for a shorter workday was not that it would perfect consent but rather that it would improve the moral and civic character of workers. Limiting by law the hours of work, they argued, would give workers more time to be citizens—to read newspapers and to participate in public affairs: "We ask for relief from Hours of Labor, which use up in the service of others, the whole day, leaving us no time to comply with the public duties which we are having thrust upon us, or for the exercise of any personal gifts or longings for refined pleasures."[59] Besides freeing up time for civic pursuits, a shorter work-day would build character indirectly, by elevating the tastes, improving the habits, and uplifting the aspirations of workers. According to Ira Steward, the leading figure in the movement for the eight-hour day, greater leisure would enable workers to compare their way of life with others and would make them less willing to accept the debased conditions of their existence. "The charm of the eight hour system," Steward argued, "is that it gives time and opportunity for the ragged—the unwashed—the ignorant and ill-mannered, to become ashamed of themselves and their standing in society." A shorter workday would give the masses the time to compare their lot with others, and to become discontented with their situation. This in turn would elevate their aspirations, and lead them to insist on higher wages. While some would spend their increased earnings and leisure on consumption, others, "wiser fellows," would devote their time and money to civic pursuits, "to study political economy, social science, the sanitary condition of the people, the prevention of crime, woman's wages, war, and the ten thousand schemes with which our age teems for the amelioration of the condition of man."[60]

McNeill also emphasized the formative case for shorter hours, hoping to transform "the habits of thought and feeling, customs and manners of the masses." The point was not simply to give workers relief from the tedium and drudgery of long workdays, but to uplift them. To disturb impoverished workers "from their sottish contentment by an agitation for more wages or less hours, is to lift them up in the level of their manhood to thoughts of better things, and to an organized demand for the same." Reducing the hours of labor would lessen intemperance, vice, and crime among the laboring classes and increase their use of newspapers and libraries, lecture rooms, and meeting halls. In time, the eight-hour day would elevate and empower workers to such an extent as to bring the demise of the wage system itself: "finally the profit upon labor shall cease, and co-operative labor [will] be inaugurated in the place of wage-labor."[61]

By 1868 seven states had enacted eight-hour laws, and Congress passed legislation declaring an eight-hour workday for all laborers employed by the federal government. But despite its legislative success, the eight-hour movement did not achieve its broader aims. Loopholes in the laws, lack of enforcement, and hostile courts undermined labor's legislative victories.[62] A similar fate met other labor legislation of the Gilded Age, especially in the courts. By the end of the century, some sixty labor laws had been struck down by state and federal courts; by 1920, about three hundred.[63]

Wage Labor in Court

The judicialization of the debate over free labor accentuated the shift from civic to voluntarist assumptions. Laissez-faire judges struck down labor laws by invoking the right of workers to exchange their labor for a wage. Defenders of the laws replied that wage labor under conditions of poverty and inequality was not truly free. The critique of wage labor as such gradually faded from view as arguments focused on the conditions of genuine consent and the role of judicial review. Notwithstanding the civic and formative aims that initially inspired the laws, those who defended labor legislation against assault by conservative courts gradually adopted the voluntarist assumptions of their laissez-faire opponents, and defended the laws as necessary to make wage labor a matter of genuine consent.

Although most judicial debate of the labor question proceeded within voluntarist assumptions, the first judicial defense of free labor under the Fourteenth Amendment reflected the republican understanding of free labor. It came in dissent, in the *Slaughter-House Cases* of 1873. The Louisiana legislature had chartered a corporation to maintain a central stockyard and slaughterhouse in New Orleans, and banned all other slaughterhouses in the area; all butchers would have to do their butchering in the designated facilities and pay the requisite fees. A group of butchers challenged the law, claiming that it violated their right to own their own slaughterhouses and carry on their trade. This right, they argued, was protected by the recently adopted Thirteenth and Fourteenth Amendments to the Constitution.[64]

The Supreme Court, in a five–four ruling, rejected their claim, holding that the Reconstruction amendments did not cast the Court as the guarantor of individual rights against state infringement. But in an influential dissent, Justice Stephen Field argued that the new amendments did empower the Court to protect fundamental rights, including the "right of free labor." Unlike the laissez-faire judges who would later invoke his dissent, Field conceived free labor as the artisan republican tradition conceived it—not as wage labor but as labor carried out by independent producers who owned their own tools or shops or means of production. If only wage labor were at stake, New Orleans' monopoly-owned slaughterhouse would not pose the same kind of threat. The state-sanctioned monopoly did not prevent the butchers from working as butchers, only from owning and operating their own slaughterhouses; it deprived them of free labor in the republican sense.[65]

According to Field, the Reconstruction amendments did more than end slavery and confer citizenship on the newly freed slaves. They also vindicated the free labor ideal in the name of which the North had fought the Civil War. It was this republican notion of free labor that Louisiana's state-chartered monopoly undermined. A butcher could no longer practice his trade as an independent producer, but would now have to work in the buildings of the favored company and pay a substantial fee. "He is not allowed to do his work in his own buildings, or to take his animals to his own stables or keep them in his own yards." Such "odious" restrictions deprived butchers of their independence. According to Field, the Fourteenth Amendment protected every citizen's equal right to pursue all lawful callings and professions. By restricting this right, Louisiana's slaughterhouse monopoly violated "the right of free labor, one of the most sacred and imprescriptible rights of man."[66]

Subsequent courts would adopt Field's view of the Fourteenth Amendment, but not his republican understanding of free labor. Like Field, they would hold that the Fourteenth Amendment required the Court to invalidate state laws that violated individual rights, including the right to free labor. Unlike Field, however, they understood free labor in its voluntarist sense—as the right of the worker to sell his labor for a wage. Although Field himself never endorsed the use of liberty of contract to strike down labor legislation, his dissent did contain one reference that laissez-faire courts seized on in support of their voluntarist view. In a footnote to his discussion of free labor, Field included a quotation from Adam Smith that linked liberty to self-ownership and the right to sell one's labor. State and federal courts that cited Field's dissent emphasized this footnote, and neglected the fact that the *Slaughter-House Cases* involved the rights of independent producers, not of wage laborers.[67]

From the 1880s to the 1930s, state and federal courts struck down scores of labor laws for violating the freedom of workers. Virtually all of these cases adopted the voluntarist conception of freedom, asserting the right of the worker to exchange his labor for a wage. In *Godcharles v. Wigeman* (1886), the Pennsylvania Supreme Court struck down a law requiring companies to pay miners and factory workers in cash rather than in scrip redeemable at company stores. The ironworkers had pressed for the law to escape their dependence on company stores that charged exorbitant prices to their captive clientele. The court invalidated the law as "an infringement alike of the rights of the employer and the employee" and "an insulting attempt to put the laborer under a legislative tutelage, which is not only degrading to his manhood, but subversive of his rights as a citizen of the United States. He may sell his labor for what he thinks best, whether money or goods, just as his employer may sell his iron or coal."[68]

In *Lochner v. New York* (1905), the voluntarist conception of free labor became federal constitutional law. In *Lochner,* the Supreme Court struck down a New York law setting maximum hours for bakery workers as "an illegal interference with the rights of individuals, both employers and employees, to make contracts regarding labor upon such terms as they may think best . . . limiting the hours in which grown and intelligent men may labor to earn their living," stated the Court, is a "mere meddlesome [interference] with the rights of the individual" and an unconstitutional violation of liberty.[69]

The Court made a similar argument in *Coppage v. Kansas* (1914), striking down a state law preventing companies from setting as a condition of employment that workers not belong to unions. The state of Kansas argued that the law was necessary to prevent workers from being coerced by employers to withdraw from unions, but the U.S. Supreme Court disagreed, insisting that a worker faced with such a choice was nonetheless "a free agent." Given the alternative of quitting the union or losing his job, the worker was "at liberty to choose what was best from the standpoint of his own interests," "free to exercise a voluntary choice." The Kansas Supreme Court had upheld the law, observing that "employees, as a rule, are not financially able to be as independent in making contracts for the sale of their labor as are employers in making contracts of purchase thereof." But the U.S. Supreme Court rejected this argument and denied that any coercion was involved. The company, after all, was not forcing the employee to accept the job. The Court acknowledged that "wherever the right of private property exists, there must and will be inequalities of fortune; and thus it naturally happens that parties negotiating about a contract are not equally unhampered by circumstances." But these inevitable inequalities did not constitute coercion and did not justify government interference with the right of employers and employees to exchange work for a wage on whatever conditions they choose.[70]

The laissez-faire constitutionalism of *Lochner* and *Coppage* offered powerful expression of the voluntarist conception of free labor that came to dominate legal and political discourse in the late nineteenth and early twentieth centuries. It was not, however, the only expression. Much of the opposition to laissez-faire orthodoxy that developed during those decades also embraced voluntarist assumptions. Dissenting judges and reform-minded commentators and activists rejected laissez-faire doctrine on the grounds that wholly unregulated labor contracts are not truly voluntary. Unlike the labor movement of the Gilded Age, they did not object to the commodification of labor, only to the unfair bargaining conditions under which the industrial worker sold his commodity. They sought not to abolish the wage system but to render it legitimate by creating conditions under which the consent of the worker would be truly free. Even among reformers, the debate about wage labor shifted from civic to contractarian terms.

The notion that legislatures might justifiably enact labor laws to equalize the bargaining position of wage laborers figured, for example, in some notable dissents to *Lochner*-era cases. Dissenting in *Lochner,* Justice John Marshall Harlan suggested that the maximum-hours statute had its origin "in the belief that employers and employees in such establishments were not upon an equal footing, and that the necessities of the latter often compelled them to submit to such exactions as unduly taxed their strength."[71] Dissenting in *Coppage,* Justice Oliver Wendell Holmes wrote: "In present conditions a workman not unnaturally may believe that only by belonging to a union can he secure a contract that shall be fair to him." That belief "may be enforced by law in order to establish the equality of position between the parties in which liberty of contract begins." A separate dissent by Justice William R. Day defended the law as an attempt "to promote the same liberty of action for the employee as the employer confessedly enjoys." Given their unequal bargaining positions, the company's requirement that the worker agree as a condition of employment to quit his union was coercive. The state was therefore justified in acting to remedy the unequal conditions that undermined true freedom of contract.[72]

Commentators outside the courts also criticized laissez-faire doctrine in the name of the voluntarist ideal implicit but unrealized in contracts for wage labor. Criticizing the line of decisions from *Godcharles* to *Lochner* and *Adair,* Roscoe Pound defended legislation "designed to give laborers some measure of practical independence, and which, if allowed to operate, would put them in a position of reasonable equality with their masters." Citing the English jurist Lord Northington, he argued that impoverished workers are unable to exercise genuine consent: "Necessitous men are not, truly speaking, free men, but, to answer a present exigency, will submit to any terms that the crafty may impose upon them."[73]

Richard Ely, an economist and reformer, also maintained that true freedom of contract requires government regulation of the conditions under which contracts are made. "Legal equality in contract is a part of modern freedom," Ely wrote. "But we have legal equality in contract with a *de facto* inequality on account of inequality of conditions lying back of contracts. It is at this point that we must take up the work of reform everywhere, but particularly in the United States." For Ely, unlike the labor leaders of the Gilded Age, the justification of eight-hour laws and other labor legislation was not to transform the moral character of workers or to abolish the wage system, but to redeem the voluntarist ideal implicit in wage labor. "While free contract must be the rule, liberty demands the social regulation of many classes of contracts. Regulation of contract conditions means establishing the 'rules of the game' for competition."[74]

The Demise of the Civic Ideal

By the turn of the century, the shift from the civic to the voluntarist ideal as the animating vision of reform was reflected in the changing character of the labor movement itself. The Knights of Labor, which challenged the wage system in the hopes of cultivating virtuous citizen-producers, enjoyed an explosion in membership in the mid-1880s, exceeding 700,000 members in 1886. Embracing the broad Jacksonian notion of the "producing classes," the Knights included skilled and unskilled laborers as well as some small merchants and manufacturers. Only "non-producers," such as lawyers, bankers, and speculators, and those associated with vice, such as saloon-keepers and gamblers, were ineligible for membership. The Knights also broke barriers of race and gender, enlisting some 60,000 black members and an even larger number of women.[75]

More than a trade union, the Knights were a reform movement that sought "to engraft republican principles" onto the industrial system, to transform the economy along lines more hospitable to self-government.[76] But the vehicle of the transformation, the cooperative system, found little sustained success. By the mid-1880s, local assemblies had established more than a hundred small cooperatives, including grocery stores, retail stores, newspapers, workshops, and factories, but most suffered a short-age of capital and lasted only a few years.[77] Beset as well by setbacks in the courts, aggressive opposition by employers, and divisions within the labor movement, the Knights declined precipitously, falling to 100,000 members by 1890. Soon thereafter, they faded into oblivion.[78]

With the demise of the Knights came a shift in the labor movement away from republican-inspired reform and toward a version of trade unionism that accepted the structure of industrial capitalism, conceded the permanence of wage labor, and sought simply to improve the living standards and working conditions of workers. "The average wage earner has made up his mind that he must remain a wage earner," declared United Mine Workers president John Mitchell in 1903, and "given up the hope of the kingdom to come, when he himself will be a capitalist."[79]

The rise of the American Federation of Labor in the 1890s signaled labor's turn from political and economic reform to trade unionism "pure and simple." "[O]pposed to broad programs of social reconstruc-tion," the trade unions "looked rather toward immediate material im-provements within the framework of existing institutions, and relied primarily on economic organization and action."[80] Under the leadership of Samuel Gompers, the AFL gave up labor's long-standing quarrel with the wage system, and turned its attention to prosperity and fairness. "We are operating under the wage system," declared Gompers in 1899. "As to what system will ever come to take its place I am not prepared to say. . . . I know that we are living under the wage system, and so long as that lasts it is our purpose to secure a continually larger share for labor."[81]

The new trade unions spoke not of the producing classes, but more bluntly of "wage-earners" or the "working class," and ended attempts to forge an alliance for reform with small businessmen and manufactur-ers. Where labor reformers such as the Knights resisted the concentra-tion of capital in large corporations, the trade unions accepted economic concentration as "a logical and inevitable feature of our modern system of industry," and sought to organize labor as a countervailing power.[82] As Gompers observed, "The two movements were inherently different." The Knights of Labor "was based upon a principle of co-operation and its purpose was reform. [It] prided itself upon being something higher and grander than a trade union or political party." Trade unions, by contrast, "sought economic betterment in order to place in the hands of wage-earners the means to wider opportunities." Their aim was not political reform but "economic betterment—today, tomorrow, in home and shop."[83]

In its waning days the Knights of Labor denounced the limited aims of the trade unions and insisted on labor's older ambitions. The Knights "is not so much intended to adjust the relationship between the employer and employee," its leader proclaimed in 1894, as to transform the economy so that "all who wish may work for themselves, independent of large employing corporations and companies. It is not founded on the question of adjusting wages, but on the question of abolishing the wage-system and the establishment of a cooperative industrial system."[84]

For his part, Gompers refused any broad statement of purpose for the trade union movement, apart from securing the economic betterment of wage-earners: "we labor men usually try to express the labor movement in practical terms. . . . I had no formula for [our] work and could not have expressed my philosophy in words. I worked intuitively." The renunciation of broad aims of political or economic reform was expressed with similar stubbornness by Adolph Strasser, president of the cigarmakers' union. Testifying before the Senate Committee on Labor and Capital in 1883, Strasser was asked about the ultimate ends of his union. "We have no ultimate ends," Strasser replied. "We are going on from day to day. We are fighting only for immediate objects—objects that can be realized in a few years. . . . We are all practical men."[85]

Although the trade unions professed no ultimate ends, they did embrace a certain conception of freedom. It was a conception that had more in common with the voluntarist vision of their industrial adversaries than with the civic vision of their artisan republican predecessors. In asserting the right to organize and strike, trade unions were not coercing employers or nonunion workers, Gompers insisted, nor were they challenging the premises of industrial capitalism; they were simply joining in voluntary association to exercise labor's market power in the same way that corporations exercised theirs. As Gompers maintained, the trade union movement drew its justification from the same conception of freedom that defenders of industry invoked: "The whole gospel of this is summed up in one phrase, a familiar one—freedom of contract."[86]

From Jefferson to Lincoln to the Knights of Labor, opponents of the wage system had argued in the name of the civic conception of freedom; free labor was labor that produced virtuous, independent citizens, capable of self-government. As that argument waned, so did the conception of freedom that inspired it. With the acceptance of wage labor as a permanent condition came a shift in American legal and political discourse from the civic to the voluntarist conception of freedom; labor was now free insofar as the worker agreed to exchange his labor for a wage. The advent of the voluntarist conception did not resolve all controversy about labor relations, but it cast the controversy in different terms. When twentieth-century reformers and conservatives debated questions of wages and work, their debates would concern the conditions of genuine consent, not the conditions for the cultivation of civic virtue.

From the standpoint of the political economy of citizenship, the voluntarist conception of free labor represented a diminished aspiration. For despite its emphasis on individual choice, it conceded as unavoidable the broader condition of dependence that the republican tradition had long resisted. It thus marked a decisive moment in America's transition from a republican public philosophy to the version of liberalism that informs the procedural republic.

As the twentieth century began, however, the procedural republic was still in formation; the political economy of citizenship had not wholly given way to a political economy of economic growth and distributive justice. Nor had American politics and law yet embraced the assumption that government must be neutral among competing conceptions of the good life. Notwithstanding the growing prominence of the voluntarist conception of freedom, the notion that government has a role in shaping the moral and civic character of its citizens persisted in the discourse and practice of American public life. In the hands of the Progressives, the formative ideal of the republican tradition found new expression. For a few decades at least, Americans continued to debate economic policy not only from the standpoint of prosperity and fairness but also from the standpoint of self-government.

7

Community, Self-Government, and Progressive Reform

The voluntarist conception of freedom that emerged in the debate over wage labor came gradually to inform other aspects of American politics and law. In the course of the twentieth century, the notion that government should shape the moral and civic character of its citizens gave way to the notion that government should be neutral toward the values its citizens espouse, and respect each person's capacity to choose his or her own ends. In the decades following World War II, for example, the voluntarist ideal figured prominently in justifications for the welfare state and the judicial expansion of individual rights. Defenders of the welfare state typically argued that respecting people's capacity to choose their ends meant providing them with the material prerequisites of human dignity, such as food and shelter, education and employment. At the same time the courts expanded the rights of free speech, religious liberty, and privacy, often in the name of respecting people's capacities to choose their beliefs and attachments for themselves.

Despite its achievements, however, the public life informed by the voluntarist self-image was unable to fulfill the aspiration to self-government. Despite the expansion of individual rights and entitlements in recent decades, Americans find to their frustration that their control over the forces that govern their lives is receding rather than increasing. Even as the liberal self-image deepens its hold on American political and constitutional practice, there is a widespread sense that we are caught in the grip of impersonal structures of power that defy our understanding and control. The triumph of the voluntarist conception of freedom has coincided, paradoxically, with a growing sense of disempowerment.

This sense of disempowerment arises from the fact that the liberal self-image and the actual organization of modern social and economic life are sharply at odds. Even as we think and act as freely choosing, independent selves, we find ourselves implicated in a network of dependencies we did not choose and increasingly reject. This condition raises with renewed force the plausibility of republican concerns. The republican tradition taught that to be free is to share in governing a political community that controls its own fate. Self-government in this sense requires political communities that control their destinies, and citizens who identify sufficiently with those communities to think and act with a view to the common good.

Whether self-government in this sense is possible under modern conditions is at best an open question. In a world of global interdependence, even the most powerful nation-states are no longer the masters of their destiny. And in a pluralist society as diverse as the United States, it is far from clear that we identify sufficiently with the good of the whole to govern by a common good. Indeed the absence of a common life at the level of the nation motivates the drift to the procedural republic. If we cannot agree on morality or religion or ultimate ends, argue contemporary liberals, perhaps we can agree to disagree on terms that respect people's rights to choose their ends for themselves. The procedural republic thus seeks to realize the voluntarist conception of freedom and also to detach politics and law from substantive moral controversy.

But the discontent and frustration that beset contemporary American politics intimate the limits of the solution the procedural republic offers. The discontent that has gathered force in recent decades undoubtedly has a number of sources, among them the disappointed expectations of a generation that came of age at a time when America stood astride the world and when the domestic economy promised an ever-rising standard of living. As economic growth has slowed in recent decades, as global interdependence has complicated America's role in the world, as political institutions have proved incapable of solving such domestic ills as crime, poverty, drugs, and urban decay, the sense of mastery that prevailed in the 1950s and early 1960s has given way to a sense of paralysis and drift.

At another level, however, beyond these particular frustrations, the predicament of liberal democracy in contemporary America may be traced to a deficiency in the voluntarist self-image that underlies it. The sense of disempowerment that afflicts citizens of the procedural republic may reflect the loss of agency that results when liberty is detached from self-government and located in the will of an independent self, unencumbered by moral or communal ties it has not chosen. Such a self, liberated though it be from the burden of identities it has not chosen, entitled though it be to the range of rights assured by the welfare state, may nonetheless find itself overwhelmed as it turns to face the world on its own resources.

If American politics is to revitalize the civic strand of freedom, it must find a way to ask what economic arrangements are hospitable to self-government, and how the public life of a pluralist society might cultivate in citizens the expansive self-understandings that civic engagement requires. It must revive, in terms relevant to our time, the political economy of citizenship. If the reigning political agenda, focused as it is on economic growth and distributive justice, leaves little room for civic considerations, it may help to recall the way an earlier generation of Americans debated such questions, in a time before the procedural republic took form.

Confronting an Age of Organization

In the last decades of the nineteenth century and the first decades of the twentieth, Americans addressed these questions with clarity and force. For it was then that the freely choosing individual self first confronted the new age of organization, suddenly national in scope. "As the network of relations affecting men's lives each year become more tangled and more distended, Americans in a basic sense no longer knew who or where they were. The setting had altered beyond their power to understand it, and within an alien context they had lost themselves."[1]

Politicians and social commentators articulated the anxieties of a time when people's understanding of themselves no longer fit the social world they inhabited. They spoke of individuals liberated from traditional communities yet swamped by circumstance, bewildered by the scale of social and economic life. Woodrow Wilson, campaigning for the presidency in 1912, said, "There is a sense in which in our day the individual has been submerged." Most men now worked not for themselves or in partnership with others, but as employees of big corporations. Under such conditions, the individual was "swallowed up" by large organizations, "caught in a great confused nexus of all sorts of complicated circumstances," "helpless" in the face of vast structures of power. In the modern world, "the everyday relationships of men are largely with great impersonal concerns, with organizations, not with other individual men. Now this is nothing short of a new social age, a new era of human relationships."[2]

The philosopher John Dewey observed that the theory of the freely choosing individual self "was framed at just the time when the individual was counting for less in the direction of social affairs, at a time when mechanical forces and vast impersonal organizations were determining the frame of things." How did this paradoxical situation arise? According to Dewey, modern economic forces liberated the individual from traditional communal ties, and so encouraged voluntarist self-understandings, but at the same time disempowered individuals and local political units. The struggle for emancipation from traditional communities was mistakenly "identified with the liberty of the individual as such; in the intensity of the struggle, associations and institutions were condemned wholesale as foes of freedom save as they were products of personal agreement and voluntary choice."[3]

Meanwhile, mass suffrage reenforced the voluntarist self-image by making it appear as if citizens held the power "to shape social relations on the basis of individual volition. Popular franchise and majority rule afforded the imagination a picture of individuals in their untrammeled individual sovereignty making the state." But this too concealed a deeper, harder reality. The "spectacle of 'free men' going to the polls to determine by their personal volitions the political forms under which they should live" was an illusion. For the very technological and industrial forces that dissolved the hold of traditional communities formed a structure of power that governed people's lives in ways beyond the reach of individual choice or acts of consent. "Instead of the independent, self-moved individuals contemplated by the theory, we have standardized interchangeable units. Persons are joined together, not because they have voluntarily chosen to be united in these forms, but because vast currents are running which bring men together." The new economic structures were "so massive and extensive" that they, not individuals or political communities or even the state, determined the course of events.[4]

Then as now, the lack of fit between the way people conceived their identities and the way economic life was actually organized gave rise to fears for the prospect of self-government. The threat to self-government took two forms. One was the concentration of power amassed by giant corporations; the other was the erosion of traditional forms of authority and community that had governed the lives of most Americans through the first century of the republic. Taken together, these developments undermined the conditions that had made self-government possible. A national economy dominated by vast corporations diminished the autonomy of local communities, traditionally the site of self-government. Meanwhile, the growth of large, impersonal cities, teeming with immigrants, poverty, and disorder, led many to fear that Americans lacked sufficient moral and civic cohesiveness to govern according to a shared conception of the good life.

The crisis of self-government and the erosion of community were closely connected. Since Americans had traditionally exercised self-government as members of decentralized communities, they experienced the erosion of community as a loss of agency, a form of disempowerment. As Robert Wiebe has observed, "The great casualty of America's turmoil late in the century was the island community. Although a majority of Americans would still reside in relatively small, personal centers for several decades more, the society that had been premised upon the community's effective sovereignty, upon its capacity to manage affairs within its boundaries, no longer functioned. The precipitant of the crisis was a widespread loss of confidence in the powers of the community."[5]

With the loss of community came an acute sense of dislocation. In an impersonal world, men and women groped for bearings. As Americans "ranged farther and farther from their communities, they tried desperately to understand the larger world in terms of their small, familiar environment." Their failure to do so fueled a mood of anxiety and frustration. "We are unsettled to the very roots of our being," wrote Walter Lippmann in 1914. "There isn't a human relation, whether of parent and child, husband and wife, worker and employer, that doesn't move in a strange situation. We are not used to a complicated civilization, we don't know how to behave when personal contact and eternal authority have disappeared. There are no precedents to guide us, no wisdom that wasn't made for a simpler age. We have changed our environment more quickly than we know how to change ourselves." At the heart of the anxiety was people's inability to make sense of the world in which they found themselves. "The modern man is not yet settled in his world," Lippmann concluded. "It is strange to him, terrifying, alluring, and incomprehensibly big."[6]

Despite the dislocation they wrought, the new forms of industry, transportation, and communication seemed to offer a new, broader basis for political community. In many ways, Americans of the early twentieth century were more closely connected than ever before. Railroads spanned the continent. The telephone, telegraph, and daily newspaper brought people into contact with events in distant places. And a complex industrial system connected people in a vast scheme of interdependence that coordinated their labors. Some saw in the new industrial and technological interdependence a more expansive form of community. "Steam has given us electricity and has made the nation a neighborhood," wrote William Allen White. "The electric wire, the iron pipe, the street railroad, the daily newspaper, the telephone, the lines of transcontinental traffic by rail and water . . . have made us all of one body—socially, industrially, politically. . . . It is possible for all men to understand one another."[7]

More sober observers were not so sure. That Americans found themselves implicated in a complex scheme of interdependence did not guarantee that they would identify with that scheme or come to share a common life with the unknown others who were similarly implicated. As the social reformer Jane Addams observed, "Theoretically, 'the division of labor' makes men more interdependent and human by drawing them together into a unity of purpose." But whether this unity of purpose is achieved depends on whether the participants take pride in their common project and regard it as their own; "the mere mechanical fact of interdependence amounts to nothing."[8]

The sociologist Charles Cooley agreed: "Although the individual, in a merely mechanical sense, is part of a wider whole than ever before, he has often lost that conscious membership in the whole upon which his human breadth depends: unless the larger life is a moral life, he gains nothing in this regard, and may lose." Moreover, in virtue of its scale, the modern industrial system actually undermines the common identity of those whose activities it coordinates. "The workman, the man of business, the farmer and the lawyer are contributors to the whole, but being morally isolated by the very magnitude of the system, the whole does not commonly live in their thought." Although new means of communication and transportation supplied "the mechanical basis" for a more extended social solidarity, it was at best an open question whether this larger commonality would be achieved. "The vast structure of industry and commerce remains, for the most part, unhumanized, and whether it proves a real good or not depends upon our success or failure in making it vital, conscious, moral."[9]

The growing gap between the scale of economic life and the terms of collective identity led social thinkers of the day to emphasize the distinction between cooperation and community. The industrial system was a cooperative scheme in the sense that it coordinated the efforts of many individuals; but unless the individuals took an interest in the whole and regarded its activity as an expression of their identity, it did not constitute a genuine community. "Men do not form a community, in our present restricted sense of that word, merely in so far as the men cooperate," wrote the philosopher Josiah Royce in 1913. "They form a community . . . when they not only cooperate, but accompany this cooperation with that ideal extension of the lives of individuals whereby each cooperating member says: 'This activity which we perform together, this work of ours, its past, its future, its sequence, its order, its sense,—all these enter into my life, and are the life of my own self writ large.'"[10]

Notwithstanding the interdependence it fostered, the modern industrial system was unlikely, Royce thought, to inspire the identification necessary to constitute a common life: "there is a strong mutual opposition between the social tendencies which secure cooperation on a vast scale, and the very conditions which so interest the individual in the common life of his community that it forms part of his own ideally extended life." Given its scale, few could comprehend much less embrace as their own the complex scheme in which they were enmeshed.

"Most individuals, in most of their work, have to cooperate as the cogs cooperate in the wheels of a mechanism."[11]

In a similar vein, John Dewey argued that "no amount of aggregated collective action of itself constitutes a community." To the contrary, modern industry and technology bound men together in an impersonal form of collective action that dismantled traditional communities without replacing them: "The Great Society created by steam and electricity may be a society, but it is no community. The invasion of the community by the new and relatively impersonal and mechanical modes of combined human behavior is the outstanding fact of modern life." More than a fact, it was also a predicament, for "the machine age in developing the Great Society has invaded and partially disintegrated the small communities of former times without generating a Great Community."[12]

For Dewey, the loss of community was not simply the loss of communal sentiments, such as fraternity and fellow feeling. It was also the loss of the common identity and shared public life necessary to self-government. American democracy had traditionally "developed out of genuine community life" based in local centers and small towns. With the advent of the Great Society came the "eclipse of the public," the loss of a public realm within which men and women could deliberate about their common destiny. According to Dewey, democracy awaited the recovery of the public, which depended in turn on forging a common life to match the scale of the modern economy. "Till the Great Society is converted into a Great Community, the Public will remain in eclipse."[13]

Progressive Reform: The Formative Ambition

Broadly speaking, the erosion of community and the threat to self-government around the turn of the century called forth two kinds of response from Progressive reformers—one procedural, the other formative. The first tried to render government less dependent on virtue among the people by shifting decision-making to professional managers, administrators, and experts. Municipal reformers sought to avoid the corruption of urban party bosses by instituting city government by nonpartisan commissioners and city managers.[14] Educational reformers sought to "take schools out of politics" by shifting authority from local citizens to professional administrators.[15] In general, Progressives looked to social science and bureaucratic techniques to accommodate and adjust the conflicting demands of modern social life. Scientists and experts, they hoped, "would constitute a neutral bar before whom people of differing outlooks could bring their conflicts, and by whose verdicts they would willingly be bound. Professionals armed with scientific method would thus make it possible to dispense with the conflict and uncertainty that had always characterized the political realm."[16]

In their attempts to detach governance from politics and to regulate competing interests by means of neutral, bureaucratic techniques, Progressive reformers gestured toward the version of liberalism that would inform the procedural republic. But even as they sought to lessen the need for government to rely on virtue among the people, Progressives retained the formative ambition of the republican tradition and sought new ways to elevate the moral and civic character of citizens. This was especially true of their various projects for urban reform. As Paul Boyer explains, the goal of Progressive reformers "was to create in the city the kind of physical environment that would gently but irresistibly mold a population of cultivated, moral, and socially responsible citizens."[17]

The struggle against urban graft and municipal corruption was not only for the sake of honest, efficient government but also for the sake of elevating the moral tone of the city and setting a proper example for new immigrants. The movement for tenement reform aimed not only at doing justice for the poor and relieving their physical suffering but also at uplifting the moral and civic character of slum dwellers. "[T]he physical conditions under which these people live lessen their power of resisting evil," stated one tenement study. Another observed that "citizens of the right type cannot be made from children who sleep in dark, windowless rooms, in dwellings much overcrowded, where privacy is unknown."[18]

Following the example of nineteenth-century landscape architect Frederick Law Olmsted, Progressive advocates of municipal parks made their case in moral terms. They argued that parks would not only enhance the beauty of the city but also promote a spirit of neighborliness among city dwellers and combat the tendency to moral degradation.[19] Similarly, the playground movement of the Progressive years had higher ambitions than providing recreation for children of the city; its aim was no less than "manufacturing good and sturdy citizenship." According to its advocates, the city playground, with its sandboxes, swings, and playing fields, "would be the womb from which a new urban citizenry—moral, industrious, and socially responsible—would emerge." As one of its champions declared, the playground could instill "more ethics and good citizenship . . . in a single week than can be inculcated by Sunday school teachers . . . in a decade."[20]

Joseph Lee, a leader of the playground movement, explained how team sports could inculcate in children "the sheer experience of citizenship in its simplest and essential form—of the sharing in a public consciousness, of having the social organization present as a controlling ideal in your heart." Play would serve as a "school of the citizen" by teaching the way in which genuine community goes beyond mere cooperation to shape the identity of the participants: "the team is not only an extension of the player's consciousness; it is a part of his personality. His participation has deepened from cooperation to membership. Not only is he now a part of the team, but the team is a part of him."[21]

A more ephemeral expression of the Progressives' formative ambition was the historical pageant, a civic spectacle that employed drama, music, and dance to depict the history of cities to their citizens. Communities across America mounted such spectacles. The largest was a pageant in St. Louis in 1914, which included a cast of 7,000 and drew audiences of 100,000 on each of four successive spring nights. Conceived as more than entertainment, such civic dramas sought to inspire among urban residents a sense of common citizenship and shared purpose. "As the first strains of melody . . . floated upon the vast audience on that rare May evening," wrote the chairman of the St. Louis pageant, "there came over all the sense of sanctified citizenship, of interest and confidence in neighbor, of pride in the city."[22]

The city planning movement of the Progressive years also reflected the attempt to elevate the moral and civic character of citizens. Domes, fountains, statues, and public architecture would serve the didactic function of inspiring civic pride and improving the moral tone of urban life. The real significance of city planning, explained a New York City official, was its "powerful influence for good upon the mental and moral development of the people." Daniel H. Burnham, Chicago's leading city planner and civic architect, argued that municipal structures should express the priority of the public good over private interests. "[G]ood citizenship," he asserted, "is the prime object of good city planning."[23] One of the most prominent public sculptures of the Progressive era was the mythic monument Civic Virtue, installed in the park facing New York's City Hall.[24]

Progressive Political Economy

Beyond the schemes of urban reform and moral uplift lay broader questions of political economy: Could democracy survive in an economy dominated by large corporations? With the "island community" in decline, what new forms of social solidarity could equip men and women to govern the vast world in which they lived? How, in short, might Americans heal the gap between the scale of modern economic life and the terms in which they conceived their identities?

Political debate in the Progressive era focused on two answers to these questions. Some sought to preserve self-government by decentralizing economic power and rendering it amenable to democratic control. Others considered economic concentration irreversible and sought to control it by enlarging the capacity of national democratic institutions.

The Decentralist Vision

The decentralizing strand of Progressivism found its ablest advocate in Louis D. Brandeis, who before his appointment to the Supreme Court was an activist attorney and outspoken critic of industrial concentration. Brandeis' primary concern was with the civic consequences of economic arrangements. He opposed monopolies and trusts, not because their market power led to higher consumer prices but because their political power undermined democratic government.

In Brandeis' view, big business threatened self-government in two ways—directly, by overwhelming democratic institutions and defying their control, and indirectly, by eroding the moral and civic capacities that equip workers to think and act as citizens. Both in his fear of concentrated power and in his concern for the formative consequences of industrial capitalism, Brandeis brought long-standing republican themes into twentieth-century debate. Like Jefferson and Jackson, he viewed concentrated power, whether economic or political, as inimical to liberty. The trusts were not the product of natural economic forces, Brandeis argued, but rather the result of favorable laws and financial manipulation. The solution was not to confront big business with big government—that would only compound "the curse of bigness"—but to break up the trusts and restore competition. Government should not try to regulate monopoly but should regulate competition to protect independent businesses from the predatory practices of monopolies and national chains. Only in this way would it be possible to sustain genuine competition and preserve a decentralized economy of locally based enterprises amenable to democratic control.[25]

Beyond the direct dangers to democracy of concentrated power, Brandeis worried about the adverse effects of industrial capitalism on the moral and civic character of workers. Like the free labor republicans of the nineteenth century, Brandeis considered industrial wage labor a form of dependence analogous to slavery. Workers in the steel industry, for example, led "a life so inhuman as to make our former Negro slavery infinitely preferable, for the master owned the slave, and tried to keep his property in working order for his own interest. The Steel Trust, on the other hand, looks on its slaves as something to be worked out and thrown aside." The results were "physical and moral degeneracy" and the corruption of American citizenship.[26]

Brandeis retained the republican conviction that free labor is not labor voluntarily undertaken in exchange for a wage, but labor carried out under conditions that cultivate the qualities of character essential to self-government. By this standard, American industrial workers could not be considered free: "Can any man be really free who is constantly in danger of becoming dependent for mere subsistence upon somebody and something else than his own exertion and conduct?" According to Brandeis, the contradiction between "our grand political liberty and this industrial slavery" could not persist for long: "Either political liberty will be extinguished or industrial liberty must be restored."[27]

For Brandeis, industrial liberty could not be achieved through shorter hours, higher wages, and better working conditions alone. Nor was it a matter of making wage labor more genuinely voluntary, through collective bargaining, or gaining for workers a greater share of the fruits of their labor, through profit sharing. Sympathetic though he was to all these reforms, Brandeis' primary concern was neither to perfect consent nor to secure distributive justice, but to form citizens capable of self-government. This formative, civic purpose could be achieved only by industrial democracy, in which workers participated in management and shared responsibility for running the business.[28]

The recognition of unions moved capital-labor relations one step beyond "industrial despotism" to a kind of "constitutional monarchy" that at least limited "the employer's formerly autocratic power." Profit sharing was a further improvement. But "full-grown industrial democracy" required a sharing of responsibility as well as of profits. "In order that collective bargaining should result in industrial democracy it must go further and create practically an industrial government," in which workers had a voice and a vote on issues of management just as citizens of a political democracy had a voice and a vote on issues of public policy.[29]

Brandeis favored industrial democracy, not for the sake of improving workers' incomes, desirable though that was, but for the sake of improving their civic capacities: "Unrest, to my mind, never can be removed—and fortunately never can be removed—by mere improvement of the physical and material condition of the workingman. . . . We must bear in mind all the time, that however much we may desire material improvement and must desire it for the comfort of the individual, that the United States is a democracy, and that we must have, above all things, men. It is the development of manhood to which any industrial and social system should be directed." For Brandeis, the formation of citizens capable of self-government was an end even higher than distributive justice. "We Americans are committed not only to social justice in the sense of avoiding . . . [an] unjust distribution of wealth; but we are committed primarily to democracy." The "striving for democracy" was inseparable from a "striving for the development of men. It is absolutely essential in order that men may develop that they be properly fed and properly housed, and that they have proper opportunities of education and recreation. We cannot reach our goal without those things. But we may have all those things and have a nation of slaves."[30]

In Brandeis' view, industrial democracy could not take root in giant corporations. "As long as there is such concentration of power no effort of the workingmen to secure democratization will be effective."[31] In line with the tradition of republican political economy, Brandeis sought to decentralize economic power, partly for the sake of restoring democratic control and also for the sake of cultivating worker-citizens capable of sharing in self-government.

Like Brandeis, Woodrow Wilson saw in the concentrated power of the trusts a threat to democracy. His "New Freedom" promised to diminish the power of monopoly over government and to restore the conditions of economic independence that had formed the basis of liberty in nineteenth-century America. From his first meeting with Brandeis in the summer of 1912, Wilson campaigned for the presidency urging that, rather than regulate monopoly as Theodore Roosevelt proposed, government should seek to restore and regulate competition.[32]

But Wilson was not an unwavering adherent of Brandeis' teaching. Unlike his counsellor, he sought to distinguish between trusts, which grew by artificial means and destroyed competition, and those big businesses that attained their size "naturally," as a result of effective competition. "I am for big business," Wilson declared, "I am against the trusts." But this distinction did not fit well with Wilson's more general argument, and he did not always observe it. Wilson's primary case against monopoly was that it frustrated democratic politics and undermined the qualities of character self-government requires. From this standpoint, what mattered were the size and power of giant corporations, not their origins. "The organization of business has become more centralized," Wilson asserted, "vastly more centralized, than the political organization of the country itself. Corporations have come to cover greater areas than states . . . have [exceeded] states in their budgets and loomed bigger than whole commonwealths in their influence over the lives and fortunes of entire communities of men. . . . What we have got to do is to disentangle this colossal 'community of interest.'"[33]

So powerful were the forces of monopoly that it was "almost an open question whether the government of the United States with the people back of it is strong enough to overcome and rule them." Wilson urged Americans to wrest the democratic prerogative from monopoly power: "If monopoly persists, monopoly will always sit at the helm of government. . . . If there are men in this country big enough to own the government of the United States, they are going to own it; what we have to determine now is whether we are big enough, whether we are men enough, whether we are free enough, to take possession again of the government which is our own. We haven't had free access to it, our minds have not touched it by way of guidance, in half a generation."[34]

His opponent, Theodore Roosevelt, proposed accepting and regulating monopoly power. Wilson attacked this course as a kind of capitulation. "We have been dreading all along the time when the combined power of high finance would be greater than the power of the government," Wilson argued. "Have we come to a time when the President of the United States or any man who wishes to be the President must doff his cap in the presence of this high finance, and say, 'You are our inevitable master, but we will see how we can make the best of it'?"[35]

Beyond the direct threat that monopoly posed to democratic government, Wilson also worried about the effects of large-scale capitalism on the moral and civic character of Americans. An economy dominated by large corporations disempowered local communities and discouraged the independence, initiative, and enterprise that equipped citizens for self-government. Although he did not display Brandeis' enthusiasm for industrial democracy, Wilson faulted the modern economy for reducing most men to the status of employee, which he did not consider wholly compatible with liberty. To this extent, he shared the formative concerns of republican political economy. "In most parts of our country," Wilson lamented, "men work, not for themselves, not as partners in the old way in which they used to work, but generally as employees . . . of great corporations." But to be "the servant of a corporation" was to "have no voice" in the policies set by a powerful few, policies often at odds with the public interest.[36]

Wilson's sympathies were with "men who are on the make rather than the men who are already made." He evoked memories of a time when most Americans were not voiceless servants of big corporations but independent laborers or entrepreneurs. That was a time before the concentration of power in vast economic units, a "time when America lay in every hamlet, when America was to be seen in every fair valley, when America displayed her great forces on the broad prairies, ran her fine fires of enterprise up over the mountainsides and down into the bowels of the earth, and eager men were everywhere captains of industry, not employees; not looking to a distant city to find out what they might do, but looking about among their neighbors, finding credit according to their character, not according to their connections."[37]

Wilson rejected the idea that a nation of employees was adequate to liberty. If America's future children "open their eyes in a country where they must be employees or nothing . . . then they will see an America such as the founders of this Republic would have wept to think of." For Wilson, restoring liberty meant restoring a decentralized economy that bred independent citizens and enabled local communities to be masters of their destinies rather than victims of economic forces beyond their control. "In all that I may have to do in public affairs in the United States I am going to think of towns . . . of the old American pattern, that own and operate their own industries. . . . My thought is going to be bent upon the multiplication of towns of that kind and the prevention of the concentration of industry in this country in such a fashion and upon such a scale that towns that own themselves will be impossible."[38]

According to Wilson, the vitality of America lay not in New York or Chicago or other great cities, but in "the enterprise of the people throughout the land," nourished by small-scale, self-sufficient "free American communities." As those communities lost control of their economic destinies to large corporations, American liberty was imperiled. "[I]f America discourages the locality, the community, the self-contained town," Wilson warned, "she will kill the nation."[39] Decentralizing economic power was essential to preserving the communities that cultivated the virtues self-government required.

The Nationalist Vision

Another branch of the Progressive movement offered a different response to the threat posed by corporate power. Rather than decentralize the economy to render it amenable to democratic control by local political units, Theodore Roosevelt proposed a "New Nationalism" to regulate big business by increasing the capacity of the national government. "Big business has become nationalized," Roosevelt declared in 1910, "and the only effective way of controlling and directing it and preventing the abuses in connection with it is by having the people nationalize the governmental control in order to meet the nationalization of the big business itself."[40]

Like Brandeis and Wilson, Roosevelt feared the political consequences of concentrated economic power. Big business corrupted government for the sake of profit and threatened to overwhelm democratic institutions. "The supreme political task of our day," Roosevelt proclaimed, "is to drive the special interests out of our public life." This task required that the citizens of the United States "control the mighty commercial forces which they have themselves called into being," and reclaim self-government from the grip of corporate power. "The corporation is the creature of the people; and it must not be allowed to become the ruler of the people."[41]

Where Roosevelt disagreed with the decentralizers was over how to restore democratic control. He considered big business an inevitable product of industrial development, and saw little point in trying to recover the decentralized political economy of the nineteenth century. Those Progressives who sought to restore a competitive economy of small units represented "a kind of rural toryism, which wishes to attempt the impossible task of returning to the economic conditions that obtained sixty years ago." They failed to recognize the necessity of industrial concentration and the need to "meet it by a corresponding increase in governmental power over big business."[42]

"Combinations in industry are the result of an imperative economic law," Roosevelt argued, "which cannot be repealed by political legislation. The effort at prohibiting all combination has substantially failed. The way out lies, not in attempting to prevent such combinations, but in completely controlling them in the interest of the public welfare." Since most big corporations operated in interstate or foreign commerce, beyond the reach of individual states, only the federal government was suited to the task of controlling them. The power of the national government had to grow to match the scale of corporate power.[43]

In its embrace of consolidated power, Roosevelt's "New Nationalism" marked a break with republican political thought. The republican tradition had taught Americans to fear concentrated power, whether economic or political, as hostile to liberty. From Jefferson to Brandeis, the political economy of citizenship in its various expressions had opposed the drift to bigness. Now Roosevelt argued that an economy of scale was here to stay, and that the only way to reclaim democratic control was to abandon the republican impulse to disperse power. Under modern economic conditions, dispersed power no longer served the cause of self-government: "People speak as if it were an innovation to nationalize control by the government of big business. The innovation came on the part of the business men who nationalized the businesses. All we wish to do on behalf of the people is to meet the nationalization of the big business by nationalized government control."[44]

But even as the New Nationalism renounced the decentralizing aspect of the republican tradition, it adhered to the formative aspect. Like republicans since the day of Jefferson, Roosevelt worried about the civic consequences of economic arrangements and sought to cultivate in citizens the qualities of character essential to self-government. Roosevelt's aim was not only to reduce the domination of government by big business, but also to enlarge the self-understandings of American citizens, to instill what he called "a genuine and permanent moral awakening," "a spirit of broad and far-reaching nationalism."[45] More than a program of institutional reform, the New Nationalism was a formative project that sought to cultivate a new sense of national citizenship.

For Roosevelt, Progressive politics was emphatically an enterprise of moral uplift. "The prime problem of our nation is to get the right type of good citizenship," he asserted. Democratic government could not be indifferent to the virtue of its people. "In a democracy like ours we cannot expect the stream to rise higher than its source. If the average man and the average woman are not of the right type, your public men will not be of the right type."[46]

Roosevelt sometimes identified the civic virtue he hoped to inspire with the strenuous dedication to duty displayed by those who fought the Civil War.[47] On other occasions, he spoke more modestly of the "homely virtues" of honesty, courage, and common sense, and the political virtues of knowing one's duties and performing them.[48] But the primary object of Roosevelt's soulcraft was to persuade his fellow citizens to rise above the material preoccupations that threatened to distract them from nobler ends. "If there is one thing which we should wish as a Nation to avoid, it is the teaching of those who would reenforce the lower promptings of our hearts, and so teach us to seek only a life of effortless ease, of mere material comfort."[49]

In his fear of luxury's power to corrupt the soul of the citizen, Roosevelt expressed a long-standing theme of republican political economy: "Material development means nothing to a nation as an end in itself. If America is to stand simply for the accumulation of what tells for comfort and luxury, then it will stand for little indeed when looked at through the vistas of the ages." Only if America treated material abundance "as the foundation on which to build the real life, the life of spiritual and moral effort and achievement," would it stand for something worth remembering. "Material well-being is a great good, but it is a great good chiefly as a means for the upbuilding upon it of a high and fine type of character, private and public."[50]

As Roosevelt was the leading spokesman for the New Nationalism, Herbert Croly was its leading philosopher. In *The Promise of American Life* (1909), Croly laid out the political theory underlying the nationalist strand of Progressivism. Unlike Brandeis and the decentralizers, Croly argued for accepting the scale of modern industrial organization and for enlarging the capacity of national democratic institutions to control it. The Jeffersonian tradition of dispersed power was now a hindrance, not a help to democratic politics. Given "the increasing concentration of American industrial, political, and social life," American government "demands more rather than less centralization." But according to Croly, the success of democracy required more than the centralization of government; it also required the nationalization of politics. The primary form of political community had to be recast on a national scale.[51]

"The nationalizing of American political, economic, and social life means something more than Federal centralization," Croly explained. It also meant inspiring in citizens a new sense of national identity, or fashioning the people "into more of a nation." This was the way to ease the gap, so acutely felt in the Progressive era, between the scale of American life and the terms of American identity. Given the national scale of the modern economy, democracy required "an increasing nationalization of the

American people in ideas, in institutions, and in spirit." An intensification of the national life would serve democracy by cultivating citizens capable of governing an economy and society now national in scale.[52]

Although Croly renounced Jefferson's notion that democracy depends on dispersed power, he shared Jefferson's conviction that economic and political arrangements should be judged by the qualities of character they promote. Repeatedly and explicitly, Croly wrote of the "formative purpose" of democratic life. More than a scheme for majority rule or individual liberty or equal rights, democracy had as its highest purpose the moral and civic improvement of the people. "Its superiority must be based upon the fact that democracy is the best possible translation into political and social terms of an authoritative and comprehensive moral idea." For Croly, the project of nationalizing the American character was "an essentially formative and enlightening political transformation." Its aim was "the gradual creation of a higher type of individual and associated life."[53]

American democracy could advance only as the nation became more of a nation, which required in turn a civic education that inspired in Americans a deeper sense of national identity. The primary instruments of this civic education were not schools as such but the institutions and practices of a national democratic life. "The national school is . . . the national life." "The nation, like the individual, must go to school; and the national school is not a lecture hall or a library," but a democratic life that aimed at a collective purpose.[54]

Far from the liberalism of the procedural republic, which seeks not to promote any particular conception of virtue or moral excellence, Croly's democratic nationalism rested on the conviction that "human nature can be raised to a higher level by an improvement in institutions and laws." The point of democracy was not to cater to people's desires but to elevate their character, broaden their sympathies, and enlarge their civic spirit. "For better or worse," Croly concluded, "democracy cannot be disentangled from an aspiration toward human perfectibility. . . . The principle of democracy is virtue."[55]

The decentralizing and the nationalizing versions of progressive reform found memorable expression in the 1912 contest between Woodrow Wilson and Theodore Roosevelt.[56] "For the only time except perhaps for

Jefferson's first election in 1800," a historian has observed, "a presidential campaign aired questions that verged on political philosophy."[57] From the standpoint of subsequent developments, however, the greater significance of the 1912 campaign lay in the assumptions the protagonists shared. Wilson and Brandeis on one side, and Croly and Roosevelt on the other, agreed despite their differences that economic and political institutions should be assessed for their tendency to promote or erode the moral qualities self-government requires. Like Jefferson before them, they worried about the sort of citizens the economic arrangements of their day were likely to produce. They argued, in different ways, for a political economy of citizenship.

The civic emphasis of their political economy sets it apart from debates familiar in our day, which focus instead on economic growth and distributive justice. This contrast can be seen more clearly in the light of a third strand of Progressive reform. For alongside the civic arguments of the decentralizers and nationalizers, a new way of thinking and talking about political economy was beginning to take shape. Although it found only tentative expression in the Progressive era, this third strand of argument would eventually set the terms of American political debate. The third voice of Progressive reform sought democracy's salvation in a different, less strenuous solidarity. It encouraged Americans to confront the impersonal world of big business and centralized markets, not as members of traditional communities or as bearers of a new nationalism, but rather as enlightened, empowered consumers.

The Consumerist Vision

As Americans struggled to find their way in an economy now national in scale, some sought a basis of shared identity and common purpose that could transcend differences of occupation, ethnicity, and class. They sought "a mundane common denominator," a "new ideology of social solidarity rooted in common experience." The common experience they appealed to was the experience of consumption.[58]

Turn-of-the-century Wisconsin Progressives, for example, based their movement on the notion that "all men and women are, after all, consumers—of high prices, defective products, and unresponsive politicians; their roles as consumers forced them to make common cause." Rather than emphasize producer-based issues, such as industrial democracy, these Progressives focused on problems that confronted people as consumers and taxpayers, such as high streetcar fares, high taxes imposed by corrupt politicians, and air pollution from the utility's power station. The reforms they advocated sought to promote the interests of consumers and taxpayers through various forms of direct democracy—direct primaries, initiative, referendum, recall, direct election of senators, and women's suffrage. Their overall aim was "a new mass politics that united men as consumers and taxpayers in opposition to the old politics that was based on ethnic and producer identities."[59]

By the early twentieth century, the citizen as consumer was a growing political presence. "[T]he real power emerging today in democratic politics is just the mass of people who are crying out against the 'high cost of living,'" wrote Walter Lippmann in 1914. "That is a consumer's cry. Far from being an impotent one, it is, I believe, destined to be stronger than the interest either of labor or of capital." Lippmann predicted that women's suffrage would increase the power of the consumer, since "[t]he mass of women do not look at the world as workers, [but] as consumers. It is they who go to market and do the shopping; it is they who have to make the family budget go around; it is they who feel shabbiness and fraud and high prices most directly." The growth of large retail organizations such as department stores, chain stores, and mail-order businesses also encouraged Americans to think and act politically as consumers. Just as large-scale production made possible the solidarity of workers, centralized retail markets made possible "the solidarity of the consumer."[60]

Lippmann did not embrace the consumer society with "unmixed joy." He deplored modern advertising as a "deceptive clamor that disfigures the scenery, covers fences, plasters the city, and blinks and winks at you through the night," evidence of the fact "that consumers are a fickle and superstitious mob, incapable of any real judgment as to what it wants." But he predicted that the consumer would nevertheless become "the real master of the political situation."[61]

Not all would share Lippmann's reservations. The historian Daniel Boorstin has chronicled the advent of "consumption communities" in almost lyrical terms, depicting their emergence in the early decades of the century as a new and buoyant episode in the American democratic experience: "Invisible new communities were created and preserved by how and what men consumed. The ancient guilds of makers, the fellowship of secrets and skills and traditions of fabricating things—muskets and cloth and horseshoes and wagons and cabinets—were outreached by the larger, more open, fellowships of consumers. . . . No American transformation was more remarkable than these new American ways of changing things from objects of possession and envy into vehicles of community."[62]

Chain stores such as A & P, Woolworth's, and Walgreen's, mail-order houses such as Montgomery Ward and Sears, and brand names such as Borden's, Campbell's, Del Monte, and Morton's salt bound countless Americans together in new communities of consumption: "Now men were affiliated less by what they believed than by what they consumed. . . . Men who never saw or knew one another were held together by their common use of objects so similar that they could not be distinguished even by their owners. These consumption communities were quick; they were nonideological; they were democratic; they were public, and vague, and rapidly shifting. . . . Never before had so many men been united by so many things." Boorstin acknowledged that "[t]he new consumption communities were . . . shallower in their loyalties, more superficial in their services" than traditional neighborhood communities. But they were nonetheless "ubiquitous, somehow touching the American consumer at every waking moment and even while he slept."[63]

The fullest statement of the consumer-based vision of Progressive reform was Walter Weyl's *New Democracy* (1912).[64] Weyl, an economist and journalist, joined with Croly and Lippmann as a founding editor of the *New Republic* and helped promote the Progressive cause championed by Theodore Roosevelt.[65] Like Croly, he sought a new, democratic solidarity to confront the undemocratic power of big business, "the plutocracy," as Weyl called it. But instead of seeking a new nationalism, Weyl saw democracy's best hope in the solidarity of consumers. Where earlier reform movements had grown out of Americans' producer identities (as farmers or artisans, small businessmen or industrial workers), reform now required rallying Americans in their role as consumers.

"In America today the unifying economic force, about which a majority, hostile to the plutocracy, is forming, is the common interest of the citizen as a consumer," Weyl declared. "The producer (who is only the consumer in another role) is highly differentiated. He is banker, lawyer, soldier, tailor, farmer, shoeblack, messenger boy. He is capitalist, workman, money lender, money borrower, urban worker, rural worker. The consumer, on the other hand, is undifferentiated. All men, women, and children who buy shoes (except only the shoe manufacturer) are interested in cheap good shoes. The consumers of most articles are overwhelmingly superior in numbers to the producers."[66]

In the past, "production seemed to be the sole governing economic fact of a man's life." People worried more about wages than about prices, and so acted politically primarily as producers. This led to policies, such as the tariff, that helped the few at the expense of the many. But the growth of monopoly capitalism diminished workers' direct interest in their product, even as it heightened their concern with rising prices. "The universality of the rise of prices has begun to affect the consumer as though he were attacked by a million gnats." According to Weyl, "[t]he chief offense of the trust" lay not in its threat to self-government, but in its "capacity to injure the consumer." This led to hope of rallying consumers to the cause of Progressive reform. "[T]he consumer, disinterred from his grave, reappears in the political arena as the 'common man,' the 'plain people,' the 'strap-hanger,' 'the man on the street,' 'the taxpayer,' the 'ultimate consumer.' Men who voted as producers are now voting as consumers."[67]

But the shift from producer-based reform to consumer-based reform was more than a new way of organizing interests. It reflected a shift in the aim of reform and in the vision of democracy underlying it. In the republican tradition of political economy that informed nineteenth-century American debate, producer identities mattered because the world of work was seen as the arena in which, for better or worse, the character of citizens was formed. Consumption, when it figured at all in republican political economy, was a thing to be moderated, disciplined, or restrained for the sake of higher ends.[68] An excess of consumption, or luxury, was often seen as a form of corruption, a measure of the loss of civic virtue. From Jefferson's agrarian republicanism to Lincoln's celebration of free labor to Brandeis' call for industrial democracy, the emphasis on producer identities reflected the attempt to form in citizens the qualities of character necessary to self-government.

A politics based on consumer identities, by contrast, changes the question. Instead of asking how to elevate or improve or restrain people's preferences, it asks how best—most fully, or fairly, or efficiently—to satisfy them. The shift to consumer-based reform in the twentieth century was thus a shift away from the formative ambition of the republican tradition, away from the political economy of citizenship. Although they did not view their movement in quite this way, the Progressives who urged Americans to identify with their roles as consumers rather than producers helped turn American politics toward a political economy of growth and distributive justice whose full expression lay decades in the future.

Weyl did not explicitly renounce the civic tradition, but he did articulate, with remarkable clarity, the link between consumer-based reform and a political economy of growth and distributive justice. Where Brandeis and Croly spoke of democracy's formative purpose, of its role in perfecting or uplifting the character of citizens, Weyl's "new democracy" undertook no formative mission. Its aim was not virtue but economic abundance and the fair distribution of abundance. The point of democracy was not to cultivate the virtue of citizens but to achieve "the widest range of economic satisfactions."[69]

"It is the increasing wealth of America," wrote Weyl, "upon which the hope of a full democracy must be based." It is economic growth, or the "social surplus," that "gives to our democratic strivings a moral impulse and a moral sanction." Weyl did not claim that maximizing national wealth was an end in itself. To the contrary, the problem with the existing pattern of economic growth was its unequal distribution. "What the people want is not wealth, but distributed wealth; not a statistical increase in the national income, but more economic satisfactions, more widely distributed."[70]

Weyl's case for a wider distribution of wealth rested on two arguments, one utilitarian, the other voluntarist, or contractarian. The utilitarian argument held that a more equal distribution would produce a higher level of overall happiness, since an extra dollar to a poor person means more than an extra dollar to a rich person. "A million dollars of commodities consumed by one overrich man gives less pleasure than would the same sum added to the expenditure of ten thousand people." Where the distribution of income and wealth is highly unequal, economic growth does not necessarily increase the general welfare; given the exploitation on which the plutocracy's prosperity is built, an increase in wealth may even decrease the general welfare. "A nearer approach to an equality of wealth and income would undoubtedly mean a vast increase in the sum total of economic satisfactions."[71]

Weyl's second argument concerned the economic prerequisites of genuine consent, especially in labor contracts. Like other labor reformers and Progressives of his day, Weyl attacked the laissez-faire orthodoxy advanced by industrialists and enforced by the *Lochner*-era courts, and did so in the name of a voluntarist conception of freedom. The new democracy would insist "on a real, economic (as well as a legal) equality between bargainers; upon a real, economic (as well as a legal) freedom." Genuine consent required a "social interpretation of rights." "A law forbidding a woman to work in the textile mills at night is a law increasing rather than restricting her liberty, simply because it takes from the employer his former right to compel her through sheer economic pressure to work at night when she would prefer to work by day."[72]

Like other reformers, Weyl argued for a progressive income tax, public spending on education, health, and other social programs, and government regulation to improve industrial working conditions. But unlike Brandeis and Croly, he argued for these reforms on terms that left the political economy of citizenship behind.

More than Brandeis or Croly, Weyl was a prophet of the procedural republic. Their democratic visions retained contact with the formative ambition of the republican tradition and with the civic conception of freedom as self-government. Thus Brandeis insisted that democracy was "possible only where the process of perfecting the individual is pursued," and Croly held that democracy "must stand or fall on a platform of possible human perfectibility." Weyl disagreed. The "new democracy" for which he spoke sought not to perfect the people or to cultivate civic virtue but rather to achieve "the widest range of economic satisfactions."[73] He argued not in the name of self-government but instead in the name of utility, fairness, and a more genuine consent than the market economy, left to its own devices, makes possible. By detaching the Progressive cause from its formative ambition and basing it instead on fair treatment for the citizen-consumer, Weyl gestured toward a political economy of growth and distributive justice that, later in the century, would set the terms of political debate.

From Citizenship to Consumer Welfare

The transition from a political economy of citizenship to one premised on consumer welfare can be seen in the fate of two attempts, one well-known, the other scarcely remembered, to curb "the curse of bigness." The first, the antitrust movement, began over a century ago and remains an instrument of public policy to this day. The second, the anti–chain store movement, provoked a flurry of legislation and debate in the 1920s and 1930s, then quickly died out. Both movements arose, at least in part, to preserve self-government by protecting local communities and independent producers from the effects of massive concentrations of economic power.

As civic considerations faded and consumerist ones became more prominent in American political economy, antitrust law survived by assuming a new function; once a way of decentralizing power for the sake of self-government, it became a way of regulating the market for the sake of competitive consumer prices. Anti–chain store laws, by contrast, displayed no similar flexibility. Unable to demonstrate their service to consumer welfare, their fate was tied to the hope that independent grocers, druggists, and shopkeepers might carry republican ideals into the twentieth century. As that hope faded, the demise of the anti-chain store movement intimated the demise of the civic strand of economic argument itself.

Anti–Chain Store Legislation

In the years following World War I, the growth of chain stores revolutionized the way Americans bought commodities. It also threatened the role of independent retailers across the land. By 1929, chains accounted for one-fifth of all retail sales and 40 percent of all grocery sales. Beginning in the late 1920s, state legislatures sought to restrict the growth of chain stores, primarily by imposing taxes that increased according to the number of stores a chain operated within the state. In Indiana, for example, chains were assessed $3 for the first store, with the rate rising to $150 for each store over twenty. In 1935 Texas levied a tax of $750 for each store over fifty, a considerable sum at a time when the average net profit per store for grocery chains was only $950.[74]

Many of the laws were struck down by state courts, but in 1931 the U.S. Supreme Court upheld a challenge to a chain store tax.[75] The favorable ruling by the Court, together with the growing economic distress on independents brought on by the Depression, quickened the pace of the movement. In 1933 some 225 chain store tax bills were proposed across the country, and 13 were enacted. By the end of the decade, more than half the states had passed some form of tax on chain stores.[76]

Opponents of the chain store system often cast their arguments in republican terms. In a series of radio broadcasts, Montaville Flowers, an antichain publicist, argued that the chain system was "contrary to the whole genius of the American people and American Government, which is local self-control of affairs." The chain store threatened self-government by producing great concentrations of economic power, destroying local communities, and undermining the status of independent shopkeepers and small businessmen. Independent retailers such as the local pharmacist traditionally served communities as leading citizens of "intelligence and character." But the chains reduced the pharmacist to a "drug clerk" beholden to a distant corporation, and so deprived the community of a trusted figure. In a similar way, the chain system "deprives hundreds of thousands of good citizens of their means of livelihood, reduces them from a status of independence to that of hirelings under humiliating regulations, thus . . . lowering the spirit of communities and the nation."[77]

While the chains reduced their employees to "cogs in big wheels," Flowers declared, independent stores stood for the free labor ideal, preserving "the open field of opportunity, the equal chance for their employees to go into business for themselves according to the blessed traditions of our country." The chains also threatened agrarian republican ideals: "The deadliest blights that ever befell the farm are the catalogues of Sears-Roebuck and Montgomery-Ward!" Farmers were fools to buy goods from the catalogues of chains, "for every time you do this you are destroying what independence you have left and binding tighter upon you the burdens of your serfdom!"[78]

Leading politicians also worried about the civic consequences of the chain store system and feared for the fate of local communities. "A wild craze for efficiency in production, sale, and distribution has swept over the land, increasing the number of unemployed, building up a caste system, dangerous to any government," said Senator Hugo L. Black of Alabama, who would later serve on the U.S. Supreme Court. "Chain groceries, chain dry-goods stores, chain clothing stores, here today and merged tomorrow—grow in size and power. . . . The local man and merchant is passing and his community loses his contribution to local affairs as an independent thinker and executive."[79]

When, in the case of *Liggett Company v. Lee* (1933), the U.S. Supreme Court struck down a portion of a Florida chain store tax law, Justice Brandeis offered an eloquent dissent that summarized the republican case against chain stores. The citizens of Florida, he reasoned, had taxed the chains not only to raise revenue but also to help independent retailers. "They may have done so merely in order to preserve competition. But their purpose may have been a broader and deeper one. They may have believed that the chain store, by furthering the concentration of wealth and of power and by promoting absentee ownership, is thwarting American ideals; that it is making impossible equality of opportunity; that it is converting independent tradesmen into clerks; and that it is sapping the resources, the vigor and the hope of the smaller cities and towns." This, Brandeis maintained, was a legitimate constitutional purpose.[80]

Many believed, Brandeis observed, that the inequality of wealth and power bred by giant corporations posed a threat to self-government, and that "only through participation by the many in the responsibilities and determinations of business can Americans secure the moral and intellectual development which is essential to the maintenance of liberty." If the citizens of Florida shared that belief, there was nothing in the Constitution to prevent them from acting on it by imposing taxes on chain stores. "To that extent," Brandeis concluded, "the citizens of each state are still masters of their destiny."[81]

The chain stores and their defenders addressed the republican arguments of their opponents but cast their main arguments in terms of consumer welfare. The notion that independent retailers embodied republican virtue was, they argued, a piece of sentimentality that did not fit the facts. Far from being a pillar of the community, the typical shopkeeper was "a dirty, illiterate, short-sighted, half-Americanized foreigner, or a sleepy, narrow-minded, dead-from-the-neck-up American," according to a writer for a chain store publication. The head of J. C. Penney observed that even as Americans romanticized "the old isolated corner store" they did their shopping at chains. Much as we might "like to go back to Uncle Henry's store and swap stories with Henry and the other idlers around the stove," few would be "willing to pay for such idleness as a tax on all the goods our family buys." Walter Lippmann also found little to mourn in the passing of the neighborhood store: "Six grocers in three blocks, dingy little butcher-shops, little retail businesses with the family living in the back room, the odor of cooking to greet you as you enter the door, fly-specks on the goods"—these were hardly conditions worth trying to preserve.[82]

As for their record of service to local communities, the chains admitted to an initial neglect that they pledged promptly to remedy. A 1931 debate manual published by the National Chain Store Association acknow-ledged that in the "pioneer stages of their development," chains "may have been a little lax in cooperating with local enterprises and community welfare," and "neglected to some degree their social responsibilities and public relations." But the chains were now avid participants in local chambers of commerce, contributors to the Community Chest, and sup-porters of the Boy Scouts and the Red Cross. They too could be good citizens.[83]

But even as the chains tried to demonstrate their good citizenship, their spokesmen argued that the true measure of the chain store's worth lay elsewhere—in its contribution to the welfare of consumers. Its primary justification was not civic but utilitarian: "what is best for the majority of the people constitutes the greatest good to the greatest number in their daily economic life." If chains "give to the consuming public better goods at lower prices, then no individual or class of individuals, no matter how their personal interests may be hurt, have the right to harass, criticize or attempt to destroy such an agency for good."[84]

All the debates about the civic role of chains—in building or damaging local communities, in increasing or reducing prospects for employment and opportunity—concerned "secondary functions of a store." Here the shift from civic to consumerist considerations found unapologetic expression. The "first duty, the largest community responsibility of a retail store," stated a chain store publication, was to benefit consumers. This was the simple fact that critics of chain stores forgot. "For to listen to them you would think that a store was only incidentally and in a sort of unimportant way, an establishment for the sale of commodities at retail prices, and that the main business of a store was to contribute to charity and build sidewalks and public meeting halls, and solve the unemployment problem." But this "belittled" the main function of a store, which was not to serve a civic purpose but to maximize the welfare of consumers by selling good products at low prices, a function "the chains are fulfilling . . . to the hilt."[85]

By the late 1930s the chain stores had successfully rallied to oppose the laws, mounting lobbying efforts and public relations campaigns and enlisting the support of consumers, farmers, and organized labor. The A & P helped defeat a 1936 California referendum calling for a chain tax by buying up a surplus crop of California produce and keeping agriculture prices high. A series of collective bargaining agreements a few years later brought labor's support to the chains. The chains suffered a temporary setback when Congress passed the Robinson-Patman Act of 1936, which restricted their ability to buy merchandise at reduced prices from wholesalers. But a 1938 proposal by Representative Wright Patman to enact a federal chain tax failed, and by the end of the decade the antichain movement had expired. While local grocers and druggists had presented themselves, not wholly convincingly, as the yeomen of their day, the last bearers of republican virtue, the chains stood instead for good products at low prices. In the face of these alternatives, the political economy of citizenship was losing its capacity to inspire.[86]

The Antitrust Movement

Antitrust law, by contrast, enjoyed a longer career, under shifting ideological auspices. Born of the political economy of citizenship, it lived on in the service of the political economy of growth and distributive justice that, by the mid-twentieth century, was ascendant. To be sure, both the civic and the consumer-oriented objections to monopoly were present from the start. Americans opposed economic concentration out of concern for self-government, and also out of fear of the high prices monopolies could extract from consumers.

Some recent commentators, opposed to the political purposes of antitrust law, have claimed that the Sherman Act was concerned solely with economic efficiency and consumer welfare.[87] But the congressional debates themselves and the broader terms of economic argument around the turn of the century suggest otherwise. When Congress debated the Sherman Antitrust Act in 1890, it sought both to protect the consumer from monopoly pricing and to preserve the decentralized economy of small businesses and trades long seen as essential to self-government. More than a matter of economic efficiency or consumer welfare, the antitrust movement reflected "the political judgment of a nation whose leaders had always shown a keen awareness of the economic foundations of politics. In this respect, the Sherman Act was simply another manifestation of an enduring American suspicion of concentrated power."[88]

For Senator John Sherman and his colleagues, the law banning combinations in restraint of trade "constituted an important means of achieving freedom from corruption and maintaining freedom of independent thinking political life, a treasured cornerstone of democratic government."[89] Sherman attacked the trusts for cheating consumers by artificially driving up prices, and also for amassing unaccountable power that threatened democratic government. The concentrated power of the trusts amounted to "a kingly prerogative, inconsistent with our form of government, and should be subject to the strong resistance of the State and national authorities. If anything is wrong this is wrong. If we will not endure a king as a political power we should not endure a king over the production, transportation, and sale of any of the necessaries of life."[90]

As Richard Hofstadter observed, "the political impulse behind the Sherman Act was clearer and more articulate than the economic theory. Men who used the vaguest language when they talked about 'the trusts' and monopolies . . . who had found no way of showing how much competition was necessary for efficiency, who could not in every case say what competitive acts they thought were fair or unfair . . . were reasonably clear about what it was that they were trying to avoid: they wanted to keep concentrated private power from destroying democratic government."[91]

Along with the direct threat posed by big corporations to democratic government, antitrust advocates worried about the indirect effects, on the moral and civic character of citizens. When reformers spoke of preserving competition, their concern was not only, or even primarily, with consumer prices, but rather with an economy of small, independent producers and with the qualities of character—of enterprise, initiative, and responsibility—that this system ideally called forth. Henry A. Stimson, a clergyman writing in 1904, called small business "a school of character second in importance only to the Church." The advent of the great corporations and trusts had brought prosperity but also a damaging "effect upon the character of many employees, who, under former conditions, would have been either managing their own business or ambitious for the opportunity of doing so." The republican tradition had long worried that a nation of hirelings and clerks could not cultivate the independence and judgment necessary to self-government. Now Stimson wondered, along similar lines, how even the corporations would manage to develop the leadership they required. Such positions "require men who have been accustomed to that independence of action and that breadth of view which only the responsibility of directing their own affairs can produce. It is a temper of mind and of spirit as far as possible from that of the lifelong clerk or employee."[92]

In a speech to a national conference on trusts in 1899, Hazen S. Pingree, governor of Michigan, denounced the trusts for their corrupting effect "upon our national life, upon our citizenship, and upon the lives and characters of the men and women who are the real strength of our republic." The strength of the republic had always resided in "the independent, individual business man and the skilled artisan and mechanic." But the trust concentrated ownership and management of business into the hands of the few, forcing once independent entrepreneurs and tradesmen to become employees of large corporations. "Their personal identity is lost. They become cogs and little wheels in a great complicated machine. . . . They may perhaps become larger cogs or larger wheels, but they can never look forward to a life of business freedom."[93]

Drawing still on the civic conception of freedom that animated the free labor ideal, Pingree accused the trust of creating "industrial slavery." The master was the director of the trust, the slave "the former merchant and business man, and the artisan and mechanic, who once cherished the hope that they might sometime reach the happy position of independent ownership of a business." Even the prosperity the trusts might bring could not justify such moral and civic degradation. "I care more for the independence and manliness of the American citizen," Pingree concluded, "than for all the gold or silver on or in the world. . . . A democratic republic cannot survive the disappearance of a democratic population."[94]

A subsequent speaker, whose defense of the trusts brought vehement protest from the audience, challenged the producer ethic espoused by Pingree and offered a glimpse of a consumerist ethic whose widespread acceptance lay several decades in the future. For George Gunton, a labor leader turned professor, the case for the trusts rested simply on their service to the public welfare, which consisted in turn of low prices for consumers and good wages for workers. By this measure, the hated Standard Oil Company, Carnegie Steel Company, and the great railroads were resounding successes. Thanks to their capital investments and economies of scale, Gunton argued, they produced better goods at lower prices than small businesses could ever have offered.[95]

As for the effect of corporations on the conditions of labor, Gunton declared bluntly that "[t]he laborer's freedom and individuality depend upon two things—permanence of employment and good wages. Wherever the employment of labor is most permanent and wages are highest, there the laborer is most intelligent, has the greatest freedom and the strongest individual identity." In a bold reversal of the free labor ethic, Gunton argued that big business made better citizens than small business. Thanks to the security of employment in large corporations, "it is there where the laborers are most independent. It is notorious that large corporations have the least influence over the opinions and individual conduct of their laborers." The small businessman, by contrast, "who does not know from quarter to quarter . . . whether he can meet his obligations, is neither as brave, as intelligent nor as free a citizen as the wage laborer in the safe employ of a large corporation." The producer ethic that bade laborers stand with independent producers against the trusts was misguided: "The laborer has not a single interest, social, economic or political, in the existence of employers with small capital."[96]

The framers of the Sherman Act left to the courts the task of defining its broad prohibition of contracts and combinations in restraint of trade, and the first decade of the law brought little enforcement.[97] In 1897, however, the Supreme Court did apply the act against a railroad rate-fixing cartel. In one of the first major antitrust opinions, Justice Rufus Wheeler Peckham held that the Sherman Act banned price-fixing even where it did not result in excessive or unreasonable prices. Even if it did not harm consumers, such price-fixing could force small, independent producers out of business, and the antitrust laws protected them too. Price-fixing that reduced consumer prices might nonetheless "[drive] out of business the small dealers and worthy men whose lives have been spent therein, and who might be unable to readjust themselves to their altered surroundings. Mere reduction in the price of the commodity dealt in might be dearly paid for by the ruin of such a class, and the absorption of control over one commodity by an all-powerful combination of capital."[98]

Robert Bork has recently argued that Peckham's mention of small producers was an unfortunate "slip" or "lapse" in an opinion otherwise concerned with maximizing consumer welfare.[99] But Peckham's opinion goes on to explain the importance of small producers in terms reminiscent of the free labor ideal. The passing from the scene of "a large number of small but independent dealers" was not only disruptive to them and their families but also a loss to the country as a whole. For even if the small businessmen displaced by big corporations could find new ways of making a living, "it is not for the real prosperity of any country that such changes should occur which result in transferring an independent business man, the head of his establishment, small though it might be, into a mere servant or agent of a corporation for selling the commodities which he once manufactured or dealt in, having no voice in shaping the business policy of the company and bound to obey orders issued by others." The loss of an independent class of producers was a civic loss not measurable in terms of consumer welfare alone.[100]

The Progressive era brought renewed energy to the antitrust movement, whose most articulate and influential spokesman in those years was Louis D. Brandeis. Unlike antitrust reformers of our day, such as consumer advocate Ralph Nader, Brandeis did not oppose the trusts in the name of the consumer. He was less concerned with lowering consumer prices than with preserving an economy of small, independent producers. Brandeis' emphasis on small producers rather than consumers as the victims of monopoly has led one critic to suggest that Brandeis should be remembered not as the "People's Lawyer" but as "the mouthpiece for retail druggists, small shoe manufacturers, and other members of the petite bourgeoisie."[101] More than a matter of special pleading, however, Brandeis' concern for the fate of small producers reflected a long tradition of republican political thought. From Jefferson to the Knights of Labor, the political economy of citizenship had sought to form the moral and civic character of Americans in their role as producers—as farmers, or artisans, or small businessmen and entrepreneurs. Brandeis' producer ethic retained this link with republican assumptions. He championed the cause of small, independent producers, not for their own sake but for the sake of preserving a decentralized economy hospitable to self-government.[102]

Of course, Brandeis did not altogether ignore arguments of economic efficiency and consumer welfare. When defenders of big business argued that trusts brought economies of scale that reduced waste and increased the efficiency of production, Brandeis replied that size often diminished efficiency. Beyond a certain point, large institutions developed a centrifugal force that defied human understanding and control.[103] "If the Lord had intended things to be big, he would have made man bigger—in brains and character."[104] As evidence of the inefficiency of size, Brandeis pointed to many attempted trusts—in the whiskey, cordage, malting, paper, leather, and steamship trades—that had either failed or met with little success. Those trusts that had succeeded—in the oil, tobacco, sugar, and steel industries—had done so not through superior efficiency but through monopoly control of markets or price-fixing. "I am so firmly convinced that the large unit is not as efficient . . . as the smaller unit," Brandeis told a Senate committee, "that I believe that if it were possible today to make the corporations act in accordance with what doubtless all of us would agree should be the rules of trade no huge corporation would be created, or if created, would be successful." Under conditions of fair competition, "these monsters would fall to the ground."[105]

But Brandeis' primary argument against the trusts looked beyond economics to considerations of self-government. Even if it could be shown that they were more efficient than small units, monopolies posed a threat to democracy that outweighed any economic benefits they might bring. Brandeis rejected the notion that bigness itself is no offense, for he believed "that our society, which rests upon democracy, cannot endure under such conditions. . . . You cannot have true American citizenship, you cannot preserve political liberty, you cannot secure American standards of living unless some degree of industrial liberty accompanies it. And the United States Steel Corporation and these other trusts have stabbed industrial liberty in the back." Some defended monopoly by pointing to the wastefulness of competition. "Undoubtedly competition involves some waste," Brandeis replied. "What human activity does not? The wastes of democracy are among the greatest obvious wastes, but we have compensations in democracy which far outweigh that waste and make it more efficient than absolutism. So it is with competition."[106]

Brandeis' distance from the consumer-oriented reform movements of our day can best be seen in his defense of resale price maintenance, a practice by which manufacturers set a retail price for their product that no distributor may discount. In 1911 the Supreme Court ruled that Dr. Miles Medical Company, which manufactured a patent medicine, could not enter into contracts with its wholesale and retail dealers requiring them to sell the patented elixir for a minimum specified price. Such agreements, the Court held, were an illegal restraint of trade under the Sherman Act. Brandeis disagreed and mounted a campaign to persuade Congress to exempt resale price maintenance contracts from antitrust restrictions. He argued that uniform retail prices of brand-name products helped protect small retailers from price-cutting by the chain stores, department stores, and mail-order houses, and so promoted a competitive economy. Banning price maintenance would enable big retailers to drive small ones out of business.[107]

Brandeis explained the benefits of price maintenance using the example of the Gillette safety razor. If Gillette could fix the retail price of its razor, no dealer could sell the item at a discount; in this sense, competition would be reduced. But as a result of the fixed price, a great many retailers, large and small, could sell Gillette razors; in this broader sense, competition would be enhanced. "Every dealer, every small stationer, every small druggist, every small hardware man, can be made a purveyor of that article . . . and you have stimulated, through the fixed price, the little man as against the department store, and as against the large unit which may otherwise monopolize that trade."[108]

For those concerned solely with consumer prices, price competition is more desirable than preserving a competitive economy in Brandeis' sense of a decentralized economy of many small producers. But for Brandeis, consumer prices were not everything. Consumers who thought so were hopelessly short-sighted. Instead of chasing after small discounts offered by price cutters, consumers would do better to buy through consumer cooperatives, to "look with suspicion upon every advertised article," and to "start a buyers' strike at any rise in price of any staple article of common consumption." The unorganized consumer, concerned only with price, was "servile, self-indulgent, indolent, ignorant," and foolishly played into the hands of monopoly. "Thoughtless or weak, he yields to the temptation of trifling immediate gain, and, selling his birthright for a mess of pottage, becomes himself an instrument of monopoly."[109]

In any event, price maintenance raised issues more important even than consumer welfare rightly understood. For according to Brandeis, the ability of manufacturers to set uniform prices made possible the decentralized economy of small, independent producers essential to democracy itself. "[T]he prohibition of price-maintenance imposes upon the small and independent producers a serious handicap," wrote Brandeis in a widely publicized article called "Cut-Throat Prices: The Competition That Kills." Prevented from setting prices through contracts with distributors, manufactures would be apt to combine with chains, cutting out small retailers. "The process of exterminating the small independent retailer already hard pressed by capitalistic combinations—the mail-order houses, existing chains of stores and the large department stores—would be greatly accelerated by such a movement. Already the displacement of the small independent business man by the huge corporation with its myriad of employees, its absentee ownership and its financier control presents a grave danger to democracy."[110]

Brandeis' campaign to exempt price maintenance agreements from antitrust law did not succeed, although Congress eventually enacted such legislation in the Miller-Tydings Fair Trade Act of 1937. The culmination of the Progressive era's antitrust movement came in 1914, with passage of the Clayton Act, which tightened restrictions on uncompetitive practices, and the establishment of the Federal Trade Commission, an administrative agency charged with investigating and regulating "unfair methods of competition." After 1914, antitrust sentiment waned. From World War I until the late New Deal, enforcement was less than vigorous, and hostility to big business figured less prominently in political debate. Massive mergers of the late 1920s increased the trend toward consolidation but did not provoke the popular protest of earlier years. The onset of the Depression brought some calls for antitrust action, but the New Deal at first suspended the antitrust laws to experiment with the government-backed cartels and price codes of the National Recovery Administration.[111]

The late 1930s brought a dramatic revival of antitrust sentiment and activism. Prompted partly by the failure of the NRA and partly by the recession of 1937, Franklin Roosevelt asked Congress in 1938 to increase funding for antitrust enforcement and to appropriate $500,000 for a comprehensive study of the concentration of economic power in American industry. In the message accompanying these requests, Roosevelt drew on both the civic and the consumer welfare strands of argument against monopoly. Invoking the civic objection, he declared that "the liberty of a democracy is not safe if the people tolerate the growth of private power to a point where it becomes stronger than their democratic state itself." At the same time, he voiced concern for the effects of monopoly on employment, distributive justice, and "the buying power of the nation as a whole."[112]

In the same year, Roosevelt appointed Thurman Arnold, a Yale law professor, to head the Antitrust Division of the Justice Department. Arnold seemed to some an unlikely choice for the post, since he had written with some sarcasm of the antitrust movement. In *The Folklore of Capitalism*, a book published in the year before his appointment, Arnold described the antitrust laws as empty rituals, "great moral gestures" that absorbed the energy of reformers but did little to slow the trend toward bigness. He ridiculed the notion that it was possible to reverse the age of organization and return to a decentralized economy of small units: "Men like Senator Borah founded political careers on the continuance of such crusades, which were entirely futile but enormously picturesque." Meanwhile, "by virtue of the very crusade against them, the great corporations grew bigger and bigger, and more and more respectable." Despite his provocative writings, Arnold was confirmed by the Senate, although Senator Borah advised him at his nomination hearing "to revise that chapter on trusts."[113]

Notwithstanding Arnold's disdain for crusades against bigness, his tenure proved to be the most vigorous period of antitrust enforcement in the nation's history. Under Theodore Roosevelt, the celebrated "trust-buster," the Antitrust Division of the Justice Department had "sallied out against the combined might of the great corporations with a staff of five lawyers and four stenographers." Largely dormant through the 1920s and early 1930s, the Antitrust Division was a mere "corporal's guard" when Arnold took office. During his first year he increased the number of lawyers from 58 to more than 100 and substantially increased the number of antitrust cases. From the adoption of the Sherman Act to 1938, the government filed an average of nine antitrust prosecutions per year; in 1940 alone, Arnold filed eighty-five. Among his cases were highly publicized actions against the dairy industry, the building and construction industry, the motion picture industry, the American Medical Association, tire manufacturers, and the fertilizer, petroleum, newsprint, billboard, typewriter, and transportation industries. By the time he left the Justice Department in 1943, Arnold "had filed (and won) more antitrust cases than the Justice Department had initiated in its entire previous history."[114]

On the surface, Arnold's unprecedented success in antitrust enforcement might seem strangely at odds with his well-known antipathy toward the movement to curb "the curse of bigness." Upon closer inspection, however, the apparent inconsistency dissolves. For Arnold's great revival of antitrust law was a revival with a difference. Unlike antimonopolists in the tradition of Brandeis, Arnold sought not to decentralize the economy for the sake of self-government but to regulate the economy for the sake of lower consumer prices. For Arnold, the purpose of antitrust law was to promote economic efficiency, not to combat the concentration of power as such. Arnold's revival of antitrust thus marked a shift in the aim of antitrust and in the political theory underlying it. For Brandeis, antitrust was an expression of the political economy of citizenship, concerned with preserving an economy of small, independent producers. For Arnold, antitrust had nothing to do with the producer ethic of the republican tradition; its purpose was to serve the welfare of consumers.[115]

Arnold was explicit about this shift of purpose. In the past, he wrote, most assumed that the antitrust laws were "designed to eliminate *the evil of bigness*. What ought to be emphasized is not the evils of size but the evils of industries which are not efficient or do not pass efficiency on to consumers. If the antitrust laws are simply an expression of a religion which condemns largeness as economic sin they will be regarded as an anachronism in a machine age. If, however, they are directed at making distribution more efficient, they will begin to make sense."[116]

For forty years, Arnold observed, Americans had debated whether big organizations were good things or bad things. But "[t]hat debate is like arguing whether tall buildings are better than low ones, or big pieces of coal better than small ones." Such questions had no meaning except in relation to some purpose, and according to Arnold, the only purpose of economic organization was the efficient production and distribution of goods. The republican tradition had attributed to economics a broader moral and political purpose, and the early advocates of antitrust, true to this tradition, had assessed economic arrangements for their tendency to form citizens capable of self-government. Arnold dismissed this "old religion" as a sentimental notion out of place in an age of mass production. He was the first major antitrust advocate to reject altogether the civic argument for antitrust and to insist exclusively on the consumerist one: "there is only one sensible test which we can apply to the privilege of [large] organization, and that is this: Does it increase the efficiency of production or distribution and pass the savings on to consumers?"[117]

Once considerations of citizenship were left behind, concentrated power was no longer objectionable as such, apart from its effect on consumer welfare. "[C]onsumers never can be convinced that size in itself is an evil. They know that the automobile they ride in could not be produced except by a large organization. They remember the time when glasses and dishes and hammers and all the things that are now sold at the ten-cent store at low prices were luxuries. They know that this efficiency in distribution could not have been accomplished without mass production and mass distribution. Consumers are unwilling to lose the advantages of a machine age because of sentimental attachment to the ideal of little business." Americans should be enlisted to support antitrust enforcement, Arnold insisted, not out of hatred of big business but out of interest in "the price of pork chops, bread, spectacles, drugs, and plumbing."[118]

Arnold revived and transformed antitrust at the very time the anti–chain store movement, its onetime political and ideological companion, was fading into oblivion. In Arnold's hands, antitrust won its place as an established legal and political institution by renouncing the small-producer ethic that had called it forth and promising instead to reduce "the price of pork chops." But beyond securing the place of antitrust in American politics and law, the shift from the civic to the consumerist ethic contained a larger significance. Though not apparent at the time, it intimated a broader change in the way Americans would think about economics and politics through the rest of the century.

Unlike republican political economy, which seeks to form in citizens the habits and dispositions that equip them for self-government, a political economy premised on consumer welfare takes people's preferences as they come; it abandons the formative ambition of the republican tradition and seeks economic arrangements that enable people to satisfy their preferences as fully and fairly as possible. Arnold's antitrust took up this new stance. Concerned as it was with the welfare of consumers, it shed the old formative ambition and attended instead to productivity and prices. In the passage from Brandeis' vision of antitrust to Arnold's can be glimpsed America's passage from the political economy of citizenship to a political economy of growth and distributive justice, from a republican public philosophy to the version of liberalism that informs the procedural republic.

Notwithstanding the growing prominence of consumer-based arguments for antitrust, the civic argument did not die out all at once or altogether. The political economy of citizenship would continue to find voice in antitrust debates, but after the 1940s and 1950s it increasingly became a minor voice, a residual expression. In a 1945 case declaring illegal Alcoa's monopoly in the aluminum industry, Judge Learned Hand recalled the formative aims of the early antitrust laws: "It is possible, because of its indirect social or moral effect, to prefer a system of small producers, each dependent for his success upon his own skill and character, to one in which the great mass of those engaged must accept the direction of a few." Hand observed that, beyond the economic reasons for forbidding monopoly, "there are others, based upon the belief that great industrial consolidations are inherently undesirable, regardless of their economic results." Among the purposes of the Sherman Act, he wrote, "was a desire to put an end to great aggregations of capital because of the helplessness of the individual before them."[119]

In 1950 Senator Estes Kefauver, sponsor of a law to tighten restrictions on mergers and acquisitions, argued that economic concentration disempowered citizens by depriving them of control over their economic and political destiny. "Local economic independence cannot be preserved in the face of consolidations such as we have had during the past few years. The control of American business is steadily being transferred, I am sorry to have to say, from local communities to a few large cities in which central managers decide the policies and the fate of the far-flung enterprises they control. Millions of people depend helplessly on their judgment. Through monopolistic mergers the people are losing power to direct their own economic welfare. When they lose the power to direct their economic welfare they also lose the means to direct their political future."[120]

Two years later, when the Senate debated legislation to protect resale price maintenance, or "fair trade laws," from judicial invalidation, Senator Hubert Humphrey offered one of the last sustained statements of the civic argument for a decentralized economy. Humphrey began by denying that such laws led to higher consumer prices. But even if they did, he argued, they would be justified for the sake of preserving the small, independent producers on whom American democracy depended: "We are not necessarily talking about whether some penny-pinching person is going to be able to save half a cent on a loaf of bread. We are talking about the kind of America we want. Do we want an America where, on the highways and byways, all we have is catalog houses? Do we want an America where the economic market place is filled with a few Frankensteins and giants? Or do we want an America where there are thousands upon thousands of small entrepreneurs, independent businessmen, and landholders who can stand on their own feet and talk back to their Government or to anyone else." The family-size farm, like the family pharmacy and hardware store, was important to preserve, not because it was more economical than the large corporation, but because it "produces good citizens, and good citizens are the only hope of freedom and democracy. So we pay a price for it. I am willing to pay that price."[121]

For a time, the civic strand of argument found continued expression in the courts. In 1962 the Supreme Court cited Kefauver's argument on behalf of small business and local control of industry in preventing the merger of two shoe companies. Chief Justice Earl Warren, writing for the Court, conceded that antitrust law protects "competition, not competitors." "But we cannot fail to recognize Congress' desire to promote competition through the protection of viable, small, locally owned businesses," he added. "Congress appreciated that occasional higher costs and prices might result from the maintenance of fragmented industries and markets. It resolved these competing considerations in favor of decentralization."[122]

A few years later the Court blocked the merger of two Los Angeles grocery chains on similar grounds, despite the fact that their combined market share was only 7.5 percent.[123] And in a 1973 case challenging an acquisition in the brewing industry, Justice William O. Douglas invoked Brandeis' civic argument against concentrated power: "Control of American business is being transferred from local communities to distant cities where men on the 54th floor with only balance sheets and profit and loss statements before them decide the fate of communities with which they have little or no relationship." Douglas offered as an example the case of Goldendale, a once-thriving community in his home state of Washington. Soon after an out-of-state giant bought a locally owned sawmill, "auditors in faraway New York City, who never knew the glories of Goldendale, decided to close the local mill and truck all the logs to Yakima. Goldendale became greatly crippled." Douglas cited the fate of Goldendale as "Exhibit A to the Brandeis concern" with the disempowering effects of monopoly on local communities. "A nation of clerks is anathema to the American antitrust dream."[124]

But these statements of the civic case for antitrust were increasingly the exception. By the 1970s and 1980s, the "antitrust dream" of a decentralized economy sustaining self-governing communities had given way to the more mundane mission of maximizing consumer welfare. The leading modern treatise of antitrust law, published in 1978, states that despite occasional judicial suggestions to the contrary, the courts have given economic efficiency priority over such "populist" goals as decentralizing the economy. "Size alone is no offense." There is "little if anything in the cases that suggests the courts have in fact been willing to pursue populist goals at the expense of competition and efficiency."[125]

For those who would look to antitrust as a promising vehicle for the political economy of citizenship in our time, the authors of the treatise offer a sobering suggestion to the contrary. It is now difficult to imagine a thoroughgoing reversal of the trend toward industrial concentration under way for at least a century. Under the circumstances, the "undeviating pursuit of wealth dispersion and small size at the expense of efficiency would be so unacceptably costly that it is out of the question." We are by now too enamored of the fruits of consumption, too far down the path of economic concentration to speak realistically of restoring an economy sufficiently dispersed to vindicate the civic ideals for which Brandeis spoke. As a practical matter, "antitrust policy is simply not going to sacrifice consumer welfare to the point of guaranteeing a very large number of producers in every market." Given that fact, it is doubtful that any tinkering around the edges could have sufficient effect on the structure of the economy to realize any meaningful gains to self-government. Given the distance we have traveled, any "plausibly acceptable interference" with existing market structures would be quite modest and "unlikely to increase power dispersion very much or to affect political life in any noticeable way. The arbitrary preservation of a few firms here or there cannot contribute significantly to the dispersion of power or to the protection of political democracy."[126]

Some such realization may underlie the fact that by the 1970s conservatives and liberals, despite their differences, shared the premise that the main purpose of antitrust policy was to promote the welfare of consumers. Robert H. Bork, a conservative legal scholar later nominated by Ronald Reagan to the Supreme Court and defeated by the Senate, wrote in 1978 that "the only legitimate goal of American antitrust law is the maximization of consumer welfare," not the "survival or comfort of small business." Bork deemed the political purpose of antitrust espoused by Brandeis and a few misguided judges "a jumble of half-digested notions and mythologies," unfounded in the law and dubious on their merits. "There is no persuasive evidence that a middle-level corporate executive is socially or politically a less desirable creature than he would be if he ran his own business." According to Bork, concern with local control and the protection of small business is an "ancient and disreputable" theory of antitrust whose enforcement would exact high costs in economic efficiency and consumer welfare.[127]

But the focus on consumerist arguments was not restricted to conservatives such as Bork. It was also found among liberal reformers such as Ralph Nader, who favored a more activist antitrust policy. Although Nader and his followers did not disparage, as did Bork, the civic tradition of antitrust, they too rested their arguments on considerations of consumer welfare. A progressive in the pro-consumer tradition of Weyl and Arnold, Nader's concern was with "citizen-consumers," not citizen-producers. According to Nader, the "modern relevance" of traditional antitrust wisdom lay in its consequences for "the prices people pay for their bread, gasoline, auto parts, prescription drugs, and houses." Mark Green, another consumer advocate, wrote that, properly focused on "pocketbook losses by consumers," the antitrust issue "becomes radically modern: Can a competitive marketplace give consumers their money's worth?" Although some may emphasize the social and political costs of corporate bigness, "the primary assumptions of antitrust enforcement" should be "efficient production and distribution—not the local farmer, local druggist, or local grocer."[128]

The widespread assumption that antitrust policy should promote consumer welfare did not of course mean the end of political controversy over antitrust. Most antitrust debate in the 1980s reflected competing conceptions of consumer welfare. For conservatives, consumer welfare and economic efficiency were one and the same; promoting consumer welfare meant maximizing total economic output, regardless of whether efficiency gains "trickled down" in the form of lower consumer prices or simply led to higher corporate profits. As Bork wrote, "consumer welfare ... is merely another term for the wealth of the nation. Antitrust thus has a built-in preference for material prosperity, but it has nothing to say about the ways prosperity is distributed or used."[129]

Liberals, on the other hand, were concerned not only with total output but also with distributive effects and issues of fairness; for them, promoting consumer welfare meant lowering consumer prices and improving product quality and safety. These different conceptions of consumer welfare led conservatives to favor less government intervention in the market, liberals more.

The Reagan administration, in line with the conservative view, sharply reduced antitrust enforcement of mergers and takeovers. William Baxter, the first head of the Reagan administration's Antitrust Division, declared: "The only goal of antitrust is economic efficiency." His successor, Charles Rule, stated that antitrust law should not insist that efficiency gains be passed on to consumers, since "it is not necessarily clear whether the consumer or the producer is more worthy of the surplus." Increased corporate profits may, after all, benefit "the proverbial widows and orphans" who are shareholders of the company. But Rule acknowledged that in the conservative conception of consumer welfare, distributive effects were of no concern anyway; it made no difference whether efficiency gains went to widows and orphans or to Wall Street tycoons: "The consumer welfare standard of the antitrust laws . . . looks to the total size of the economic pie . . . not merely to the size of the individual pieces."[130]

Liberals, including consumer advocates and some Democrats in Congress, replied that antitrust law should be concerned not only with maximizing total wealth but with preventing unfair transfers of wealth from consumers to firms with market power. They were concerned not only with the size of the economic pie but also with the way the pieces were distributed.[131] In some cases monopolies, by limiting output and raising prices, produce inefficiencies that actually reduce total output. In other cases they produce efficiency gains that boost corporate profits without lowering consumer prices. This leads to "large aggregate economic growth without commensurate growth in consumer value."[132] Liberals emphasized this "transfer cost" of monopoly: "When consumers pay excessive prices, income from the consuming public is redistributed to the shareholders of particular corporations." The conservatives' claim that widows and orphans and other ordinary Americans may be among the beneficiaries of higher corporate profits ignores the fact that the vast majority of corporate stock is actually owned by a tiny fraction of the wealthiest Americans.[133]

These competing views of consumer welfare led in the 1980s to a debate over retail price-fixing that illustrated how radically the terms of antitrust debate had changed. The issue of retail price-fixing, or resale price maintenance, goes back a long way. When the Supreme Court ruled in 1911 that Dr. Miles Company could not fix the price at which retailers sold its popular elixir, Brandeis protested that without price maintenance, the chains would drive small druggists out of business. In 1937 Congress finally agreed and enacted the Miller-Tydings Fair Trade Act, which exempted resale price maintenance from antitrust law. In 1952, led by Hubert Humphrey, Congress strengthened the fair trade act. In 1975 Congress, in a bipartisan flush of pro-consumer sentiment, repealed it.[134]

In the 1980s the question of retail price-fixing arose again, in slightly different form. At issue was the ability of powerful retailers, such as department stores, to fix prices by pressuring manufacturers to refuse brand-name merchandise to discounters who undercut their prices. The 1911 *Dr. Miles* decision had made price-fixing illegal, but the Reagan Justice Department refused to enforce it, arguing that businesses should, for the sake of efficiency, be free to use their market power to negotiate prices as they please. Democrats in Congress, led by Senator Howard Metzenbaum of Ohio and Representative Jack Brooks of Texas, disagreed. They wanted the government to crack down on vertical price fixing, thus lowering prices to consumers. If the economy was to revive quickly, said Brooks, "it will be because people won't have to pay the Bloomingdale's price for a product."[135] For Progressives of old, the chains had been the villains, cut-throat competitors whose discounts would destroy the small, independent druggists and grocers and small businessmen on whom democracy depended. For modern liberals, the discounters had become the heroes, whose low prices enabled consumers to avoid paying the Bloomingdale's price.

Had the protagonists paused to reflect on the origins of the policies they defended, they might have been puzzled by the company they were keeping. The shifting terms of political discourse over the course of the century had made for strange ideological bedfellows. In the name of economic efficiency and deference to the market, the Reagan conservatives defended a policy once championed by Brandeis and Hubert Humphrey, progressive advocates of small producers and the civic case for antitrust. In the name of lower consumer prices, liberals and consumer groups defended the discounting chain stores once despised by progressives as destructive of a decentralized economy of independent producers. That the paradox was scarcely noticed may be a measure of the passing of the public philosophy that gave antitrust its first occasion.

8

Liberalism and the Keynesian Revolution

So familiar are the terms of our economic debates—about prosperity and fairness, employment and inflation, taxes and spending, budget deficits and interest rates—that they seem natural, even timeless. If economic policy is not about the size and distribution of national wealth, what else could it be about? But looking back across the century, it is striking to recall how novel are the economic questions that command our attention. The economic arguments of our day bear little resemblance to the issues that divided Theodore Roosevelt and Woodrow Wilson, Herbert Croly and Louis D. Brandeis. They were concerned with the structure of the economy and debated how to preserve democratic government in the face of concentrated economic power. We are concerned with the overall level of economic output and debate how to promote economic growth while assuring broad access to the fruits of prosperity.

In retrospect, it is possible to identify the moment when our economic questions displaced theirs. As the case of antitrust suggests, the late 1930s brought the beginning of a shift in the terms of economic debate, from considerations of self-government to considerations of consumer welfare. At about the same time, national economic policy as a whole underwent a similar transformation. Beginning in the late New Deal and culminating in the early 1960s, the political economy of growth and distributive justice displaced the political economy of citizenship.

Competing Visions of New Deal Reform

As the New Deal began, political debate continued to reflect the alternatives defined in the Progressive era. When Franklin Roosevelt took office in the midst of the Depression, two traditions of reform offered competing approaches to economic recovery. One group of reformers, heirs to the New Freedom and the philosophy of Brandeis, sought to decentralize the economy through antitrust and other measures aimed at restoring competition. Another group, indebted to the New Nationalism, sought to rationalize the economy through national economic planning. They argued that concentrated power was an inevitable feature of a modern economy; what was needed was systematic planning and rational control of the industrial system. Among the planners, there was much disagreement about who should do the planning. Industrialists favored a kind of business commonwealth scheme by which self-governing trade associations would regulate output and prices, as during World War I. Others, such as New Deal economist Rexford G. Tugwell, wanted government or other public agencies, not business, to do the planning.[1]

Despite their differences, both the planners and the antitrusters assumed that overcoming the Depression required a change in the structure of industrial capitalism. They also agreed that the concentration of power in the economy, left to its own devices, posed a threat to democratic government. Like Croly and Brandeis before them, they differed on how best to preserve democracy in the face of economic power—whether to form a rival concentration of power in the national government, or to decentralize economic power in hopes of making it accountable to local political units.

These competing approaches persisted, unresolved, through much of the New Deal. In different policies and different moods, Roosevelt experimented with both, never fully embracing or rejecting either. In the end, however, neither the planners nor the antitrusters prevailed. Recovery, when it came, was due not to structural reform but to massive government spending. World War II supplied the occasion for the spending, Keynesian economics the rationale. But Keynesian fiscal policy had a political appeal that appeared even before the war demonstrated its economic success. For unlike the various proposals for structural reform,

Keynesian economics offered a way for government to control the economy without having to choose among controversial conceptions of the good society. Where earlier reformers had sought economic arrangements that would cultivate citizens of a certain kind, Keynesians undertook no formative mission; they proposed simply to accept existing consumer preferences and to regulate the economy by manipulating aggregate demand.

The political appeal of Keynesian fiscal policy can best be understood against the background of conflicting visions of reform that struggled for preeminence within the early New Deal. At first it seemed the planners would prevail. "More and more the movement of things in 1933 favored those who contended that industrial growth had produced an organic economy requiring national control." The administration's first major reform measure asserted federal planning authority over agriculture. The Agricultural Adjustment Administration (AAA), established in 1933, supervised prices and production levels of basic commodities. In hopes of boosting farm prices and stabilizing the agricultural economy, the AAA subsidized farmers for reducing production. When the program began, the government ordered cotton farmers to plow under a quarter of their crop and pig farmers to destroy 6 million pigs—measures that brought uncomprehending protest from a nation suffering hunger and privation. Other measures provided credit to farmers and brought electrical power to rural areas. Although parts of the AAA were invalidated by the Supreme Court, the federal government's role in the agricultural economy, through price supports, credit programs, and other policies, would continue.[2]

Roosevelt's second major initiative extended the planning philosophy to the industrial economy. In 1933 Congress passed the National Industrial Recovery Act, an attempt to reorganize American industry through a new system of cooperation among business, labor, and government. Roosevelt hailed it as "the most important and far-reaching legislation ever enacted by the American Congress." The act established the National Recovery Administration (NRA) to oversee the cooperative scheme, and the Public Works Administration (PWA) to spend $3.3 billion on public works.[3]

The NRA's planning mission was to negotiate two sets of agreements with the nation's major industries. One set of agreements would commit employers to minimum wages, maximum hours, collective bargaining, and the abolition of child labor, thus reducing unemployment, improving working conditions, and increasing purchasing power. At the same time, the NRA suspended the antitrust laws to enable industry groups to negotiate agreements setting minimum prices for their products and in some cases restricting output. These price codes, set by trade associations with government supervision, would, at least in theory, save responsible employers from being undercut by greedy competitors who refused to pay their workers a decent wage.[4]

When piecemeal, industry-by-industry negotiations proved inadequate to the task of prompting recovery, the flamboyant head of the NRA, the retired general Hugh S. Johnson, launched a nationwide campaign to pledge all employers to a blanket agreement to uphold NRA standards on wages and hours. Employers who took the pledge could display the NRA's "Blue Eagle" insignia in their windows and on their products. Consumers were urged to sign a pledge of their own promising to buy only from Blue Eagle merchants. Unable to mandate compliance, Johnson sought to enlist public support for NRA codes by inspiring among Americans the same patriotic fervor called forth in times of war. Noting that the Depression had brought more suffering to more Americans than the Great War, Johnson launched a mass movement drawing "on the power and the willingness of the American people to act together as one person in an hour of great danger."[5]

The high point of the campaign was a massive Blue Eagle parade in New York City in September 1933. "In the greatest march in the city's history," writes Arthur Schlesinger, Jr., "a quarter of a million men and women streamed down Fifth Avenue, while a million and a half more lined the streets, watching and cheering." Night fell, but "[s]till the marchers came—CCC boys in olive drab; life insurance men and telephone linemen; stock brokers and chorus girls; brewers walking under red flares and bands playing 'Happy Days Are Here Again.' On it went till midnight in a pandemonium of ticker tape, enthusiasm, and fellowship. The flight of the Blue Eagle had reached its zenith."[6]

But the cheers did not last. By 1934 public criticism of the NRA was mounting. Business disliked the requirements for collective bargaining, consumers were angry over price increases, and labor complained that the

NRA was overly sympathetic to business. The code authorities that set price and production agreements, intended to represent labor and the public, were dominated in practice by well-organized trade associations. NRA labor standards were commonly violated, and enforcement was weak. Critics objected that the NRA amounted to government-sanctioned price-fixing by big business. A review board chaired by the lawyer Clarence Darrow concluded, much to the fury of General Johnson, that the NRA was an instrument of monopoly. Beset by criticism, Johnson himself became increasingly erratic and was finally eased out by Roosevelt. But by now public enthusiasm for the NRA had waned, and new leadership could do little to improve its fortunes. In the *Schechter* decision of 1935, the Supreme Court put an end to the NRA, ruling unconstitutional its broad delegation of code-making authority. Roosevelt criticized the Court in public but privately expressed a sense of relief. "It has been an awful headache," he conceded to an associate.[7]

With the demise of the NRA, the New Deal entered a new phase, in which the planning impulse faded and the decentralizing strand of reform assumed greater prominence. "The early New Deal had accepted the concentration of economic power as the central and irreversible trend of the American economy and had proposed the concentration of political power as the answer." As Tugwell, a leading planner, had declared, "The old sentiment of fear of big business has become unnecessary. . . . We have turned our backs on competition and have chosen control." The "Second New Deal," as some called the post-NRA period, gave greater voice to those who retained the old fear of big business and also mistrusted government planning.[8]

Of early New Deal measures, only securities industry reform and the Tennessee Valley Authority (TVA) had reflected the philosophy of the decentralizers. The Securities and Exchange Commission, established in 1934, was not a planning body but a regulatory agency charged with preventing Wall Street abuses and promoting fair competition in the securities market. The TVA, a 1933 program to bring cheap power and flood control to rural areas, did involve government planning. But from the standpoint of the decentralizers, it also represented an experiment in decentralized administration and regional development and a way of encouraging small, integrated communities in which workers might remain attached to the land while also gaining access to electricity, transportation, and modern technology.[9]

A leading figure of the later New Deal was Felix Frankfurter, Harvard law professor, Brandeis disciple, and FDR confidant. Frankfurter, whose views reflected the progressivism of Wilson and Brandeis, "believed in a world of small business, economic independence, and government action to restore and preserve free competition." In the aftermath of the *Schechter* decision, Frankfurter, along with the many students and proteges he had placed in the administration, gained greater influence. He argued that business-government cooperation had failed and urged Roosevelt to speak out against big business, to invigorate antitrust, and to tax large corporations.[10]

One expression of the new antitrust emphasis was Roosevelt's proposal, in 1935, to break up the great utility holding companies that enabled a small group of powerful investors to control local power companies. In his message to Congress urging passage of the holding-company bill, Roosevelt echoed the Brandeisian charge that big business threatens democracy. The holding companies deprived local communities of control over their public utilities, he argued, and gave "tyrannical power" to a favored few. "It is time to make an effort to reverse that process of the concentration of power which has made most American citizens, once traditionally independent owners of their own businesses, helplessly dependent for their daily bread upon the favor of a very few, who, by devices such as holding companies, have taken for themselves unwarranted economic power. I am against private socialism of concentrated private power as thoroughly as I am against governmental socialism. The one is equally as dangerous as the other." Though weakened somewhat by intense industry lobbying, the Public Utility Holding Company Act represented a victory for the opponents of economic concentration.[11]

Another attack on concentrated power and wealth was contained in Roosevelt's 1935 tax message to Congress, which called for increased inheritance and gift taxes, higher income taxes for the wealthy, and a graduated corporate income tax that would increase with the size of the business. To some extent, these proposals responded to growing support for Senator Huey Long's "Share the Wealth" campaign and invoked considerations of distributive justice. Roosevelt's message referred, for example, to "social unrest and a deepening sense of unfairness" in American life and stressed the need for a just distribution of the tax burden and a "fairly distributed national prosperity." But beyond the issue of distributive justice, Roosevelt also emphasized the civic consequences of concentrated power and wealth: "Great accumulations of wealth . . . amount to the perpetuation of great and undesirable concentration of control in a relatively few individuals over the employment and welfare of many, many others." As the founders rejected inherited political power, Americans now rejected inherited economic power.[12]

Roosevelt's tax proposals provoked a torrent of business opposition, which succeeded in weakening the bill that finally emerged from Congress. In the end, the Revenue Act of 1935 did little to redistribute wealth or to stem the tide of bigness. Roosevelt's attempt the following year to tax undistributed corporate profits brought a similar struggle and only modest results. Although the tax battles of 1935 and 1936 represented a new commitment to oppose bigness in the name of small competitive enterprise, they did little if anything to decentralize the economy.[13]

Still, FDR entered the 1936 campaign in full voice against big business and concentrated power. Accepting renomination by the Democratic convention, he attacked the "economic royalists" who were using their vast power to undermine American democracy. The American Revolution had overthrown political tyranny and won for each citizen "the right with his neighbors to make and order his own destiny through his own Government." But the modern age of machinery and railroads, of steam and electricity, of mass production and mass distribution, had enabled new tyrants to build kingdoms "upon concentration of control over material things." And before long, "the privileged princes of these new economic dynasties, thirsting for power, reached out for control over Government itself."[14]

The "new industrial dictatorship" deprived the people of control over the hours they worked, the wages they received, and the conditions of their labor. For those who tilled the soil, the "small measure of their gains was decreed by men in distant cities." Monopoly destroyed opportunity, and "individual initiative was crushed in the cogs of a great machine." Political equality was rendered "meaningless in the face of economic inequality. A small group had concentrated into their own hands an almost complete control over other people's property, other people's money, other people's labor—other people's lives." The New Deal took as its mandate to redeem American democracy from the despotism of economic power.[15]

FDR won reelection in a landslide in 1936, only to confront, in the first year of his second term, a new and severe economic downturn. The recession of 1937 began with the sharpest decline of industrial production on record, followed by a steep drop in the stock market. The administration, confident that recovery was under way, suddenly faced a new crisis. Roosevelt had inherited the first depression; now he had one of his own. As he groped to respond, the same bewildering array of alternatives presented themselves. "Should industry be atomized and concentrated economic power dispersed? Should it be organized and rationalized so that the businessmen themselves might engage in economic planning? Or would it be necessary to transfer economic power to the state or to non-business groups? And did any of these alternatives offer a real solution?"[16]

Among the various schools of reform, the antimonopolists offered the most influential diagnosis. The new recession proved that big business, left to its own devices, would restrict output and impose artificially high "administered prices" on consumers, thus diminishing purchasing power. Some alleged that the corporate world had intentionally brought on the recession to sabotage the New Deal. Only a vigorous campaign of trust-busting and regulation, it followed, could restore the economy to health. "Thus, on the surface at least, the most powerful impulse within the New Deal beginning early in 1938 was the revival of the old crusade against 'monopoly.' Rhetorical assaults on economic concentration echoed throughout the administration as New Dealers tried to forge an explanation for the setbacks of the year before."[17]

In a 1938 message to Congress, Roosevelt sounded traditional antimonopoly themes in asking for increased spending on antitrust enforcement and for a comprehensive study of the concentration of economic power in American industry. "[T]he liberty of a democracy is not safe," he declared, "if the people tolerate the growth of private power to a point where it becomes stronger than their democratic state itself." At about the same time, Roosevelt appointed Thurman Arnold to head the Antitrust Division of the Justice Department, where he invigorated enforcement.[18]

But events belied the seeming triumph of Brandeisian reform. As we have seen, Arnold's antitrust enforcement, vigorous though it was, aimed at lowering consumer prices, not at decentralizing the economy or reducing the political power of big business. "His success in using the antitrust laws to police rather than forestall 'bigness' was a serious, perhaps final, blow to the old concept of those laws as the route to genuine decentralization." Nor did antitrust prove an effective means of promoting recovery. "[A]s a means of stimulating economic expansion, Arnold's antitrust campaign could only be adjudged a failure. Even if it had not been derailed by the war, it was too cumbersome, too rigid, and too slow."[19]

The massive study of monopoly urged by Roosevelt also failed to generate effective policies for restoring a competitive economy of independent producers. The Temporary National Economic Committee (TNEC), as it was known, labored for three years, called 655 witnesses, produced eighty volumes of testimony, published forty-four monographs, but in the end offered little in the way of concrete conclusions. For all the ammunition it assembled, commented *Time* magazine, "the committee rolled a rusty BB gun into place [and] pinged at the nation's economic problems." As Alan Brinkley writes, "The feeble conclusion of the TNEC inquiry illustrated the degree to which the antimonopoly enthusiasms of 1938 had faded by 1941. But the character of the inquiry during its three years of striving illustrated how the rhetoric of antimonopoly, even at its most intense, had ceased to reflect any real commitment to decentralization."[20]

The decentralizers, then, were only the apparent winners of the policy struggles of the late 1930s. The more lasting triumph belonged to advocates of a different course, a path to recovery that abandoned attempts at structural reform and focused instead on government spending. The way to lift the economy from depression, they argued, was to employ the tools of fiscal policy to promote economic growth by stimulating consumer demand.

The Spending Solution

Of course, government spending to ease depression was not in itself a new idea. Many of the programs of the early New Deal involved spending, from farm price supports to the Tennessee Valley Authority to the $3.3 billion for public works. But FDR had considered these expenditures as emergency measures necessary to carry out particular projects, not as a way of stimulating the economy as a whole. In the case of public works, for example, he resisted advice to spend more, insisting that the number of useful public projects was limited. More important, he doubted that such spending would have any "indirect effects" beyond the construction jobs actually created. Roosevelt therefore considered the public works program a "stop-gap" measure, not a "pump-priming" measure designed to boost purchasing power and increase aggregate demand.[21]

Far from being an early apostle of Keynesian economics, Roosevelt adhered to the conventional wisdom that stressed the importance of balanced budgets. During the 1932 campaign he denounced Herbert Hoover for running a deficit and condemned excessive government spending in words that, decades later, could easily have been mistaken for those of conservative Republicans such as Barry Goldwater or Ronald Reagan: "I accuse the present Administration of being the greatest spending Administration in peace times in all our history. It is an Administration that has piled bureau on bureau, commission on commission," all at the expense of the American taxpayer. "It is committed to the idea that we ought to center control of everything in Washington as rapidly as possible—Federal control." Candidate Roosevelt promised to remedy this excess by reducing the cost of federal government operations by 25 percent. "I regard reduction in Federal spending as one of the most important issues of this campaign. In my opinion it is the most direct and effective contribution that Government can make to business."[22]

More than a piece of campaign rhetoric, Roosevelt's commitment to a balanced budget persisted as a refrain, unrealized though it was, throughout much of his presidency. Those among his advisers, such as Marriner Eccles, who urged spending as a way to economic recovery, found themselves "colliding with one of the few economic doctrines which Roosevelt held in a clear way—that an unbalanced budget was bad." Nor was Roosevelt much influenced by the advice of the founder of modern fiscal policy, John Maynard Keynes. When the celebrated British economist visited FDR in the White House in 1934, the president seemed more mystified than impressed. "He left a whole rigamarole of figures,"

Roosevelt complained to Labor secretary Frances Perkins. "He must be a mathematician rather than a political economist." Keynes, for his part, later told Perkins that he had "supposed the President was more literate, economically speaking."[23]

As late as 1937, Roosevelt sided with those of his advisers, led by Treasury secretary Henry Morgenthau Jr., who urged spending cuts to balance the budget. It was not until 1938, after the economic collapse, that Roosevelt reluctantly adopted a policy of deficit spending designed to boost the purchasing power of consumers. Acceding to the arguments of pro-spending advisers such as Eccles and Harry Hopkins, he asked Congress for $4.5 billion in additional appropriations. More significant than the amount was the new rationale. Roosevelt had presented earlier New Deal expenditures as temporary measures meeting emergency needs, such as work relief, until structural reforms produced recovery. Now, for the first time, he justified spending as itself the instrument of recovery. "We suffer primarily from a failure of consumer demand because of a lack of buying power," Roosevelt said in a fireside chat explaining the new policy. It was therefore up to government to "create an economic upturn" by making "definite additions to the purchasing power of the Nation." Government spending would not only help those who received government-funded jobs; it would act "as a trigger to set off private activity," thus increasing the national income by far more than the amount of the expenditure itself.[24]

Roosevelt's turn to spending as an instrument of recovery marked a break with the assumptions that informed the early New Deal. For five years the New Deal had sought recovery through various programs designed to reform the structure of the economy. Now, under the pressure of a new recession and with few practical alternatives remaining, Roosevelt reluctantly adopted what amounted to Keynesian fiscal policy. Despite his break with fiscal orthodoxy, however, he resisted the more massive spending that full-fledged Keynesianism would have required. The economy improved somewhat in late 1938, then leveled off in 1939; about 10 million people remained unemployed, over one-sixth of the labor force. Full economic recovery, and the ultimate demonstration of the effects of fiscal stimulus, awaited the far larger government expenditures of World War II.[25]

In the meantime, Keynes's teachings acquired increasing influence among American economists and policymakers. In 1938 a group of young economists at Harvard and Tufts published a report that summed up the new wisdom. The gradual economic recovery from 1933 to 1937 was due less to the direct effects of New Deal programs—the temporary jobs, the farm subsidies, the public projects—than to the broader secondary effects of deficit spending on the economy as a whole. When government spending was curtailed in 1937, recession followed. The problem with the New Deal was simply its failure to spend enough to bring recovery. The economists urged that government spending no longer be viewed as a temporary emergency device but as a permanent policy to compensate as necessary for slack in the private economy. They also called for measures to redistribute income, through old-age benefits, subsidies for education and health, and unemployment compensation, to increase the purchasing power of lower-income families.[26]

World War II brought a growing consensus that government should employ fiscal policy to assure full employment during times of peace as well as war. This conviction was embraced by Democrats and Republicans alike. During the 1944 presidential campaign, the Republican candidate Thomas Dewey declared, "We Republicans are agreed that full employment shall be a first objective of national policy." He also endorsed government spending as a way of achieving this objective: "If at any time there are not sufficient jobs in private employment to go around, then government can and must create additional job opportunities because there must be jobs for all in this country of ours." After the war, the new consensus on using fiscal policy to assure prosperity was embodied in the Employment Act of 1946, which declared it "the continuing policy and responsibility of the Federal Government" to "promote maximum employment, production, and purchasing power."[27]

By the end of World War II the central issues of economic policy had little to do with the debates that had preoccupied Americans from the Progressive era to the New Deal. The old debates about how to reform industrial capitalism faded from the scene, and the macroeconomic issues familiar in our day came to the fore. By 1960 most economists and policymakers agreed that "the chief economic problem of the country was to achieve and maintain high and rapidly rising total output." Steps to make the distribution of income more equal were also deemed desirable, but secondary to the aim of full employment and economic growth.[28]

Debate would continue, of course, about the relative claims of economic growth and distributive justice, about trade-offs between inflation and unemployment, about tax policies and spending priorities. But these debates reflected the assumption that economic policy is concerned above all with the size and distribution of national wealth. The old questions about what economic arrangements are hospitable to self-government ceased to be the subject of national debate. With the triumph of fiscal policy, the political economy of citizenship gave way to the political economy of growth and distributive justice.

Keynesian Economics and the Procedural Republic

More than a matter of economics alone, the advent of the new political economy marked a decisive moment in the demise of the republican strand of American politics and the rise of contemporary liberalism. According to this liberalism, government should be neutral among the conceptions of the good life, in order to respect persons as free and independent selves, capable of choosing their ends for themselves. As Keynesian fiscal policy emerged from the late 1930s to the early 1960s, it both reflected this liberalism and deepened its hold on American public life. Although those who practiced Keynesian economics did not defend it in precisely these terms, the new political economy displayed two features of the liberalism that defines the procedural republic. First, it offered policymakers and elected officials a way to "bracket," or set aside, controversial conceptions of the good life, and so promised a consensus that programs for structural reform could not offer. Second, by abandoning the ambition of inculcating certain habits and dispositions, it denied government a stake in the moral character of its citizens and affirmed the notion of persons as free and independent selves, capable of choice. The Keynesian revolution can thus be seen as the counterpart in political economy of the liberalism that emerged in constitutional law after World War II, as the economic expression of the procedural republic.

Avoiding Political Controversy

The first sense in which Keynesian economics displayed the aspiration to neutrality characteristic of the procedural republic concerned contending visions of economic reform. From the late 1930s to the early 1960s, Keynesian fiscal policy appealed to policymakers as a way of avoiding the intractable controversies among advocates of various reforms and spokesmen for various sectors of the economy. This political advantage contributed to Roosevelt's decision to adopt the spending policy of 1938. Unlike competing proposals for structural reform, the spending solution was one upon which most New Dealers—planners and decentralizers as well as Keynesians—could agree. Even conservatives regarded deficit spending as less objectionable than efforts to decentralize the economy or to impose national economic planning. Because of the conflicting goals that divided New Deal reformers, which reflected in turn conflicting moral and political visions, "policy makers found that it was extremely difficult to reach a common basis of agreement." In the face of this disagreement about ends, "the spending solution became increasingly attractive."[29]

Although the New Deal began as an attempt, or series of attempts, to reform the structure of industrial capitalism, New Dealers failed in the end, as Ellis Hawley has written, "to arrive at any real consensus about the origins and nature of economic concentration, the effects of it, or the methods of dealing with it. In 1939, in fact, they seemed to be even more divided than they had been in 1933. Perhaps . . . they were wrestling with a problem for which there was no real solution." In response to this predicament, the Roosevelt administration, beset by conflicting ideologies and divergent goals, opted for a solution that was neutral with respect to those controversies. "It shied away from drastic institutional reform and came to rely primarily on the spending solution."[30]

The hope of avoiding long-standing political controversies also contributed to the appeal of Keynesianism in the postwar years. The planning efforts undertaken during World War II diminished Americans' confidence in the ability of the state to manage the economy directly. Meanwhile, the wartime expansion proved the powerful effect of massive fiscal stimulus. "The route to full employment, the war seemed to demonstrate, was not state management of capitalist institutions, but fiscal policies that would promote consumption and thus stimulate economic growth." As Brinkley observes, Keynesian economics offered a way to "manage the economy without managing the institutions of the economy." Growth did not require government intervention in the management of industry, only the indirect manipulation of the economy through the use of fiscal and monetary policy. "Such measures were not (as some liberals had once believed) simply temporary stopgaps, keeping things going until some more basic solution could be found; they were themselves the solution."[31]

For those postwar liberals who called themselves New Dealers, it was this procedural liberalism of the late 1930s and the 1940s, not the reform ideologies of the early New Deal, that they appropriated and affirmed. "They largely ignored the New Deal's abortive experiments in economic planning, its failed efforts to create harmonious associational arrangements, its vigorous if short-lived antimonopoly and regulatory crusades, its open skepticism toward capitalism and its captains, its overt celebration of the state." Instead, "postwar liberals celebrated the New Deal for having discovered solutions to the problems of capitalism that required no alteration in the structure of capitalism; for having defined a role for the state that did not intrude it too far into the economy."[32] The late New Deal sought to avoid rather than embrace controversial conceptions of political and economic reform, and it was this strategy of avoidance that came to define the procedural republic.

The postwar emphasis on economic growth and full employment not only enabled New Deal reformers to agree among themselves; it also provided a basis for agreement between liberals and conservatives. "Full employment became the flag around which every one could rally. This permitted the subordination of other more controversial and divisive goals and policies." The agreement among postwar liberals and conservatives on the goal of full employment helped elevate fiscal policy as the agreed-upon means. "Fiscal policy promised to be fairly efficient in achieving the full employment goal while being, at least in some variants, neutral with respect to more divisive goals," according to Herbert Stein, an economist who later served as chairman of the Council of Economic Advisors under Richard Nixon. "One could be for active use of fiscal policy to promote high employment without being pro-business or anti-business, or pro-planning or anti-planning. Disputes over these other issues could continue, and did, but no one had to, or could afford to, let his insistence on these other positions stand in the way of supporting a more or less neutral policy for full employment."[33]

The Keynesian revolution came to fruition with the tax cut recommended by President John F. Kennedy in 1962, finally enacted in 1964. Kennedy entered the White House a believer in balanced budgets, but the slow pace of economic recovery during his first year, together with the influence of his Keynesian advisers, soon persuaded him of the need to stimulate the economy. Many in the administration, including Kennedy himself, would have preferred to provide fiscal stimulus through increased government spending, in order to boost the economy while at the same time meeting pressing public needs. But conservatives and businessmen, still devoted to budget-balancing, opposed new spending. Mindful of the political climate, Kennedy opted for a tax cut instead. The conservatives, who liked tax reduction even more than they liked balanced budgets, offered little opposition.[34]

The tax cut led to an economic expansion that lasted for the rest of the decade and came to be regarded as a textbook case of successful Keynesian fiscal management. But beyond its economic success, the Kennedy tax cut symbolized the political appeal of modern fiscal policy, in particular its neutrality with respect to competing political ends. "In the calm which has followed a new national consensus," an economist wrote in 1966, "it is possible to see at last that Keynesian economics is not conservative, liberal, or radical. The techniques of economic stimulation and stabilization are simply neutral administrative tools capable of distributing national income either more or less equitably . . . and increasing or decreasing the importance of the public sector of the economy."[35]

The clearest expression of faith in the new economics as a neutral instrument of national governance was offered by Kennedy himself. Speaking to a White House economic conference in 1962, he argued that modern economic problems could best be resolved if people bracketed, or set aside, their political and ideological convictions. "Most of us are conditioned for many years to have a political viewpoint, Republican or Democratic—liberal, conservative, moderate. The fact of the matter is that most of the problems, or at least many of them, that we now face are technical problems, are administrative problems. They are very sophisticated judgments which do not lend themselves to the great sort of 'passionate movements' which have stirred this country so often in the past."[36]

A few weeks later, in a commencement address at Yale University, Kennedy elaborated this theme. "The central domestic issues of our time," he observed, "are more subtle and less simple" than the large moral and political issues that commanded the nation's attention in earlier days. "They relate not to basic clashes of philosophy or ideology but to ways and means of reaching common goals. . . . What is at stake in our economic decisions today is not some grand warfare of rival ideologies which will sweep the country with passion but the practical management of a modern economy." Kennedy urged the country "to face technical problems without ideological preconceptions," to focus on "the sophisticated and technical issues involved in keeping a great economic machinery moving ahead."[37]

Of course, Keynesian economics is not neutral, strictly speaking, with respect to all political ends. To the contrary, it avowedly promotes the end of prosperity, or economic growth. But affirming growth as an end is nonetheless consistent with the idea of avoiding controversial conceptions of the good life, in two respects. First, at least as it functioned as an aim of American politics from the late 1930s to the 1960s, economic growth was a sufficiently general end as to be neutral with respect to the more particular ends advanced by, say, planners and decentralizers or business and labor. Whatever their particular conceptions of the good society, partisans of various political and economic persuasions seemed to agree that increasing the overall level of national wealth would make it easier to realize their particular ends. The notion that economic growth serves all social and political ends well would be challenged in later years, by environmentalists among others, but it did seem to underlie the consensus on Keynesian fiscal policy that developed from the late 1930s to the early 1960s.[38]

Abandoning the Formative Project

The second sense in which promoting growth expresses neutrality among ends ties the new political economy more deeply and distinctly to the public philosophy of the procedural republic. Whereas the first sense of neutrality applies at the level of competing public policies, the second concerns the wants, desires, interests, and ends that men and women bring to public life. Keynesian fiscal policy is neutral in this second sense in its assumption that government should not form or revise, or for that matter even judge, the interests and ends its citizens espouse; rather, it should enable them to pursue these interests and ends, whatever they may be, consistent with a similar liberty for others. It is this assumption above all that distinguishes the political economy of growth from the political economy of citizenship, and links Keynesian economics to contemporary liberalism.

Those who practiced and championed the new political economy did not describe their project in exactly these terms. But in the course of explaining and justifying their views, they did articulate three themes of the Keynesian revolution that, taken together, reveal the contours of the new public philosophy that Keynesian economics brought to prominence. One was the shift from production to consumption as the primary basis of political identity and focus of economic policy. The second was the rejection of the formative project characteristic of earlier reform movements and the republican tradition generally. The third was the embrace of the voluntarist conception of freedom and the conception of persons as free and independent selves, capable of choosing their ends for themselves.

Of the three themes, the emphasis on consumption was closest to the surface and found most explicit expression among Keynesians. In his famous work, *The General Theory of Employment, Interest, and Money*, Keynes declared what he took to be obvious, that "consumption . . . is the sole end and object of all economic activity." Leading New Dealers made similar pronouncements. Harold Ickes, Roosevelt's secretary of the Interior and head of the WPA, argued that government should direct its efforts toward improving the lot of the consumer: "The major part of the activity of all of us is that of consuming. It is as consumers that we all have a common interest, regardless of what productive work we may be engaged in. . . . We work in order to earn so that we may consume." In the late 1930s Thurman Arnold, as we have seen, shifted the aim of antitrust enforcement to improving consumer welfare.[39]

Alvin Hansen, one of the leading promulgators of Keynesianism among American economists, stressed increased consumption as the key to a prosperous postwar economy. Writing in 1943, he argued that maintaining full employment after the war would require substantial public expenditures, especially for construction. But since a high level of construction cannot continue indefinitely, "it is important to develop a high-consumption economy so that we can achieve full employment and utilize effectively our increasing productive power. . . . We must raise the propensity to consume." Postwar prosperity depended on building an economy "capable of matching mass consumption with mass production."[40]

Keynes's claim that consumption is the sole end of all economic activity, obvious though it seems, runs counter to one of the main assumptions of republican political thought. According to the republican tradition, one of the ends of economic activity is the cultivation of conditions hospitable to self-government. From Jefferson to Brandeis, republicans worried more about conditions of production than about conditions of consumption because they viewed the world of work as the arena in which, for better or for worse, the character of citizens was formed. The activity of consumption was not decisive for self-government in the same way. To the extent that consumption figured at all in republican political economy, it did so as a thing to be moderated or restrained, a potential source of corruption.

Keynesians, by contrast, focused on consumption and wanted to increase "the propensity to consume." In this sense, they too sought to change people's behavior. But the change they sought did not involve reforming people's character—making them more profligate, for example—or changing the content of their wants and desires. Keynesian economics sought to increase the propensity to consume, not by changing individual preferences but by managing aggregate demand. "A higher propensity to consume can in part be achieved by a progressive tax structure combined with social security, social welfare, and community consumption expenditures," Hansen wrote, "and by achieving continuous high levels of employment at rising wages commensurate with increasing productivity. The assurance of sustained employment tends to make people spend a larger proportion of their current income." Not a new civic virtue but rather increased consumer confidence and a more widely distributed purchasing power would induce people to spend more and lead the country "forward toward a high-consumption economy."[41]

The Keynesians' focus on the level of aggregate demand thus enables government to be neutral with respect to the content of consumers' wants and desires. John Kenneth Galbraith, arguing that America's "affluent society" of the 1950s gave excessive priority to private consumption over public spending, well described this assumption. The theory of consumer demand takes consumer wants as "given data." The economist's task "is merely to seek their satisfaction," to maximize the goods that supply the wants. "He has no need to inquire how these wants are formed," or for that matter to judge how important or legitimate they are. The theory of consumer demand "divorce[s] economics from any judgment on the goods with which it [is] concerned."[42] The resolutely nonjudgmental character of Keynesian demand management is the first theme of the new economics that intimates the liberalism of the procedural republic.

The second theme of Keynesian political economy that connects it to contemporary liberalism is its rejection of the formative ambition of the civic tradition. This aspect of the new political economy, while closely related to the emphasis on consumption, found less explicit articulation at the time. Although many liberals of the New Deal and postwar period sensed that their politics differed in important ways from earlier progressive movements, few took note of the passing of the formative ideal as such. Among those who did was the political commentator Edgar Kemler. He compared the New Deal with earlier reform traditions and wrote of "the deflation of American ideals." "Whatever may be said about the old Mugwump reform movement, it cannot be denied that it was calculated to improve the character of the citizen." By the time of the New Deal, however, "the era of uplift" had given way to "the era of social engineering." "We withdrew human character from the range of our reforms."[43]

Kemler viewed this shift as "the most important aspect of the deflation of American ideals. It is most clearly seen, I think, in the changed character of political education. We no longer care to develop the individual as a unique contributor to a democratic form. We want him as a private in an army cooperating with all the other privates. The old Jeffersonian emphasis on schools for citizenship and on self-government has changed to a Rooseveltian emphasis on response to a heroic leadership." Kemler conceded that, with the rise of the modern economy, the deflation of American ideals was perhaps inevitable. "Let us be reasonable," he sardonically concluded. "Inspiration comes from many sources—from clergymen, teachers, writers, musicians, poets, artists. Let them demonstrate the virtues and let them mold the character of our citizenry. Politicians have other things to do."[44]

For the most part, the formative ambition simply fell away, unmourned and undisputed, as civic considerations faded from political debate. Rexford Tugwell, a Columbia economist and leading figure of the early New Deal, was one of the few to offer an explicit argument for abandoning the formative project. "It has always seemed to me arrogant to assume that we have any right or power to change people at all," he told a national convention of social workers in 1934. "People are pretty much the same, with respect to their basic wants, urges and passions, as they were five thousand years ago. . . . When we talk of social change, we talk of changing . . . institutions, not the men who use them."[45]

A generation earlier, Croly had argued that "democracy cannot be disentangled from an aspiration toward human perfectibility," and Brandeis had maintained, in similar terms, that democracy "is possible only where the process of perfecting the individual is pursued." This measures their distance from the procedural republic, which is premised on the faith that democracy can manage without the aspiration to moral improvement after all. Tugwell spoke on behalf of the new faith. The New Deal differed from earlier reform movements in precisely this respect; it sought better to satisfy Americans' wants and ends, not to elevate or improve them. "The New Deal is attempting to do nothing to *people*," Tugwell insisted, "and does not seek at all to alter their way of life, their wants and desires."[46]

From the standpoint of contemporary liberalism, the rejection of the formative project is not the deflation but rather the revision of American ideals, a revision in favor of the liberal conception of freedom. According to the republican tradition, freedom depends on self-government, which requires in turn certain qualities of character, certain moral and civic virtues. Liberals object that according government a role in molding the character of its citizens opens the way to coercion and fails to respect persons as free and independent selves, capable of choosing their ends for themselves. Implicit in the liberals' rejection of the formative project, then, is a rival conception of freedom, what might be called the voluntarist conception.

This suggests the third theme of Keynesian economics that gestures toward the liberalism of the procedural republic. Defenders of the new political economy did not simply abandon the formative ambition of earlier reformers; they affirmed in its place the voluntarist conception of freedom. Since the nineteenth century, the voluntarist conception of freedom had been invoked by defenders of classical, or laissez-faire liberalism; government intervention in the workings of the market economy, they claimed, violated freedom by failing to let workers and employers choose for themselves the terms on which they exchanged labor for wages. By the late nineteenth century, reformist liberals also adopted the voluntarist conception. They argued that, contrary to the claims of laissez-faire liberals, truly voluntary choice presupposed a fair bargaining position between the parties to a contract, which in some cases justified government regulation.[47]

Keynes now advanced this tradition of reformist liberalism by proposing a way for government to regulate aggregate demand without regulating the choices individual consumers made. Like the laissez-faire liberals who abhorred his views, Keynes justified his economics in the name of the voluntarist conception of freedom. Though sometimes seen as being "in conflict with the earlier tradition of economic liberalism, the complete Keynesian program can, instead, be regarded as its culmination." As the economist Fred Hirsch aptly observed, "Keynes completed the corrections to laissez-faire that were needed to validate what laissez-faire was designed to do," namely, to respect people's freedom to choose their ends for themselves.[48]

Keynes considered it an important advantage of his theory that the government intervention it sanctioned was consistent with respect for individual choice: "If the community's aggregate rate of spending can be regulated, the way in which personal incomes are spent and the means by which demand is satisfied can be safely left free and individual. . . . [This is] the only way to avoid the destruction of choice." Keynes acknowledged that "the central controls necessary to ensure full employment will, of course, involve a large extension of the traditional functions of government." But there would still remain, he argued, "a wide field for the exercise of private initiative and responsibility." "[A]bove all, individualism, if it can be purged of its defects, is the best safeguard of personal liberty," since "it greatly widens the field for the exercise of personal choice." Although "the enlargement of the functions of government" might seem "to be a terrific encroachment on individualism," Keynes insisted it was the only practical alternative to "the destruction of existing economic forms in their entirety" and the only way to preserve a scheme based on individual choice.[49]

The ideals and self-images implicit in a way of life often escape the notice of those who live by them. It is not surprising, therefore, that few among the American Keynesians explicitly addressed the transition from the civic to the voluntarist conception of freedom. David Lilienthal, the first director of the Tennessee Valley Authority, may have come closest. His varied reflections on the political economy of his day reflected the moment of passage. Writing in 1943, Lilienthal drew on the civic conception of freedom in describing the TVA as an expression of grass-roots democracy. The TVA decentralized decision-making power; it recognized that each citizen "wants to be able not only to express his opinion freely, but to know that it carries some weight; to know that there are some things that he decides, or has a part in deciding, and that he is a needed and useful part of something far bigger than he is. . . . By that act of joint effort, of citizen participation, the individual's essential freedom is strengthened." Centralized administration, whether in government or in business, posed a threat to this freedom. It "promotes remote and absentee control, and thereby increasingly denies to the individual the opportunity to make decisions and to carry those responsibilities by which human personality is nourished and developed. I find it impossible to comprehend how democracy can be a living reality if people are remote from their government . . . or if the control and direction of making a living—industry, farming, the distribution of goods—is far removed from the stream of life and from the local community."[50]

By the 1950s Lilienthal had recast his hopes for freedom in voluntarist terms. Writing in defense of big business, he sought to refute the "outdated" fear that bigness was antithetical to freedom: "The times call for a rousing affirmation that Bigness can be made the means of promoting and furthering not only our nation's productivity but more important still the freedom and the well-being of its individual citizens." For more than a century, republican critics of wage labor had argued that industrial capitalism deprived workers of the independence essential to self-government. Lilienthal now replied that independence should no longer be sought in the world of work but instead in the realms of leisure and consumption. "Largely because of the productivity of Bigness most of man's independence need no longer come from his job directly." As a result of the spectacular increase in leisure, "the total percentage of a man's week *which is his own* has markedly increased." When, thanks to the productivity of large-scale industry, the hours of labor fall from sixty per week to forty-four, "we have thereby added sixteen hours to each man's independence every week. In those added hours he is his 'own boss,' not in the sense of the man who owns his own business, but potentially in an even more meaningful sense."[51]

The freedom Lilienthal celebrated was something other than the civic freedom that inspired the political economy of citizenship: "By freedom I mean essentially *freedom to choose* to the maximum degree possible." This freedom, not simply the production and consumption of a great many goods, was the highest purpose of the American economic system and the ultimate justification of big business: "Freedom of choice in economic matters means freedom to choose between competing ideas or services or goods. It means the maximum freedom to choose one job or one profession or one line of business as against some other. It means a maximum range of choice for the consumer when he spends his dollar." More than economic or business acts alone, these choices expressed a higher moral ideal: "They are the mark of men who are free, as free as in society it is possible or workable for men to be."[52]

Even as he affirmed the voluntarist ideal that animates the procedural republic, the old New Dealer offered a valedictory for the political economy of citizenship: "There was an old dream: the independent man in his own little shop or business. It *was* a good dream." But now "[t]here is a new dream: a world of great machines, with man in control, devising and making use of these inanimate creatures to build a new kind of independence. . . . Bigness can become an expression of the heroic size of man himself as he comes to a new-found greatness."[53]

9

The Triumph and Travail of the Procedural Republic

As Keynesian fiscal policy rose to prominence after World War II, the civic strand of economic argument faded from American political discourse. Economic policy attended more to the size and distribution of the national product and less to the conditions of self-government. Americans increasingly viewed economic arrangements as instruments of consumption, not as schools for citizenship. The formative ambition gave way to the more mundane hope of increasing and dispersing the fruits of prosperity. Rather than cultivate virtuous citizens, government would take people's wants and desires as given, and pursue policies aimed at satisfying them as fully and fairly as possible.

From the standpoint of the republican tradition, the demise of the political economy of citizenship constituted a concession, a deflation of American ideals, a loss of liberty. Republican political theory teaches that to be free is to share in governing a political community that controls its own fate. Self-government in this sense requires political communities that control their destinies, and citizens who identify sufficiently with those communities to think and act with a view to the common good. Cultivating in citizens the virtue, independence, and shared understandings such civic engagement requires is a central aim of republican politics. To abandon the formative ambition is thus to abandon the project of liberty as the republican tradition conceives it.

Animated by the civic conception of freedom, Americans from Jefferson to Lincoln to Brandeis and Croly and Theodore Roosevelt had struggled to assert democratic mastery over economic power and to cultivate in citizens the virtues that would suit them to self-government. Now Americans seemed ready to give up the struggle, or, more precisely, to give up the conception of freedom that made the struggle necessary. For with the demise of the political economy of citizenship came a shift from the civic to the voluntarist conception of freedom.

Confronted with an economy too vast to admit republican hopes of mastery, and tempted by the prospect of prosperity, Americans of the postwar years found their way to a new understanding of freedom. According to this conception, our liberty depends not on our capacity as citizens to shape the forces that govern our collective destiny but rather on our capacity as persons to choose our values and ends for ourselves.

By the late twentieth century, the eclipse of the civic strand of freedom would fuel a growing discontent with democratic institutions, a widespread sense that common purposes and shared understandings were eroding, and a gnawing fear that, individually and collectively, Americans were losing control of the forces that governed their lives. But it did not seem that way at first. As the procedural republic took form after World War II, Americans did not experience the new public philosophy as disempowering. To the contrary, in the day of its arrival, the procedural republic appeared not as a concession but rather as a triumph of agency and self-command. This was due partly to the historical moment, and partly to the liberating promise of the voluntarist conception of freedom.

The Moment of Mastery

The procedural republic was born at a rare moment of American mastery. As World War II came to a close, the United States stood astride the world, an unrivaled global power. In a radio address to the nation on the day of Japan's surrender, President Harry Truman could declare without hyperbole that America possessed "the greatest strength and the greatest power which man has ever reached."[1]

As America's primacy in the world conferred a sense of collective mastery, the performance of the domestic economy gave Americans a sense of command over their individual destinies. The gross national product rose from \$231 billion in 1947 to \$504 billion in 1960 to \$977 billion in 1970. In the two decades from 1948 to 1968, the average rate of economic growth, adjusted for inflation, was 4 percent per year, a record without precedent in the history of nations. Birthrates rose rapidly from the 1940s to the late 1950s and remained at high levels through the early 1960s. Home ownership jumped from 44 percent in 1940 to 62 percent by 1960. "If Americans around 1947 concluded that economic growth was once again possible," writes Michael Barone, "around 1964 they decided it was more or less inevitable. The business cycle, it seemed, had been abolished." Equipped with the tools of Keynesian demand management, policymakers "seemed to have discovered the secret of producing sustained economic growth without inflation or recession."[2]

More than a matter of material prosperity, the buoyant economy of the postwar years, together with America's power in the world, accustomed a generation of Americans to see themselves as masters of their circumstance. Although events would soon confound their heady confidence, this was a generation "brought up to believe, at home or abroad, that whatever Americans wished to make happen would happen."[3]

Nowhere was the assertion of agency more explicit than in the stirring rhetoric of John F. Kennedy. He campaigned for the presidency during an interlude of anxiety brought on in the late 1950s by the launching of the Soviet satellite Sputnik, the recession of 1957–58, the alleged "missile gap" with Russia, and growing concern that the United States was losing its edge in the Cold War. In the face of these worries, Kennedy promised to reassert American purpose and will, to get the country moving again. "My campaign for the Presidency is founded on a single assumption," he declared, "the assumption that the American people are tired of the drift in our national course, that they are weary of the continual decline in our national prestige . . . and that they are ready to move again." Accepting his party's nomination, he called on Americans to summon "the nerve and the will" to prevail in "a race for mastery of the sky and the rain, the ocean and the tides, the far side of space and the inside of men's minds."[4]

Kennedy's inaugural address gave eloquent expression to a generation's conviction that it possessed powers of Promethean proportions. "The world is very different now," Kennedy proclaimed. "For man holds in his mortal hands the power to abolish all forms of human poverty and all forms of human life." If both sides in the Cold War could surmount their differences, they could deploy the wonders of science to "explore the stars, conquer the deserts, eradicate disease, tap the ocean depths and encourage the arts and commerce." But in the meantime, America would exercise its power with boundless resolve: "Let every nation know, whether it wishes us well or ill, that we shall pay any price, bear any burden, meet any hardship, support any friend, oppose any foe to assure the survival and the success of liberty. This much we pledge—and more."[5]

A few months later, in a similar spirit, Kennedy proposed that the United States send a man to the moon. The reasons he offered for embarking on this project had mostly to do with the display of American power and will. No other space project would be "more impressive to mankind," and none would be "so difficult or expensive to accomplish." The mission mattered less for any tangible results it might bring than as an assertion of collective agency and resolve. "No one can predict with certainty what the ultimate meaning will be of mastery of space," Kennedy acknowledged. But the prospect of mastery and the "dedication, organization and discipline" necessary to achieve it were reasons enough to try. The success of the project required that "every scientist, every engineer, every serviceman, every technician, contractor, and civil servant [give] his personal pledge that this nation will move forward, with the full speed of freedom, in the exciting adventure of space."[6]

Kennedy presented his summons to American purpose as the mission of a new generation, poised to claim the future. In retrospect, however, his "New Frontier" stands as a monument to a fading vision of American power and will, a final expression of the mid-century moment when Americans viewed themselves as masters of their destiny. For even as Kennedy challenged Americans to ask what they could do for their country, the civic resources of American life were becoming attenuated; the political economy of citizenship was losing its hold, crowded out by the imperatives of growth and the public philosophy of the procedural republic. As Kennedy himself acknowledged, the economic problems of the day did not lend themselves to the "passionate movements" that had stirred the country in the past, but involved "sophisticated, technical questions . . . which are beyond the comprehension of most men."[7]

And so, for a time, the special circumstances of American life in the two decades after World War II obscured the passing of the civic conception of freedom. But when the moment of mastery subsided—when the rigors of the early Cold War eased and the economy faltered and the authority of government began to unravel—Americans were left ill equipped to contend with the dislocation and disempowerment that they confronted.

The Voluntarist Promise

Beyond the bounty of American power, the promise of mastery in the postwar decades had another, deeper source in the public philosophy of contemporary liberalism. This is the liberalism that asserts the priority of the right over the good; government should be neutral among competing conceptions of the good life in order to respect persons as free and independent selves, capable of choosing their own ends. The voluntarist conception of freedom that inspires this liberalism holds out a liberating vision, a promise of agency that could seemingly be realized even under conditions of concentrated power.

Inspired by the civic conception of freedom, republicans had railed against "the curse of bigness," worried about the gap between the terms of political community and the scale of economic life, and struggled, in the face of moral and cultural differences, to forge common purposes and ends. The voluntarist conception of freedom seemed to demand no such exertions. If government could provide a framework of rights, neutral among ends, then citizens could pursue their own values and ends, consistent with a similar liberty for others. At a time when the social and economic facts of modern life threatened to consign republican freedom to the realm of nostalgia, Americans found their way to a conception of freedom that did not depend, as the civic conception did, on dispersed power.

If freedom depends on a framework of rights, neutral among ends, within which people can pursue their own vision of the good life, it remains to ask what rights such a framework requires. Does voluntarist freedom mandate respect for civil and political rights alone, such as freedom of speech, religious liberty, trial by jury, and voting rights? Or does it also require certain social and economic rights, such as rights to education, employment, housing, and health care? From the 1940s to the 1990s, different people would offer different answers to this question. But whatever their views on the scope and content of individual rights, most would justify their arguments in terms of the voluntarist conception of freedom.

This marked a change in the terms of political discourse. Through much of the nineteenth century, Americans had argued about how to instill in citizens the virtues that would equip them for self-government. By the second half of the twentieth century, Americans argued instead about what rights would enable persons to choose their own values and ends. In time, the political agenda defined by the voluntarist conception of freedom proved unable to address the aspiration to self-government and so lost its capacity to inspire. At first, however, it gave energy and purpose to a far-reaching project of moral and political improvement.

The new public philosophy found its first sustained expression in court. In 1940 the U.S. Supreme Court upheld a local law requiring schoolchildren to salute the flag, even in the case of Jehovah's Witnesses who raised a religious objection. Justice Felix Frankfurter invoked the formative mission of the republican tradition. The Constitution did not prevent school districts from inculcating in young citizens "the binding tie of cohesive sentiment" on which liberty depends. Three years later the Court changed course and struck down a compulsory flag salute. It now appealed to a different conception of freedom: liberty depended not on cultivating virtue but rather on placing certain rights beyond the reach of majorities. Moreover, government could not impose on its citizens any particular conception of the good life: "no official, high or petty, can prescribe what shall be orthodox in politics, nationalism, religion, or other matters of opinion." Patriotism would now be a matter of choice, not of inculcation, a voluntary act by free and independent selves.[8]

After World War II, as liberal assumptions displaced the civic strand of economic argument, a similar transition unfolded in constitutional law. Beginning in the 1940s, the Supreme Court assumed its now familiar role of protecting individual rights against government infringement and of defining rights according to the requirement that government be neutral on questions of the good life. In 1947 the Court stated for the first time that government must be neutral toward religion. In subsequent decades it justified this neutrality in the name of the voluntarist conception of freedom: "religious beliefs worthy of respect are the product of free and voluntary choice by the faithful."[9] During the same period the Court broadened its protection of free speech, relying less on its importance for self-government and more on its importance for self-expression, making "the choice of the speech by the self the crucial factor in justifying protection."[10] And in a series of decisions from the 1960s to the 1980s the Court enforced, in the name of autonomy and freedom of choice, a right of privacy that prevents government from trying to legislate morality in matters of contraception and abortion.

The version of liberalism that asserts the priority of the right over the good was not restricted to the province of constitutional law. It also figured prominently in the justification of the American welfare state as it emerged from the New Deal to the present. At first glance it is not clear how this liberalism could play such a role. The welfare state's intervention in the market economy might seem at odds with the attempt to be neutral among ends. Moreover, the case for the public provision of certain goods to all citizens would seem to require a strong ethic of mutual obligation and shared citizenship, a highly developed sense of solidarity and common purpose.[11] In Britain, for example, the welfare state drew not only on the socialist traditions of the Labour party but also on the preliberal, communal traditions of Tory conservativism. As Samuel H. Beer wrote of British politics in the mid-1960s, "Old traditions of strong government, paternalism, and the organic society have made easier the massive reassertion of state power that has taken place in recent decades, often under Conservative auspices."[12]

The advocates of the American welfare state, by contrast, did not rely on an ethic of civic or communal obligation; they appealed instead to the voluntarist conception of freedom. Their case for expanding social and economic rights did not depend on cultivating a deeper sense of shared citizenship but rather on respecting each person's capacity to choose his or her own values and ends.

Franklin Roosevelt did appeal on occasion to an expansive sense of national community. "We have been extending to our national life the old principle of the local community," he proclaimed in 1933. "We are saying, 'Is this practice, is this custom, something which is being done at the expense of the many?' And the many are the neighbors. In a national sense the many, the neighbors, are the people of the United States as a whole." Speaking to an audience of Young Democrats in 1935, he urged them to embrace an ethic of cooperation and mutual advancement. Once Americans had pursued "the dream of the golden ladder—each individual for himself." But the new generation had a different dream: "Your advancement, you hope, is along a broad highway on which thousands of your fellow men and women are advancing with you."[13]

But Roosevelt took care not to rest the case for federal social policy on any such communal ethic. For example, the Social Security Act was not defended as a welfare program but was carefully designed to resemble a private insurance scheme, funded by payroll "contributions" rather than general tax revenues. Later conceding that the regressive payroll taxes were bad economics, FDR emphasized that their purpose was political: "We put those payroll contributions there so as to give the contributors a legal, moral, and political right to collect their pensions and their unemployment benefits. With those taxes in there, no damn politician can ever scrap my social security program."[14]

In 1944, in his last State of the Union address, Roosevelt laid out what became the agenda for the welfare state that would emerge in subsequent decades. He called it "an economic bill of rights." As the industrial economy expanded, the political rights enumerated in the Constitution had proven inadequate to assure freedom. Among the social and economic rights necessary to "true individual freedom" were "the right to a useful and remunerative job . . . the right to earn enough to provide adequate food and clothing and recreation . . . the right of every family to a decent home, the right to adequate medical care . . . the right to adequate protection from the economic fears of old age, sickness, accident, and unemployment . . . the right to a good education." For Roosevelt, these rights depended for their justification not on strong notions of communal obligation, but instead on the idea that "necessitous men are not free men." Certain material conditions were prerequisites for the freedom of each person to choose his ends for himself.[15]

From Harry Truman's "Fair Deal" to Lyndon Johnson's "Great Society," the American welfare state unfolded, sometimes fitfully, along roughly the lines that FDR envisioned. Federal aid to education, low-income housing, Medicare, Medicaid, food stamps, job training, and expansions of Social Security, unemployment insurance, and public assistance went a considerable way toward fulfilling the project of liberal reform. Consistent with Roosevelt's suggestion, the argument for these programs—like the argument against them—was typically cast in terms of individual rights and the voluntarist conception of freedom.

In advancing the rationale for the Great Society, Lyndon Johnson drew on a number of arguments, including the ideal of national community.[16] He spoke of "forging in this country a greater sense of union," of learning "to submerge our individual differences to the common good," of turning Americans' "unity of interest into unity of purpose, and unity of goals into unity in the Great Society." In a metaphor that would recur in Democratic rhetoric for a generation, Johnson described the nation as "a family" that "takes care of all its members in time of adversity," its people "bound together by common ties of confidence and affection."[17]

Johnson's evocation of national community might seem to embrace the nationalizing tradition of Progressive reform and to set him apart from the liberalism of the procedural republic. Like Progressives from Herbert Croly to FDR, Johnson sought not only to expand the role of the federal government but also to deepen Americans' sense of national belonging, "to make the nation more of a nation."[18] The primary purpose of politics, he declared, was "to elevate our national life," to "help perfect the unity of the people," to engage Americans in "a common enterprise, a cause greater than themselves. . . . Without this, we will simply become a nation of strangers."[19]

On closer inspection, however, Johnson's political vision shared less with the formative tradition than with the version of liberalism that, by the 1960s, increasingly set the terms of American political discourse. Earlier proponents of the formative project had sought to shape the character of citizens through concrete practices and institutions, ranging from the common school to industrial democracy and other economic arrangements thought hospitable to the habits of self-rule. For Johnson, by contrast, the call to national community was more abstract and hortatory. To its credit, Johnson's ethic of national community did serve as a way of trying to explain why whites should accord equal rights to blacks and why the affluent should support policies designed to help the poor.[20] But despite its promise to answer "the hunger for community,"[21] the Great Society was primarily concerned with promoting abundance and fair access to the fruits of abundance; it offered little that might form in citizens the virtues that would equip them for self-government.

The one aspect of the Great Society that did recall the political economy of citizenship was the community action program of the War on Poverty. This program sought to enlarge the civic capacity of the poor by encouraging their participation in antipoverty programs at the local level. For Johnson, however, the program was an uncomfortable anomaly, and when community action groups came into conflict with Democratic mayors and other local officials, he abandoned it.[22]

In Johnson's vision of national community, the formative project of the Progressive tradition can be seen giving way to the voluntarist project of contemporary liberalism. One expression of the drift to the procedural republic can be found in the conception of citizenship Johnson affirmed. For Johnson, perfecting the unity of the nation meant encouraging Americans to set aside or rise above identities tied to region, race, religion, or class. The ideal American citizen would think and act as a kind of universal person, unencumbered by particular identities and attachments. Johnson's ideal was "an America that knows no North or South, no East or West," "a united nation, divided neither by class nor by section nor by color." As an example of "the politics of unity" he espoused, Johnson recalled the gathering of high government and military officials at the White House during the Cuban missile crisis. What impressed him most was the way they deliberated without reference to the particular backgrounds or communities from which they came: "You couldn't tell from anyone's comment what their religion was or what their party was, and you could not even observe from their accent where they were from."[23]

Even as he appealed to the ideal of national community, Lyndon Johnson defended the Great Society in the name of the voluntarist conception of freedom. In this lies a further link to the liberalism of the procedural republic. Johnson disputed the claim made by conservative critics that the federal government had become "a major menace to individual liberty. . . . The truth is—far from crushing the individual, government at its best liberates him from the enslaving forces of his environment."

Thanks to the achievements of Democratic reform, "every American is freer to shape his own activities, set his own goals, do what he wants with his own life, than at any time in the history of man."[24]

Accepting his party's nomination in 1964, Johnson echoed Roosevelt's argument that economic security is a prerequisite for individual liberty: "The man who is hungry, who cannot find work or educate his children, who is bowed by want—that man is not fully free." Johnson defended the project of liberal reform in the name of enabling people to choose and pursue their ends for themselves: "For more than 30 years, from social security to the war against poverty, we have diligently worked to enlarge the freedom of man. And as a result, Americans tonight are freer to live as they want to live, to pursue their ambitions, to meet their desires . . . than at any time in all of our glorious history."[25]

The notion that government should respect people's rights to choose their own values and ends was not unique to defenders of the welfare state. It was also invoked by laissez-faire critics of the welfare state such as the conservative Republican Barry Goldwater and the economist Milton Friedman. It thus set the terms of national political debate. Goldwater's 1964 campaign against Johnson posed one of the clearest ideological contrasts in recent presidential elections. But despite his opposition to such liberal causes as the war on poverty, the progressive income tax, and even Social Security, Goldwater shared with liberals the voluntarist conception of freedom.[26]

"The choices that govern [a person's] life are choices that *he* must make: they cannot be made by any other human being, or by a collectivity of human beings," wrote Goldwater in a 1960 manifesto, *The Conscience of a Conservative*. "If the Conservative is less anxious than his Liberal brethren to increase Social Security 'benefits,' it is because he is more anxious than his Liberal brethren that people be free throughout their lives to spend their earnings when and as they see fit." The only legitimate functions of government were those that made it "possible for men to follow their chosen pursuits with maximum freedom." According to Goldwater, these functions were limited to such things as maintaining order, providing for the national defense, and enforcing private property rights. Other government activities, such as taxing the rich to help the poor, amounted to coerced charity, a violation of freedom. "How can a man be truly free . . . if the fruits of his labor are not his to dispose of, but are treated, instead, as part of a common pool of public wealth?" Those who believed in welfare programs should contribute as they saw fit to private charity, not confiscate the money of "fellow citizens who may have different ideas about their social obligations."[27]

The economist Milton Friedman offered a scholarly version of the positions Goldwater espoused. Instead of embracing the term "conservative," however, Friedman insisted that opposing the welfare state in the name of individual freedom was being true to liberalism in its classic, nineteenth-century sense. "I find it hard, as a liberal, to see any justification for graduated taxation solely to redistribute income," Friedman wrote. "This seems a clear case of using coercion to take from some in order to give to others and thus to conflict head-on with individual freedom." Requiring persons to contribute to their own retirement through the Social Security system was also an unjust infringement on freedom. "If a man knowingly prefers to live for today, to use his resources for current enjoyment, deliberately choosing a penurious old age, by what right do we prevent him from doing so? We may argue with him, seek to persuade him that he is wrong, but are we entitled to use coercion to prevent him from doing what he chooses to do?"[28]

Friedman opposed on similar grounds a wide range of policies, including housing subsidies, the minimum wage, national parks, publicly owned and operated toll roads, and laws requiring the licensing of doctors, pharmacists, and other occupational groups. Thoroughgoing though it was, Friedman's critique of the welfare state shared with its defenders the voluntarist conception of freedom. Government programs of recent decades were wrong for imposing on some the values of others, for failing to respect people's desires "to live their lives by their own values."[29]

Liberalism and Welfare Rights

Welfare advocates also worried that existing programs of public assistance were infringing people's liberty. But the threat they saw was to the freedom of the recipient, not to the freedom of the taxpayer. Unlike Social Security,

Aid to Families with Dependent Children (AFDC), the primary welfare program, was open only to the poor who met certain conditions. These eligibility conditions, as well as the level of benefits, varied widely from state to state. The discretionary character of AFDC benefits rendered recipients vulnerable to removal from welfare roles on various grounds and enabled states to use eligibility requirements to express moral judgments about who was and was not a worthy recipient of assistance. For example, some states denied welfare to unmarried women found cohabiting with a man, a provision enforced by "midnight raids" of recipients' homes. For liberal reformers, such practices constituted a double violation of individual liberty. Not only did the odious means of enforcement involve a gross infringement on privacy, but the attempt to regulate the moral character of welfare recipients was an unjust case of "legislating morality," a failure to respect each person's capacity to choose his or her own way of life. Welfare reformers of the 1960s and 1970s therefore urged that welfare be established as a basic right of citizenship and that states be limited with regard to the eligibility criteria they could impose.[30]

In an influential article titled "The New Property," Yale law professor Charles Reich argued that benefits such as unemployment compensation, public assistance, and old-age insurance should be regarded not as government largesse but as rights, subject to the same legal protections accorded traditional property rights. "Only by making such benefits into rights can the welfare state achieve its goal of providing a secure minimum basis for individual well-being and dignity in a society where each man cannot be wholly the master of his own destiny." Treating welfare as a right would serve freedom not only by assuring a certain level of economic security but also by limiting the capacity of states "to impose a standard of moral behavior on beneficiaries."[31]

Edward Sparer, a leading welfare-rights litigator, included among the aims of poverty law "the right to choose one's own standards of morality." "No more invidious invasion of the rights of welfare subjects exists," he wrote, "than the ubiquitous tendency to impose upon the welfare recipient standards of morality which are a matter of free choice for other citizens. . . . The constant search for a man sleeping in the female's house, prompting the midnight raids and early morning visits, reflects not only a search for sources of support, but an angry moral judgment."[32]

For a time, the U.S. Supreme Court moved in the direction that welfare reformers advocated. In *King v. Smith* (1968), the Warren Court struck down an Alabama rule that cut off welfare payments to unmarried mothers and their children if the mother cohabited with a man. Central to the Court's holding was the notion that no state could use its welfare regulations to impose moral judgments or standards of behavior on recipients. Alabama had defended its regulation partly on grounds of "discouraging immorality and illegitimacy." But as Chief Justice Earl Warren explained, "these state interests are not presently legitimate justifications for AFDC disqualification. Insofar as this or any similar regulation is based on the State's asserted interest in discouraging illicit sexual behavior and illegitimacy, it plainly conflicts with federal law and policy."[33]

Warren acknowledged that earlier public welfare programs had distinguished between the "worthy poor" and those deemed unworthy of support. Congressional reports on the Social Security Act of 1935 indicated "that States participating in AFDC were free to impose eligibility requirements relating to the 'moral character' of applicants." From the 1930s to the 1950s, many states adopted "judgmental" regulations of this kind, disqualifying families for illicit sexual behavior by the mother or the presence of illegitimate children. But in the 1960s, rulings by the Department of Health, Education and Welfare and congressional amendments to the Social Security Act limited the ability of states to impose such restrictions. "[F]ederal public welfare policy now rests on a basis considerably more sophisticated and enlightened than the 'worthy-person' concept of earlier times," Warren concluded. In the light of recent federal policy, "it is simply inconceivable . . . that Alabama is free to discourage immorality and illegitimacy by the device of absolute disqualification of needy children."[34]

In two subsequent cases the Court seemed implicitly to recognize a constitutional right to welfare. In *Shapiro v. Thompson* (1969), it struck down state residency requirements for welfare eligibility. The Court argued that such requirements violated the constitutional right to travel between states. Some commentators, noting the Court's statement that residency requirements effectively denied to some "the very means to subsist—food, shelter, and other necessities of life," argued that the ruling implicitly recognized a right to welfare.[35]

In *Goldberg v. Kelly* (1970), the Court held that a state could not terminate a person's welfare benefits without a prior hearing to determine eligibility. To terminate aid without such a hearing "may deprive an eligible recipient of the very means by which to live while he waits." Writing for the Court, Justice William Brennan rejected "the argument that public assistance benefits are 'a privilege and not a right.'" Citing Reich, Brennan observed: "It may be realistic today to regard welfare entitlements more like 'property' than a 'gratuity.'" Public assistance, Brennan stated, "is not mere charity."[36]

In *Dandridge v. Williams* (1970), however, the Burger Court reversed the movement toward treating welfare as a constitutional right. Upholding a Maryland regulation setting the maximum AFDC grant at a level below the established need of some families, the Court rejected the notion that a fundamental right was at stake: "here we deal with state regulation in the social and economic field, not affecting freedoms guaranteed by the Bill of Rights."[37] Although the Supreme Court refused to recognize a constitutional right to welfare, federal courts continued throughout the 1970s to employ statutory interpretation to review federal and state welfare policies, broaden eligibility standards, and raise benefits.[38]

Meanwhile, the version of liberalism that asserts the priority of the right over the good found further expression in general public debate about welfare during the 1960s and 1970s, especially among those who favored replacing welfare with a guaranteed income for all citizens. Some economists viewed a cash payment as a more efficient form of assistance than various categorical programs.[39] But beyond the appeal of efficiency, many liberals considered a guaranteed income the best way of respecting the freedom of the poor to choose their values and ends for themselves. Not only would such a policy assure to all citizens the economic prerequisite for the meaningful exercise of their civil and political rights; it would do so in a way that avoided the contentious struggle over eligibility requirements and the moral judgments they typically imposed.

Robert Theobald, an influential advocate of the guaranteed income, emphasized its importance in terms of the voluntarist conception of freedom. Each individual should be ensured "the maximum of freedom in his choice of action compatible with the needs of the society. Such a degree of freedom can only be obtained if the individual is provided with sufficient resources to enable him to live with dignity." Government should therefore "adopt the concept of an absolute constitutional right to income. This would guarantee to every citizen of the United States . . . the right to an income from the federal government sufficient to enable him to live with dignity." Unlike welfare, a guaranteed income would not seek to form moral character or shape behavior or cultivate virtue but rather would enable recipients to choose their values and ends for themselves. It offered "money rather than moral uplift." It would reflect "the fundamental American belief in the right and the ability of the individual to decide what he wishes and ought to do."[40]

Liberal reformers echoed the argument that Americans were entitled to a minimum income as a matter of right and that the right should be provided in a way that did not impose on recipients any particular conception of the good life. William Ryan of New York, a leading congressional advocate of welfare reform, argued that "a guaranteed annual income is not a privilege. It should be a right to which every American is entitled." He opposed any attempt to condition income maintenance on the requirement that recipients work. Such requirements were coercive and objectionable, since "forced work is alien to individual choice and freedom." In testimony to Congress, liberal church groups opposed not only work requirements but any mandatory job training, family planning programs, or measures to determine paternity and locate missing fathers. Such requirements, they objected, "attempt to legislate morality." "Assistance should not be used to enforce a particular code of behavior." All persons, including the poor, "should have the freedom to choose how they may express the meaning of their lives."[41]

In 1969 President Richard Nixon proposed a Family Assistance Plan that closely resembled a guaranteed income, providing $1,600 per year for a family of four. The plan passed the House but died in the Senate, where liberals objected that its benefits were too low and conservatives objected that its work incentives were too weak. Welfare reform remained a vexed issue into the 1980s and 1990s, when sentiment grew for work requirements and other measures to transform the lives of the poor.[42]

The Self-Image of the Age

The version of liberalism that informed American political and constitutional debate in the decades after World War II found its fullest philosophical statement in the 1970s, most notably in John Rawls's *Theory of Justice*. Against the utilitarian assumptions that dominated much twentieth-century Anglo-American philosophy, Rawls argued that certain individual rights are so important that they outweigh considerations of the general welfare or the will of the majority. Thus "the rights secured by justice are not subject to political bargaining or the calculus of social interests."[43]

The notion that certain individual rights outweigh utilitarian considerations is not, of course, unique to the liberalism of the procedural republic. Rights can be defended on a number of grounds, including the grounds that respecting certain rights is a way of cultivating civic virtue or of encouraging among citizens certain worthy practices or beliefs or qualities of character. A right to free speech might be defended, for example, on the grounds that it makes possible the political debate and deliberation on which self-government depends. Similarly, the right to religious liberty might be defended on the grounds that religious practice and belief are important features of the good life and thus worthy of special protection.

But Rawls did not defend rights on grounds such as these. To the contrary, he argued that rights should not depend for their justification on any particular conception of the good life. According to Rawls, a just society does not try to cultivate virtue or impose on its citizens any particular ends. Rather, it provides a framework of rights, neutral among ends, within which persons can pursue their own conceptions of the good, consistent with a similar liberty for others. This is the claim that the right is prior to the good, and it is this claim that defines the liberalism of the procedural republic.[44]

Closely connected to the claim for the priority of the right is the voluntarist conception of freedom. As Rawls explained, it is precisely because we are free and independent selves, capable of choosing our ends for ourselves, that we need a framework of rights that is neutral among ends. When government seeks to promote virtue or to shape the moral character of its citizens, it imposes on some the values of others and so fails to respect our capacity to choose our own values and ends. On the voluntarist view, the rights to free speech and religious liberty are important, not because the activities they protect are specially worthy but rather because these rights respect the capacity of persons to choose their beliefs and opinions for themselves. This brings out the liberating vision underlying the insistence that government be neutral among ends. "A moral person is a subject with ends he has chosen, and his fundamental preference is for conditions that enable him to frame a mode of life that expresses his nature as a free and equal rational being as fully as circumstances permit." As the right is prior to the good, so the self is prior to its ends. "It is not our aims that primarily reveal our nature," but rather the rights we would agree to respect if we could abstract from our aims. "For the self is prior to the ends which are affirmed by it; even a dominant end must be chosen from among numerous possibilities."[45]

If government must be neutral among ends in order to respect persons as freely choosing, individual selves, unclaimed by moral ties antecedent to choice, it is a further question what rights the ideal of the neutral state requires. Here too the philosophical debate of the 1970s paralleled the political debate over rights that unfolded from the New Deal through the Great Society. Some, including Rawls, argued in defense of the welfare state. For government to be neutral among ends meant allowing only those social and economic inequalities that work to the advantage of the least advantaged members of society. The distribution of talents and endowments that leads some to flourish and others to fail in the market economy is "arbitrary from a moral point of view." Respecting persons as free and independent selves therefore requires a structure of rights and entitlements that compensates for the arbitrariness of fortune.[46]

Others, such as Robert Nozick in *Anarchy, State, and Utopia,* argued against the welfare state. A laissez-faire liberal in the tradition of Barry Goldwater and Milton Friedman, Nozick held that respecting rights means denying the state a role in the redistribution of income and wealth. The just distribution is whatever one results from the voluntary exchanges that transpire in a market society. "From each as they choose, to each as they are chosen." Despite their differences about distributive justice, Nozick agreed with Rawls that individual rights outweigh utilitarian considerations and that government should be neutral among ends in order to respect people's capacity to choose and pursue their own values and ends.[47] Like the political debate they brought to philosophical clarity, theirs was a debate within the terms of the voluntarist conception of freedom.

The liberal self-image underlying the procedural republic found more vivid if less edifying expression in the pop psychology and self-help literature of the 1970s. It was here that the liberating promise of the voluntarist conception of freedom assumed its most extravagant form. According to Dr. Wayne Dyer, a best-selling author of the 1970s, the road to happiness and freedom begins with the insight that "you are the sum total of your choices." Self-mastery consists in viewing every aim and attachment, every feeling and thought, as the product of choice. Viewing every emotion "as a choice rather than as a condition of life" is "the very heart of personal freedom." It is likewise with thought: "You have the power to think whatever you choose to allow into your head. If something just 'pops' into your head . . . you still have the power to make it go away." Morality and religion, properly understood, are also the products of choice. Organized religion, a symptom of "approval-seeking needs," produces behavior that "you haven't chosen . . . freely." Preferable is "a veritable religion of the self in which an individual determines his own behavior" without "needing the approval of an outside force."[48]

According to the political theory of contemporary liberalism, government should neither shape nor judge the character of its citizens. According to Dr. Dyer, people should adopt the same nonjudgmental stance even in their intimate relations. The essence of love is the "willingness to allow those that you care for to be what they choose for themselves." Such love "involves no imposition of values on the loved one." Such independent selves would inspire new lyrics for popular love songs. Instead of singing "Can't stop loving you," they would croon, "I can stop loving you, but at this point I choose not to."[49]

Notwithstanding their nonjudgmental pose, however, Dr. Dyer's unencumbered selves do insist that those they love live up to the ideal of independence. They "want those they love to be independent, to make their own choices, and to live their lives for themselves." They "see independence as superior to dependence in all relationships. . . . They refuse to be dependent, or depended upon, in a mature relationship."[50]

If caricature can be clarifying, Dyer's ideal of the person sums up the liberating promise that animates the procedural republic. The happy, healthy selves he invites us to admire "are strikingly independent. . . . Their relationships are built upon mutual respect for the right of an individual to make decisions for himself." They are tolerant, nonjudg-mental, except toward those who affirm the dependence they despise. "They have no oughts for others. They see everyone as having choices, and those petty things that drive others insane are simply the results of someone else's decision." Alert to the fact that people often disagree about values, they are quick to bracket controversial questions and so waste little time engaging in moral discourse or debate: "They aren't arguers or hot-headed debaters; they simply state their views, listen to others and recognize the futility of trying to convince someone else to be as they are. They'll simply say, 'That's all right; we're just different. We don't have to agree.' They let it go at that without any need to win an argument or persuade the opponent of the wrongness of his posi-tion."[51]

Unencumbered by moral ties they have not chosen, Dyer's ideal selves know no solidarity: "Their values are not local. They do not identify with the family, neighborhood, community, city, state, or country. They see themselves as belonging to the human race, and an unemployed Austrian is no better or worse than an unemployed Californian. They are not patriotic to a special boundary; rather they see themselves as a part of the whole of humanity."[52]

More than health and happiness, those who live according to Dr. Dyer's precepts can attain "total mastery" of their lives.[53] Far from the republican freedom of exercising self-government, however, the mastery at issue has mostly to do with personal relations or activities of consump-tion—standing up to surly department store clerks, returning a steak without being intimidated by rude waiters, and so on. In this lies the pathos of the voluntarist project as it had unfolded by the 1970s. For even as Americans yearned for mastery in their personal lives, the public life informed by the voluntarist vision was haunted by the fear that the prospect of collective agency was slipping away.

The Loss of Mastery

By the 1970s, the version of liberalism that asserts the priority of the right over the good had become the reigning American public philosophy. The notion that government should be neutral among competing conceptions of the good life in order to respect people's rights to choose their own values and ends figured prominently in political discourse and constitutional law. The image of persons as free and independent selves, unencumbered by moral or political ties they have not chosen, found expression in politics, economics, law, philosophy, and the broader public culture. Older, republican understandings of citizenship and freedom did not disappear altogether but were now a minor strand in American public discourse.

But notwithstanding its liberating vision, the public philosophy of contemporary liberalism was unable to secure the liberty it promised. The triumph of the voluntarist conception of freedom coincided with a growing sense of disempowerment. Despite the expansion of rights and entitlements and despite the achievements of the political economy of growth and distributive justice, Americans found to their frustration that they were losing control of the forces that governed their lives. At home and abroad, events spun out of control, and government seemed helpless to respond. At the same time, the circumstances of modern life were eroding those forms of community—families and neighborhoods, cities and towns, civic and ethnic and religious communities—that situate people in the world and provide a source of identity and belonging.

Taken together, these two fears—for the loss of self-government and the erosion of community—defined the anxiety of the age. It was an anxiety that the reigning political agenda, with its attenuated civic resources, was unable to answer or even address. This failure fueled the discontent that has beset American democracy from the late 1960s to the present day. Those political figures who managed to tap the mood of discontent did so by reaching beyond the terms of contemporary liberalism; some sought a response in a recovery of republican themes.

History seldom marks its moments with precision; the lines it etches in time are often blurry and difficult to discern. The year 1968, however, was an exception. For it was then that America's moment of mastery expired. Theodore White began his chronicle of the tumultuous politics of 1968 by describing the glassed-in wall maps and clattering teletypes of the Pentagon's National Military Command Center, where the U.S. military monitors the readiness of American forces and weapons around the globe. "Here, enshrined like myth, in January, 1968, was the visible symbol of American faith: that the power of the United States can be curbed by no one, that the instruments of American government need but the will to act and it is done." As White observed, "In 1968 this faith was to be shattered—the myth of American power broken, the confidence of the American people in their government, their institutions, their leadership, shaken as never before since 1860."[54]

The first episode in the shattering of faith came at the end of January, when reports of a Communist offensive in Vietnam came across the command center's teletypes. On the day of the Vietnamese New Year (Tet), Viet Cong forces mounted a stunning attack on Saigon and other South Vietnamese strongholds, invading even the supposedly impregnable American embassy. That night on the evening news, Americans, long assured by their government that the United States was winning the war, saw the shocking scene of Viet Cong troops in the U.S. embassy. The next day they witnessed the gruesome spectacle of a South Vietnamese officer shooting a Viet Cong prisoner in the head, an image that came to symbolize the brutality of the war.[55]

Although the Tet offensive actually ended in a costly defeat for Communist forces, it had a devastating effect on Americans' confidence in Lyndon Johnson's conduct of the war. In the weeks after Tet, antiwar sentiment grew, Johnson's popularity plummeted, and even the measured CBS newscaster Walter Cronkite called for de-escalation. Meanwhile, the 1968 political season unfolded in a series of bewildering and ultimately violent events. In the New Hampshire primary, antiwar senator Eugene McCarthy, challenging a president of his own party, nearly defeated Lyndon Johnson. Polls showed that McCarthy's votes came not only from opponents of the war but also from hawks disillusioned with Johnson's Vietnam quagmire. A few days later, Robert Kennedy declared his candidacy. At the end of March, Johnson, his presidency battered not only by the war but also by the domestic unrest it had provoked, shocked the country by announcing his withdrawal from the campaign.[56]

Four days later, Martin Luther King Jr. was assassinated in Memphis. Riots broke out in urban ghettos across the country; forty-three people died, and more than 20,000 were arrested. The next month, on the night of his victory in the California primary, Robert Kennedy was assassinated in Los Angeles. Vice President Hubert Humphrey went on to win the Democratic nomination in August, but violent clashes between police and antiwar protesters outside the Chicago convention hall defined the occasion. In November, Richard Nixon, appealing to Americans' desire for "law and order," was elected president.[57]

The mood of discontent and disillusion that descended upon American politics in 1968 had been building for several years. The inner-city riots, campus protests, and antiwar demonstrations of the mid-1960s intimated the unraveling of faith in existing arrangements. These protests and disorders, and the fears they aroused, fostered a growing sense that events were spinning out of control and that government lacked the moral or political authority to respond. In 1968 the disillusion spread beyond the ghettos and the campuses to a broader American public. The heady sense of mastery so prevalent in earlier decades gave way to the conviction that "events are in the saddle and ride mankind."[58] Americans began to think of themselves less as agents than as instruments of larger forces that defied their understanding and control. As James Reston wrote, "Washington is now the symbol of the helplessness of the present day. . . . The main crisis is not Vietnam itself, or in the cities, but in the feeling that the political system for dealing with these things has broken down."[59]

The decades that followed did not allay that sense of helplessness. At home and abroad, events of the 1970s and 1980s only deepened Americans' fears that, individually and collectively, they were losing control of the forces that governed their lives. The Watergate break-in and cover-up; Nixon's resignation under threat of impeachment; the fall of Saigon, as Americans and South Vietnamese clamored desperately to board the few departing helicopters; the inflation of the 1970s; the OPEC oil shock; the ensuing energy shortage and gasoline lines; the Iranian hostage-taking and failed rescue mission; the terrorist killing of 241 American marines in their barracks in Beirut; the stagnation of middle-class incomes; the gaping federal budget deficit; and the persistent inability of government to deal with crime, drugs, and urban decay: all further eroded Americans' faith that they were the masters of their destiny.

These events took a devastating toll on Americans' trust in government.[60] In 1964, 76 percent of Americans believed they could trust the government in Washington to do what is right most of the time; three decades later, only 20 percent did.[61] In 1964, just under half of Americans thought that government wasted a lot of the taxpayers' money; by the 1990s, four out of five thought so. In 1964, fewer than one in three Americans believed government was run by a few big interests rather than for the benefit of all the people; by the 1990s, three-fourths of Americans thought government was run by and for the few.[62] When John Kennedy was elected president, most Americans believed that public officials cared what they thought; three decades later, most Americans did not.[63]

Groping to Address the Discontent

As disillusion with government grew, politicians groped to articulate frustrations and discontents that the reigning political agenda did not capture. Those who tapped the mood of discontent differed as sharply in their politics as George Wallace and Robert Kennedy, Jimmy Carter and Ronald Reagan. But for all their differences, those who succeeded all drew on themes that reached beyond the terms of contemporary liberalism and spoke to the loss of self-government and community.

The Politics of Protest: George C. Wallace

Prominent among the early practitioners of the politics of protest was George Wallace, the fiery southern populist who in 1963, as governor of Alabama, proclaimed "segregation now, segregation tomorrow, segregation forever" and vowed to "stand in the schoolhouse door" to prevent the desegregation of the University of Alabama.[64] Running as a third-party candidate for president in 1968, and in the Democratic primaries in 1972, Wallace voiced the resentments of white working-class voters who felt threatened by crime and race riots, victimized by forced busing to integrate public schools, angered by student protests and antiwar demonstrations, and disempowered by permissive courts and arrogant federal bureaucrats. He spoke, he said, for the "average man in the street, this man in the textile mill, this man in the steel mill, this barber, the beautician, the policeman on the beat."[65]

Beyond the undeniable element of racism in Wallace's appeal lay a broader protest against the powerlessness many Americans felt toward a distant federal government that regulated their lives but seemed helpless to stem the social turmoil and lawlessness that troubled them most.[66] Wallace exploited the fact that neither major party was addressing this sense of disempowerment. There was "not a dime's worth of difference," Wallace charged, between national Democrats and Republicans, who would rather listen to "some pointy-headed pseudo-intellectual who can't even park his bicycle straight" than to ordinary citizens. "They've looked down their noses at the average man on the street too long . . . they say, 'We've gotta write a guideline, we've gotta tell you when to get up in the morning, we've gotta tell you when to go to bed at night.' And we gonna tell both national parties the average man on the street in Tennessee and Alabama and California don't need anybody to write him a guideline to tell him when to get up."[67]

Although he railed against the power of the federal government, Wallace was no laissez-faire conservative. He favored tax reform and supported increases in Social Security, unemployment compensation, and the minimum wage. Like earlier populists, he protested against concentrated wealth and economic power: "We're sick and tired of the average citizen being taxed to death while these multibillionaires like the Rockefellers and the Fords and the Mellons and Carnegies go without paying taxes."[68]

Wallace offered blunt remedies for social unrest. Professors calling for revolution and students raising money for Communists should be thrown into "a good jail somewhere." Unruly political protesters might be dealt with by "a good crease in the skull." As for the "anarchist" who tried to block the president's car, Wallace promised, "If any demonstrator lies down in front of my car when I'm President, that'll be the last car he lays down in front of."[69]

Beyond cracking down on dissenters, Wallace proposed scaling back the power of the federal government, which he claimed was dominated by an elite that scorned the values of ordinary Americans: "I'm sick and tired of some professors and some preachers and some judges and some newspaper editors having more to say about my everyday life . . . than I have to say about it myself." He would summon the Washington bureaucrats and "take away their briefcases and throw them in the Potomac River." The "beatnik mob in Washington" had "just about destroyed not only local government but the school systems of our country," prompting a "backlash against big government." Wallace pledged to reverse the trend toward federal power: "We are going to turn back to you, the people of the states, the right to control our domestic institutions."[70]

Wallace's candidacy revealed the dark side of the politics of powerlessness, but his electoral success alerted mainstream politicians to a gathering discontent they could ill afford to ignore.[71] As a third-party candidate in 1968, Wallace drew close to 10 million votes and carried five states. Before being shot while campaigning in the 1972 Democratic primaries, he drew more popular votes than any other Democrat, winning five primaries and finishing second in five others.[72] Although Wallace offered little in the way of plausible solutions, he was among the first to tap the discontent of a growing number of Americans who believed that the familiar debates between Democrats and Republicans, liberals and conservatives, did not address the issues that mattered most. The reigning political agenda, which still bore the imprint of the New Deal and the Great Society, had mostly to do with competing notions of individual rights and different ways of managing the relation between the welfare state and the market economy. It had little to say to those who feared they were losing control of their lives to vast structures of impersonal power while the moral fabric of neighborhood and community unraveled around them.

Civic Stirrings: Robert F. Kennedy

Of all the presidential candidates of recent decades who sought to articulate the inchoate frustrations that beset American politics, the one who offered the most compelling political vision was Robert F. Kennedy. The alternative he offered was drawn from the republican tradition of politics that contemporary liberalism had largely eclipsed. As attorney general under his brother, John Kennedy, and later as a U.S. senator from New York, Robert Kennedy was widely identified with the version of liberalism that set the terms of political discourse in the 1960s. But in the last few years of his life, Kennedy became a trenchant critic of the assumptions underlying the American welfare state.[73]

Kennedy observed that by the mid-1960s the federal government had largely fulfilled the agenda of liberal reform: "The inheritance of the New Deal is fulfilled. There is not a problem for which there is not a program. There is not a problem for which money is not being spent. There is not a problem or a program on which dozens or hundreds or thousands of bureaucrats are not earnestly at work."[74] But despite the success of the liberal project, and perhaps partly because of it, Americans found themselves the victims of large, impersonal forces beyond their control. Kennedy linked this loss of agency to the erosion of self-government and the sense of community that sustains it.

Kennedy sought to redress the loss of agency by decentralizing political power. This marked a departure from the liberalism of his day. From the 1930s to the 1960s, liberals had viewed increased federal power as an instrument of freedom.[75] The concentration of power in the national government and the expansion of individual rights and entitlements had gone hand in hand. Liberals defended the growth of federal power as essential to securing the basic rights of citizens—including civil rights and certain economic rights—against infringement by local majorities. Otherwise, they argued, local governments might act to deprive people of their rights, by allowing segregation, for example, or denying welfare benefits on illegitimate grounds. Those like Wallace, who opposed desegregation, or Goldwater, who opposed social and economic entitlements, often called for states' rights and local control as a way of opposing federal policies they disliked.

Robert Kennedy's case for decentralization was different. Since he was an advocate of civil rights and federal spending to help the poor, his worry about federal power did not spring from opposition to the ends it served. Rather, it reflected the insight that even a realized welfare state cannot secure the part of freedom bound up with sharing in self-rule; it cannot provide, and may even erode, the civic capacities and communal resources necessary to self-government. In the mounting discontents of American public life, Kennedy glimpsed the failure of liberal politics to attend to the civic dimension of freedom.

In terms reminiscent of Brandeis' attack on "the curse of bigness," Kennedy criticized the concentration of power in both the modern economy and the bureaucratic state. "Even as the drive toward bigness [and] concentration . . . has reached heights never before dreamt of in the past," he told an audience in rural Minnesota, "we have come suddenly to realize how heavy a price we have paid . . . in [the] growth of organizations, particularly government, so large and powerful that individual effort and importance seem lost; and in loss of the values of . . . community and local diversity that found their nurture in the smaller towns and rural areas of America. . . . Bigness, loss of community, organizations and society grown far past the human scale—these are the besetting sins of the twentieth century, which threaten to paralyze our capacity to act. . . . Therefore, the time has come . . . when we must actively fight bigness and overconcentration, and seek instead to bring the engines of government, of technology, of the economy, fully under the control of our citizens."[76]

A politics of more manageable proportions was not only an idyll for rural America. It also informed Kennedy's approach to the crisis of the cities. Underlying the plight of urban America, he told a Senate subcommittee, was "the destruction of the sense, and often the fact, of community, of human dialogue, the thousand invisible strands of common experience and purpose, affection and respect, which tie men to their fellows. It is expressed in such words as community, neighborhood, civic pride, friendship."[77]

In recent decades, Democrats who have evoked the ideal of community—from Lyndon Johnson to Walter Mondale and Mario Cuomo—have typically appealed to the national community.[78] But Robert Kennedy doubted that the nation was a sufficient vehicle for the kind of community self-government requires: "Nations or great cities are too huge to provide the values of community. Community demands a place where people can see and know each other, where children can play and adults work together and join in the pleasures and responsibilities of the place where they live." Such communities were disappearing in the modern world, leaving their inhabitants dislocated and disempowered. "The world beyond the neighborhood has become more impersonal and abstract," beyond the reach of individual control: "cities, in their tumbling spread, are obliterating neighborhoods and precincts. Housing units go up, but there is no place for people to walk, for women and their children to meet, for common activities. The place of work is far away through blackened tunnels or over impersonal highways. The doctor and lawyer and government official is often somewhere else and hardly known. In far too many places—in pleasant suburbs as well as city streets—the home is a place to sleep and eat and watch television; but the community is not where we live. We live in many places and so we live nowhere."[79]

In describing the ways in which crime and joblessness plague life in the urban ghetto, Kennedy emphasized their civic consequences. Beyond the physical danger it posed, the tragedy of crime was that it destroyed the public spaces, such as neighborhoods and communities, that are essential to self-government: "The real threat of crime is what it does to ourselves and our communities. No nation hiding behind locked doors is free, for it is imprisoned by its own fear. No nation whose citizens fear to walk their own streets is healthy, for in isolation lies the poisoning of public participation." Similarly, the problem with unemployment was not simply that the jobless lacked an income but that they could not share in the common life of citizenship: "Unemployment means having nothing to do—which means having nothing to do with the rest of us. To be without work, to be without use to one's fellow citizens, is to be in truth the Invisible Man of whom Ralph Ellison wrote."[80]

Drawing on the voluntarist conception of freedom, many liberals of the day argued that the solution to poverty was welfare, ideally in the form of a guaranteed minimum income that imposed no conditions and made no judgments about the lives recipients led. Respecting persons as free and independent selves, capable of choosing their own ends, meant providing each person as a matter of right a certain measure of economic security. Kennedy disagreed. Unlike many liberals, he did not draw his inspiration from the voluntarist conception of freedom. His primary concern was with the civic dimension of freedom, the capacity to share in self-government. On these grounds, he rejected welfare and a guaranteed income as inadequate.

Although welfare might alleviate poverty, it did not equip persons with the moral and civic capacities to share in full citizenship. Welfare was perhaps "our greatest domestic failure," Kennedy argued, because it rendered "millions of our people slaves to dependency and poverty, waiting on the favor of their fellow citizens to write them checks. Fellowship, community, shared patriotism—these essential values of our civilization do not come from just buying and consuming goods together. They come from a shared sense of individual independence and personal effort." The solution to poverty was not a guaranteed income paid by the government but "dignified employment at decent pay, the kind of employment that lets a man say to his community, to his family, to his country, and most important, to himself, 'I helped to build this country. I am a participant in its great public ventures.'" A guaranteed income, whatever good it might do, "simply cannot provide the sense of self-sufficiency, of participation in the life of the community, that is essential for citizens of a democracy."[81]

Kennedy's proposal for bringing jobs to the inner city reflected his broader aim of restoring a political economy of citizenship. Rather than a government jobs program directed from Washington, Kennedy proposed federal tax breaks for businesses that opened plants in impoverished areas, an idea recently revived as "enterprise zones." But Kennedy did not propose to rely on market forces alone. Even if tax incentives succeeded in prompting outside enterprises to invest in the ghetto, this would do little to give residents control of their communities. Kennedy therefore proposed the creation of Community Development Corporations, community-run institutions that would direct development in accordance with local needs. Such corporations might finance construction of low-cost housing, health clinics, parks, even shopping centers and movie theaters, and also arrange job training so that local workers could carry out the construction. The aim of the program was civic as well as economic: to help "the ghetto to become a community—a functioning unit, its people acting together on matters of mutual concern, with the power and resources to affect the conditions of their own lives."[82]

In one of the first major experiments along these lines, Kennedy enlisted government, corporate, and foundation support to launch a community development corporation in the Bedford-Stuyvesant section of Brooklyn, the second-largest black ghetto in the country. More than a project of economic development, Kennedy saw Bedford-Stuyvesant as "an experiment in politics, an experiment in self-government. Indeed, it is above all a chance to bring government back to the people of the neighborhood."

Kennedy recalled Jefferson's proposal to regenerate civic virtue by dividing the country into small political districts, or "wards," within which Americans could take charge of their local affairs and learn the habits and the skills of citizenship. Community development corporations and other neighborhood bodies, given sufficient responsibilities and support, might be a way of translating Jefferson's republican vision to modern times, of reversing "the growing accumulation of power and authority in the central government in Washington, and [returning] that power of decision to the American people in their own local communities."[83]

Alone among the major politicians of his day, Robert Kennedy diagnosed the disempowerment that afflicted American public life as a symptom of the erosion of civic practices and ideals. Partly as a result, Kennedy's candidacy resonated across two constituencies of discontent—white ethnics and blacks—that since his death have often been at odds. In the Indiana primary, for example, he won 86 percent of the black vote and also swept the seven counties that had given George Wallace his greatest support in 1964. Once described as "the last liberal politician who could communicate with white working-class America," Kennedy was in any case the only candidate of protest—from Wallace to Reagan to Jesse Jackson—who "was able to talk to the two polarities of powerlessness at the same time."[84]

In the decades that followed, Jimmy Carter and Ronald Reagan won the presidency by speaking to the frustrations that Americans felt toward government and politicians. Both campaigned as outsiders to Washington who would restore American confidence and pride. In the end, their presidencies did little to change the conditions underlying the discontents they tapped as candidates. Their differing attempts to diagnose these discontents shed light nonetheless on the political condition we still confront.

Moralism and Managerialism: Jimmy Carter

Carter campaigned, in the wake of Watergate and Gerald Ford's pardon of Richard Nixon, as an outsider to the Washington establishment who would restore Americans' faith in government. Americans had lost confidence in their government, Carter argued, because it had been deceitful and inefficient. He offered two remedies—one moral, the other managerial. The first emphasized honesty and openness, the second efficiency and competence.[85] Carter's moral appeal was expressed in his famous pledge never to lie to the American people. But the honesty and openness Carter promised was more than a matter of personal probity. It was also intended as a cure for the distance between the people and their government, a distance that Americans increasingly experienced as disempowering.

In this respect Carter's vision departed from the republican tradition and reflected the public philosophy of his day. The republican tradition taught that a certain distance between the people and their government was unavoidable, even desirable—provided that distance was filled with mediating institutions that gathered people together and equipped them to share in self-rule. This was the insight that animated the formative project from Jefferson's ward system to Robert Kennedy's community development corporations. Carter's politics did not draw on this tradition. Rather than mediate and order the distance between the people and the government, Carter proposed to close it. His call for honesty and openness stood for this larger ambition—to collapse the distance between government and the governed, to approach a kind of transparence, or immediacy, between the presidency and the people.

Carter expressed this aspiration in a number of ways. He wanted "to strip away the secrecy," to "tear down the wall that exists between our people and our government," to have a nation that was "honest and sensitive [and] open." Even "the smallest lie, the smallest misleading statement" he might commit as President could have a devastating effect. He would seek to avoid such transgressions by "tying" himself directly to the people: "I don't ever want there to be any powerful, big shot political intermediary between me and the average citizen of this country. We've got to be melded together."[86]

The second aspect of Carter's program traced the disillusion with government to its inefficiency: "We now have a bloated bureaucratic mess in Washington. It's going to take an outsider to correct it." Carter promised to make government more efficient, economical, and manageable: "We must give top priority to a drastic and thorough revision of the federal bureaucracy, to its budgeting system and to the procedures for constantly analyzing the effectiveness of its many varied services. Tight businesslike management and planning techniques must be instituted and maintained, utilizing the full authority and personal involvement of the president himself."[87] Critics soon derided Carter for being all too true to his technocratic promise, as he checked the arithmetic of the federal budget and personally reviewed requests to use the White House tennis court.[88] But the deeper difficulty lay elsewhere.

However different their tone, the moralism and managerialism that defined Carter's politics shared this defect: neither addressed the purposes or ends that government should serve. Consistent with the public philosophy of the procedural republic, Carter's program of honesty and efficiency bracketed, or abstracted from, any substantive moral or political ends. More than a technocratic conceit, Carter's moralism and managerialism had the political advantage of avoiding ideological controversy. Carter repeatedly emphasized the nonideological character of his politics: "I don't believe in wasting money. I do believe in tough, competent management. . . . I also believe in delivering services to those people who need those services in an efficient, economical, and sensitive way. That is not liberal or conservative. It's just good government."[89]

Some faulted Carter for conducting a "passionless presidency."[90] The real problem was that, true to his campaign, his was a purposeless presidency. Honesty and efficiency, however admirable, are not ends but ways of pursuing ends; they do not in themselves constitute a governing vision. Lacking any substantive governing purpose, Carter's presidency was all the more vulnerable to events at home and abroad that deepened Americans' sense of disempowerment.

The first such event unfolded gradually, as rising consumer prices brought an extended episode of double-digit inflation, only the second since the days following World War II. Prompted partly by higher energy prices, the annual rate of inflation rose steadily from 7 percent in May 1978 to 14.8 percent in March 1980.[91] Beyond shrinking the purchasing power of consumers, the mounting inflation further eroded Americans' confidence that they were the masters of their destiny. The civic consequences of inflation were nowhere better described than in the *Economic Report of the President* of January 1979. "One of the major tasks of a democratic government is to maintain conditions in which its citizens have a sense of command over their own destiny," the report stated. During an inflation, people watch in frustration as the value of their pay or pension is eroded "by a process that is beyond their control." It is difficult enough to plan for the future in the best of times. But "[w]hen the value of the measuring rod with which we do our planning—the purchasing power of the dollar—is subject to large and unpredictable shrinkage, one more element of command over our own future slips away. It is small wonder that trust in government and in social institutions is simultaneously eroded."[92]

The sense that events were spinning out of control was heightened by the oil shock of 1979, brought on by the overthrow of the shah of Iran and sharp price increases by other oil-producing states of the Middle East. Oil, which had sold on the world market for $3.41 a barrel in 1973, rose to $14.54 by 1978, and reached $30 a barrel in 1980.[93] The oil shock not only contributed to U.S. inflation but also drove home to Americans how dependent was their way of life on cheap energy supplied by foreign nations over which they had little control. Frustration with this condition reached panic proportions when, in the spring and summer of 1979, gasoline shortages led to long lines and rationing schemes at gas stations across the country.

President Carter, aware that the gas shortage was deepening the anger and disillusion of the American electorate, recast a planned speech on the energy crisis to address the larger crisis of confidence in American public life. "The erosion of our confidence in the future is threatening to destroy the social and political fabric of America," he declared. People were losing faith "not only in government itself but in their ability as citizens to serve as the ultimate rulers and shapers of our democracy." What could be done to change this condition? Carter's answer consisted mainly of exhortation: "We simply must have faith in each other, faith in our ability to govern ourselves, and faith in the future of this Nation. Restoring that faith and that confidence to America is now the most important task we face."[94]

Carter's address became known as the "malaise" speech (although he never used that term), and many criticized him for blaming his troubles on the anxious mood of the American people.[95] But the speech was actually a cogent statement of the discontent that had been building for over a decade. Its weakness was not that it shifted blame but that it failed to offer a direction for American politics that might address the discontent he aptly described.

A few months later the gas lines receded, but the unraveling of faith, and of the Carter presidency, continued. In the crowning indignity of Carter's luckless tenure, a mob of demonstrators in Iran took fifty-three Americans hostage at the U.S. embassy in Teheran. Walter Cronkite began closing the CBS newscast each night by counting the days the hostages had been held—a count that stretched to the end of Carter's term—and ABC kept the humiliating spectacle before the public with a daily late-night report that became the long-running program "Nightline." The hostage crisis, and the rescue mission that failed in the desert, seemed to confirm yet again that a nation accustomed to mastery had lost control of its destiny.[96]

Libertarian versus Communal Conservatism: Ronald Reagan

Ronald Reagan was elected on the promise to restore American mastery. Unbound by the strictures of the procedural republic, his rhetoric resonated with the ideals of self-government and community. For a time, his appeal to American pride and resolve, combined with the salubrious effects of economic recovery, seemed to reverse the trend toward ever-increasing disillusion with government. In the end, however, his presidency did little to change the conditions underlying the discontent. The policies he advanced did not attend to the features of modern life that posed the gravest threats to the prospect of collective agency and the fabric of community. The "morning in America" proclaimed in Reagan's gauzy campaign commercials of 1984 proved a false dawn, and by the end of the 1980s Americans' frustration with their political condition continued to mount.[97]

Although Reagan ultimately failed to allay the discontent he tapped, it is instructive nonetheless to consider the source of his appeal and the way it departed from the reigning terms of political discourse. Reagan's achievement was to bring together in a single voice two contending strands in American conservatism. The first, the libertarian or laissez-faire conservatism of Barry Goldwater and Milton Friedman, holds that people should be free to do as they please as long as they do not harm others. This is the conservatism that celebrates the "free market" and talks of getting government out of people's lives. It rejects the notion that government should form the character of its citizens, and so fits comfortably with the assumptions of the procedural republic. Rather than seek to cultivate virtue, this conservativism affirms the voluntarist conception of freedom. As Reagan once declared, in his libertarian voice, "We believe that liberty can be measured by how much freedom Americans have to make their own decisions—even their own mistakes."[98]

The second strand of Reagan's conservatism fit uneasily with the first and gestured beyond the terms of the procedural republic. This part of his politics evoked a civic or communal ethic favored by cultural conservatives and the religious right. Where libertarian conservatives reject the formative project, communal conservatives believe government should attend to the character of its citizens. The first seek a greater role for markets in public life, the second a greater role for morals.

Communal conservatism of the Reagan era found its most conspicuous expression in the strident voice of Jerry Falwell and his "Moral Majority." Falwell railed against rampant moral decay in American life, which he associated with feminism, abortion, homosexuality, pornography, sexual permissiveness, secular humanism, rock music, and the lack of prayer in public schools. "The hope of reversing the trends of decay in our republic now lies with the Christian public in America," Falwell declared. "We cannot expect help from the liberals." "While it is true that we are not a theocracy," Falwell allowed, "we nevertheless are a nation that was founded upon Christian principles. . . . We need to define and articulate the issues of sin and sinful living, which are destroying our nation today." Asked if such a program would lead to "censorship or a kind of Christian Nazism," Falwell offered the uncomforting reply that "we cannot allow an immoral minority of our population to intimidate us on moral issues. People who take a weak stand on morality inevitably have weak morals."[99]

Communal conservatism found more attractive expression in the writings of columnist George F. Will. Arguing that "statecraft is soulcraft," he criticized liberals and conservatives alike for assuming that government should be neutral on moral questions. "Just as all education is moral education because learning conditions conduct, much legislation is moral legislation because it conditions the action and the thought of the nation in broad and important spheres in life." Unlike Falwell, who sought America's salvation in a rebirth of Christian morality, Will sought to cultivate civic virtue, the "dispositions, habits and mores" on which free government depends. By virtue he meant "good citizenship, whose principal components are moderation, social sympathy and willingness to sacrifice private desires for public ends." Against the laissez-faire conservatism of his day, Will sought to revive for conservative politics the formative ambition of the republican tradition.[100]

In their hostility toward government, conservatives had come to agree with liberals that political institutions "should strive to be indifferent to, or neutral about, the 'inner life'—the character—of the citizenry." For example, as many liberals defended abortion rights by claiming that government should be neutral on moral questions, many conservatives defended laissez-faire economic policies by claiming that government should be neutral toward the outcomes the market economy generates. This was a mistake, argued Will, for it is neither possible nor desirable for government to be neutral on moral questions. The attempt to avoid the formative aspects of politics had impoverished political discourse, eroded social cohesion, and heightened Americans' dislike of government. "Our sense of citizenship," Will observed, "has become thin gruel." Conservatives would do better, he maintained, to stop despising government and to articulate a version of the welfare state hospitable to conservative values and likely to nurture the qualities of character on which good citizenship depends.[101]

Reagan drew, in different moods and moments, on both the libertarian and communal strands of American conservativism. Like Goldwater, he viewed the welfare state as a violation of individual liberty and rejected the notion that public assistance was a right or entitlement of the needy. But for all his talk of individual liberty and market solutions, it was the communal strand of Reagan's politics that enabled him to speak to the discontents of the time. The most resonant part of his political appeal lay in his skillful evocation of communal values—of family and neighborhood, religion and patriotism. What set Reagan apart from laissez-faire conservatives also set him apart from the liberal public philosophy of the day. This was his ability to identify with Americans' yearnings for a common life of larger meanings on a smaller, less impersonal scale than the procedural republic provides.

Reagan spoke to the loss of mastery and the erosion of community. Challenging Republican incumbent Gerald Ford in 1976, Reagan criticized those "in our nation's capital [who] would have us believe we are incapable of guiding our own destiny." His 1980 presidential campaign was above all about mastery, about countering the sense of powerlessness that afflicted the Carter presidency. "The prevailing view in America is that no one is in control," Reagan's pollster observed. "The prevailing impression given by the White House is that no one can be in control." The Reagan campaign would "convey the clearest possible message that Reagan stands for leadership and control."[102]

Accepting his party's nomination in 1980, Reagan denounced the view "that our nation has passed its zenith." He rejected the notion that "the federal government has grown so big and powerful that it is beyond the control of any president." And he expressed alarm that the main question for American foreign policy was "no longer, 'Should we do something?', but 'Do we have the capacity to do *anything?*'" In a world that seemed to defy human agency and control, Reagan promised to rekindle the American spirit, to reassert "our national will and purpose," to "recapture our destiny, to take it into our own hands."[103]

Reagan linked the sense of disempowerment with the erosion of community and the unraveling of those sources of moral authority and shared identity intermediate between the individual and the nation. Campaigning for the 1976 Republican nomination, Reagan called for "an end to giantism, for a return to the human scale—the scale that human beings can understand and cope with; the scale of the local fraternal lodge, the church congregation, the block club, the farm bureau." In terms reminiscent of Brandeis, Reagan praised the "locally-owned factory, the small businessman, who personally deals with his customers and stands behind his product, the farm and consumer cooperative, the town or neighborhood bank that invest in the community, the union local. . . . It is this activity on a small, human scale that creates the fabric of community."[104]

Reagan's 1980 Republican platform elaborated this theme. It pledged to "reemphasize those vital communities like the family, the neighborhood, [and] the workplace" that reside "between government and the individual," and to encourage the "rebirth of citizen activity in neighborhoods and cities across the land." During his presidency Reagan spoke repeatedly of restoring "the values of family, work, neighborhood, and religion." Announcing his candidacy for reelection in 1984, he declared: "America is back and standing tall. We've begun to restore great American values—the dignity of work, the warmth of family, the strength of neighborhood."[105]

Reagan blamed big government for disempowering citizens and undermining community: "Our citizens feel they've lost control of even the most basic decisions made about the essential services of government, such as schools, welfare, roads, and even garbage collection. And they're right." He also claimed that big government contributed to crime and moral decay by crowding out the institutions of civil society that had in the past "shaped the character of our people." Citing commentators who stressed the need for such mediating institutions, he argued that government had "preempt[ed] those mitigating [sic] institutions like family, neighborhood, church, and school—organizations that act as both a buffer and a bridge between the individual and the naked power of the state."[106]

Reagan's solution was a "New Federalism" that would shift power from the federal government to states and localities. A revitalized federal system would restore people's control over their lives by locating power closer to home. A less intrusive national government would leave room for local forms of community to flourish. Meanwhile, a Task Force on Private Sector Initiatives would explore ways to promote private charity and community service.[107]

The communal strand of Reagan's politics recalled the long-standing republican worry about concentrated power. But Reagan revived this tradition with a difference. Previous advocates of republican political economy had worried about big government and big business alike. For Reagan, by contrast, the curse of bigness attached to government alone. Even as he evoked the ideal of community, he had little to say about the corrosive effects of capital flight or the disempowering consequences of economic power organized on a vast scale. As Christopher Lasch observed, "Reagan's rhetorical defense of 'family and neighborhood' could not be reconciled with his championship of unregulated business enterprise, which has replaced neighborhoods with shopping malls and super-highways." For all his invocation of tradition, "his program aimed to promote economic growth and unregulated business enterprise, the very forces that have undermined tradition."[108]

For their part, Reagan-era Democrats did not challenge Reagan on this score, nor did they otherwise join the debate about community and self-government. Tied to the terms of rights-oriented liberalism, they missed the mood of discontent. They criticized Reagan's economic policy for favoring the rich, but failed to address Americans' larger fears that they were losing control of their lives and that the moral fabric of community was unraveling around them. At times, Democrats seemed determined to avoid moral concerns altogether, as when Michael Dukakis said of his 1988 campaign against George Bush: "this election isn't about ideology. It's about competence." When Democrats did articulate the moral vision underlying their politics, they spoke mostly of fairness and distributive justice. Recurring to the familiar terms of debate between Democrats and Republicans, they argued that Reagan had given "his rich friends enough tax relief to a buy a Rolls-Royce" and then asked the average American "to pay for the hub caps."[109]

In the face of Reagan's potent appeal, these complaints, valid though they were, lacked the moral or civic resonance to inspire. Sensing this lack of resonance, Democrats sometimes cast their case for fairness in communal terms. Both Walter Mondale, Reagan's 1984 Democratic challenger, and New York governor Mario Cuomo appealed to the ideal of national community and the ethic of sharing that it implied. Both drew, as Lyndon Johnson had done, on the metaphor of the nation as a family. "Let's be a community," Mondale declared, "a family where we care for one another. Let us end this selfishness, this greed, this new championship of caring only for yourself." In his keynote address to the 1984 Democratic convention, Cuomo argued that the nation's moral purpose could be found in "the idea of family," which meant sharing benefits and burdens for the good of all: "We believe we must be the family of America, recognizing that at the heart of the matter we are bound one to another, that the problems of a retired schoolteacher in Duluth are *our* problems. That the future of the child in Buffalo is *our* future. The struggle of a disabled man in Boston to survive, to live decently, is *our* struggle. The hunger of a woman in Little Rock *our* hunger."[110]

By the 1980s, however, the ideal of national community had lost its capacity to inspire, at least for purposes of distributive justice. Reformers since the turn of the century had sought, sometimes successfully, to cultivate a deeper sense of national community. But now the nation proved too vast to sustain more than a minimal commonality, too distant to summon the enlarged social sympathies a more generous welfare state required.

Nor was it suited to answer the rising discontent. The anxieties of the age concerned the erosion of those communities intermediate between the individual and the nation, such as families and neighborhoods, cities and towns, schools and congregations. American democracy had long relied on associations like these to cultivate a public spirit that the nation alone cannot command. As the republican tradition taught, local attachments can serve self-government by engaging citizens in a common life beyond their private pursuits, by forming the habit of attending to public things. They enable citizens, in Tocqueville's phrase, to "practice the art of government in the small sphere within [their] reach."[111]

Ideally at least, the reach extends as the sphere expands. Civic capacities first awakened in neighborhoods and town halls, churches and synagogues, trade unions and social movements, find broader expression. For example, the civic education and social solidarity cultivated in the black Baptist churches of the South were a crucial prerequisite for the civil rights movement that ultimately unfolded on a national scale. What began as a bus boycott in Montgomery later became a general challenge to segregation in the South, which led in turn to a national campaign for equal citizenship and the right to vote. More than a means of winning the vote, the movement itself was a moment of self-government, an instance of empowerment. It offered an example of the civic engagement that can flow from local attachments and communal ties.

But the public philosophy of Reagan-era Democrats lacked the civic resources to answer the aspiration for self-government. Democrats, once the party of dispersed power, had learned in recent decades to view intermediate communities with suspicion. Too often such communities had been pockets of prejudice, outposts of intolerance, places where the tyranny of the majority held sway. And so, from the New Deal to the civil rights movement to the Great Society, the liberal project was to use federal power to vindicate individual rights that local communities failed to protect. The individual and the nation advanced hand in hand.

This unease with the middle terms of civic life left Democrats ill-equipped to attend to the erosion of self-government. The conception of national community they affirmed bore only a distant relation to the republican tradition. For them, community mattered not for sake of cultivating virtue or equipping citizens for self-rule, but rather for the sake of providing a rationale for the welfare state. Detached from the formative ideal of the republican tradition, it offered a way of explaining why the pursuit of economic growth should be tempered by certain distributive concerns. But it offered no way to reinvigorate civic life, no hope for reconstituting the political economy of citizenship.

The civic and communal strand of Reagan's rhetoric enabled him to succeed, where Democrats failed, to tap the mood of discontent. But in the end Reagan's presidency did little to alter the conditions underlying the discontent. He governed more as market conservative than as civic conservative. The less fettered capitalism he favored did nothing to repair the moral fabric of families, neighborhoods, or communities.[112] The "New Federalism" he proposed was not adopted, and in any case did not address the disempowerment that local communities—and even nations—now confronted as they struggled to contend with global economic forces beyond their control. And while economic growth continued in the 1980s, spurred partly by massive federal deficits, the fruits of that growth were no longer widely shared. In the decades after World War II, when Americans could believe they were the masters of their destiny, the gains from economic growth had reached across the economic spectrum. From 1979 to 1992, by contrast, 98 percent of the $826 billion increase in household incomes went to the top fifth of the population. Most American families lost ground.[113] Not surprisingly, Americans' frustration with politics continued to mount.[114]

Conclusion: In Search of a Public Philosophy

Republican Freedom: Difficulties and Dangers

Any attempt to revitalize the civic strand of freedom must confront two sobering objections. The first doubts it is possible to revive republican ideals; the second doubts it is desirable. The first objection holds that, given the scale and complexity of the modern world, it is unrealistic to aspire to self-government as the republican tradition conceives it. From Aristotle's polis to Jefferson's agrarian ideal, the civic conception of freedom found its home in small and bounded places, largely self-sufficient, inhabited by people whose conditions of life afforded the leisure, learning, and commonality to deliberate well about public concerns. But we do not live that way today. To the contrary, we live in a highly mobile continental society, teeming with diversity. Moreover, even this vast society is not self-sufficient but is situated in a global economy whose frenzied flow of money and goods, information and images, pays little heed to nations, much less neighborhoods. How, under conditions such as these, could the civic strand of freedom possibly take hold?

In fact, this objection continues, the republican strand of American politics, for all its persistence, has often spoken in a voice tinged with nostalgia. Even as Jefferson valorized the yeoman farmer, America was becoming a manufacturing nation. And so it was with the artisan republicans of Jackson's day, the apostles of free labor in Lincoln's time, the producer-citizens of the Knights of Labor, and the shopkeepers and pharmacists Brandeis defended against the curse of bigness. In each of these cases—or so one might argue—republican ideals found their expression at the last moment, too late to offer feasible alternatives, just in time to offer an elegy for a lost cause. If the republican tradition is irredeemably nostalgic, then whatever its capacity to illuminate the defects of liberal politics, it offers little that could lead us to a richer civic life.

The second objection argues that even were it possible to recover republican ideals, to do so would not be desirable. That the civic strand of our tradition has given way in recent decades to a liberal public philosophy is not necessarily cause for regret. All things considered, it may represent a change for the better. Critics of the republican tradition might even concede that the procedural republic comes with a certain loss of community and self-government, and still insist that this is a price worth paying for the toleration and individual choice the procedural republic makes possible.

Underlying this objection are two related worries about republican political theory as traditionally conceived. The first is that it is exclusive; the second is that it is coercive. Both worries flow from the special demands of republican citizenship. If sharing in self-rule requires the capacity to deliberate well about the common good, then citizens must possess certain excellences—of character, judgment, and concern for the whole. But this implies that citizenship cannot be indiscriminately bestowed. It must be restricted to those who either possess the relevant virtues or can come to acquire them.

Some republican theorists have assumed that the capacity for civic virtue corresponds to fixed categories of birth or condition. Aristotle, for example, considered women, slaves, and resident aliens unworthy of citizenship because their nature or roles deprived them of the relevant excellences. Similar arguments were offered in nineteenth-century America by defenders of property qualifications for voting, southern defenders of slavery, and nativist opponents of citizenship for immigrants.[1] All linked republican notions of citizenship to the further assumption that some group or other—the propertyless, or African-Americans, or Catholic immigrants—were, by nature or condition or conviction, incapable of the virtues good citizenship requires.

But the assumption that the capacity for virtue is incorrigible, tied to roles or identities fixed in advance, is not intrinsic to republican political theory, and not all republicans have embraced it. Some have argued that good citizens are made, not found, and have rested their hopes on the formative project of republican politics. This is especially true of the democratic versions of republican thought that arose with the Enlightenment. When the incorrigibility thesis gives way, so does the tendency of republican politics to sanction exclusion.

As the tendency to exclusion recedes, however, the danger of coercion looms larger. Of the two pathologies to which republican politics is prone, modern democracies are more likely to suffer the second. For given the demands of republican citizenship, the more expansive the bounds of membership, the more demanding the task of cultivating virtue. In Aristotle's polis, the formative task was to cultivate virtue among a small group of people who shared a common life and a natural bent for citizenship. When republican thought turns democratic, however, and when the natural bent of persons to be citizens can no longer be assumed, the formative project becomes more daunting. The task of forging a common citizenship among a vast and disparate people invites more strenuous forms of soulcraft. This raises the stakes for republican politics and heightens the risk of coercion.

This peril can be glimpsed in Rousseau's account of the formative undertaking necessary to a democratic republic. The task of the founder, or great legislator, he writes, is no less than "to change human nature, to transform each individual . . . into a part of a larger whole from which this individual receives, in a sense, his life and his being." The legislator "must deny man his own forces" in order to make him reliant on the community as a whole. The more each person's individual will is "dead and obliterated," the more likely he is to embrace the general will. "Thus if each citizen is nothing and can do nothing except in concert with all the others . . . one can say that the legislation has achieved the highest possible point of perfection."[2]

The coercive face of soulcraft is by no means unknown among American republicans. For example, Benjamin Rush, a signer of the Declaration of Independence, wanted "to convert men into republican machines" and to teach each citizen "that he does not belong to himself, but that he is public property."[3] But civic education need not take so harsh a form. In practice, successful republican soulcraft involves a gentler kind of tutelage. For example, the political economy of citizenship that informed nineteenth-century American life sought to cultivate not only commonality but also the independence and judgment to deliberate well about the common good. It worked not by coercion but by a complex mix of persuasion and habituation, what Tocqueville called "the slow and quiet action of society upon itself."[4]

What separate Rousseau's republican exertions from the civic practices described by Tocqueville are the dispersed, differentiated character of American public life in Tocqueville's day and the indirect modes of character formation this differentiation allowed. Unable to abide disharmony, Rousseau's republican ideal seeks to collapse the distance between persons so that citizens stand in a kind of speechless transparence, or immediate presence to one another. Where the general will prevails, the citizens "consider themselves to be a single body," and there is no need for political argument. "The first to propose [a new law] merely says what everybody has already felt; and there is no question of intrigues or eloquence" to secure its passage. Given the unitary character of the general will, deliberation at its best issues in silent unanimity: "The more harmony reigns in the assemblies, that is to say, the closer opinions come to unanimity, the more dominant too is the general will. But long debates, dissensions, and tumult betoken the ascendance of private interests and the decline of the state." Since the common good does not admit of competing interpretations, disagreement signals corruption, a falling away from the common good.[5]

It is this assumption—that the common good is unitary and uncontestable—not the formative ambition as such, that inclines Rousseau's politics to coercion. It is, moreover, an assumption that republican politics can do without. As America's experience with the political economy of citizenship suggests, the civic conception of freedom does not render disagreement unnecessary. It offers a way of conducting political argument, not transcending it.

Unlike Rousseau's unitary vision, the republican politics Tocqueville describes is more clamorous than consensual. It does not despise differentiation. Instead of collapsing the space between persons, it fills this space with public institutions that gather people together in various capacities, that both separate and relate them.[6] These institutions include the townships, schools, religions, and virtue-sustaining occupations that form the "character of mind" and "habits of the heart" a democratic republic requires. Whatever their more particular purposes, these agencies of civic education inculcate the habit of attending to public things. And yet given their multiplicity, they prevent public life from dissolving into an undifferentiated whole.[7]

So the civic strand of freedom is not necessarily exclusive or coercive. It can sometimes find democratic, pluralistic expression. To this extent, the liberal's objection to republican political theory is misplaced. But the liberal worry does contain an insight that cannot be dismissed: Republican politics is risky politics, a politics without guarantees. And the risks it entails inhere in the formative project. To accord the political community a stake in the character of its citizens is to concede the possibility that bad communities may form bad characters. Dispersed power and multiple sites of civic formation may reduce these dangers but cannot remove them. This is the truth in the liberal's complaint about republican politics.

The Attempt to Avoid the Formative Project

What to make of this complaint depends on the alternatives. If there were a way to secure freedom without attending to the character of citizens, or to define rights without affirming a conception of the good life, then the liberal objection to the formative project might be decisive. But is there such a way? Liberal political theory claims that there is. The voluntarist conception of freedom promises to lay to rest, once and for all, the risks of republican politics. If liberty can be detached from the exercise of self-government and conceived instead as the capacity of persons to choose their own ends, then the difficult task of forming civic virtue can finally be dispensed with. Or at least it can be narrowed to the seemingly simpler task of cultivating toleration and respect for others.

On the voluntarist conception of freedom, statecraft no longer needs soulcraft, except in a limited domain. Tying freedom to respect for the rights of freely choosing selves would dampen old disputes about how to form the habits of self-rule. It would spare politics the ancient quarrels about the nature of the good life. Once freedom is detached from the formative project, "the problem of setting up a state can be solved even by a nation of devils," in Kant's memorable words. "For such a task does not involve the moral improvement of man."[8]

But the liberal attempt to detach freedom from the formative project confronts problems of its own, problems that can be seen in both the theory and the practice of the procedural republic. The philosophical difficulty lies in the liberal conception of citizens as freely choosing, independent selves, unencumbered by moral or civic ties antecedent to choice. This vision cannot account for a wide range of moral and political obligations that we commonly recognize, such as obligations of loyalty or solidarity. By insisting that we are bound only by ends and roles we choose for themselves, it denies that we can ever be claimed by ends we have not chosen—ends given by nature or God, for example, or by our identities as members of families, peoples, cultures, or traditions.

Some liberals concede we may be bound by obligations such as these, but insist they apply to private life alone and have no bearing on politics. But this raises a further difficulty. Why insist on separating our identity as citizens from our identity as persons more broadly conceived? Why should political deliberation not reflect our best understanding of the highest human ends? Don't arguments about justice and rights unavoidably draw on particular conceptions of the good life, whether we admit it or not?

The problems in the theory of procedural liberalism show up in the practice it inspires. Over the past half-century, American politics has come to embody the version of liberalism that renounces the formative ambition and insists government should be neutral toward competing conceptions of the good life. Rather than tie liberty to self-government and the virtues that sustain it, the procedural republic seeks a framework of rights, neutral among ends, within which individuals can choose and pursue their own ends.

But the discontent that besets American public life today illustrates the inadequacy of this solution. A politics that brackets morality and religion too completely soon generates its own disenchantment. Where political discourse lacks moral resonance, the yearning for a public life of larger meaning finds undesirable expression. Groups like the Moral Majority seek to clothe the naked public square with narrow, intolerant moralisms. Fundamentalists rush in where liberals fear to tread. The disenchantment also assumes more secular forms. Absent a political agenda that addresses the moral dimension of public questions, attention becomes riveted on the private vices of public officials. Political discourse becomes increasingly preoccupied with the scandalous, the sensational, and the confessional as purveyed by tabloids, talk shows, and eventually the mainstream media as well. In cannot be said that the public philosophy of contemporary liberalism is wholly responsible for these tendencies. But its vision of political discourse is too spare to contain the moral energies of democratic life. It creates a moral void that opens the way for intolerance and other misguided moralisms.

A political agenda lacking substantive moral discourse is one symptom of the public philosophy of the procedural republic. Another is the loss of mastery. The triumph of the voluntarist conception of freedom has coincided with a growing sense of disempowerment. Despite the expansion of rights in recent decades, Americans find to their frustration that they are losing control of the forces that govern their lives. This has partly to do with the insecurity of jobs in the global economy, but it also reflects the self-image by which we live. The liberal self-image and the actual organization of modern social and economic life are sharply at odds. Even as we think and act as freely choosing, independent selves, we confront a world governed by impersonal structures of power that defy our understanding and control. The voluntarist conception of freedom leaves us ill equipped to contend with this condition. Liberated though we may be from the burden of identities we have not chosen, entitled though we may be to the range of rights assured by the welfare state, we find ourselves overwhelmed as we turn to face the world on our own resources.

The inability of the reigning political agenda to address the erosion of self-government and community reflects the impoverished conceptions of citizenship and freedom implicit in our public life. The procedural republic that has unfolded over the past half-century can now be seen as an epic experiment in the claims of liberal as against republican political thought. Our present predicament lends weight to the republican claim that liberty cannot be detached from self-government and the virtues that sustain it, that the formative project cannot be dispensed with after all. The procedural republic, it turns out, cannot secure the liberty it promises because it cannot inspire the moral and civic engagement self-government requires.

If the public philosophy of contemporary liberalism fails to answer democracy's discontent, it remains to ask how a renewed attention to republican themes might better equip us to contend with our condition. How would a political agenda informed by the civic strand of freedom differ from the one that now prevails? Is self-government in the republican sense even possible under modern conditions? If so, what economic and political arrangements would it require, and what qualities of character would be necessary to sustain them?

How American politics might recover its civic voice is not wholly a speculative matter. Although the public philosophy of the procedural republic predominates in our time, it has not extinguished the civic understanding of freedom. Around the edges of our political discourse and practice, hints of the formative project can still be glimpsed. As the reigning political agenda lost energy in the 1980s and 1990s, these residual civic impulses quickened. Americans of various ideological persuasions groped to articulate a politics that reached beyond the terms of the procedural republic and spoke to the anxieties of the time.

These gropings, however partial and inchoate, gesture nonetheless toward the kind of political debate that would accord greater attention to republican themes. These expressions of Americans' persisting civic aspirations have taken two forms; one emphasizes the moral, the other the economic prerequisites of self-government. The first is the attempt, coming largely but not wholly from the right, to revive virtue, character-formation, and moral judgment as considerations in public policy and political discourse. The second involves a range of efforts, coming mostly though not entirely from the left, to contend with economic forces that disempower communities and threaten to erode the social fabric of democratic life.

The Recrudescence of Virtue

From the 1930s to the 1980s, conservatives criticized the welfare state in the name of the voluntarist conception of freedom. However desirable old-age pensions or school lunches or aid to the poor might be, argued conservatives such as Milton Friedman and Barry Goldwater, it was a violation of liberty to use state power to coerce taxpayers to support these causes against their will. By the mid-1980s, however, the conservative argument began to change. Increasingly, conservatives focused their criticism on the moral and civic consequences of federal social policy. For a time, debate over public policy had proceeded without reference to the formative project, reflecting the conviction that government should be neutral among competing conceptions of the good life. But now social commentators observed "a deepening concern for the development of character in the citizenry," and a "growing awareness that a variety of public problems can only be understood—and perhaps addressed—if they are seen as arising out of a defect in character formation."[9]

Nowhere was the recrudescence of virtue more pronounced than in debates about welfare. Welfare policy was a failure, many now argued, not because it coerced taxpayers but because it bred dependence among recipients and rewarded immoral and irresponsible behavior.[10] In the 1960s and 1970s it was widely held that public assistance programs should not impose any particular moral judgment about family arrangements or sexual behavior but simply enable recipients to choose their values for themselves. In 1965 Daniel Patrick Moynihan, then assistant secretary of Labor under Lyndon Johnson, wrote a report citing the alarming rate of out-of-wedlock births among blacks and calling for a national effort to enhance "the stability of the Negro American family."[11] Much of the protest that greeted the report attacked its judgmental aspect.[12] "My major criticism of the report is that it assumes that middle class American values are the correct ones for everyone in America," said Floyd McKissick, director of the Congress on Racial Equality (CORE). "Just because Moynihan believes in the middle class values doesn't mean that they are the best for everyone in America." Even sympathetic commentators averred that "it would have been well to reduce the discussion of illegitimacy" because of "its inevitable overtones of immorality."[13]

Three decades later, the terms of debate had changed. Welfare reform efforts of the 1980s and 1990s reflected a departure from the "nonjudgmental" approach of earlier years, a "new willingness to discuss sensitive, value-laden issues," and a greater effort to "reorder the personal lives of the poor."[14] Advocates of a civic conception of social policy argued that work requirements were essential, not for the sake of saving money but for the sake of including welfare recipients in the common obligations of citizenship.[15] As Moynihan, now a senior U.S. senator, declared, "you're talking here about what is the central task of any society: to produce citizens."[16]

For civic conservatives of the 1980s and 1990s, a renewed concern for the formative project extended beyond welfare to education, crime, and other aspects of public policy. William J. Bennett, secretary of Education and drug czar in the Reagan and Bush administrations, noted "a seismic shift" in American political discourse of the 1990s: "A set of issues once thought beyond the purview of politics—the social issues, the moral issues, the family issues—is now suddenly driving the public debate." Bennett applauded this shift and called for "public policies that once again make the connection between our deepest beliefs and our legislative agenda."[17]

The notion that public life should express the moral convictions and shape the moral character of citizens might seem at odds with the conservative's instinct for smaller, less intrusive government. But Bennett insisted that these conservative purposes were compatible. Statecraft could be soulcraft without big government, provided that families, schools, and churches served as the primary agents of character formation. Bennett blamed big government for weakening these instruments of moral and civic education. Government should be limited, he argued, "not only, or even primarily, for fiscal reasons, but because the 'nanny state' has eroded self-reliance and encouraged dependency, crowding out the character-forming institutions and enfeebling us as citizens."[18]

Beyond the baleful effects of big government, civic conservatives alleged that the public philosophy of contemporary liberalism was itself a source of moral decline. The notion that government must be neutral among competing moral and religious visions had taken a corrosive toll on American public life. It had made for a "naked public square," inhospitable to religion and empty of moral purposes larger than the pursuit of individual rights and entitlements.[19] In the area of education, the contagion of "value neutrality" had led schools to abandon their traditional role as "incubators of civic and personal virtue." The flight from public moral judgment had abetted the epidemic of drug use, a scourge that proved the folly of thinking that government "can be neutral regarding human character and personal responsibility."[20]

The abiding shame of American life, the urban ghetto, also attested to the poverty of a public life bereft of authoritative moral judgment, civic conservatives maintained. Glenn Loury, a prominent black intellectual, lamented the fact that American political discourse "fail[s] to engage questions of personal morality," of "character and values. . . . The public debate gives only muted voice to the judgment that it is wrong to be sexually promiscuous, to be indolent and undisciplined, to be disrespectful of legitimate authority, or to be unreliable, untruthful, or unfaithful." Given government's abdication of moral instruction, Americans must look to other sources of moral teaching, such as families and churches. "Until these institutions are restored, the behavioral problems of the ghetto will remain."[21] Absent an appeal to spiritual and religious precepts, Loury saw little hope of teaching ghetto youths to abstain from sex, drugs, and violence: "successful efforts at reconstruction in ghetto communities invariably reveal a religious institution, or set of devout believers, at the center of the effort."[22]

Liberals came more reluctantly to the revolt against the procedural republic. By the 1990s, however, Americans' discontent with their moral and civic condition was too pervasive to ignore. Bill Clinton was elected to the presidency in 1992 as a "New Democrat," stressing responsibility as well as rights. What set him apart from Democrats such as Michael Dukakis, Walter Mondale, and Jimmy Carter had less to do with his stand on particular issues than with his ability, at least at moments, to transcend the terms of the procedural republic. Speaking in the Memphis church where Martin Luther King Jr. had preached before his assassination, President Clinton ventured onto moral and spiritual terrain that liberals of recent times had sought to avoid. Restoring work to the life of the inner city was essential, he explained, not only for the income it brings but also for its character-forming effects, for the discipline, structure, and pride that work confers on family life. He also acknowledged that even the best efforts government might make to deal with crime, drugs, violence, and the breakdown of the family would achieve little without changes people must make "from the inside out," changes that reach "the values, the spirit, the soul."[23]

On other occasions Clinton continued to trespass on value-laden territory once occupied by conservatives and the religious right. "Our problems go way beyond the reach of government," he declared in his 1994 State of the Union Address. "They are rooted in the loss of values, in the disappearance of work, and the breakdown of our families and communities."[24] Among the sources of family breakdown was the soaring number of children born outside of marriage. Clinton allowed that former vice president Dan Quayle had been right when he maintained that having children out of wedlock was wrong and that government should act to discourage it.[25]

Other members of Clinton's administration, however, continued to display the nonjudgmental reflex characteristic of contemporary liberalism. Surgeon General Joycelyn Elders refused to condemn out-of-wedlock births, stating: "Everyone has different moral standards. You can't impose your standards on someone else." Donna Shalala, secretary of Health and Human Services, was unable to suppress the old reflex even as she endorsed her president's position. "I don't like to put this in moral terms," she conceded, "but I do believe that having children out of wedlock is just wrong."[26]

Other Democrats of the 1990s joined the call to restore moral and religious discourse to public life and to repair the character-forming agencies of civil society. The political agenda of recent decades, mainly concerned with adjudicating the roles of market and government, did not address the loss of community and the erosion of civic life. U.S. senator Bill Bradley called for a politics that focused more on the institutions of civil society. Neither the market nor government was "equipped to solve America's central problems, which are the deterioration of our civil society and the need to revitalize our democratic process." Politics should be concerned, he urged, with restoring "churches, schools, fraternities, community centers, labor unions, synagogues, sports leagues, PTAs, libraries, and barber shops" as "civic spaces," sites of deliberation about the common good. The "distinctive moral language of civil society"—the language of community, family, citizenship, and mutual obligation—should play a more prominent role "in our public conversation."[27]

Reviving the Political Economy of Citizenship

Those in the 1990s who spoke of virtue and soulcraft emphasized the moral and cultural prerequisites of self-government. Others emphasized the economic prerequisites. They worried, as many civic conservatives did not, about the way the modern economy disempowered communities and eroded the social fabric essential to democracy. Their search for economic arrangements conducive to community and self-government went beyond familiar arguments about prosperity and fairness and recalled the terms of debate that informed the political economy of citizenship.

The Civic Case against Inequality

One gesture toward a political economy of citizenship could be seen in a growing concern with the civic consequences of economic inequality. By the 1990s the gap between rich and poor was approaching levels unknown in American society since the 1920s. The sharpest increase in inequality unfolded from the late 1970s to the 1990s. From 1950 to 1978, rich and poor alike had shared in the gains from economic growth; real family income doubled for lower-, middle-, and upper-income Americans, confirming the economist's maxim that a rising tide lifts all boats. From 1979 to 1993, however, this maxim ceased to hold. Almost all of the increase in household incomes during this period went to the richest fifth of the population. Most Americans lost ground.[28] The distribution of wealth also showed increasing inequality. In 1992 the richest 1 percent of the population owned 42 percent of total private wealth, up from 34 percent a decade earlier, and more than twice the concentration of wealth in Britain.[29]

Some blamed the rising inequality on Reagan-era tax policy, which lowered income taxes for the wealthy while increasing taxes—including Social Security, state, and local taxes—that fall more heavily on lower- and middle-income taxpayers. Others pointed to an increasingly competitive global economy that rewarded highly educated workers but eroded the wages of low-skill laborers.[30] Whatever the explanation, the growing gap between rich and poor occasioned a new set of arguments about why inequality matters and what should be done about it. Some of these arguments went beyond the terms of the procedural republic and revived the civic strand of economic argument.

One argument against wide disparities of income and wealth, familiar in American politics of recent decades, is based on fairness or distributive justice. This argument, consistent with the public philosophy of contemporary liberalism, reflects the voluntarist conception of freedom. According to this view, a just society provides a framework of rights, neutral among ends, within which individuals are free to choose and pursue their own conceptions of the good life. This notion of justice requires that government do more than maximize the general welfare by promoting economic growth. It also requires that government assure each person a measure of social and economic security sufficient to the meaningful exercise of choice. Absent fair social and economic conditions, persons cannot truly be free to choose and pursue their own values and ends. In this way, the liberal's emphasis on fairness and distributive justice reflects the voluntarist conception of freedom.

But fairness to freely choosing, independent selves is not the only reason to worry about inequalities of income and wealth. A second reason draws not on the liberal but on the republican conception of freedom. The republican tradition teaches that severe inequality undermines freedom by corrupting the character of both rich and poor and destroying the commonality necessary to self-government. Aristotle held that persons of moderate means make the best citizens. The rich, distracted by luxury and prone to ambition, are unwilling to obey, while the poor, shackled by necessity and prone to envy, are ill suited to rule. A society of extremes lacks the "spirit of friendship" self-government requires: "Community depends on friendship; and when there is enmity instead of friendship, men will not even share the same path." Rousseau argued, on similar grounds, that "no citizen should be so rich as to be capable of buying another citizen, and none so poor that he is forced to sell himself." Although absolute equality is impossible, a democratic state should "[t]olerate neither rich men nor beggars," for these two estates "are equally fatal to the common good."[31]

As the gap between America's rich and poor deepened in the 1980s and 1990s, the civic case against inequality found at least tentative expression. Robert B. Reich, secretary of Labor in the Clinton administration, argued that the imperatives of technological change and global competition required greater federal spending on job training and education. The decline of the middle class could be reversed if American workers acquired the skills the new economy prized.[32] In a book he wrote shortly before taking office, however, Reich acknowledged a serious obstacle to this solution. A national commitment to invest more in the education and training of American workers presupposed a national sense of mutual responsibility that could no longer be assumed. As rich and poor grew further apart, their sense of shared fate diminished, and with it the willingness of the rich to invest, through higher taxes, in the skills of their fellow citizens.[33]

More than a matter of money, the new inequality gives rise, Reich observed, to increasingly separate ways of life. Affluent professionals gradually secede from public life into "homogeneous enclaves" where they have little contact with those less fortunate than themselves. "As public parks and playgrounds deteriorate, there is a proliferation of private health clubs, golf clubs, tennis clubs, skating clubs," accessible only to paying members. As the children of the prosperous enroll in private schools or in relatively homogeneous suburban schools, urban public schools are left to the poor. By 1990, for example, 45 percent of children in New York City public schools were on welfare. As municipal services decline in urban areas, residents and businesses in upscale districts manage to insulate themselves from the effects by assessing themselves surtaxes to provide private garbage collection, street cleaning, and police protection unavailable to the city as a whole. More and more, the affluent evacuate public spaces, retreating to privatized communities defined largely by income level, or by the zip code direct-mail marketers use to target likely customers. As one such marketer proclaims, "Tell me someone's zip code and I can predict what they eat, drink, and drive—even think."[34]

Reich's concern with the erosion of national community had mostly to do with the obstacle this posed for worthy federal spending. For him, as for advocates of national community such as Mario Cuomo, community was important not for the sake of forming citizens equipped for self-rule but rather for the sake of inspiring the ethic of sharing a more generous welfare state required. In this respect it fit within the terms of the reigning political agenda.

But Reich's account of the communal consequences of inequality highlights a defect in American life that also bears on the prospect of self-government. The secession of the affluent from the public sphere not only weakens the social fabric that supports the welfare state; it also erodes civic virtue more broadly conceived. The republican tradition long viewed the public realm not only as a place of common provision but also as a setting for civic education. The public character of the common school, for example, consisted not only in its financing but also in its teaching; ideally at least, it was a place where children of all classes would mix and learn the habits of democratic citizenship. Even municipal parks and playgrounds were once seen not only as places of recreation but also as sites for the promotion of civic identity, neighborliness, and community.[35]

As affluent Americans increasingly buy their way out of reliance on public services, the formative, civic resources of American life diminish. The deterioration of urban public schools is perhaps the most conspicuous and damaging instance of this trend. Another is the growing reliance on private security services, one of the fastest-growing occupational categories of the 1980s. So great was the demand for security personnel in shopping malls, airports, retail stores, and residential communities that by 1990 the number of private security guards nationwide exceeded the number of public police officers.[36] "The nation, in effect, is putting less emphasis on controlling crime for everyone—the job of publicly employed police officers—and more emphasis on private police officers who carve out secure zones for those who pay for such protection."[37] Even children's recreation is subject to these privatizing forces. Far from the spirit of the playground movement of the Progressive era is the new franchise business of "pay-per-use" playgrounds. For $4.95 per hour per child, parents can now take their children to private playcenters, often in shopping malls. "Playgrounds are dirty," one pay-for-play proprietor explains. "We're indoors; we're padded; parents can feel their child is safe."[38]

Civic conservatives have not, for the most part, acknowledged that market forces, under conditions of inequality, erode those aspects of community life that bring rich and poor together in public places and pursuits. Many liberals, largely concerned with distributive justice, have also missed the civic consequences of growing inequality. A politics attentive to the civic strand of freedom might try "to restrict the sphere of life in which money matters" and shore up the public spaces that gather people together in common experiences and form the habits of citizenship. Such a politics would worry less about the distribution of income as such, and more "about rebuilding, preserving, and strengthening community institutions in which income is irrelevant, about preventing their corruption by the forces of the market." It would encourage "class-mixing institutions" like public schools, libraries, parks, community centers, public transportation, and national service. Although such policies might also be favored by welfare-state liberals, the emphasis and justification would differ. A more civic-minded liberalism would seek communal provision less for the sake of distributive justice than for the sake of affirming the membership and forming the civic identity of rich and poor alike.[39]

Community Development Corporations

Some gestures toward a political economy of citizenship can be seen in the shifting terms of political discourse. Others can be glimpsed in pockets of political activism that defy the trend toward civic disengagement and try to contend with economic forces that disempower communities and undermine civic life. One range of examples is offered by community development corporations (CDCs). Begun in the mid-1960s as an alternative to large-scale government programs of urban renewal, CDCs are nonprofit corporations designed to give low-income communities a voice in shaping their economic destinies. Among the first and best-known was the Bedford-Stuyvesant Restoration Corporation of Brooklyn, initiated by Robert Kennedy as a means of economic revitalization and also as "an experiment in self-government." Governed by boards of local residents and business leaders, CDCs promote the economic development of the neighborhoods they serve by funding housing projects, new businesses, job training, and other social services.[40] When, in the 1980s, the Reagan administration cut their major sources of federal support, CDCs survived by relying more heavily on private investment, foundation funding, and financing from community banks. By the 1990s the thousand-plus CDCs in operation had achieved some success in reviving depressed communities. Whether, as some hoped, CDCs might be a vehicle for more self-reliant local and regional economies and greater democratic control, remained to be seen.[41]

Sprawlbusters

Another recent example of the political economy of citizenship recalls the long-forgotten anti–chain store movement of the 1930s. Then, opponents of national chains such as Sears Roebuck and A & P argued that the proliferation of chain stores undermined self-government by destroying local businesses and replacing independent shopkeepers with hirelings and clerks. In the 1990s, opponents of Wal-Mart and other discount superstores voiced similar concerns. As of 1994 Wal-Mart, with 2,400 stores and annual sales of $80 billion, was the largest retailer in the country.[42] So pervasive were its massive, boxlike structures and vast parking lots at highway interchanges across the land that, in the words of *Time* magazine, it was "redesigning the social structure of rural and small-town American more than any other force besides nature."[43] As Americans flocked to buy brand-name merchandise at discount prices, many downtown merchants were forced out of business. Critics complained not only of the ugly sprawl and environmental blight the superstores wrought, but also of the damage they did to the civic landscape.[44] "In older town centers, retail was the glue that connected a myriad of public places—government offices, parks, schools, libraries, and so forth. The intermingling of retail and community facilities created a setting for repetitive chance encounters with friends and neighbors that built and strengthened community bonds." The arrival of megastores accessible only by automobile destroyed these settings and "contributed to the atrophy of community and neighborhood activities."[45] The damage was compounded when Wal-Mart entered a community, destroyed local businesses, and then moved out in search of higher profits elsewhere. Residents were left with vacant sprawl, a downtown of shuttered stores, and a heightened sense of being victims of forces beyond their control.[46]

When, in the 1990s, Wal-Mart sought to expand beyond its base in the South and Midwest, it met resistance from community activists who opposed the zoning changes the big-box stores require. In Greenfield,

Massachusetts, local voters, turning out in record numbers, narrowly defeated a 1993 referendum that would have permitted Wal-Mart to enter the New England town.[47] Veterans of the successful Greenfield campaign joined Wal-Mart opponents in other communities across the country in a coalition of "Sprawl-busters," sharing tactics and experiences. By the mid-1990s these activists were engaging Wal-Mart and other retail giants in over a hundred local battles against megastore development. Like the antichain activists of old, they argued for the priority of civic values over consumer values. As one activist declared, "I'd rather have a viable community than a cheap pair of underwear."[48]

The New Urbanism

Another contemporary movement that expresses civic aspirations recalls the town planning efforts of the Progressive era. A growing number of urban planners, architects, citizens' groups, and regional planning agencies are exploring ways to build communities more hospitable to a vibrant civic life. Advocates of the New Urbanism, as the movement is called, seek to reverse the pattern of suburban development that has unfolded since the end of World War II. Prompted by the automobile, government highway subsidies, and Americans' desire to retreat to a private life at a safe distance from urban centers, the spread of suburbs carried with it mounting costs: long commutes for working people, isolation for children and elderly persons who cannot drive, traffic congestion and air pollution, the segregation of neighborhoods by class, race, and generation, the sense of placelessness bred by homogeneous chain stores, office parks, and subdivisions.[49]

The New Urbanists worry that suburban arrangements leave little room for the public settings in which people of different ages, incomes, and races encounter one another in the course of their daily lives. "By isolating people in houses and cars and by segregating households into homogeneous enclaves, the late twentieth century suburban metropolis has done little to replace the urban vitality it so aggressively displaced, and little to foster desperately needed civic responsibility in our increasingly diverse society." Some view the rise of the suburb as reflecting and furthering the depreciation of American life: "Our faith in government and the fundamental sense of commonality at the center of any vital democracy is seeping away in suburbs designed more for cars than people, more for market segments than communities." The ultimate expression of this tendency is the growing number of gated communities, walled-off enclaves of private parks, roads, police, and schools, open only to residents.[50]

The New Urbanists build communities that offer some of the virtues of traditional towns. They place housing, parks, and schools within walking distance of shops, civic services, jobs, and public transportation, not only for convenience but also to encourage the encounters that promote a common life. "Without the pedestrian, a community's common ground— its parks, sidewalks, squares, and plazas—become useless obstructions to the car." Instead of the arterials and highways that speed cars in and out of suburbs, the New Urbanists favor gridlike street patterns that promote pedestrian and bicycle traffic, tame car traffic with frequent stops, and knit neighborhoods and communities together on a human scale. Another tenet of the New Urbanism that highlights its civic aspirations is to design neighborhoods around central public spaces and accord primacy to town halls, libraries, schools, and other civic buildings. "We must return meaning and stature to the physical expression of our public life. From streets and parks to plazas, village squares, and commercial centers, the Commons defines the meeting ground of a neighborhood and its local identity." By the 1990s, dozens of developments inspired by the New Urbanism had been built or planned across the country, from the town of Seaside on Florida's panhandle to Laguna West in Sacramento County, California.[51]

Community Organizing

One of the most promising expressions of the civic strand of freedom can be found in the work of the Industrial Areas Foundation (IAF), a network of community-based organizations that teach residents of poor communities how to engage in effective political activity. The IAF traces its origins to Saul Alinsky, the well-known community organizer of the 1940s and 1950s, who brought his aggressive style of organizing to the slums behind the stockyards of Chicago. Alinsky stressed the importance of building on local "pockets of power" such as unions, religious groups, ethnic and civic groups, small business associations, and political organizations. In recent decades, however, most traditional bases of civic activity in inner cities have eroded, leaving religious congregations the only vital institutions in many communities. As a result, Alinsky's successors in the IAF have organized primarily around congregations, especially Catholic and Protestant churches.[52]

The most influential modern IAF organization is Communities Organized for Public Service (COPS), a citizens' group founded in 1974 in the impoverished Hispanic neighborhoods of San Antonio. Its base in Catholic parishes provides not only a stable source of funds, participants, and leaders but also a shared moral language as a starting point for political discourse.[53] The leaders COPS identifies and trains are not established political figures or activists but those accustomed to working in community-sustaining institutions like school PTAs and church councils. Often they are women "whose lives by and large have been wrapped up in their parishes and their children. What COPS has been able to do is to give them a public life and a public visibility, to educate, to provide the tools whereby they can participate in the political process."[54]

By equipping its members to deliberate about community needs and to engage in political activity, COPS brought a billion dollars' worth of improvements for roads, schools, sewers, parks, and other infrastructure to long-neglected neighborhoods of San Antonio. Together with a network of affiliated organizations throughout Texas, it helped pass statewide legislation reforming public education, health care, and farm safety. By 1994 the IAF had spawned some forty grass-roots organizations in seventeen states. Like civic conservatives, IAF leaders stressed the importance of mediating institutions such as families, neighborhoods, and churches, and the character-forming role such institutions can play. For the IAF, however, these structures were points of departure for political activity, ways of linking the moral resources of community life to the exercise of freedom in the republican sense.[55]

As these disparate expressions of the republican tradition suggest, the case for reviving the civic strand of freedom is not that it would make for a more consensual politics. There is no reason to suppose that a politics organized around republican themes would command a greater measure of agreement than does our present politics. As the reigning political agenda invites disagreement about the meaning of neutrality, rights, and truly voluntary choice, a political agenda informed by civic concerns would invite disagreement about the meaning of virtue and the forms of self-government that are possible in our time. Some would emphasize the moral and religious dimensions of civic virtue, while others would emphasize the ways in which economic arrangements and structures of power hinder or promote the exercise of self-rule. The political divisions arising in response to these issues would probably differ from those that govern the debate over the welfare state. But political divisions there would surely be. A successful revival of republican politics would not resolve our political disputes; at best, it would invigorate political debate by grappling more directly with the obstacles to self-government in our time.

Global Politics and Particular Identities

But suppose the civic aspirations that roil our present politics did find fuller voice and succeeded in reorienting the terms of political discourse. What then? What is the prospect that a revitalized politics could actually alleviate the loss of mastery and the erosion of community that lie at the heart of democracy's discontent? Politics is an unpredictable activity, so it is difficult to say with certainty. But even a politics that engaged rather than avoided substantive moral discourse, that attended to the civic consequences of economic inequality, that strengthened the mediating institutions of civil society—even such a politics would confront a daunting obstacle. This obstacle consists in the formidable scale on which modern economic life is organized and the difficulty of constituting the democratic political authority necessary to govern it.

This difficulty actually involves two related challenges. One is to devise political institutions capable of governing the global economy. The other is to cultivate the civic identities necessary to sustain those institutions, to supply them with the moral authority they require. It is not obvious that both these challenges can be met.

In a world where capital and goods, information and images, pollution and people, flow across national boundaries with unprecedented ease, politics must assume transnational, even global forms, if only to keep up. Otherwise, economic power will go unchecked by democratically sanctioned political power. Nation-states, traditionally the vehicles of self-government, will find themselves increasingly unable to bring their citizens' judgments and values to bear on the economic forces that govern their destinies. The disempowering of the nation-state in relation to the global economy may be one source of the discontent that afflicts not only American politics but other democracies around the world.

If the global character of the economy suggests the need for transnational forms of governance, however, it remains to be seen whether such political units can inspire the identification and allegiance—the moral and civic culture—on which democratic authority ultimately depends. In fact there is reason to doubt that they can. Except in extraordinary moments, such as war, even nation-states find it difficult to inspire the sense of community and civic engagement self-government requires. Political associations more expansive than nations, and with fewer cultural traditions and historical memories to draw upon, may find the task of cultivating commonality more difficult still.

Even the European Community, one of the most successful experiments in supranational governance, has so far failed to cultivate a common European identity sufficient to support its mechanisms of economic and political integregation. Advocates of further European integration worry about the "democratic deficit" that arises when expert commissioners and civil servants rather than elected representatives conduct most of the Community's business. Such an "attenuated political scene," Shirley Williams observes, misses "the anger, the passion, the commitment, and the partisanship that constitute the lifeblood of politics." It makes for a "businessman's Europe," not a "citizens' Europe." Czech president Vaclav Havel emphasizes the absence of shared moral purpose: "Europe today lacks an ethos. . . . There is no real identification in Europe with the meaning and purpose of integration." He calls upon pan-European institutions "to cultivate the values from which the spirit and ethos of European integration might grow."[56]

In certain ways, the challenge to self-government in the global economy resembles the predicament American politics faced in the early decades of the twentieth century. Then as now, there was a gap, or lack of fit, between the scale of economic life and the terms in which people conceived their identities, a gap that many experienced as disorienting and disempowering. Americans long accustomed to taking their bearings from small communities suddenly found themselves confronting an economy that was national in scope. Political institutions lagged behind, inadequate to life in a continental society. Then as now, new forms of commerce and communication spilled across familiar political boundaries and created networks of interdependence among people in distant places. But the new interdependence did not carry with it a new sense of community. As Jane Addams observed, "the mere mechanical fact of interdependence amounts to nothing."[57]

Addams' insight is no less apt today. What railroads, telegraph wires, and national markets were to her time, satellite hookups, CNN, cyberspace, and global markets are to ours—instruments that link people in distant places without necessarily making them neighbors or fellow citizens or participants in a common venture. Converting networks of communication and interdependence into a public life worth affirming is a moral and political matter, not a technological one.

Given the similarity between their predicament and ours, it is instructive to recall the solution they pursued. Confronted with an economy that threatened to defy democratic control, Progressives such as Theodore Roosevelt and Herbert Croly and their New Deal successors sought to increase the powers of the national government. If democracy were to survive, they concluded, the concentration of economic power would have to be met by a similar concentration of political power. But this task involved more than the centralization of government; it also required the nationalization of politics. The primary form of political community had to be recast on a national scale. Only in this way could they hope to ease the gap between the scale of social and economic life and the terms in which people conceived their identities. Only a strong sense of national community could morally and politically underwrite the extended involvements of a modern industrial order. The "nationalizing of American political, economic, and social life," Croly wrote, was "an essentially formative and enlightening political transformation." America would become more of a democracy only as it became "more of a nation . . . in ideas, in institutions, and in spirit."[58]

It is tempting to think that the logic of their solution can be extended to our time. If the way to deal with a national economy was to strengthen the national government and cultivate a sense of national citizenship, perhaps the way to deal with a global economy is to strengthen global governance and to cultivate a corresponding sense of global, or cosmopolitan citizenship.

Internationally minded reformers have already begun to articulate this impulse. In 1995 the Commission on Global Governance, a group of twenty-eight public officials from around the world, published a report stressing the need to strengthen international institutions. Global interdependence was growing, they observed, driven by powerful technological and economic forces. But the world's political structures had not kept pace. The Commission called for new international institutions to deal with economic and environmental issues, a "people's assembly" that might ultimately be elected by the people of the world, a scheme of international taxation to finance activities of global goverance, and greater authority for the World Court. Mindful of the need to cultivate an ethic adequate to its project, the Commission also called for efforts to "foster global citizenship," to inspire "broad acceptance of a global civic ethic," to transform "a global neighborhood based on economic exchange and improved communications into a universal moral community."[59]

Other commentators of the 1990s saw in international environmental, human rights, and women's movements the emergence of a "global civil society" that might serve as a counterweight to the power of global markets and media. According to political scientist Richard Falk, such movements hold promise for a new "global citizenship . . . premised upon global or species solidarity." "This spirit of global citizenship is almost completely deterritorialized," he observes. It has nothing to do with loyalty to a particular political community, whether city or state, but aspires instead to the ideal of "one-world community." Philosopher Martha Nussbaum argues, in a similar spirit, for a civic education that cultivates cosmopolitan citizenship. Since national identity is "a morally irrelevant characteristic," students should be taught that their "primary allegiance is to the community of human beings in the entire world."[60]

The cosmopolitan ideal rightly emphasizes the humanity we share and directs our attention to the moral consequences that flow from it. It offers a corrective to the narrow, sometimes murderous chauvinism into which ethnic and national identities can descend. It reminds wealthy nations that their obligations to humanity do not end at the water's edge. It may even suggest reasons to care for the planet that go beyond its use to us. All this makes the cosmopolitan ideal an attractive ethic, especially now that the global aspect of political life requires forms of allegiance that go beyond nations.

Despite these merits, however, the cosmopolitan ideal is flawed, both as a moral ideal and as a public philosophy for self-government in our time. The notion that universal identities must always take precedence over particular ones has a long and varied history. Kant tied morality to respect for persons as rational beings independent of their particular characteristics, and Marx identified the highest solidarity as that of man with his species-being. Perhaps the clearest statement of the cosmopolitan ethic as a moral ideal is the one offered by the Enlightenment philosopher Montesquieu: "If I knew something useful to me, but prejudicial to my family, I would reject it from my soul. If I knew something useful to my family but not to my country, I would try to forget it. If I knew something useful to my country, but prejudicial to Europe, or useful to Europe but prejudicial to humankind, I would regard it as a crime. . . . [For] I am a man before I am a Frenchman, or rather . . . I am necessarily a man, while I am a Frenchman only by chance."[61]

If our encompassing loyalties should always take precedence over more local ones, then the distinction between friends and strangers should ideally be overcome. Our special concern for the welfare of friends would be a kind of prejudice, a measure of our distance from universal human concern. Montesquieu does not shrink from this conclusion. "A truly virtuous man would come to the aid of the most distant stranger as quickly as to his own friend," he writes. "If men were perfectly virtuous, they wouldn't have friends."[62]

It is difficult to imagine a world in which persons were so virtuous that they had no friends, only a universal disposition to friendliness. The problem is not simply that such a world would be difficult to bring about but that it would be difficult to recognize as a human world. The love of humanity is a noble sentiment, but most of the time we live our lives by smaller solidarities. This may reflect certain limits to the bounds of moral sympathy. More important, it reflects the fact that we learn to love humanity not in general but through its particular expressions.

J. G. Herder, the German Romantic philosopher, was among the first to affirm differences of language, culture, and national identity as distinctive expressions of our humanity. He was scornful of the cosmopolitan citizen whose devotion to humankind is wholly abstract: "The savage who loves himself, his wife and child, with quiet joy, and in his modest way works for the good of his tribe" is "a truer being than that shadow of a man, the refined citizen of the world, who, enraptured with the love of all his fellow-shadows, loves but a chimera." In practice, Herder writes, it is the savage in his poor hut who welcomes the stranger. "The inundated heart of the idle cosmopolite, on the other hand, offers shelter to nobody." Charles Dickens also caught the folly of the unsituated cosmopolitan in his description of Mrs. Jellyby, the character in Bleak House who woefully neglects her children while pursuing charitable causes overseas. She was a woman "with handsome eyes," Dickens writes, "though they had a curious habit of seeming to look a long way off. As if . . . they could see nothing nearer than Africa."[63]

To affirm as morally relevant the particular communities that locate us in the world, from neighborhoods to nations, is not to claim that we owe nothing to persons as persons, as fellow human beings. At their best, local solidarities gesture beyond themselves toward broader horizons of moral concern, including the horizon of our common humanity. The cosmopolitan ethic is wrong, not for asserting that we have certain obligations to humanity as a whole but rather for insisting that the more universal communities we inhabit must always take precedence over more particular ones.

Most of us find ourselves claimed, at one time or another, by a wide range of different communities, some overlapping, others contending. When obligations conflict, there is no way of deciding in advance, once and for all, which should prevail. Deciding which of one's identities is properly engaged—as parent or professional, follower of a faith or partisan of a cause, citizen of one's country or citizen of the world—is a matter of moral reflection and political deliberation that will vary according to the issue at stake. The best deliberation will attend to the content of the claims, their relative moral weight, and their role in the narratives by which the participants make sense of their lives. Montesquieu to the contrary, such claims cannot simply be ranked according to the size or scope of the community that gives rise to them. No general principle of much practical use can rank obligations in advance, and yet some responses to moral and political dilemmas are better—more admirable or worthy or fitting—than others. Unless this were so, there would be no point, and no burden, in deliberation itself.

The moral defect of the cosmopolitan ethic is related to its political defect. For even as the global economy demands more universal forms of political identity, the pull of the particular reasserts itself. Even as nations accede to new institutions of global governance, they confront rising demands from ethnic, religious, and linguistic groups for various forms of political recognition and self-determination. These demands are prompted in part by the dissolution of the empires that once contained them, such as the Soviet Union. But the growing aspiration for the public expression of communal identities may also reflect a yearning for political identities that can situate people in a world increasingly governed by vast and distant forces.

For a time, the nation-state promised to answer this yearning, to provide the link between identity and self-rule. In theory at least, each state was a more or less self-sufficient political and economic unit that gave expression to the collective identity of a people defined by a common history, language, or tradition. The nation-state laid claim to the allegiance of its citizens on the ground that its exercise of sovereignty expressed their collective identity.

In the contemporary world, however, this claim is losing its force. National sovereignty is eroded from above by the mobility of capital, goods, and information across national boundaries, the integration of world financial markets, the transnational character of industrial production. At the same time, national sovereignty is challenged from below by the resurgent aspirations of subnational groups for autonomy and self-rule. As their effective sovereignty fades, nations gradually lose their hold on the allegiance of their citizens. Beset by the integrating tendencies of the global economy and the fragmenting tendencies of group identities, nation-states are increasingly unable to link identity and self-rule. Even the most powerful states cannot escape the imperatives of the global economy; even the smallest are too heterogeneous to give full expression to the communal identity of any one ethnic or national or religious group without oppressing others who live in their midst.

Given the limits of cosmopolitan politics, the attempt to save democracy by globalizing citizenship, as Progressives once sought to save democracy by nationalizing citizenship, is unlikely to succeed. The analogy between the globalizing impulse of our time and the nationalizing project of theirs holds to this extent: We cannot hope to govern the global economy without transnational political institutions, and we cannot expect to sustain such institutions without cultivating more expansive civic identities. This is the moment of truth in the cosmopolitan vision. Human rights conventions, global environmental accords, and world bodies governing trade, finance, and economic development are among the undertakings that will depend for public support on inspiring a greater sense of engagement in a shared global destiny.

But the cosmopolitan vision is wrong to suggest that we can restore self-government simply by pushing sovereignty and citizenship upward. The hope for self-government lies not in relocating sovereignty but in dispersing it. The most promising alternative to the sovereign state is not a one-world community based on the solidarity of humankind, but a multiplicity of communities and political bodies—some more, some less extensive than nations—among which sovereignty is diffused. The nation-state need not fade away, only cede its claim as sole repository of sovereign power and primary object of political allegiance. Different forms of political association would govern different spheres of life and engage different aspects of our identities. Only a regime that disperses sovereignty both upward and downward can combine the power required to rival global market forces with the differentiation required of a public life that hopes to inspire the reflective allegiance of its citizens.

In some places, dispersing sovereignty may entail according greater cultural and political autonomy to subnational communities—such as Catalans and Kurds, Scots and Québecois—even while strengthening and democratizing transnational structures, such as the European Union. Or it may involve modes of devolution and subsidiarity along geographic rather than ethnic and cultural lines. Arrangements such as these may ease the strife that arises when state sovereignty is an all-or-nothing affair, absolute and indivisible, the only meaningful form of self-determination.

In the United States, which never was a nation-state in the European sense, proliferating sites of political engagement may take a different form. America was born of the conviction that sovereignty need not reside in a single place. From the start, the Constitution divided power among branches and levels of government. Over time, however, we too have pushed sovereignty and citizenship upward, in the direction of the nation.

The nationalizing of American political life occurred largely in response to industrial capitalism. The consolidation of economic power called forth the consolidation of political power. Present-day conservatives who rail against big government often ignore this fact. They wrongly assume that rolling back the power of the national government would liberate individuals to pursue their own ends instead of leaving them at the mercy of economic forces beyond their control.

Conservative complaints about big government find popular resonance, but not for the reasons conservatives articulate. The American welfare state is politically vulnerable because it does not rest on a sense of national community adequate to its purpose. The nationalizing project that unfolded from the Progressive era to the New Deal to the Great Society succeeded only in part. It managed to create a strong national government but failed to cultivate a shared national identity. As the welfare state developed, it drew less on an ethic of social solidarity and mutual obligation and more on an ethic of fair procedures and individual rights. But the liberalism of the procedural republic proved an inadequate substitute for the strong sense of citizenship the welfare state requires.

If the nation cannot summon more than a minimal commonality, it is unlikely that the global community can do better, at least on its own. A more promising basis for a democratic politics that reaches beyond nations is a revitalized civic life nourished in the more particular communities we inhabit. In the age of NAFTA, the politics of neighborhood matters more, not less. People will not pledge allegiance to vast and distant entities, whatever their importance, unless those institutions are somehow connected to political arrangements that reflect the identity of the participants.

This is reason to consider the unrealized possibilities implicit in American federalism. We commonly think of federalism as a constitutional doctrine that, once dormant, has recently been revived by conservatives who would shift power from the federal government to the states. But federalism is more than a theory of intergovernmental relations. It also stands for a political vision that offers an alternative to the sovereign state and the univocal political identities such states require. It suggests that self-government works best when sovereignty is dispersed and citizenship formed across multiple sites of civic engagement. This aspect of federalism informs the pluralist version of republican politics. It supplies the differentiation that separates Tocqueville's republicanism from Rousseau's, that saves the formative project from slipping into coercion.

Rousseau conceived political community as an undifferentiated whole and so insisted that citizens conform to the general will. Tocqueville stressed the republican benefits of political bodies intermediate between the individual and the state, such as townships. "The native of New England is attached to his township because it is independent and free," he wrote. "He takes a part in every occurrence in the place; he practices the art of government in the small sphere within his reach; he accustoms himself to those forms without which liberty can only advance by revolutions; he imbibes their spirit; he acquires a taste for order, comprehends the balance of powers, and collects clear practical notions on the nature of his duties and the extent of his rights." Practicing self-government in small spheres, Tocqueville observed, impels citizens to larger spheres of political activity as well.[64]

Jefferson spoke for a similar vision when he worried, late in life, that the Constitution did not make adequate provision for the cultivation of civic virtue. Even the states, and for that matter the counties, were too distant to engage the civic energies and affection of the people. In order "to nourish and perpetuate" the republican spirit, Jefferson proposed dividing the counties into wards, local self-governing units that would permit direct political participation. By "making every citizen an acting member of the government," the ward system would "attach him by his strongest feelings to the independence of his country, and its republican constitution." The "division and subdivision of duties" among federal, state, county, and ward republics was not only a way of avoiding the abuse of power. It was also, for Jefferson, a way of cementing the whole by giving each citizen a part in public affairs.[65]

Jefferson's ward system was never adopted, and the New England township Tocqueville admired has faded in power and civic significance. But the political insight underlying their federalism remains revelant today. This is the insight that proliferating sites of civic activity and political power can serve self-government by cultivating virtue, equipping citizens for self-rule, and generating loyalties to larger political wholes. If local government and municipal institutions are no longer adequate arenas for republican citizenship, we must seek such public spaces as may be found amidst the institutions of civil society—in schools and workplaces, churches and synagogues, trade unions and social movements.

Public spaces such as these were indispensable to the finest expression of republican politics in our time, the civil rights movement of the 1950s to mid-1960s. In retrospect, the republican character of the civil rights movement is easily obscured. It unfolded at just the time when the procedural republic was taking form. Partly as a result, Americans learned the lessons of the movement through the lens of contemporary liberalism: Civil rights was about nondiscrimination and equality before the law, about vindicating individual rights against the prejudices of local communities, about respecting persons as persons, regardless of their race, religion, or other particular characteristics.

But this is not the whole story. To assimilate the civil rights movement to the liberalism of the procedural republic is to miss its most important lessons for our time. More than a means to equal rights, the movement itself was a moment of empowerment, an instance of the civic strand of freedom. The laws that desegregated public facilities and secured voting rights for blacks served freedom in the voluntarist sense—the freedom to choose and pursue one's purposes and ends. But the struggle to win these rights displayed a higher, republican freedom—the freedom that consists in acting collectively to shape the public world.[66]

Beyond the legal reforms it sought, the civil rights movement undertook a formative project; it aimed at the moral and civic "transformation of a whole people." As Martin Luther King Jr. explained, "When legal contests were the sole form of activity, the ordinary Negro was involved as a passive spectator. His interest was stirred, but his energies were unemployed. Mass marches transformed the common man into the star performer. . . . The Negro was no longer a subject of change; he was the active organ of change."[67]

The formative aspect of republican politics requires public spaces that gather citizens together, enable them to interpret their condition, and cultivate solidarity and civic engagement. For the civil rights movement, these public spaces were provided by the black churches of the South. They were the sites of the mass meetings, the civic education, the prayer and song, that equipped blacks to join in the boycotts and the marches of the movement.[68]

We commonly think of the civil rights movement as finding its fruition in the civil rights and voting rights laws passed by Congress. But the nation would never have acted without a movement whose roots lay in more particular identities and places. Moreover, the movement offered a vision of republican citizenship that went beyond the right to vote. Even after the Voting Rights Act was won, King hoped for a public life that might realize the intimations of republican freedom present in the civil rights movement at its best: "How shall we turn the ghettos into a vast school? How shall we make every street corner a forum . . . every house-worker and every laborer a demonstrator, a voter, a canvasser and a student? The dignity their jobs may deny them is waiting for them in political and social action."[69]

Beyond Sovereign States and Sovereign Selves

The global media and markets that shape our lives beckon us to a world beyond boundaries and belonging. But the civic resources we need to master these forces, or at least to contend with them, are still to be found in the places and stories, memories and meanings, incidents and identities, that situate us in the world and give our lives their moral particularity.

The public philosophy by which we live bids us to bracket these attachments, to set them aside for political purposes, to conduct our political debates without reference to them. But a procedural republic that banishes moral and religious argument from political discourse makes for an impoverished civic life. It also fails to answer the aspiration for self-government; its image of citizens as free and independent selves, unencumbered by moral or civic ties they have not chosen, cannot sustain the public spirit that equips us for self-rule.

Since the days of Aristotle's polis, the republican tradition has viewed self-government as an activity rooted in a particular place, carried out by citizens loyal to that place and the way of life it embodies. Self-government today, however, requires a politics that plays itself out in a multiplicity of settings, from neighborhoods to nations to the world as a whole. Such a politics requires citizens who can think and act as multiply-situated selves. The civic virtue distinctive to our time is the capacity to negotiate our way among the sometimes overlapping, sometimes conflicting obligations that claim us, and to live with the tension to which multiple loyalties give rise. This capacity is difficult to sustain, for it is easier to live with the plurality between persons than within them.

The republican tradition reminds us that to every virtue there corresponds a characteristic form of corruption or decay. Where civic virtue consists in holding together the complex identities of modern selves, it is vulnerable to corruption of two kinds. The first is the tendency to fundamentalism, the response of those who cannot abide the ambiguity associated with divided sovereignty and multiply-encumbered selves. To the extent that contemporary politics puts sovereign states and sovereign selves in question, it is likely to provoke reactions from those who would banish ambiguity, shore up borders, harden the distinction between insiders and outsiders, and promise a politics to "take back our culture and take back our country," to "restore our sovereignty" with a vengeance.[70]

The second corruption to which multiply-encumbered citizens are prone is the drift to formless, protean, storyless selves, unable to weave the various strands of their identity into a coherent whole. Political community depends on the narratives by which people make sense of their condition and interpret the common life they share; at its best, political deliberation is not only about competing policies but also about competing interpretations of the character of a community, of its purposes and ends. A politics that proliferates the sources and sites of citizenship complicates the interpretive project. At a time when the narrative resources of civic life are already strained—as the soundbites, factoids, and disconnected images of our media-saturated culture attest—it becomes increasingly difficult to tell the tales that order our lives. There is a growing danger that, individually and collectively, we will find ourselves slipping into a fragmented, storyless condition. The loss of the capacity for narrative would amount to the ultimate disempowering of the human subject, for without narrative there is no continuity between present and past, and therefore no responsibility, and therefore no possibility of acting together to govern ourselves.

Since human beings are storytelling beings, we are bound to rebel against the drift to storylessness. But there is no guarantee that the rebellions will take salutary form. Some, in their hunger for story, will be drawn to the vacant, vicarious fare of confessional talk shows, celebrity scandals, and sensational trials. Others will seek refuge in fundamentalism. The hope of our time rests instead with those who can summon the conviction and restraint to make sense of our condition and repair the civic life on which democracy depends.

Notes

1. The Public Philosophy of Contemporary Liberalism

1. Only 20 percent of Americans believe they can trust the government in Washington to do what is right most of the time; *Gallup Poll Monthly*, February 1994, p. 12. Three-fourths say they are dissatisfied with the way the political process is working; *Gallup Poll Monthly*, September 1992. A similar percentage believe that government is run by a few big interests rather than for the benefit of all; Alan F. Kay et al., "Steps for Democracy," *Americans Talk Issues*, March 25, 1994, p. 9.

2. See John Rawls, *A Theory of Justice* (Cambridge, Mass.: Harvard University Press, 1971); Ronald Dworkin, "Liberalism," in Stuart Hampshire, ed., *Public and Private Morality* (Cambridge: Cambridge University Press, 1978), pp. 114–143; idem, *Taking Rights Seriously* (Cambridge, Mass.: Harvard University Press, 1977); Robert Nozick, *Anarchy, State, and Utopia* (New York: Basic Books, 1977); Bruce Ackerman, *Social Justice in the Liberal State* (New Haven: Yale University Press, 1980).

3. The term "procedural republic" was suggested to me by Judith N. Shklar.

4. On the meaning of "liberal" as used in contemporary American politics, see Ronald D. Rotunda, *The Politics of Language* (Iowa City: Iowa University Press, 1986).

5. Chapters 2–4 tell the first story; Chapters 5–9 tell the second.

6. Aristotle, *The Politics*, trans. Ernest Barker, book 3, chap. 9 (London: Oxford University Press, 1946), p. 119.

7. Ibid., pp. 119–120.

8. In this section I draw on my introduction to Michael Sandel, ed., *Liberalism and Its Critics* (Oxford: Basil Blackwell, 1984), pp. 1–11.

9. John Stuart Mill, *On Liberty* (1859), chap. 1.

10. For a sampling of arguments for and against utilitarianism, see Amartya Sen and Bernard Williams, eds., *Utilitarianism and Beyond* (Cambridge: Cambridge University Press, 1982).

11. See Immanuel Kant, *Groundwork of the Metaphysics of Morals* (1785), trans.

H. J. Paton (New York: Harper and Row, 1956); idem, *Critique of Practical Reason* (1788), trans. L. W. Beck (Indianapolis: Bobbs-Merrill, 1956); idem, "On the Common Saying: 'This May Be True in Theory, But It Does Not Apply in Practice,'" in *Kant's Political Writings*, ed. Hans Reiss (Cambridge: Cambridge University Press, 1970), pp. 61–92.

12. Rawls, *A Theory of Justice*, pp. 3–4.
13. Dworkin, "Liberalism," p. 136.
14. Rawls, *A Theory of Justice*, p. 560.
15. George Kateb, "Democratic Individuality and the Claims of Politics," *Political Theory*, 12 (August 1984), 343.
16. John Rawls, "Kantian Constructivism in Moral Theory," *Journal of Philosophy*, 77 (Summer 1980), 543.
17. John Rawls, "Fairness to Goodness," *Philosophical Review*, 84 (October 1985), 537.
18. Ibid.
19. Rawls, *A Theory of Justice*, p. 312, and, generally, pp. 310–315. See also Friedrich A. Hayek, *The Constitution of Liberty* (Chicago: University of Chicago Press, 1960), chap. 7; and Nozick, *Anarchy, State, and Utopia*, pp. 155–160.
20. Rawls, *A Theory of Justice*, pp. 108–117.
21. Ibid., p. 114.
22. See Michael J. Sandel, *Liberalism and the Limits of Justice* (Cambridge: Cambridge University Press, 1982), pp. 179–183.
23. Alasdair MacIntyre, *After Virtue* (Notre Dame: University of Notre Dame Press, 1981), pp. 204–206.
24. Lee quoted in Douglas Southall Freeman, *R. E. Lee* (New York: Charles Scribner's Sons, 1934), pp. 443, 421. See also the discussions of Lee in Morton Grodzins, *The Loyal and the Disloyal* (Chicago: University of Chicago Press, 1965), pp. 142–143; and Judith Shklar, *Ordinary Vices* (Cambridge, Mass.: Harvard University Press, 1984), p. 160.
25. Rawls, *A Theory of Justice*, pp. 101–102.
26. See Nozick, *Anarchy, State, and Utopia*, p. 228.
27. Ralph Waldo Emerson, "Self Reliance," in Emerson, *Essays and Lectures* (New York: Library of America, 1983), p. 262.
28. The view I describe here as minimalist liberalism is represented by John Rawls's recent book, *Political Liberalism* (New York: Columbia University Press, 1993), and his article "Justice as Fairness: Political Not Metaphysical," *Philosophy & Public Affairs*, 14 (1985), 223–251. It is also presented, in a somewhat different version, in Richard Rorty, "The Priority of Democracy to Philosophy," in *The Virginia Statute for Religious Freedom*, ed. Merrill D. Peterson and Robert C. Vaughan (Cambridge: Cambridge University Press, 1988). The quotation is from Rawls, "Justice as Fairness," p. 230.
29. Rawls, *Political Liberalism*, p. 31; see generally pp. 29–35.
30. Ibid., pp. xvi–xxviii.
31. Rawls, "Justice as Fairness," p. 230; Rorty, "Priority of Democracy," p. 257.

32. I draw in this discussion from Michael J. Sandel, "Political Liberalism," *Harvard Law Review,* 107 (1994), 1765–94.

33. Paul M. Angle, ed., *Created Equal? The Complete Lincoln-Douglas Debates of 1858* (Chicago: University of Chicago Press, 1958), pp. 369, 374.

34. Ibid., p. 390.

35. Ibid., p. 392.

36. Ibid., p. 389.

2. Rights and the Neutral State

1. Aristotle, *The Politics,* trans. Ernest Barker (London: Oxford University Press, 1946), bks. 1 and 3. For a contemporary statement of the "strong" republican view, see Hannah Arendt, *The Human Condition* (Chicago: University of Chicago Press, 1958).

2. See Niccolò Machiavelli, *The Discourses,* ed. Bernard Crick, trans. Leslie J. Walker (Harmondsworth: Penguin Books, 1970); and the illuminating discussion of Machiavelli in this connection in Quentin Skinner, "The Paradoxes of Political Liberty," in *The Tanner Lectures on Human Values* (Cambridge: Cambridge University Press, 1985), pp. 227–250.

3. Isaiah Berlin, "Two Concepts of Liberty," in Berlin, *Four Essays on Liberty* (London: Oxford University Press, 1969), pp. 129–130.

4. Thomas Hobbes, *Leviathan* (1651), ed. C. B. Macpherson (Harmondsworth: Penguin Books, 1968), part II, chap. 21, p. 266.

5. See Ronald Dworkin, "Liberalism," in Stuart Hampshire, ed., *Public and Private Morality* (Cambridge: Cambridge University Press, 1978), p. 127: "What does it mean for the government to treat its citizens as equals? That is, I think, the same question as the question of what it means for the government to treat all its citizens as free, or as independent, or with equal dignity. In any case, it is a question that has been central to political theory at least since Kant."

6. Laurence Tribe, *American Constitutional Law* (Mineola, N.Y.: Foundation Press, 1978), pp. 2–3. See also Louis Henkin, "Constitutional Fathers, Constitutional Sons," *Minnesota Law Review,* 60 (1976), 1113–47.

7. Alexis de Tocqueville, *Democracy in America* (1835), ed. Phillips Bradley (New York: Alfred A. Knopf, 1945), vol. 1, chap. 5, p. 61.

8. Only rarely since the New Deal has the Supreme Court struck down an act of Congress on federalist grounds. One was a law granting eighteen-year-olds the right to vote in state elections, *Oregon v. Mitchell,* 400 U.S. 410 (1970); another was a minimum-wage law for state and municipal employees, *National League of Cities v. Usery,* 426 U.S. 833 (1976). The first was overturned a year later by constitutional amendment (26), and the second was overruled by the Court itself in 1985. In *United States v. Lopez,* 115 S.Ct. 1365 (1995), a closely divided Court struck down a federal law banning the possession of guns near schools.

9. I am indebted in this section to the excellent accounts provided in Bernard Bailyn, *The Ideological Origins of the American Revolution* (Cambridge, Mass.: Harvard Uni-

versity Press, 1967), pp. 175–198; and Gordon S. Wood, *The Creation of the American Republic, 1776–1787* (Chapel Hill: University of North Carolina Press, 1969), pp. 259–305.

10. An American Tory, Charles Inglis, *The True Interest of America* (Philadelphia, 1776), p. 18, quoted in Bailyn, *Ideological Origins*, p. 175; Blackstone, *Commentaries*, vol. 1, p. 126, quoted in Wood, *Creation of the American Republic*, p. 261.

11. Bailyn, *Ideological Origins*, p. 176.

12. Otis quoted in Bernard Bailyn, ed., *Pamphlets of the American Revolution* (Cambridge, Mass.: Harvard University Press, 1965), p. 412.

13. James Otis, *The Rights of the British Colonies Asserted and Proved* (Boston, 1764), ibid., pp. 447, 454.

14. Ibid., pp. 454–455, 448.

15. Samuel Adams, quoted in Wood, *Creation of the American Republic*, p. 266.

16. *Four Letters on Interesting Subjects* (1776), ibid., p. 267.

17. Bailyn, *Ideological Origins*, pp. 186–187.

18. [John Dickinson,] *An Address to the Committee of Correspondence in Barbados* (Philadelphia, 1766), ibid., p. 187.

19. See Donald S. Lutz, *Popular Consent and Popular Control* (Baton Rouge: Louisiana State University Press, 1980), pp. 61, 65–67; and Willi Paul Adams, *The First American Constitutions* (Chapel Hill: University of North Carolina Press, 1980), pp. 146–147. Lutz observes that early constitutions used prescriptives such as "should" and "ought" in declarations of rights, and imperatives such as "shall" in setting forth institutions of government.

20. W. F. Dodd, "The First State Constitutional Conventions, 1776–1783," *American Political Science Review*, 2 (November 1908), 551, 558. See also Lutz, *Popular Consent*, p. 82; and Wood, *Creation of the American Republic*, p. 307.

21. Thomas Jefferson, *Notes on the State of Virginia* (1787), in *Jefferson Writings*, ed. Merrill D. Peterson (New York: Library of America, 1984), pp. 246–250.

22. New Jersey Constitution of 1776, Articles XXIII, XXII, in Ben Perley Poore, ed., *The Federal and State Constitutions, Colonial Charters, and Other Organic Laws of the United States* (Washington, D.C.: U.S. Government Printing Office, 1877), p. 1313.

23. North Carolina Constitution of 1776, Article XLIV, ibid., p. 1414; Pennsylvania Constitution of 1776, secs. 46, 47, ibid., p. 1548; Delaware Constitution of 1776, Article 30, ibid., p. 278.

24. [Thomas Tudor Tucker,] *Conciliatory Hints, Attempting by a Fair State of Matters, to Remove Party Prejudice* (1784), quoted in Wood, *Creation of the American Republic*, p. 281.

25. Max Farrand, ed., *The Records of the Federal Convention of 1787* (New Haven: Yale University Press, 1966), vol. 2, pp. 587–588.

26. Ibid., p. 588.

27. James Wilson, quoted in John Bach McMaster and Frederick D. Stone, eds., *Pennsylvania and the Federal Constitution* (Philadelphia: Historical Society of Pennsylvania, 1888), p. 253.

28. This argument was advanced by James Wilson, ibid., pp. 143–144, and by Alexan-

der Hamilton in *The Federalist* no. 84 (1788), ed. Jacob E. Cooke (Middletown, Conn.: Wesleyan University Press, 1961), pp. 578–579. Anti-Federalist replies to this argument include "A Federal Republican," in Herbert J. Storing, ed., *The Complete Anti-Federalist,* 7 vols. (Chicago: University of Chicago Press, 1981), vol. 3, p. 85; "An Old Whig," ibid., p. 24; "Essays of Brutus," ibid., vol. 2, p. 374; and "Letters from the Federal Farmer," ibid., pp. 247–250, 323–328.

29. Hamilton, *The Federalist* no. 84, pp. 578–579.

30. Benjamin Rush, quoted in McMaster and Stone, *Pennsylvania and the Federal Constitution,* pp. 294–295.

31. Storing, *The Complete Anti-Federalist,* vol. 2, p. 231. See also p. 261.

32. "Letters of Agrippa," ibid., vol. 4, p. 111.

33. Jefferson to Madison, December 20, 1787, in *Jefferson Writings,* p. 916.

34. See David A. J. Richards, *Toleration and the Constitution* (New York: Oxford University Press, 1986), p. 291n.

35. "Address by Denatus," in Storing, *The Complete Anti-Federalist,* vol. 5, p. 263; see also "Letters of Centinel," ibid., vol. 2, p. 152.

36. Leonard W. Levy, *Constitutional Opinions: Aspects of the Bill of Rights* (New York: Oxford University Press, 1986), pp. 111–112.

37. "A Federal Republican," in Storing, *The Complete Anti-Federalist,* vol. 3, p. 85 (emphasis added).

38. Samuel Chase, ibid., vol. 2, p. 14.

39. James Madison, *Federalist* no. 48, p. 335.

40. Madison to Jefferson, October 17, 1788, in Marvin Meyers, ed., *The Mind of the Founder: Sources of the Political Thought of James Madison,* rev. ed. (Hanover, N.H.: University Press of New England, 1981), p. 157.

41. Madison, *Federalist* nos. 10 and 48, pp. 62–64, 335.

42. See Charles F. Hobson, "The Negative on State Laws: James Madison, the Constitution, and the Crisis of Republican Government," *William and Mary Quarterly,* 36 (April 1979), 215–235. The quotation is from Madison to Washington, April 16, 1787, at p. 219.

43. *Annals,* 1st Cong., 1st sess., August 17, 1789, reprinted in Charles S. Hyneman and George W. Carey, eds., *A Second Federalist* (Columbia: University of South Carolina Press, 1967), p. 275.

44. Ibid., April 8, 1789, p. 272.

45. Anti-Federalists in Virginia succeeded in delaying ratification for two years. See Levy, *Constitutional Opinions,* pp. 122–124.

46. *Barron v. Baltimore,* 7 Peters 243 (1833).

47. Henkin, "Constitutional Fathers, Constitutional Sons," p. 1118. See also Tribe, *American Constitutional Law,* pp. 3–4; and Edward S. Corwin, *The Twilight of the Supreme Court* (New Haven: Yale University Press, 1934), p. 78.

48. *Lamont v. Postmaster General,* 381 U.S. 301 (1965).

49. *Dred Scott v. Sandford,* 19 Howard 393 (1857).

50. *Slaughter-House Cases,* 83 U.S. (16 Wallace) 36, 78 (1873).

51. Ibid. at 89, 105.

52. *Allgeyer v. Louisiana,* 165 U.S. 578, 589 (1897).

53. Tribe, *American Constitutional Law,* p. 435.

54. *Lochner v. New York,* 198 U.S. 45 (1905).

55. *Adkins v. Children's Hospital,* 261 U.S. 525 (1923).

56. *Adair v. United States,* 208 U.S. 161 (1908); and *Coppage v. Kansas,* 236 U.S. 1 (1915).

57. *Coppage,* 236 U.S. at 17–18.

58. See *Meyer v. Nebraska,* 262 U.S. 390, 399 (1923); and *Pierce v. Society of Sisters,* 268 U.S. 510 (1925).

59. *Morehead v. New York ex rel. Tipaldo,* 298 U.S. 587 (1936).

60. *West Coast Hotel Co. v. Parrish,* 300 U.S. 379 (1937).

61. Gerald Gunther, *Constitutional Law,* 11th ed. (Mineola, N.Y.: Foundation Press, 1985), p. 472.

62. The phrase is Justice Miller's in the *Slaughter-House Cases,* 83 U.S. (16 Wallace) 36, 78 (1873).

63. *Truax v. Corrigan,* 257 U.S. 312, 344 (1921). See also Holmes's dissents in *Lochner,* 198 U.S. at 75; *Adair,* 208 U.S. at 191–192; *Coppage,* 236 U.S. at 27; and *Tyson and Brother v. Banton,* 273 U.S. 418, 447 (1927).

64. *Holmes-Laski Letters,* ed. Mark DeWolfe Howe (Cambridge, Mass.: Harvard University Press, 1953), vol. 1, p. 249.

65. *Schenck v. United States,* 249 U.S. 47 (1919).

66. *Abrams v. United States,* 250 U.S. 616, 628 (1919).

67. *Gilbert v. Minnesota,* 254 U.S. 325, 343 (1920).

68. Brandeis concurring in *Whitney v. California,* 274 U.S. 357, 373 (1927). For an illuminating discussion of these cases, see Robert M. Cover, "The Left, the Right and the First Amendment: 1918–1928," *Maryland Law Review,* 40 (1981), 349–388.

69. *Gitlow v. California,* 268 U.S. 652, 672–673 (1924).

70. *Otis v. Parker,* 187 U.S. 606, 608–609 (1903).

71. *Lochner,* 198 U.S. at 75–76.

72. *Abrams,* 250 U.S. at 629.

73. See, e.g., *Police Department of Chicago v. Mosley,* 408 U.S. 92, 95 (1972): "Above all else, the First Amendment means that government has no power to restrict expression because of its message, its ideas, its subject matter, or its content."

74. *United States v. Carolene Products Co.,* 304 U.S. 144, 152 n. 4 (1938).

75. Ibid.

76. *Adamson v. California,* 332 U.S. 46 (1947).

77. *Palko v. Connecticut,* 302 U.S. 319 (1937).

78. See *Duncan v. Louisiana,* 391 U.S. 145 (1968).

79. *Carolene Products,* 304 U.S. 144, 152 n. 4 (1938). This part of the footnote has generated a literature proportionate to its influence. See especially John Hart Ely, *Democracy and Distrust* (Cambridge, Mass.: Harvard University Press, 1980); Robert M. Cover, "The Origins of Judicial Activism in the Protection of Minorities," *Yale Law Journal,* 91 (1982), 1287–1316; and Bruce A. Ackerman, "Beyond Carolene Products," *Harvard Law Review,* 98 (1985), 713–746.

80. See, e.g., Gunther, *Constitutional Law,* pp. 472–475; and Henry J. Abraham, *Freedom and the Court,* 4th ed. (New York: Oxford University Press, 1982), chap. 2.
81. See, e.g., Tribe, *American Constitutional Law,* p. 574: "The time may come when constitutional law will answer the scholar's question, 'Why education and not golf?' with the only reply that is likely to make human sense—'Because education is more important.'"
82. *Coppage,* 236 U.S. at 9.
83. Ibid. at 14.
84. Holmes dissenting in ibid. at 27. The Court's opinion in *West Coast Hotel* also notes this legislative purpose. The Progressive response to laissez-faire economics is discussed in Sidney Fine, *Laissez Faire and the General Welfare State* (Ann Arbor: University of Michigan Press, 1956), esp. pp. 376, 383.
85. Franklin D. Roosevelt, "An Economic Bill of Rights," January 11, 1944, in *The Public Papers and Addresses of Franklin D. Roosevelt,* ed. Samuel I. Rosenman, 13 vols. (New York: Random House, 1938–1950), vol. 13, p. 32.
86. Dworkin, "Liberalism," pp. 133–134.
87. *Minersville School District v. Gobitis,* 310 U.S. 586 (1940).
88. *West Virginia State Board of Education v. Barnette,* 319 U.S. 624, 638 (1943).
89. Ibid. at 642.
90. Ibid. at 644.

3. Religious Liberty and Freedom of Speech

1. *Abington Township School District v. Schempp,* 374 U.S. 203, 226 (1963).
2. *Epperson v. Arkansas,* 393 U.S. 97, 104–104 (1968).
3. *Everson v. Board of Education of Ewing Township,* 330 U.S. 1, 24 (1947), Justice Jackson dissenting.
4. *Abington,* 374 U.S. at 221.
5. *Walz v. Tax Commission of the City of New York,* 397 U.S. 664, 669 (1970).
6. *Wallace v. Jaffree,* 472 U.S. 38, 60 (1985).
7. See, for example, John Locke, *A Letter concerning Toleration* (1689), ed. James H. Tully (Indianapolis: Hackett, 1983); and John Rawls, "Justice as Fairness: Political not Metaphysical," *Philosophy & Public Affairs,* 14 (Summer 1985), 249.
8. *Everson,* 330 U.S. at 16. The quotation is from Jefferson's letter to the Baptists of Danbury, Connecticut, January 1, 1802, in *Jefferson Writings,* ed. Merrill D. Peterson (New York: Library of America, 1984), p. 510.
9. *McCollum v. Board of Education,* 333 U.S. 203, 247 (1948), Justice Reed dissenting.
10. *Abington,* 374 U.S. at 203.
11. *McCollum,* 333 U.S. at 203.
12. In *Everson,* 330 U.S.
13. Unlike European religious establishments, the American versions, at least after the Revolution, were multiple rather than exclusive establishments, allowing support for more than a single denomination. Some states established Protestantism, others

Christianity, as the religion eligible for tax support. See Leonard W. Levy, *The Establishment Clause* (New York: Macmillan, 1986), chap. 2.

14. See Mark DeWolfe Howe, *The Garden and the Wilderness* (Chicago: University of Chicago Press, 1965), chap. 1; and Wilbur G. Katz, *Religion and American Constitutions* (Evanston, Ill.: Northwestern University Press, 1964), p. 9.

15. *Jefferson Writings,* p. 347.

16. See Leo Pfeffer, *Church, State, and Freedom,* rev. ed. (Boston: Beacon Press, 1967), pp. 108–111; and Levy, *The Establishment Clause,* pp. 51–61.

17. See Richard E. Morgan, *The Supreme Court and Religion* (New York: Free Press, 1972), pp. 30–31. The Maryland case was *Torcaso v. Watkins,* 367 U.S. 488 (1961).

18. Kent quoted in Pfeffer, *Church, State, and Freedom,* p. 665.

19. *Permoli v. New Orleans,* 44 U.S. 589, 609 (1845).

20. Levy, *The Establishment Clause,* p. 122.

21. Anson Phelps Stokes and Leo Pfeffer, *Church and State in the United States,* rev. ed. (New York: Harper and Row, 1964), pp. 433–434; Pfeffer, *Church, State, and Freedom,* pp. 146–147; Morgan, *The Supreme Court and Religion,* pp. 50–51.

22. *Reynolds v. United States,* 98 U.S. 145, 164 (1878).

23. *Cantwell v. Connecticut,* 310 U.S. 296, 303 (1940).

24. *Everson,* 330 U.S. at 16.

25. Ibid. at 15–16.

26. A recent exception is Justice Rehnquist's dissent in *Wallace,* 472 U.S. at 91.

27. *Everson,* 330 U.S. at 19.

28. *Abington,* 374 U.S. at 225, 313. In *Engel v. Vitale,* 370 U.S. 421 (1962), by contrast, Stewart had defended school prayer by appealing not to neutrality but to "the history of the religious traditions of our people" and "the deeply entrenched and highly cherished spiritual traditions of our Nation."

29. *Epperson,* 393 U.S. at 113.

30. Ibid. The dispute over the proper interpretation of neutrality also arose in *Edwards v. Aguillard,* 482 U.S. 578 (1987), a case involving a Louisiana law mandating "balanced treatment" of creationism and evolution in the public schools.

31. *Wallace,* 472 U.S. at 60, 85. In a separate dissent, Justice Rehnquist challenged the assumption, accepted since *Everson,* that the establishment clause requires government to be neutral between religion and irreligion; ibid. at 99.

32. *McGowan v. Maryland,* 366 U.S. 420, 448 (1961).

33. *Lynch v. Donnelly,* 465 U.S. 668, 681, 683 (1984). In *Marsh v. Chambers,* 463 U.S. 783 (1983), the Court upheld the Nebraska legislature's practice of opening each day with a prayer by a chaplain paid by the state, citing the long history of the practice. Writing in dissent, Justice Brennan construed the decision as carving out a narrow exception to establishment clause doctrine.

34. *McGowan,* 366 U.S. at 572–573.

35. *Lynch,* 465 U.S. at 727.

36. *McCollum,* 333 U.S. at 212.

37. *Everson,* 330 U.S. at 59, Justice Rutledge dissenting.

38. *Abington,* 374 U.S. at 245, Justice Brennan concurring.

39. Roger Williams quoted in Howe, *The Garden and the Wilderness,* pp. 6–7.
40. *Engel,* 370 U.S. at 432.
41. Concurring opinion in *Abington,* 374 U.S. at 259.
42. *Everson,* 330 U.S. at 53, 59, Justice Rutledge dissenting.
43. *McCollum,* 333 U.S. at 216–217.
44. *Zorach v. Clauson,* 343 U.S. 306, 319 (1952), Justice Black dissenting.
45. *Cantwell,* 310 U.S. at 303.
46. *Abington,* 374 U.S. at 222, 317, Justice Clark for the Court, Justice Stewart in dissent.
47. Gail Merel, "The Protection of Individual Choice: A Consistent Understanding of Religion under the First Amendment," *University of Chicago Law Review,* 45 (1978), 806.
48. Alan Schwarz, "No Imposition of Religion: The Establishment Clause Value," *Yale Law Journal,* 77 (1968), 728.
49. David A. J. Richards, *Toleration and the Constitution* (New York: Oxford University Press, 1986), p. 140.
50. *Allegheny County v. ACLU,* 492 U.S. 573, 634 (1989).
51. *Lee v. Weisman,* 112 S.Ct. 2649, 2665 (1992).
52. *Wallace,* 472 U.S. at 52–53; emphasis added.
53. *Wolman v. Walter,* 433 U.S. 229, 263 (1977), Justice Powell concurring and dissenting. See also Chief Justice Burger's dissent in *Meek v. Pittenger,* 421 U.S. 349 (1975).
54. See President Ronald Reagan's "State of the Union Address," January 27, 1987, in *Public Papers of the Presidents of the United States: Ronald Reagan, 1987* (Washington, D.C.: U.S. Government Printing Office, 1989), vol. 1, p. 59; and, generally, Richard E. Morgan, *The Politics of Religious Conflict* (Washington, D.C.: University Press of America, 1980).
55. Laurence Tribe, *American Constitutional Law* (Mineola, N.Y.: Foundation Press, 1978), p. 885.
56. James Madison, *Memorial and Remonstrance against Religious Assessments* (1785), in Marvin Meyers, ed., *The Mind of the Founder,* rev. ed. (Hanover, N.H.: University Press of New England, 1981), pp. 6–13.
57. In 1779 Jefferson asserted that God "chose not to propagate" religion by coercion, "as was in his Almighty power to do, but to extend it by its influence on reason alone"; *Jefferson Writings,* p. 346.
58. Ibid.
59. Locke, *Letter concerning Toleration,* p. 46. Jefferson's argument may also have reflected the influence of the eighteenth-century philosopher Thomas Hutcheson, whose account of belief is discussed in Morton White, *The Philosophy of American Revolution* (New York: Oxford University Press, 1978), pp. 195–202.
60. Madison, *Memorial and Remonstrance,* p. 7.
61. The civic consequences of religion vary widely, of course, according to political circumstance and the particular religion. For a favorable account of the civic consequences of religion in nineteenth-century America, see Alexis de Tocqueville, *Democracy in America* (1835), trans. Henry Reeve, ed. Phillips Bradley (New York: Alfred A. Knopf, 1945), vol. 1, pp. 299–314.

62. The phrase is from John Rawls, "Kantian Constructivism in Moral Theory," *Journal of Philosophy*, 77 (September 1980), 543.

63. *Thornton v. Caldor, Inc.*, 474 U.S. 703 (1985).

64. Ibid., Burger at 710, O'Connor at 711.

65. *Sherbert v. Verner*, 374 U.S. 398, 409 (1963). Three justices argued that the decision was inconsistent with *Braunfeld v. Brown*, 336 U.S. 599 (1961), where the Court had refused to exempt Orthodox Jewish store owners from Sunday blue laws, even though this meant they had to forgo business two days each week instead of one. Other employment compensation cases decided in line with *Sherbert* are *Thomas v. Review Board of Indiana Employment Security Div.*, 450 U.S. 707 (1981); and *Hobbie v. Unemployment Appeals Comm'n of Florida*, 480 U.S. 136 (1987).

66. *United States v. Seeger*, 380 U.S. 163, 166 (1965).

67. *Gillette v. United States*, 401 U.S. 437, 454 (1971). See also *Welsh v. United States*, 398 U.S. 333 (1970).

68. *Gillette*, 401 U.S. at 454.

69. *Wisconsin v. Yoder*, 406 U.S. 205, 220 (1972).

70. *Goldman v. Weinberger*, 475 U.S. 503, 507–509 (1986).

71. *Employment Division v. Smith*, 494 U.S. 872, 879, 885 (1990).

72. Ibid. at 886, 885, 888.

73. Ibid. at 890.

74. *Congressional Quarterly Weekly Report*, 51 (October 30, 1993), 2984; ibid., November 6, 1993, p. 3057. See also Angela C. Carmella, "The Religious Freedom Restoration Act," *Religion & Values in Public Life*, 3 (Winter 1995), 5–7.

75. *Young v. American Mini Theatres, Inc.*, 427 U.S. 50, 67 (1976).

76. *Herbert v. Lando*, 441 U.S. 153, 184–185 (1979), Justice Brennan dissenting.

77. *Police Department of the City of Chicago v. Mosley*, 408 U.S. 92, 95 (1972). I leave aside the question whether the content neutrality doctrine prohibits "subject matter" as well as "viewpoint" restrictions. That debate in any case presupposes that government must be neutral with respect to speech, and involves competing conceptions of neutrality. See Geoffrey R. Stone, "Content Regulation and the First Amendment," *William and Mary Law Review*, 25 (1983), 189–252.

78. Gerald Gunther, *Constitutional Law*, 11th ed. (Mineola, N.Y.: Foundation Press, 1985), devotes 491 of 1633 pages to freedom of expression.

79. For discussion of free speech cases before World War I, see David M. Rabban, "The First Amendment in Its Forgotten Years," *Yale Law Journal*, 90 (1981), 514–596.

80. Leonard W. Levy, *Emergence of a Free Press* (New York: Oxford University Press, 1985), p. 268.

81. Jefferson to Abigail Adams, September 4, 1804, quoted in ibid., p. 307.

82. See Paul L. Murphy, *World War I and the Origin of Civil Liberties in the United States* (New York: W. W. Norton, 1979), pp. 30–31.

83. The "clear and present danger" standard was introduced by Holmes in *Schenck v. United States*, 249 U.S. 47 (1919), a case upholding convictions of antidraft agitators during World War I.

84. See *Abrams v. United States*, 250 U.S. 616 (1919), Justice Holmes dissenting.

85. The Court first stated that the Fourteenth Amendment protects freedom of speech from infringement by the States in *Gitlow v. New York*, 268 U.S. 652 (1925). Early cases reversing convictions for subversive advocacy include *Fiske v. Kansas*, 274 U.S. 380 (1927); *Stromberg v. California*, 283 U.S. 359 (1931); *DeJonge v. Oregon*, 299 U.S. 353 (1937); and *Herndon v. Lowry*, 301 U.S. 242 (1937).

86. The phrase is from Harry Kalven, "Metaphysics of the Law of Obscenity," *Supreme Court Review*, 1960, p. 10.

87. *Chaplinsky v. New Hampshire*, 315 U.S. 568, 572 (1942).

88. *Valentine v. Chrestensen*, 316 U.S. 52 (1942).

89. *Beauharnais v. Illinois*, 343 U.S. 250, 266 (1952).

90. *Roth v. United States*, 354 U.S. 476 (1957).

91. See, e.g., Frederick Schauer, "Codifying the First Amendment: New York v. Ferber," *Supreme Court Review*, 1982, p. 285. Laurence Tribe offers a qualified version of this argument in *American Constitutional Law*, p. 671.

92. Thomas Emerson, *The System of Freedom of Expression* (New York: Random House, 1970), p. 326.

93. *New York Times Co. v. Sullivan*, 376 U.S. 254 (1964).

94. *Stanley v. Georgia*, 394 U.S. 557, 564 (1969).

95. See *Cohen v. California*, 403 U.S. 15 (1971); *Gooding v. Wilson*, 405 U.S. 518 (1972); *Rosenfeld v. New Jersey*, 408 U.S. 901 (1972).

96. *Virginia Pharmacy Board v. Virginia Consumer Council*, 425 U.S. 748 (1976).

97. Discussed above, Chapter 2.

98. *Mosley*, 408 U.S. at 95–96.

99. Stone, "Content Regulation and the First Amendment," p. 189.

100. *Erznoznik v. City of Jacksonville*, 422 U.S. 205, 211, 214–215 (1975).

101. *Consolidated Edison Company of New York v. Public Service Commission of New York*, 447 U.S. 530, 536–537 (1980).

102. *Texas v. Johnson*, 491 U.S. 397 (1989).

103. *R.A.V. v. City of St. Paul, Minnesota*, 112 S.Ct. 2538, 2541, 2549 (1992). Other cases employing the content neutrality doctrine include *Carey v. Brown*, 447 U.S. 455, 461–465 (1980); *Virginia Pharmacy Board*, 425 U.S. at 771; *Heffron v. International Society for Krishna Consciousness, Inc.*, 452 U.S. 640, 647–649 (1981); and *American Mini Theatres*, 427 U.S. at 67–73, 82.

104. Louis Henkin, "Morals and the Constitution: The Sin of Obscenity," *Columbia Law Review*, 63 (1963), 395.

105. Ronald Dworkin, "Is There a Right to Pornography?" *Oxford Journal of Legal Studies*, 1 (Summer 1981), 197. See also Richards, *Toleration and the Constitution*, p. 206: "Prohibitions on access of consenting adults to pornographic materials are rendered centrally suspect by the nonneutral and now highly controversial moral judgments invoked both in identifying what is obscene and in justifying suppression."

106. *Roth*, 354 U.S. at 476.

107. *Paris Adult Theatre I v. Slaton*, 413 U.S. 49, 57–58 (1973).

108. Ibid. at 59, quoting Alexander Bickel, *The Public Interest*, 22 –(Winter 1971), 25–26.

109. Ibid. at 69; emphasis added.
110. *Erznoznik*, 422 U.S.
111. *American Mini Theatres*, 427 U.S. at 70.
112. Ibid. at 71.
113. *City of Renton v. Playtime Theatres, Inc.*, 475 U.S. 41 (1986).
114. Ibid.
115. *Abrams*, 250 U.S. at 630, Justice Holmes dissenting.
116. *Whitney v. California*, 274 U.S. 357, 375 (1926), Justice Brandeis concurring. Brandeis also attributed to the founders the belief that "the final end of the State [is] to make men free to develop their faculties"; ibid. Some contemporary commentators see this as an early statement of the recent "self-fulfillment" rationale discussed later in this chapter. In the context of Brandeis' opinion, however, it suggests a notion of freedom essentially connected to the good of self-government.
117. Alexander Meiklejohn, *Free Speech and Its Relation to Self-Government* (New York: Harper, 1948), pp. 88–89. Meiklejohn later interpreted political speech broadly, to include philosophy and the sciences, literature, and the arts. See Meiklejohn, "The First Amendment Is an Absolute," *Supreme Court Review*, 1961, pp. 255–257. For a narrower view, see Robert Bork, "Neutral Principles and Some First Amendment Problems," *Indiana Law Journal*, 47 (1971), 1.
118. *Garrison v. Louisiana*, 379 U.S. 64, 74–75 (1964): "speech concerning public affairs is more than self-expression; it is the essence of self-government." *Richard Newspapers v. Virginia*, 448 U.S. 555, 587 (1980), Justice Brennan concurring: "the First Amendment embodies more than a commitment to free expression and communicative interchange for their own sakes; it has a *structural* role to play in securing and fostering our republican system of government."
119. Richards, *Toleration and the Constitution*, p. 168. See also idem, "Free Speech and Obscenity Law: Toward a Moral Theory of the First Amendment," *University of Pennsylvania Law Review*, 123 (1974), 62: "[The] value of free expression, in this view, rests on its deep relation to self-respect arising from autonomous self-determination."
120. C. Edwin Baker, "Scope of the First Amendment Freedom of Speech," *U.C.L.A. Law Review*, 25 (1978), 993.
121. *Cohen*, 403 U.S. at 24–25. Justice Harlan also offered the more plausible argument that display of the jacket should be protected as political speech; ibid. at 18, 24, 26.
122. *Mosley*, 408 U.S. at 96.
123. *Doe v. Bolton*, 410 U.S. 179, 211 (1973), Justice Douglas concurring.
124. *Herbert*, 441 U.S. at 183n, Justice Brennan dissenting.
125. *First National Bank of Boston v. Bellotti*, 435 U.S. 765, 807 (1978). White was dissenting from a ruling invalidating a Massachusetts law restricting corporate spending to influence the outcome of referendums. He also defended the law on the less sweeping and more compelling grounds that a state need not allow corporations, which amass wealth as a result of special advantages conferred by the state, to use that wealth to acquire an unfair advantage in the political process; ibid. at 809.

126. Peter Berger, "On the Obsolescence of the Concept of Honour," *European Journal of Sociology*, 11 (1970), 344.

127. Robert C. Post, "The Social Foundations of Defamation Law: Reputation and the Constitution," *California Law Review*, 74 (1986), 699–700.

128. David Riesman, "Democracy and Defamation: Control of Group Libel," Columbia Law Review, 42 (1942), 730.

129. Race Relations Act of 1965, *Public General Acts*, 1965, chap. 73. See Anthony Dickey, "English Law and Race Defamation," *New York Law Forum*, 14 (1968), 9.

130. Riesman, "Democracy and Defamation," p. 730.

131. *Chaplinsky*, 315 U.S. at 571–572; emphasis added.

132. *Beauharnais*, 343 U.S.

133. Ibid. at 258–259, 261.

134. Ibid. at 263; emphasis added.

135. Ibid. at 272–274, Justice Black dissenting.

136. Ibid. at 299, 302–303, Justice Jackson dissenting; emphasis added.

137. This debate is recounted in Donald Alexander Downs, *Nazis in Skokie* (Notre Dame: University of Notre Dame Press, 1985), chap. 3.

138. David Hamlin, quoted in ibid., p. 37. For the ACLU perspective, see David Hamlin, *The Nazi/Skokie Conflict: A Civil Liberties Battle* (Boston: Beacon Press, 1980).

139. *Collin v. Smith*, 447 F. Supp. 676, 686–687 (1978); *Collin v. Smith*, 578 F.2d 1197, 1202 (1978).

140. *Collin*, 578 F.2d at 1202.

141. *Collin*, 447 F. Supp. at 686–688, 693–697. The Supreme Court refused to review the case, but Justice Blackmun dissented, observing that "*Beauharnais* has never been overruled or formally limited in any way"; *Smith v. Collin*, 436 U.S. 953 (1978).

142. General Ordinances nos. 24, 1984, and 35, 1984, Code of Indianapolis and Marion County, Indiana, quoted in *American Booksellers Association, Inc., v. Hudnut*, 598 F. Supp. 1316, 1320 (1984).

143. Ibid. at 1320, 1322.

144. Catharine A. MacKinnon, "Not a Moral Issue," *Yale Law & Policy Review*, 2 (1984), 326.

145. See, e.g., *The Report of the Commission on Obscenity and Pornography* (Washington, D.C.: U.S. Government Printing Office, 1970).

146. MacKinnon, "Not a Moral Issue," p. 338.

147. *American Booksellers*, 598 F. Supp. at 1330–31.

148. Ibid. at 1335–36.

149. *American Booksellers Association, Inc. v. Hudnut*, 771 F.2d 323, 328–329, 332, 325 (1985).

150. Compare Ronald Dworkin's defense of race-conscious admissions policies, distinguishing the "benign" quotas of the 1970s from the racist and anti-Semitic quotas of the 1940s. Since, on liberal theory, the distinction cannot be based on the worthiness of the purpose the policy serves, it must be based on such elaborate grounds as a theory distinguishing "internal" from "external" preferences; Dworkin, *Taking Rights Seriously* (Cambridge, Mass.: Harvard University Press, 1977), chap. 9.

151. *Williams v. Wallace*, 240 F. Supp. 100, 108, 106 (1965).

152. For discussion of the case, see Frank M. Johnson, "Civil Disobedience and the Law," *Tulane Law Review*, 44 (1969), 9–10.

4. Privacy Rights and Family Law

1. *Roe v. Wade*, 410 U.S. 113, 162, 153 (1973).

2. *Thornburgh v. American College of Obstetricians*, 476 U.S. 747, 777 (1986), Justice Stevens concurring.

3. June Aline Eichbaum, "Towards an Autonomy-Based Theory of Constitutional Privacy," *Harvard Civil Rights–Civil Liberties Law Review*, 14 (1979), 365.

4. David Richards, "The Individual, the Family, and the Constitution: A Jurisprudential Perspective," *New York University Law Review*, 55 (April 1980), 31.

5. Kenneth L. Karst, "The Freedom of Intimate Association," *Yale Law Journal*, 89 (1980), 641. On the connection between privacy and autonomy rights, see also J. Harvie Wilkinson III and G. Edward White, "Constitutional Protection for Personal Lifestyles," *Cornell Law Review*, 63 (1977), 563–625; Louis Henkin, "Privacy and Autonomy," *Columbia Law Review*, 74 (1974), 1410–33; and Rogers M. Smith, "The Constitution and Autonomy," *Texas Law Review*, 60 (February 1982), 175–205.

6. *Carey v. Population Services International*, 431 U.S. 678, 687 (1977).

7. *Thornburgh*, 476 U.S. at 772.

8. *Doe v. Bolton*, 410 U.S. 179, 211 (1973), Justice Douglas concurring.

9. *Kelley v. Johnson*, 425 U.S. 238, 251 (1976), Justice Marshall dissenting.

10. *Bowers v. Hardwick*, 478 U.S. 186, 205 (1986), Justice Blackmun dissenting.

11. *Whalen v. Roe*, 429 U.S. 589, 599–600 (1977).

12. *Roberts v. United States Jaycees*, 468 U.S. 609, 618–619 (1984).

13. Ibid. at 619.

14. Samuel Warren and Louis Brandeis, "The Right to Privacy," *Harvard Law Review*, 4 (1890), 193–220.

15. Alpheus T. Mason, *Brandeis: A Free Man's Life* (New York: Viking Press, 1946), p. 70.

16. Warren and Brandeis, "The Right to Privacy," p. 196.

17. See William L. Prosser, "Privacy," *California Law Review*, 48 (1960), 338–423.

18. *Meyer v. Nebraska*, 262 U.S. 390 (1923); and *Pierce v. Society of Sisters*, 268 U.S. 510 (1925).

19. *Olmstead v. United States*, 277 U.S. 438, 478 (1927), Justice Brandeis dissenting. Brandeis' position was not vindicated until 1967, when in *Katz v. United States*, 389 U.S. 347 (1967), the Supreme Court ruled that unauthorized wiretaps violate the Fourth Amendment.

20. *Skinner v. Oklahoma*, 316 U.S. 535 (1942).

21. *Poe v. Ullman*, 367 U.S. 497, 519–521 (1961), Justice Douglas dissenting.

22. Ibid. at 519: "If a State banned completely the sale of contraceptives in drug stores,

the case would be quite different. . . . The present law, however, deals not with sale, not with manufacture, but with *use*."

23. Ibid. at 545, Justice Harlan dissenting.

24. Ibid. at 545–546.

25. Ibid. at 553–554.

26. *Griswold v. Connecticut*, 381 U.S. 479, 485–486 (1965).

27. Ibid. at 486.

28. *Eisenstadt v. Baird*, 405 U.S. 438 (1972).

29. Ibid. at 453.

30. Ibid. The Court's opinion in *Eisenstadt* camouflages the shift from the old privacy to the new with a false hypothetical premise: "If under *Griswold* the distribution of contraceptives to married persons cannot be prohibited, a ban on distribution to unmarried persons would be equally impermissible." But *Griswold* did not hold that distribution to married persons cannot be prohibited.

31. *Roe*, 410 U.S. at 153.

32. *Planned Parenthood of Missouri v. Danforth*, 428 U.S. 52, 69, 74–75 (1976).

33. *Planned Parenthood v. Casey*, 112 S.Ct. 2791 (1992).

34. *Carey*, 431 U.S. at 687. Emphasis in quotations from *Eisenstadt* and *Roe* added by Court in *Carey*.

35. *Carey*, 431 U.S. at 688.

36. *Thornburgh*, 476 U.S. at 772.

37. *Casey*, 112 S.Ct. at 2807.

38. *Bowers*, 478 U.S. at 190–191, 196.

39. Ibid. at 204–205, 211, Justice Blackmun dissenting. In striking down a similar sodomy law, a New York State court also gave clear expression to the idea that government must be neutral among competing conceptions of morality and religion: "it is not the function of the Penal Law in our governmental policy to provide either a medium for the articulation or the apparatus for the intended enforcement of moral or theological values"; *People v. Onofre*, 51 N.Y.2d 476, 488 (1980).

40. John Rawls, "Justice as Fairness: Political not Metaphysical," *Philosophy & Public Affairs*, 14 (Summer 1985), 245.

41. *Roe*, 410 U.S. at 159.

42. Ibid. at 159–160.

43. Ibid. at 162.

44. Ibid. at 163.

45. *Thornburgh*, 476 U.S. at 796, 790, Justice White dissenting. Justice Harlan suggested a similar way of bracketing the moral controversy over contraception in *Poe*, 367 U.S. at 547: "the very controversial nature of these questions would, I think, require us to hesitate long before concluding that the Constitution precluded Connecticut from choosing as it has among these various views."

46. *Thornburgh*, 476 U.S. at 777–778, Justice Stevens concurring.

47. The phrase is from Rawls, "Justice as Fairness," p. 231.

48. *Bowers*, 478 U.S.

49. Ibid. at 191.

50. *Griswold,* 381 U.S. at 486.

51. *Bowers,* 478 U.S. at 217.

52. Ibid. at 218–219.

53. *Hardwick v. Bowers,* 760 F.2d 1202 (1985).

54. Ibid. at 1211–12. Another case that upheld gay rights on substantive rather than voluntarist grounds was *Braschi v. Stahl Associates Co.,* 543 N.E.2d 49 (N.Y. 1989). The New York Court of Appeals ruled that a rent-control law prohibiting the eviction of "family" members upon the death of the tenant protected gay life partners. More than "mere roommates," gay partners were analogous to legally married spouses, not because they had chosen to live together but because of "the totality of the relationship as evidenced by the dedication, caring and self-sacrifice of the parties"; ibid. at 54–55.

55. See *Eisenstadt,* 405 U.S. at 453; and *Carey,* 431 U.S. at 687.

56. *Stanley v. Georgia,* 394 U.S. 557, 564–566 (1969); ibid. at 568: "The right to receive information and ideas, *regardless of their social worth,* is fundamental to our free society . . . the States retain broad power to regulate obscenity; that power simply does not extend to mere possession by the individual in the privacy of his own home" (emphasis added).

57. *Onofre,* 51 N.Y.2d at 488.

58. *Bowers,* 478 U.S. at 191, 199.

59. Carl E. Schneider, "Moral Discourse in Family Law," *Michigan Law Review,* 83 (1985), 1807–08.

60. Illuminating accounts of these developments include ibid.; Mary Ann Glendon, *The New Family and the New Property* (Toronto: Butterworths, 1981); Lenore J. Weitzman, *The Divorce Revolution* (New York: Free Press, 1985); and Herbert Jacob, *Silent Revolution* (Chicago: University of Chicago Press, 1988).

61. Schneider, "Moral Discourse in Family Law," p. 1808.

62. Weitzman, *The Divorce Revolution,* pp. 4–7.

63. Ibid., p. 27 and, generally, pp. 15–41.

64. Ibid., p. 24.

65. Ibid., pp. 32–33. Figures are for Los Angeles County.

66. Ibid., pp. 36–37.

67. Schneider, "Moral Discourse in Family Law," p. 1809; Weitzman, *The Divorce Revolution,* pp. 41–43.

68. Weitzman, *The Divorce Revolution,* pp. 43–46, 167, Glendon, *The New Family,* pp. 52–57; Schneider, "Moral Discourse in Family Law," p. 1810. The Uniform Marriage and Divorce Act provides that maintenance awards shall be determined "without regard to marital misconduct"; sec. 308(b), 9A U.L.A. 160 (1979).

69. U.S. Bureau of the Census, "Divorce, Child Custody, and Child Support," in *Current Population Reports,* Series P-23, no. 84 (Washington, D.C., 1979), cited in Glendon, *The New Family,* p. 69.

70. Weitzman, *The Divorce Revolution,* pp. 267 (figures for Los Angeles County, 1978) and 262, citing U.S. Bureau of the Census, "Child Support and Alimony: 1981," *Current Population Reports,* Series P-23, no. 124 (Washington, D.C., 1983).

71. *Zablocki v. Redhail*, 434 U.S. 374 (1978).

72. The number of states with filial responsibility statutes declined from thirty-eight in 1956 to twenty-seven in 1980. See Schneider, "Moral Discourse in Family Law," p. 1813; and Glendon, *The New Family*, pp. 49–51. On grandparents' visiting rights, see S. Con. Res. 40, 98th Cong., 1st sess. (1983), cited in Schneider, p. 1858, n. 212.

73. Weitzman, *The Divorce Revolution*, pp. 186, 265, 338–339, 362. Alimony and standard-of-living figures are for Los Angeles County, 1977 and 1978. Child-support figure is for the United States, 1981, reported in U.S. Bureau of the Census, "Child Support and Alimony: 1981."

74. Arland Thornton and Deborah Freedman, "The Changing American Family," *Population Bulletin*, 38, no. 4 (October 1983), p. 10.

75. See "Elements of Child-Support Bill Pass," *Congressional Quarterly Almanac*, 50 (1994), 375.

76. John Rawls, *A Theory of Justice* (Cambridge, Mass.: Harvard University Press, 1971), p. 311.

77. Thornton and Freedman, "The Changing American Family," pp. 3, 7.

78. Samuel Preston, "Children and the Elderly: Divergent Paths for America's Dependents," *Demography*, 21 (November 1984), 435, 443–444. The figure for 1992 is from National Center for Health Statistics, "Advance Report of Final Natality Statistics, 1992," *Monthly Vital Statistics Report*, 43, no. 5, supp. (1994).

79. Joseph Veroff, Elizabeth Douvan, and Richard A. Kulka, *The Inner American: A Self-Portrait from 1957 to 1976* (New York: Basic Books, 1981), pp. 147, 201. Figures are based on national surveys conducted in 1957 and 1976.

80. Ibid., p. 200.

81. Ibid., pp. 209, 215, 239–240, 531. Women, however, showed an increased concern for providing children material support, possibly as a reflection of the increase in female-headed households.

82. Leo F. Buscaglia, *Personhood: The Art of Being Fully Human* (New York: Fawcett Columbine, 1978), p. 100.

83. Veroff, Douvan, and Kulka, *The Inner American*, p. 141.

84. Weitzman, *The Divorce Revolution*, pp. 169, 177. Alimony is more frequent for housewives of long marriages who have never held a job, but even in this category, over a third of women are awarded no alimony. Figures are for Los Angeles County, 1977.

85. Weitzman, *The Divorce Revolution*, p. 372.

86. Rawls, *A Theory of Justice*, pp. 264–265.

87. John Rawls, "Fairness to Goodness," *Philosophical Review*, 84 (October 1975), 550.

88. This argument is made in William J. Goode, "Individual Investments in Family Relationship over the Coming Decades," *Tocqueville Review*, 6, no. 1 (1984), 51–83. For an opposing view, see Theodore Caplow et al., *Middletown Families* (Minneapolis: University of Minnesota Press, 1982), pp. 322–334.

89. This contrast is a major theme of Glendon, *The New Family*, esp. pp. 1–8, 151–170, 198.

90. Veroff, Douvan, and Kulka, *The Inner American,* p. 55.
91. For a classic statement of this view, see Alexis de Tocqueville, *Democracy in America* (1835), trans. Henry Reeve, ed. Phillips Bradley (New York: Alfred A. Knopf, 1945), vol. 1, chap. 5.
92. See Grant Gilmore, *The Death of Contract* (Columbus: Ohio State University Press, 1974); and P. S. Atiyah, *The Rise and Fall of Freedom of Contract* (Oxford: Clarendon Press, 1979).
93. Lawrence Friedman, *Contract Law in America* (Madison: University of Wisconsin Press, 1965), pp. 23–24.
94. Atiyah, *Rise and Fall,* p. 724. For an account of similar developments in other areas of private law, see Gilmore, *The Death of Contract,* p. 94; Glendon, *The New Family,* pp. 215–227; Lawrence M. Friedman, *Total Justice* (New York: Russell Sage Foundation, 1985); and Robert A. Baruch Bush, "Between Two Worlds: The Shift from Individual to Group Responsibility in the Law of Causation of Injury," *U.C.L.A. Law Review,* 33 (1986), 1473.
95. Atiyah, *Rise and Fall,* pp. 687, 725–726.

5. Economics and Virtue in the Early Republic

1. Thomas Jefferson, *Notes on the State of Virginia* (1787), in *Jefferson Writings,* ed. Merrill D. Peterson (New York: Library of America, 1984), pp. 290–291.
2. Drew R. McCoy, "The Virginia Port Bill of 1784," *Virginia Magazine of History and Biography,* 83 (July 1975), 288–290.
3. Ibid., pp. 295–296.
4. George Mason, quoted in Drew R. McCoy, *The Elusive Republic: Political Economy in Jeffersonian America* (Chapel Hill: University of North Carolina Press, 1980), p. 16. See also McCoy, "The Virginia Port Bill of 1784," pp. 299–300.
5. John Adams to Mercy Warren, April 16, 1776, *Warren-Adams Letters,* ed. Worthington C. Ford (Boston: Massachusetts Historical Society, 1917), vol. 1, p. 222.
6. Benjamin Franklin to Messrs. The Abbés Chalut and Arnaud, April 17, 1787, quoted in McCoy, *The Elusive Republic,* p. 80.
7. Adams to Mercy Warren, January 8, 1776, *Warren-Adams Letters,* vol. 1, p. 202.
8. Ibid.
9. See Gordon S. Wood, *The Creation of the American Republic, 1776–1787* (Chapel Hill: University of North Carolina Press, 1969), pps. 46–124.
10. Ibid., p. 36.
11. Bernard Bailyn, *The Ideological Origins of the American Revolution* (Cambridge, Mass.: Harvard University Press, 1967), pp. 94–95.
12. Wood, *Creation of the American Republic,* pp. 53, 55, 58, 91–124.
13. Ibid., pp. 393–429. George Washington, quoted in Gordon S. Wood, "Interests and Disinterestedness in the Making of the Constitution," in Richard Beeman, Stephen Botein, and Edward C. Carter II, eds., *Beyond Confederation: Origins of the Consti-*

tution and American National Identity (Chapel Hill: University of North Carolina Press, 1987), p. 71.

14. Wood, "Interests and Distinterestedness," pp. 73–77.

15. Ibid., pp. 75–77.

16. James Madison, "Vices of the Political System of the United States" (1787), in Marvin Meyers, ed., *The Mind of the Founder: Sources of the Political Thought of James Madison,* rev. ed. (Hanover, N.H.: University Press of New England, 1981), p. 63.

17. Benjamin Rush, *Plan for the Establishment of Public Schools* (1786), in Frederick Rudolph, ed., *Essays on Education in the Early Republic* (Cambridge, Mass.: Harvard University Press, 1965), pp. 14, 17.

18. Wood, "Interests and Disinterestedness," pp. 80–81.

19. Alexander Hamilton, *The Continentalist* (1782), quoted in Gerald Stourzh, *Alexander Hamilton and the Idea of Republican Government* (Stanford: Stanford University Press, 1970), p. 70. Noah Webster, *An Examination into the Leading Principles of the Federal Constitution* (1787), quoted in ibid., p. 230, n. 104. See also Wood, *Creation of the American Republic,* p. 610.

20. James Madison, *Federalist* no. 51 (1788), in *The Federalist,* ed. Jacob E. Cooke (Middletown, Conn.: Wesleyan University Press, 1961), p. 349.

21. Ibid.

22. See Wood, "Interests and Disinterestedness," pp. 82–85.

23. Madison, "Vices of the Political System of the United States," p. 63; idem, *Federalist* no. 10 (1787), p. 60.

24. Madison, "Vices of the Political System of the United States," p. 65; idem, *Federalist* no. 10, p. 64.

25. Madison, *Federalist* no. 10, p. 64. See Wood, "Interests and Disinterestedness," p. 92.

26. Madison, *Federalist* no. 10, p. 62.

27. Hamilton, quoted in Stourzh, *Hamilton and Idea of Republican Government,* p. 175. On the general point, see Stourzh, pp. 171–205.

28. Hamilton, *Federalist* no. 7 (1788), p. 488. See the discussion in Stourzh, *Hamilton and Idea of Republican Government,* pp. 95–106.

29. Madison, *Federalist* no. 10, p. 62.

30. Madison, in Jonathan Elliot, ed., *The Debates in the Several State Conventions on the Adoption of the Federal Constitution* (New York: Burt Franklin, 1888), vol. 3, pp. 536–537.

31. Washington, "Farewell Address," September 19, 1796, in Noble E. Cunningham, Jr., ed., *The Early Republic, 1789–1828* (Columbia: University of South Carolina Press, 1968), p. 53.

32. Hamilton, *Federalist* no. 27, pp. 173–174.

33. Two excellent studies of the role of republican themes in the economic debates of the early republic, to which I am much indebted, are Lance Banning, *The Jeffersonian Persuasion* (Ithaca: Cornell University Press, 1978); and McCoy, *The Elusive Republic.* Other valuable discussions of republicanism and economic policy in this period

can be found in Steven Watts, *The Republic Reborn: War and the Making of Liberal America, 1790–1820* (Baltimore: Johns Hopkins University Press, 1987); John R. Nelson, Jr., *Liberty and Property: Political Economy and Policymaking in the New Nation, 1789–1812* (Cambridge, Mass.: Harvard University Press, 1987); Joyce Appleby, *Capitalism and a New Social Order: The Republican Vision of the 1790s* (New York: New York University Press, 1984); Richard Buel, Jr., *Securing the Revolution: Ideology in American Politics, 1789–1815* (Ithaca: Cornell University Press, 1972); and Rowland Berthoff, "Independence and Attachment, Virtue and Interest: From Republican Citizen to Free Enterpriser, 1787–1837," in Richard L. Bushman et al., eds., *Uprooted Americans: Essays to Honor Oscar Handlin* (Boston: Little, Brown, 1979), pp. 97–124. Since my aim is simply to show how certain civic themes—especially the formative ambition of the republican tradition—figured in the economic debates of the early republic, I leave aside the question, much debated among intellectual historians, of the influence on American politics of the "court-country" debates of eighteenth-century England, or the relative influence of Locke versus Machiavelli, James Harrington, and Viscount Bolingbroke. See J. G. A. Pocock, *The Machiavellian Moment: Florentine Political Thought and the Atlantic Republican Tradition* (Princeton: Princeton University Press, 1975); idem, "Virtue and Commerce in the Eighteenth Century," *Journal of Interdisciplinary History,* 3 (1972), 119–134; Isaac Kramnick, *Republicanism and Bourgeois Radicalism: Political Ideology in Late Eighteenth-Century England and America* (Ithaca: Cornell University Press, 1990); John Patrick Diggins, *The Lost Soul of American Politics: Virtue, Self-Interest, and the Foundation of Liberalism* (New York: Basic Books, 1984); Thomas L. Pangle, *The Spirit of Modern Republicanism: The Moral Vision of the American Founders and the Philosophy of Locke* (Chicago: University of Chicago Press, 1988); Lance Banning, "Jeffersonian Ideology Revisited: Liberal and Classical Ideas in the New American Republic," *William and Mary Quarterly,* 43 (January 1986), 3–19; Joyce Appleby, "Republicanism in Old and New Contexts," ibid., pp. 20–34.

34. Alexander Hamilton, *Report Relative to a Provision for the Support of Public Credit* (1790), in *The Reports of Alexander Hamilton,* ed. Jacob E. Cooke (New York: Harper and Row, 1964), pp. 1–45.
35. Ibid., p. 14. See Banning, *The Jeffersonian Persuasion,* pp. 134–140.
36. Hamilton, "Notes on the Advantages of a National Bank," quoted in Banning, *The Jeffersonian Persuasion,* pp. 136–137.
37. "The Tablet," *Gazette of the United States,* April 24, 1790, quoted in ibid., p. 137.
38. See Banning, *The Jeffersonian Persuasion,* pp. 126–160.
39. The story is told by Jefferson in *The Anas* (1791–1806), in *Jefferson Writings,* pp. 670–671.
40. See Banning, *The Jeffersonian Persuasion,* p. 204.
41. Jefferson to Washington, May 23, 1792, in *Jefferson Writings,* pp. 986–987.
42. Anonymous pamphlet, *A Review of the Revenue System* (1794), quoted in Banning, *The Jeffersonian Persuasion,* p. 227.
43. "For the General Advertiser" (1794), quoted in ibid., p. 230.

44. John Taylor, *An Inquiry into the Principles and Policy of the Government of the United States* (1814), ed. Loren Baritz (Indianapolis: Bobbs-Merrill, 1969), pp. 48–49.

45. Banning, *The Jeffersonian Persuasion,* p. 181.

46. McCoy, *The Elusive Republic,* p. 126.

47. Ibid., pp. 120–132.

48. Ibid., pp. 120–184.

49. Hamilton (December 1774), quoted in Stourzh, *Hamilton and Idea of Republican Government,* p. 195.

50. Hamilton in the Federal Convention (June 22, 1787), in Max Farrand, ed., *The Records of the Federal Convention of 1787* (New Haven: Yale University Press, 1966), vol. 1, p. 381. See also Stourzh, *Hamilton and Idea of Republican Government,* p. 79.

51. Hamilton, *Federalist* no. 72 (1788), p. 488. See also Stourzh, *Hamilton and Idea of Republican Government,* p. 102.

52. Banning, *The Jeffersonian Persuasion,* p. 140.

53. McCoy, *The Elusive Republic,* pp. 137–147.

54. Ibid., pp. 182–183.

55. Ibid., pp. 185–187.

56. Ibid., pp. 199–203.

57. Jefferson quoted in ibid., p. 203.

58. John Taylor, *A Defense of the Measures of the Administration of Thomas Jefferson* (1804), quoted in Watts, *The Republic Reborn,* pp. 26–27.

59. See McCoy, *The Elusive Republic,* p. 204; and Stourzh, *Hamilton and Idea of Republican Government,* pp. 191–192.

60. See McCoy, *The Elusive Republic,* p. 199.

61. Hamilton (1803), quoted in ibid., p. 200, and in Stourzh, *Hamilton and Idea of Republican Government,* p. 193. See also Appleby, *Capitalism and a New Social Order,* p. 94.

62. See McCoy, *The Elusive Republic,* pp. 216–221.

63. Ibid., p. 210.

64. See Watts, *The Republic Reborn,* pp. 83–84, 90–91, 101–103, 151–160, 240–249, 260, 269, 284.

65. See Linda K. Kerber, *Federalists in Dissent: Imagery and Ideology in Jeffersonian America* (Ithaca: Cornell University Press, 1980), pp. 173–215.

66. William Crafts, "Oration Delivered in St. Michael's Church" (1812), quoted in ibid., p. 94; Fisher Ames, "On the Dangers of American Liberty" (1805), quoted in ibid., p. 201; Edward Rutledge to J. Rutledge, January 23, 1798, quoted in ibid., p. 200.

67. Arthur St. Clair, "Address to the Territorial Legislature," November 5, 1800, quoted in ibid., p. 209; Timothy Pickering to George Cabot, January 29, 1804, quoted in ibid., p. 211; Archibald Henderson, "Speech in the North Carolina House of Commons," December 11, 1807, quoted in ibid., p. 213.

68. *Pennsylvania Journal* (Philadelphia), December 10, 1767, quoted in Edmund S. Morgan, "The Puritan Ethic and the American Revolution," *William and Mary*

Quarterly, 24 (October 1967), 10. See the entire article by Morgan, pp. 3–43; John F. Kasson, *Civilizing the Machine: Technology and Republican Values in America, 1776–1900* (Harmondsworth: Penguin Books, 1976), p. 9; and McCoy, *The Elusive Republic,* pp. 64–66.

69. McCoy, *The Elusive Republic,* pp. 65, 107–109.

70. Benjamin Rush, "Speech to the United Company of Philadelphia for Promoting American Manufactures" (1775), reprinted in Michael Brewster Folsom and Steven D. Lubar, eds., *The Philosophy of Manufactures: Early Debates over Industrialization in the United States* (Cambridge, Mass.: MIT Press, 1982), pp. 6–7. See also Kasson, *Civilizing the Machine,* pp. 9–10.

71. See McCoy, *The Elusive Republic,* pp. 104–119; and Kasson, *Civilizing the Machine,* pp. 14–21.

72. Jefferson, *Notes on the State of Virginia* (1787), in *Jefferson Writings,* pp. 290–291.

73. Jefferson to John Jay, August 23, 1785, ibid., p. 818.

74. See Kasson, *Civilizing the Machine,* pp. 24–25; and Thomas Bender, *Toward an Urban Vision: Ideas and Institutions in Nineteenth-Century America* (Baltimore: Johns Hopkins University Press, 1975), pp. 22–23.

75. Noah Webster, *Sketches of American Policy* (1785), quoted in McCoy, *The Elusive Republic,* pp. 111–112.

76. "An Oration delivered at Petersburgh . . .," *American Museum,* 2 (November 1787), quoted in Kasson, *Civilizing the Machine,* p. 18. See ibid., pp. 17–19.

77. Tench Coxe, "Address to an Assembly Convened to Establish a Society for the Encouragement of Manufactures and the Useful Arts" (Philadelphia, 1787), in Folsom and Lubar, *The Philosophy of Manufactures,* pp. 45, 55. See also Kasson, *Civilizing the Machine,* pp. 28–32.

78. Coxe, "Address," pp. 55–57, 61–62.

79. Hamilton, *Report on Manufactures* (December 5, 1791), in Cooke, *Reports of Alexander Hamilton,* p. 118.

80. James Madison, "Republican Distribution of Citizens," *National Gazette,* March 5, 1792, in Meyers, *The Mind of the Founder,* p. 185.

81. George Logan, *A Letter to the Citizens of Pennsylvania . . .,* 2d ed. (Philadelphia, 1800), quoted in McCoy, *The Elusive Republic,* p. 223.

82. Tench Coxe (August 6, 1810), quoted in Watts, *The Republic Reborn,* p. 255.

83. Tench Coxe, *An Essay on the Manufacturing Interest of the United States . . .* (Philadelphia, 1804), quoted in Watts, *The Republic Reborn,* p. 253.

84. Jefferson to Mr. Lithson, January 4, 1805, in Folsom and Lubar, *The Philosophy of Manufactures,* p. 26.

85. Henry Clay, "Speech on Domestic Manufactures," March 26, 1810, in Folsom and Lubar, *The Philosophy of Manufactures,* pp. 168–170. See also McCoy, *The Elusive Republic,* pp. 231–232; and Watts, *The Republic Reborn,* pp. 88–90.

86. *Address of the American Society for the Encouragement of Manufactures, to the People of the United States* (1817), in Folsom and Lubar, *The Philosophy of Manufactures,* p. 207.

87. Jefferson to Benjamin Austin, January 9, 1816, in *Jefferson Writings,* p. 1371.

88. *Connecticut Courant* (Hartford), April 6, 1808, quoted in McCoy, *The Elusive Republic*, p. 220.

89. *Monthly Anthology, and Boston Review* (1809), quoted in ibid.

90. Philip Barton Key, *Annals of Congress*, 11th Cong., 2d sess., House, p. 1906 (April 18, 1810), quoted in Kerber, *Federalists in Dissent*, p. 186.

91. Daniel Webster (1814), in Folsom and Lubar, *The Philosophy of Manufactures*, pp. 196–197.

92. Henry Clay to William Schouler, November 10, 1843, quoted in Bender, *Toward an Urban Vision*, p. 41.

93. Nathan Appleton, *Introduction of the Power Loom, and Origin of Lowell* (Lowell, 1858), p. 15, quoted in Kasson, *Civilizing the Machine*, p. 69. See generally Kasson, pp. 66–79.

94. Kasson, *Civilizing the Machine*, p. 78.

95. Ibid., p. 70.

96. Henry Miles, quoted in Paul Boyer, *Urban Masses and Moral Order in America, 1820–1920* (Cambridge, Mass.: Harvard University Press, 1978), p. 79.

97. Edward Everett, "Fourth of July at Lowell" (1830), reprinted in Folsom and Lubar, *The Philosophy of Manufactures*, pp. 283–284, 292.

98. Amos Lawrence, quoted in Bender, *Toward an Urban Vision*, p. 49.

99. See Kasson, *Civilizing the Machine*, pp. 81–86; and Bender, *Toward an Urban Vision*, pp. 41, 47–49.

100. Quoted in Kasson, *Civilizing the Machine*, p. 93.

101. *Voice of Industry*, September 4, 1845, quoted in ibid., p. 97.

102. Kasson, *Civilizing the Machine*, pp. 99–100.

103. Ibid., pp. 102–104.

104. Bender, *Toward an Urban Vision*, pp. 103–104.

105. For the views of Democrats and Whigs on wealth, distribution, and economic inequality see Lawrence Frederick Kohl, *The Politics of Individualism: Parties and the American Character in the Jacksonian Era* (New York: Oxford University Press, 1989), pp. 186–227.

106. Orestes Augustus Brownson, "The Laboring Classes" (1840), reprinted in Joseph L. Blau, ed., *Social Theories of Jacksonian Democracy* (Indianapolis: Bobbs-Merrill, 1954), p. 306.

107. New York *Evening Post*, October 21, 1834, quoted in Kohl, *The Politics of Individualism*, pp. 202–203.

108. Richard Hildreth, *Theory of Politics* (New York, 1853), in Blau, *Social Theories of Jacksonian Democracy*, p. 367.

109. Edward Everett, "Accumulation, Property, Capital, Credit" (1838), in Everett, *Orations and Speeches*, vol. 2 (Boston: Little, Brown, 1850), pp. 301–302.

110. "Introduction," *United States Magazine and Democratic Review*, October 1837, reprinted in Blau, *Social Theories of Jacksonian Democracy*, pp. 26–28.

111. See Marvin Meyers, *The Jacksonian Persuasion* (Stanford: Stanford University Press, 1957), pp. 186–188.

112. Andrew Jackson, "Veto Message," July 10, 1832, in James D. Richardson, ed.,

Messages and Papers of the Presidents, vol. 2 (Washington, D.C.: U.S. Government Printing Office, 1896), p. 590.

113. Ibid.

114. In urging the rapid settlement of public lands, however, Jackson did invoke the traditional Jeffersonian agrarian ideal: "The wealth and strength of a country are its population, and the best part of that population are the cultivators of the soil. Independent farmers are everywhere the basis of society and the true friends of liberty"; "Fourth Annual Message," December 4, 1832, ibid., p. 600.

115. For accounts of Jackson's war against the Bank of the United States in the context of republican themes, see Harry L. Watson, *Liberty and Power: The Politics of Jacksonian America* (New York: Hill and Wang, 1990), pp. 133–148; and Meyers, *The Jacksonian Persuasion,* pp. 10–17, 101–120.

116. Jackson, "Farewell Address," March 4, 1837, in James D. Richardson, ed., *Messages and Papers of the Presidents,* vol. 3 (Washington, D.C.: U.S. Government Printing Office, 1899), pp. 303–304.

117. Ibid., p. 302.

118. Orestes Brownson (1838), quoted in Kohl, *The Politics of Individualism,* p. 109.

119. Jackson, "Removal of the Public Deposits," September 18, 1833, in Richardson, *Messages and Papers of the Presidents,* vol. 3, p. 19.

120. Jackson, "Seventh Annual Message," December 7, 1835, ibid., p. 166.

121. Jackson, "Farewell Address," March 4, 1837, ibid., p. 305.

122. Meyers, *The Jacksonian Persuasion,* pp. 31–32. See also Watson, *Liberty and Power,* pp. 237–241; and Kohl, *The Politics of Individualism,* pp. 60–62.

123. Meyers, *The Jacksonian Persuasion,* p. 233.

124. Watson, *Liberty and Power,* p. 243.

125. Ibid., p. 149.

126. Henry Clay, "On the Removal of the Public Deposits," December 26, 1833, in Daniel Mallory, ed., *The Life and Speeches of Henry Clay,* vol. 2 (New York: Van Amringe and Bixby, 1844), p. 145. See also Watson, *Liberty and Power,* p. 156; and Daniel Walker Howe, *The Political Culture of the American Whigs* (Chicago: University of Chicago Press, 1979), p. 87.

127. Clay, "On the State of the Country from the Effects of the Removal of the Deposits," March 14, 1834, in Mallory, *Life and Speeches,* vol. 2, p. 199.

128. Watson, *Liberty and Power,* pp. 158–159; and Howe, *Political Culture of American Whigs,* pp. 87–91.

129. The relation of the American Whigs to the "country-party" tradition of English politics is elaborated in Howe, *Political Culture of American Whigs,* pp. 77–80. For a challenge to this view, see John Diggins, *The Lost Soul of American Politics: Virtue, Self-Interest, and the Foundations of Liberalism* (New York: Basic Books, 1984), pp. 105–118.

130. See Watson, *Liberty and Power,* pp. 59–60, 76–77, 113–114; and Howe, *Political Culture of American Whigs,* pp. 137–138.

131. Rufus Choate, quoted in Howe, *Political Culture of American Whigs,* p. 101.

132. Abbot Lawrence to Henry Clay, quoted in Kohl, *The Politics of Individualism,* p. 139.

133. Quoted in Howe, *Political Culture of American Whigs*, p. 101.

134. Quoted in Kohl, *The Politics of Individualism*, p. 139.

135. Clay, "On the Public Lands," June 20, 1832, in Mallory, *Life and Speeches*, vol. 2, pp. 84–85. See also Howe, *Political Culture of American Whigs*, p. 138.

136. Webster to Citizens of Worcester County, Massachusetts, January 23, 1844, in *Writings and Speeches of Daniel Webster*, 18 vols. (Boston: Little, Brown, 1903), vol. 16, p. 423. See also Kohl, *The Politics of Individualism*, pp. 142–143.

137. Webster, "Objects of the Mexican War," March 23, 1848, in *Writings and Speeches*, vol. 10, p. 32. See also Kohl, *The Politics of Individualism*, p. 136.

138. Howe, *Political Culture of American Whigs*, p. 101.

139. Howe, *Political Culture of American Whigs*, pp. 20–21, 32–37, 153–159, 210, 218–220; Kohl, *The Politics of Individualism*, pp. 72–78, 99, 105, 152–154; Paul Boyer, *Urban Masses and Moral Order in America, 1820–1920* (Cambridge, Mass.: Harvard University Press, 1978), pp. 1–64.

140. Daniel Webster to Professor Pease, June 15, 1852, in *Writings and Speeches*, vol. 16, p. 655. See also Kohl, *The Politics of Individualism*, p. 154.

141. Daniel D. Barnard, *The Social System* (1848), in Daniel Walker Howe, ed., *The American Whigs: An Anthology* (New York: John Wiley & Sons, 1973), pp. 106–107.

142. Horace Mann, "Oration Delivered before the Authorities of the City of Boston," July 4, 1842, in Mary Mann, ed., *Life and Works of Horace Mann*, vol. 4 (Boston: Lee and Shepard, 1891), pp. 366, 355–356.

143. Mann, *Ninth Annual Report of the Secretary of the Board of Education of Massachusetts* (1845), ibid., p. 4.

144. Mann, "Fourth of July Oration," ibid., pp. 365–366; idem, *Twelfth Annual Report* (1848), ibid., p. 289.

145. Madison, *Federalist* no. 10, p. 62.

146. Jackson, "Farewell Address," March 4, 1837, in Richardson, *Messages and Papers of the Presidents*, vol. 3, pp. 298, 305–306.

147. Mann, *Twelfth Annual Report*, in *Life and Works*, vol. 4, p. 271; idem, "Fourth of July Oration," ibid., p. 366.

148. Mann, "Fourth of July Oration," ibid., pp. 359–360.

6. Free Labor versus Wage Labor

1. See Sean Wilentz, "The Rise of the American Working Class, 1776–1877," in J. Carroll Moody and Alice Kessler-Harris, eds., *Perspectives on American Labor History* (De Kalb: Northern Illinois University Press, 1989), pp. 83–109; Wilentz, *Chants Democratic: New York City and the Rise of the American Working Class, 1788–1850* (Princeton: Princeton University Press, 1984), pp. 61–103; Daniel T. Rodgers, *The Work Ethic in Industrial America, 1850–1920* (Chicago: University of Chicago Press, 1974), pp. 30–64.

2. Wilentz, *Chants Democratic*, pp. 90–95. See also idem, "Rise of American Working Class," pp. 87–88.

3. Idem, "Rise of American Working Class," p. 87. See also idem, "Artisan Republican Festivals and the Rise of Class Conflict in New York City, 1788–1837," in Michael H. Frisch and Daniel J. Walkowitz, eds., *Working-Class America* (Urbana: University of Illinois Press, 1983), pp. 39–45; Wilentz, *Chants Democratic*, pp. 105–216; Bruce Laurie, *Artisans into Workers: Labor in Nineteenth-Century America* (New York: Hill and Wang, 1989), pp. 15–46, 63–64.

4. GTU president John Commerford, quoted in Wilentz, "Artisan Republican Festivals," p. 59, and in idem, *Chants Democratic*, p. 245; on the general point, see ibid., pp. 217–296.

5. Quoted in Laurie, *Artisans into Workers,* p. 64.

6. Wilentz, "Artisan Republican Festivals," pp. 60, 61–65; idem, *Chants Democratic*, pp. 145–171.

7. Two excellent accounts of the debates over wage labor to which I am much indebted are Eric Foner, *Politics and Ideology in the Age of the Civil War* (New York: Oxford University Press, 1980), pp. 57–76; and Rodgers, *Work Ethic in Industrial America*, pp. 30–64.

8. Orestes Brownson, "The Laboring Classes" (1840), reprinted in Joseph L. Blau, ed., *Social Theories of Jacksonian Democracy* (Indianapolis: Bobbs-Merrill, 1954), pp. 309, 306–307, 310; see also Foner, *Politics and Ideology,* p. 60.

9. William Lloyd Garrison, quoted in Foner, *Politics and Ideology,* pp. 62–63.

10. William Jay, *An Inquiry into the Character and Tendency of the American Colonization and American Anti-Slavery Societies* (1835), reprinted in Walter Hugins, ed., *The Reform Impulse, 1825–1850* (Columbia: University of South Carolina Press, 1972), pp. 168–169. See also Foner, *Politics and Ideology,* p. 64.

11. See Foner, *Politics and Ideology,* pp. 64–65.

12. Albert Brisbane, *The Liberator,* September 5, 1846, quoted in ibid., p. 63.

13. George Henry Evans, *The Liberator,* September 4, 1846, quoted in Aileen S. Kraditor, *Means and Ends in American Abolitionism* (New York: Pantheon Books, 1967), p. 248; see also Foner, *Politics and Ideology,* p. 70. For an account of Evans and the National Reformers in relation to republican ideals, see William B. Scott, *In Pursuit of Happiness: American Conceptions of Property from the Seventeenth to the Twentieth Century* (Bloomington: Indiana University Press, 1977), pp. 53–70.

14. William West, *The Liberator,* September 25, 1846, quoted in Foner, *Politics and Ideology,* p. 70; see also Kraditor, *Means and Ends in American Abolitionism,* pp. 248–249.

15. Garrison, *The Liberator,* March 26, 1847, quoted in Foner, *Politics and Ideology,* pp. 70–71; and in Kraditor, *Means and Ends in American Abolitionism,* pp. 249–250.

16. Wendell Phillips, *The Liberator,* July 9, 1847, quoted in Kraditor, *Means and Ends in American Abolitionism,* p. 250; see also Foner, *Politics and Ideology,* pp. 70–72.

17. John C. Calhoun, "Speech on the Reception of Abolition Petitions," U.S. Senate, February 6, 1837, reprinted in Eric L. McKitrick, ed., *Slavery Defended: The Views of the Old South* (Englewood Cliffs, N.J.: Prentice-Hall, 1963), pp. 12–13, 18–19. See also George Fitzhugh, "Sociology for the South," in ibid., p. 48; and Larry E.

Tise, *Proslavery: A History of the Defense of Slavery in America, 1701–1840* (Athens: University of Georgia Press, 1987), pp. 308–362.

18. George Fitzhugh, *Cannibals All! or, Slaves without Masters* (1857), ed. C. Vann Woodward (Cambridge, Mass.: Harvard University Press, 1960), pp. 52, 17.

19. Ibid., pp. 18, 32.

20. Ibid., pp. 72, 222–224.

21. James Henry Hammond, "Speech on the Admission of Kansas," U.S. Senate, March 4, 1858, reprinted in McKitrick, *Slavery Defended*, p. 123.

22. Rodgers, *Work Ethic in Industrial America*, p. 33.

23. Ibid., pp. 34–35.

24. Foner, *Politics and Ideology*, p. 72.

25. Ibid. See generally idem, *Free Soil, Free Labor, Free Men: The Ideology of the Republican Party before the Civil War* (London: Oxford University Press, 1970).

26. *New York Times*, May 19, 1854, quoted in Foner, *Free Soil, Free Labor*, p. 95. On the slave power argument generally, see ibid., pp. 73–102, 309; and idem, *Politics and Ideology*, pp. 41–50.

27. Foner, *Free Soil, Free Labor*, pp. 90–91.

28. Ibid., pp. 9–39.

29. Ibid.; Carl Schurz quoted on p. 11, Zachariah Chandler on p. 17.

30. Ibid., pp. 40–65.

31. Ibid.; William Seward quoted on pp. 69–70, Theodore Sedgwick on p. 310.

32. Ibid., p. 266; on the role of racism in antislavery politics, see generally ibid., pp. 58–65, 261–300.

33. Ibid.; George Rathburn quoted on p. 61, David Wilmot on pp. 60, 267. On the racial views of the Barnburners and Free Soilers, see Foner, *Politics and Ideology*, pp. 77–93.

34. Frederick Douglass, quoted in Foner, *Politics and Ideology*, p. 49.

35. Fitzhugh, *Cannibals All!* p. 201.

36. Abraham Lincoln, "First Debate with Stephen A. Douglas," Ottawa, Illinois, August 21, 1858, in *The Collected Works of Abraham Lincoln*, ed. Roy P. Basler, 8 vols. (New Brunswick, N.J.: Rutgers University Press, 1953), vol. 3, p. 16; see also ibid., p. 402. On Republican views of the rights of blacks, see Foner, *Free Soil, Free Labor*, pp. 214–216, 290–295.

37. Lincoln, "Speech at Kalamazoo, Michigan," August 27, 1856, in *Collected Works*, vol. 2, p. 364.

38. Idem, "Annual Message to Congress," December 3, 1861, ibid., vol. 5, pp. 51–52; see also "Speech at Indianapolis, Indiana," September 19, 1859, ibid., vol. 3, pp. 468–469; "Address before Wisconsin State Agricultural Society," September 30, 1859, ibid., pp. 477–478; "Speech at Dayton, Ohio," September 17, 1859, ibid., p. 459.

39. Idem, "Annual Message to Congress," ibid., vol. 5, pp. 52–53; see also "Address before Wisconsin Agricultural Society," vol. 3, pp. 478–479; "Speech at New Haven, Connecticut," March 6, 1860, vol. 4, pp. 24–25.

40. Foner, *Politics and Ideology*, pp. 73–74.

41. Ibid., pp. 32–33.
42. Rodgers, *Work Ethic in Industrial America*, p. 33.
43. *New York Times*, February 22, 1869, quoted in David Montgomery, *Beyond Equality: Labor and the Radical Republicans, 1862–1872* (Urbana: University of Illinois Press, 1981), pp. 25–26. For discussion of the transition to an economy of wage-earners, see ibid., pp. 3–44.
44. Ibid., pp. 28–30, 448–452.
45. Terence V. Powderly, "Address to the General Assembly of the Knights of Labor" (1880), reprinted in Powderly, *The Path I Trod* (New York: Columbia University Press, 1940), p. 268; George E. McNeill, ed., *The Labor Movement: The Problem of Today* (Boston: A. M. Bridgman, 1887), p. 454.
46. McNeill, *The Labor Movement*, pp. 485, 483, 495; see also ibid., p. 462.
47. William H. Sylvis, "Address Delivered at Chicago, January 9, 1865," in James C. Sylvis, ed., *The Life, Speeches, Labors and Essays of William H. Sylvis* (Philadelphia: Claxton, Remsen & Haffelfinger, 1872), p. 129.
48. Ibid., pp. 130, 148, 150; see also Montgomery, *Beyond Equality*, pp. 228–229.
49. Sylvis, "Address Delivered at Chicago," p. 168; Powderly, "Address to the Knights of Labor," p. 269; McNeill, *The Labor Movement*, pp. 496, 466.
50. Terence V. Powderly, *Thirty Years of Labor, 1859–1889* (Columbus, Ohio: Excelsior, 1889), p. 453; Sylvis, "Address Delivered at Chicago," p. 169; Robert Howard, quoted in Leon Fink, *Workingmen's Democracy: The Knights of Labor and American Politics* (Urbana: University of Illinois Press, 1983), p. 10. On the cultural activities of the Knights, see ibid., pp. 3–15; and David Montgomery, "Labor and the Republic in Industrial America: 1860–1920," *Le mouvement social*, no. 111 (1980), 204–205.
51. E. L. Godkin, "The Labor Crisis," *North American Review*, 105 (July 1867), 186. On Godkin and the relation of middle-class reformers to the labor movement generally, see Montgomery, *Beyond Equality*, pp. 237–249; Rodgers, *Work Ethic in Industrial America*, pp. 32–33, 42–45; and William E. Forbath, "The Ambiguities of Free Labor: Labor and the Law in the Gilded Age," *Wisconsin Law Review*, 1985, pp. 787–791.
52. Godkin, "The Labor Crisis," pp. 206–209.
53. Ibid., pp. 212, 197; idem, "The Eight-Hour Muddle," *The Nation*, 4 (May 9, 1867), 374; idem, "The Labor Crisis," p. 213.
54. E. L. Godkin, "The Labor Crisis," *The Nation*, 4 (April 25, 1867), 335; idem, "The Eight-Hour Movement," *The Nation*, 1 (October 26, 1865), 517; idem, "The Working-Men and Politicians," *The Nation*, 5 (July 4, 1867), 11–12.
55. Godkin, "The Labor Crisis," *North American Review*, pp. 181–182, 184, 186.
56. Ibid., pp. 189–190.
57. Ibid., pp. 179, 190–191; idem, "The Labor Crisis," *The Nation*, p. 335.
58. McNeill, *The Labor Movement*, pp. 478–480; see also Montgomery, *Beyond Equality*, p. 252.
59. Letter from a working man to the Bureau of Labor Statistics, quoted in ibid., pp. 237–238.

60. Ira Steward, "Poverty," *American Federationist,* 9 (April 1902), 159–160; idem, *A Reduction of Hours an Increase of Wages* (Boston: Boston Labor Reform Association, 1865), reprinted in Commons, *Documentary History of American Industrial Society,* vol. 9, pp. 291, 295; see generally ibid., pp. 284–301. On Steward and the eight-hour movement, see Montgomery, *Beyond Equality,* pp. 239–260; and Forbath, "Ambiguities of Free Labor," pp. 810–812.

61. McNeill, *The Labor Movement,* pp. 472–474, 482.

62. See Montgomery, *Beyond Equality,* pp. 296–334.

63. William E. Forbath, *Law and the Shaping of the American Labor Movement* (Cambridge, Mass.: Harvard University Press, 1991), pp. 38, 177–192.

64. *Slaughter-House Cases,* 83 U.S. (16 Wallace) 36 (1873).

65. Ibid. at 110. For his account of the republican background to Field's dissent in *Slaughter-House,* I am indebted to Forbath, "Ambiguities of Free Labor," pp. 772–782.

66. *Slaughter-House,* 83 U.S. at 90–92, 109–110.

67. Ibid. at 110. See Forbath, "Ambiguities of Free Labor," pp. 779–782.

68. *Godcharles v. Wigeman,* 113 Pa. St. 431, 6 A. 354, 356 (1886). See also *Ritchie v. People,* 115 Ill. 98, 40 N.W. 454 (1895). A New York case, *In re Jacobs,* 98 N.Y. 98 (1885), struck down a law prohibiting the manufacture of cigars in tenements. Although the laborers involved were sweated outworkers rather than self-employed artisans, the court argued that the law deprived them of the right to pursue their trade. See Forbath, "Ambiguities of Free Labor," pp. 795–800; and idem, *Law and Shaping of American Labor Movement,* pp. 39–49.

69. *Lochner v. New York,* 198 U.S. 45, 61 (1905). In an earlier case, *Allgeyer v. Louisiana* (1896), the Court had ruled that the Fourteenth Amendment protects individual liberty against state infringement, although that case did not involve wage labor.

70. *Coppage v. Kansas,* 236 U.S. 1, 8–9, 12, 14, 17 (1914). See also *Adair v. United States,* 208 U.S. 161, 174–175 (1908).

71. *Lochner,* 198 U.S. at 69.

72. *Coppage,* 236 U.S. at 26–27, 38–41. See also *Holden v. Hardy,* 169 U.S. 366, 397 (1898).

73. Roscoe Pound, "Liberty of Contract," *Yale Law Journal,* 18 (May 1909), 471–472, quoting Lord Northington from *Vernon v. Bethell,* 2 Eden, 110, 113.

74. Richard T. Ely, *Property and Contract in their Relations to the Distribution of Wealth,* vol. 2 (New York: Macmillan, 1914), pp. 603, 731–732; see also ibid., pp. 568–569, 588–589, 604–605, 638, 697–698, and 722. On the similar views of other "new-school economists" of the late nineteenth century, see Sidney Fine, *Laissez Faire and the General-Welfare State* (Ann Arbor: University of Michigan Press, 1956), pp. 198–251.

75. Gerald N. Grob, *Workers and Utopia* (Chicago: Northwestern University Press, 1961), pp. 52–59, 109; Fink, *Workingmen's Democracy,* pp. 9, 25, 36n; Laurie, *Artisans into Workers,* pp. 157–163; Victoria Hattam, "Economic Visions and Political Strategies: American Labor and the State, 1865–1896," *Studies in American Political Development,* 4 (1990), 90–93.

76. McNeill, *The Labor Movement,* p. 456.

77. Grob, *Workers and Utopia*, pp. 46–47; Rodgers, *Work Ethic in Industrial America*, p. 44; Laurie, *Artisans into Workers*, p. 155.

78. Laurie, *Artisans into Workers*, p. 174; Hattam, "Economic Visions and Political Strategies," pp. 123–128; Grob, *Workers and Utopia*, pp. 119–137.

79. John Mitchell, quoted in Rodgers, *Work Ethic in Industrial America*, p. 39.

80. Grob, *Workers and Utopia*, p. 37.

81. Samuel Gompers, "Testimony before Industrial Commission," Washington, D.C., April 18, 1899, reprinted in Gompers, *Labor and the Employer* (New York: E. P. Dutton, 1920), p. 291.

82. Samuel Gompers, "Labor and Its Attitude toward Trusts," *American Federationist*, 14 (1907), 881; Hattam, "Economic Visions and Political Strategies," pp. 100–106. For references to "wage-earners" and the "wage-earning classes," see Samuel Gompers, *Seventy Years of Life and Labor*, vol. 1 (New York: E. P. Dutton, 1925), pp. 284, 334.

83. Gompers, *Seventy Years of Life and Labor*, pp. 244, 286.

84. James R. Sovereign (1894), quoted in John R. Commons, *History of Labour in the United States*, vol. 2 (1918; reprint, New York: Augustus M. Kelly, 1966), pp. 494–495.

85. Gompers, *Seventy Years of Life and Labor*, p. 335; Adolph Strasser, quoted in Fink, *Workingmen's Democracy*, p. 8.

86. Samuel Gompers, "Justice Brewer on Strikes and Lawlessness," *American Federationist*, 8 (1901), 122; see generally Forbath, *Law and Shaping of American Labor Movement*, pp. 128–135.

7. Community, Self-Government, and Progressive Reform

1. Robert H. Wiebe, *The Search for Order, 1877–1920* (New York: Hill and Wang, 1967), pp. 42–43.

2. Woodrow Wilson, *The New Freedom* (1913; reprint, Englewood Cliffs, N.J.: Prentice-Hall, 1961), pp. 20–21, 164.

3. John Dewey, *The Public and Its Problems* (1926), reprinted in *The Later Works of John Dewey, 1925–1953*, ed. Jo Ann Boydston, vol. 2 (Carbondale: Southern Illinois University Press, 1984), pp. 295–297.

4. Ibid., pp. 298–301.

5. Wiebe, *The Search for Order*, p. 44.

6. Ibid., p. 12; Walter Lippmann, *Drift and Mastery* (1914; reprint, Englewood Cliffs, N.J.: Prentice-Hall, 1961), pp. 92, 118.

7. William Allen White, *The Old Order Changeth* (New York: Macmillan, 1910), pp. 250, 252–253. On the response of Progressive intellectuals to the question of community, see Jean B. Quandt, *From the Small Town to the Great Community* (New Brunswick, N.J.: Rutgers University Press, 1970).

8. Jane Addams, *Democracy and Social Ethics* (New York: Macmillan, 1907), pp. 210–211.

9. Charles Horton Cooley, *Social Organization* (New York: Charles Scribner's Sons, 1929), pp. 385, 244.

10. Josiah Royce, *The Problem of Christianity,* vol. 2 (New York: Macmillan, 1913), pp. 85–86.

11. Ibid., pp. 84, 88.

12. Dewey, *The Public and Its Problems,* pp. 330, 296, 314.

13. Ibid., pp. 304, 324, and, generally, pp. 304–350.

14. See James Weinstein, *The Corporate Ideal in the Liberal State, 1900–1918* (Boston: Beacon Press, 1968), pp. 92–116.

15. See David Tyack and Elisabeth Hansot, *Managers of Virtue: Public School Leadership in America, 1820–1980* (New York: Basic Books, 1982), pp. 106–108.

16. R. Jeffrey Lustig, *Corporate Liberalism: The Origins of Modern American Political Theory, 1890–1920* (Berkeley: University of California Press, 1982), p. 153 and, generally, pp. 150–194. See also Wiebe, *The Search for Order,* pp. 133–176; and Daniel T. Rodgers, "In Search of Progressivism," *Reviews in American History,* 10 (December 1982), 113–132.

17. Paul Boyer, *Urban Masses and Moral Order in America, 1820–1920* (Cambridge, Mass.: Harvard University Press, 1978), p. 190 and, generally, pp. 189–292.

18. Ibid., pp. 168–171, 195–201, 233–236; and Robert B. Fairbanks, *Making Better Citizens: Housing Reform and the Community Development Strategy in Cincinnati, 1890–1960* (Urbana: University of Illinois Press, 1988), p. 25.

19. Boyer, *Urban Masses,* pp. 236–241. For Olmstead's views, see Frederick Law Olmsted, "Public Parks and the Enlargement of Towns" (1870), reprinted in Nathan Glazer and Mark Lilla, eds., *The Public Face of Architecture: Civic Culture and Public Spaces* (New York: Free Press, 1987), pp. 222–263; and in Thomas Bender, *Toward an Urban Vision: Ideas and Institutions in Nineteenth-Century America* (Baltimore: Johns Hopkins University Press, 1975), pp. 160–187.

20. Boyer, *Urban Masses,* pp. 243, 242, 244, and, generally, pp. 242–251.

21. Joseph Lee, *Charities and the Commons* (1907), quoted in Cooley, *Social Organization,* pp. 34–35.

22. Boyer, *Urban Masses,* p. 259 and, generally, pp. 256–260. A full history of the pageant movement can be found in David Glassberg, *American Historical Pageantry: The Uses of Tradition in the Early Twentieth Century* (Chapel Hill: University of North Carolina Press, 1990).

23. Boyer, *Urban Masses,* pp. 270, 275 (Daniel H. Burnham), and, generally, pp. 261–276.

24. See Michele H. Bogart, *Public Sculpture and the Civic Ideal in New York City, 1980–1930* (Chicago: University of Chicago Press, 1989), pp. 258–270.

25. See Osmond K. Fraenkel, ed., *The Curse of Bigness: Miscellaneous Papers of Louis D. Brandeis* (New York: Viking Press, 1935), pp. 100–181; Philippa Strum, *Louis D. Brandeis: Justice for the People* (Cambridge, Mass.: Harvard University Press, 1984), pp. x–xi, 142–153, 337–353, 390–396.

26. Louis D. Brandeis, "Big Business and Industrial Liberty" (1912), in Fraenkel, *The Curse of Bigness,* p. 38.

27. Idem, "The Road to Social Efficiency" (1911), quoted in Strum, *Louis D. Brandeis,* p. 170; idem, "Big Business and Industrial Liberty," p. 39.

28. For a fine account of Brandeis' views on industrial democracy, see Strum, *Louis D. Brandeis,* pp. 159–195.

29. Louis D. Brandeis, "How Far Have We Come on the Road to Industrial Democracy?—An Interview" (1913), in Fraenkel, *The Curse of Bigness,* p. 47; idem, "Testimony before the United States Commission on Industrial Relations" (1915), ibid., pp. 78–79, 83.

30. Idem, "Testimony," pp. 73, 81.

31. Ibid., p. 80.

32. On Brandeis' influence on Wilson's economic views, see Arthur S. Link, *Woodrow Wilson and the Progressive Era, 1910–1917* (New York: Harper & Row, 1954), pp. 20–21; John Milton Cooper Jr., *The Warrior and the Priest: Woodrow Wilson and Theodore Roosevelt* (Cambridge, Mass.: Harvard University Press, 1983), pp. 193–198; Strum, *Louis D. Brandeis,* pp. 196–223.

33. Wilson, speech at Sioux City, Iowa, September 17, 1912, quoted in Cooper, *The Warrior and the Priest,* p. 198. See also Woodrow Wilson, *The New Freedom,* ed. William E. Leuchtenburg (Englewood Cliffs, N.J.: Prentice-Hall, 1961), p. 102, 112–113, and the editor's introduction, pp. 10–11.

34. Idem, *The New Freedom,* pp. 121, 165–166.

35. Ibid., p. 121.

36. Ibid., p. 20.

37. Ibid., pp. 26–27.

38. Ibid., pp. 166–167.

39. Ibid., p. 167.

40. Theodore Roosevelt, "Speech at Denver," August 29, 1910, in William E. Leuchtenburg, ed., *The New Nationalism* (Englewood Cliffs, N.J.: Prentice-Hall, 1961), p. 53.

41. Idem, "Speech at St. Paul," September 6, 1910, in ibid., p. 85; "Speech at Osawatomie," August 31, 1910, ibid., p. 27; "Speech at Syracuse," September 17, 1910, ibid., p. 171.

42. Roosevelt to Alfred W. Cooley, August 29, 1911, quoted in George E. Mowry, *The Era of Theodore Roosevelt, 1900–1912* (New York: Harper & Row, 1958), p. 55.

43. Roosevelt, "Speech at Osawatomie," p. 29; "Speech at St. Paul," p. 79.

44. Idem, "Speech at Denver," pp. 53–54.

45. Idem, "Speech at Osawatomie," pp. 38, 36.

46. Ibid., p. 39; idem, "Speech at the Milwaukee Auditorium," September 7, 1910, in Leuchtenburg, *The New Nationalism,* p. 141. See also idem, "Speech at Sioux Falls," September 3, 1910, ibid., p. 93.

47. Idem, "At Unveiling of Statue to McClellan at Washington," May 2, 1907, in Roosevelt, *Presidential Addresses and State Papers,* vol. 6 (New York: Review of Reviews, 1910), pp. 1236–37; also idem, "Speech at Osawatomie," pp. 38–39.

48. Idem, "Speech at St. Paul," p. 84; "Speech at Osawatomie," p. 39; "Speech at Sioux

Falls," p. 95; "Speech at Pueblo," August 30, 1910, in Leuchtenburg, *The New Nationalism,* p. 145.

49. Idem, "At Unveiling of Statue to McClellan," p. 1232.

50. Ibid.; idem, "Speech at Syracuse," p. 173.

51. Croly, *The Promise of American Life* (1909; Indianapolis: Bobbs-Merrill, 1965), pp. 272–275. The relation between Croly and Roosevelt and the question of who influenced whom are discussed in Charles Forcey, *The Crossroads of Liberalism: Croly, Weyl, Lippmann, and the Progressive Era, 1900–1925* (New York: Oxford University Press, 1961), pp. 121–139; and Cooper, *The Warrior and the Priest,* p. 147.

52. Croly, *The Promise of American Life,* pp. 273, 212, 271.

53. Ibid., pp. 207–208, 273, 280.

54. Ibid., pp. 286, 407.

55. Ibid., pp. 399, 454; see also pp. 208, 400.

56. Wilson was the Democratic nominee, Roosevelt the candidate of the Progressive, or "Bull Moose," party. The Republican incumbent, William Howard Taft, relegated to the sidelines of the campaign, finished third.

57. Cooper, *The Warrior and the Priest,* p. 141.

58. Wiebe, *The Search for Order,* p. 158; David P. Thelen, *The New Citizenship: Origins of Progressivism in Wisconsin, 1885–1900* (Columbia: University of Missouri Press, 1972), p. 82.

59. Thelen, *The New Citizenship,* pp. 82, 288, 308. See generally Thelen's distinction between producer- and consumer-based movements of Progressive era reform, ibid., pp. 1–2.

60. Lippmann, *Drift and Mastery,* pp. 54–55.

61. Ibid., pp. 52–53, 54.

62. Daniel J. Boorstin, *The Americans: The Democratic Experience* (New York: Vintage Books, 1973), p. 89.

63. Ibid., pp. 89–90, 112, and, generally, pp. 89–164.

64. Walter E. Weyl, *The New Democracy* (New York: Macmillan, 1912).

65. See Forcey, *The Crossroads of Liberalism,* esp. pp. 3–5, 52–56.

66. Weyl, *The New Democracy,* p. 250.

67. Ibid., pp. 250–251.

68. Examples range from the nonconsumption and nonimportation movements of the colonial period to Theodore Roosevelt's exhortations against materialism. See Edmund S. Morgan, "The Puritan Ethic and the American Revolution," *William and Mary Quarterly,* 24 (October 1967), 33–43; Gordon S. Wood, *The Creation of the American Republic, 1776–1787* (New York: W. W. Norton, 1969), pp. 91–125; and Cooper, *The Warrior and the Priest,* pp. 112–117.

69. Weyl, *The New Democracy,* p. 150.

70. Ibid., pp. 191, 195, 145.

71. Ibid., pp. 145–146.

72. Ibid., pp. 152–153, 161, 164.

73. Louis D. Brandeis, "Letter to Robert W. Bruere," February 25, 1922, in Fraenkel,

The Curse of Bigness, pp. 270–271; Croly, *The Promise of American Life,* p. 400; Weyl, *The New Democracy,* p. 150.

74. Joseph Cornwall Palamountain Jr., *The Politics of Distribution* (Cambridge, Mass.: Harvard University Press, 1955), pp. 159–160; Maurice W. Lee, *Anti-Chain-Store Tax Legislation* (Chicago: University of Chicago Press, 1939), pp. 5–24; Thomas W. Ross, "Store Wars: The Chain Tax Movement," *Journal of Law & Economics,* 29 (April 1986), 125–127.

75. *State Board of Commissioners v. Jackson,* 283 U.S. 527 (1931).

76. Palamountain, *The Politics of Distribution,* pp. 160–162; Lee, *Anti-Chain-Store Tax Legislation,* pp. 25–26.

77. Montaville Flowers, *America Chained* (Pasadena: Montaville Flowers Publicists, 1931), pp. 65, 35, 131, 82.

78. Ibid., pp. 94–95, 172, 231.

79. Hugo L. Black, quoted in Boorstin, *The Americans: The Democratic Experience,* pp. 111–112.

80. *Liggett Company v. Lee,* 288 U.S. 517 (1933), Justice Brandeis dissenting, reprinted in Fraenkel, *The Curse of Bigness,* p. 171.

81. Ibid., pp. 178–179.

82. Christine Frederick, "Listen to This Sophisticated Shopper!" *Chain Store Age,* 1 (June 1925), 36, quoted in Rowland Berthoff, "Independence and Enterprise: Small Business in the American Dream," in Stuart W. Bruchey, ed., *Small Business in American Life* (New York: Columbia University Press, 1980), p. 28. E. C. Sams, "The Chain Store is a Public Necessity," in E. C. Buehler, ed., *A Debate Handbook on the Chain Store Question* (Lawrence: University of Kansas, 1932), p. 100; see also Berthoff, "Independence and Enterprise," p. 28. Lippmann, *Drift and Mastery,* p. 55.

83. E. C. Buehler, *Chain Store Debate Manual* (New York: National Chain Store Association, 1931), pp. 40–41; John Somerville, *Chain Store Debate Manual* (New York: National Chain Store Association, 1930), pp. 20–21; see also Boorstin, *The Americans: The Democratic Experience,* p. 112.

84. Albert H. Morrill, "The Development and Effect of Chain Stores," in Buehler, *Debate Handbook on Chain Store Question,* pp. 145–146.

85. Somerville, *Chain Store Debate Manual,* pp. 16–17.

86. Palamountain, *The Politics of Distribution,* pp. 168–187; Lee, *Anti-Chain-Store Tax Legislation,* pp. 24–26; Ross, "Store Wars," pp. 127, 137.

87. The leading example is Robert H. Bork, *The Antitrust Paradox* (New York: Basic Books, 1978), pp. 15–66.

88. Richard Hofstadter, "What Happened to the Antitrust Movement?" in Earl F. Cheit, ed., *The Business Establishment* (New York: John Wiley & Sons, 1964), p. 125. See also David Millon, "The Sherman Act and the Balance of Power," *Southern California Law Review,* 61 (1988), 1219–92; and Robert Pitofsky, "The Political Content of Antitrust," *University of Pennsylvania Law Review,* 127 (1979), 1051–75.

89. Hans B. Thorelli, *The Federal Antitrust Policy* (Stockholm: Akademisk Avhandling, 1954), p. 227.

90. John B. Sherman, quoted in *Congressional Record,* 51st Cong., 1st sess., 21 (March

21, 1890), 2457, reprinted in Earl W. Kintner, ed., *The Legislative History of the Federal Antitrust Laws and Related Statutes,* Part I, 9 vols. (New York: Chelsea House, 1978), vol. 1, p. 117.

91. Hofstadter, "What Happened to the Antitrust Movement?" p. 125.

92. Henry A. Stimson, "The Small Business as a School of Manhood," *Atlantic Monthly,* 93 (1904), 337–340. See also Berthoff, "Independence and Enterprise," pp. 35–36.

93. Hazen S. Pingree, quoted in *Chicago Conference on Trusts* (Chicago: Civic Federation of Chicago, 1900), pp. 263–267. See also Berthoff, "Independence and Enterprise," pp. 34–35.

94. Pingree quoted in *Chicago Conference on Trusts,* pp. 266–267.

95. George Gunton, quoted in ibid., pp. 276–285. See also Berthoff, "Independence and Enterprise," p. 35.

96. Gunton quoted in *Chicago Conference on Trusts,* pp. 281–282.

97. See Ellis W. Hawley, "Antitrust," in Glenn Porter, ed., *Encyclopedia of American Economic History,* vol. 2 (New York: Charles Scribner's Sons, 1980), pp. 773–774; Phillip Areeda and Louis Kaplow, *Antitrust Analysis: Problems, Text, Cases,* 4th ed. (Boston: Little, Brown, 1988), pp. 58–59.

98. *United States v. Trans-Missouri Freight Association,* 166 U.S. 290, 323 (1897).

99. Bork, *The Antitrust Paradox,* pp. 21–26.

100. *Trans-Missouri Freight Association,* 166 U.S. at 323–324.

101. Thomas K. McCraw, "Rethinking the Trust Question," in McCraw, ed., *Regulation in Perspective: Historical Essays* (Cambridge, Mass.: Harvard University Press, 1981), p. 54.

102. See Strum, *Louis D. Brandeis,* pp. x–xi, 142–153, 390–396. Unsympathetic though he is to Brandeis' arguments against bigness, McCraw does distinguish between Brandeis' political and economic arguments, though without reference to the republican tradition. See McCraw, "Rethinking the Trust Question," pp. 1–55; and idem, *Prophets of Regulation* (Cambridge, Mass.: Harvard University Press, 1984), pp. 80–142.

103. Louis D. Brandeis, testimony, December 14, 1911, in U.S. Senate, *Report of the Committee on Interstate Commerce, Pursuant to Senate Resolution 98: Hearings on Control of Corporations, Persons, and Firms Engaged in Interstate Commerce,* 62nd Cong., 2nd sess. (Washington, D.C.: U.S. Government Printing Office, 1912), pp. 1146–48; idem, "Competition," *American Legal News,* 44 (January 1913), reprinted in Fraenkel, *The Curse of Bigness,* pp. 112–124.

104. Louis D. Brandeis to Elizabeth Brandeis Rauschenbush, November 19, 1933, quoted in Strum, *Louis D. Brandeis,* p. 391.

105. Brandeis, testimony, *Report of the Committee on Interstate Commerce,* pp. 1148, 1170; idem, "Competition," pp. 114–118. See also Strum, *Louis D. Brandeis,* pp. 147–150; McCraw, "Rethinking the Trust Question," pp. 28–38; and idem, *Prophets of Regulation,* pp. 94–101.

106. Brandeis, testimony, *Report of the Committee on Interstate Commerce,* pp. 1166–67, 1155, 1174; idem, "Competition," p. 116.

107. The case is *Dr. Miles Medical Co. v. John D. Park & Sons Co.,* 220 U.S. 373 (1911).

On Brandeis and resale price maintenance, see McCraw, *Prophets of Regulation,* pp. 101–108.

108. Louis D. Brandeis, testimony, May 15, 1912, before the House Committee on Patents, quoted in McCraw, *Prophets of Regulation,* pp. 102–103.

109. Louis D. Brandeis to George Soule, April 22, 1923, quoted in Strum, *Louis D. Brandeis,* pp. 192–193; Brandeis, "Cut-Throat Prices: The Competition That Kills," *Harper's Weekly,* November 15, 1913, reprinted in Brandeis, *Business—A Profession* (Boston: Small, Maynard, 1914), p. 254.

110. Brandeis, "Cut-Throat Prices," pp. 252–253.

111. Areeda and Kaplow, *Antitrust Analysis,* pp. 58–61; McCraw, *Prophets of Regulation,* pp. 114–152; Hofstadter, "What Happened to the Antitrust Movement?" pp. 114–115; Hawley, "Antitrust," pp. 776–779.

112. Franklin D. Roosevelt, "Recommendations to the Congress to Curb Monopolies and the Concentration of Economic Power," April 29, 1938, in *The Public Papers and Addresses of Franklin D. Roosevelt,* ed. Samuel I. Rosenman, vol. 7 (New York: Macmillan, 1941), pp. 305–315.

113. Thurman W. Arnold, *The Folklore of Capitalism* (New Haven: Yale University Press, 1937), pp. 207–217, 221, 228–229; Ellis W. Hawley, *The New Deal and the Problem of Monopoly* (Princeton: Princeton University Press, 1966), pp. 421–423.

114. Hawley, *The New Deal and Monopoly,* pp. 420–455; Hofstadter, "What Happened to the Antitrust Movement?" pp. 114–115; Alan Brinkley, "The New Deal and the Idea of the State," in Steven Fraser and Gary Gerstle, eds., *The Rise and Fall of the New Deal Order, 1930–1980* (Princeton: Princeton University Press, 1989), pp. 89–90.

115. Thurman W. Arnold, *The Bottlenecks of Business* (New York: Reynal & Hitchcock, 1940), pp. 1–19, 116–131, 260–297; Hawley, *The New Deal and Monopoly,* pp. 421–429; Brinkley, "New Deal and Idea of State," pp. 89–91.

116. Arnold, *The Bottlenecks of Business,* pp. 3–4.

117. Ibid., pp. 122, 125.

118. Ibid., p. 123.

119. *United States v. Aluminum Co. of America,* 148 F.2d 416, 427, 428 (2d Cir. 1945).

120. Estes Kefauver, Senate debate, *Congressional Record,* 81st Cong., 2d sess., 96 (December 12, 1950), 16433, 16452, reprinted in Kintner, *Legislative History of Federal Antitrust Laws,* Part I, vol. 4, p. 3581. See also remarks by Rep. Emanuel Cellar, House debate, *Congressional Record,* 81st Cong., 1st Sess., 95 (August 15, 1949), 11484, 11486, reprinted in Kintner, p. 3476. The bill was the Cellar-Kefauver Act of 1950.

121. Hubert H. Humphrey, Senate debate, *Congressional Record,* 82d Cong., 2d sess., 98 (July 1–2, 1952), 8741, 8823, reprinted in Kintner, *Legislative History of Federal Antitrust Laws,* Part I, vol. 1, pp. 807–808, 832. The bill was the McGuire Act of 1952.

122. *Brown Shoe Co., Inc. v. United States,* 370 U.S. 293, 315–316, 344 (1962).

123. *United States v. Von's Grocery Co.,* 384 U.S. 270, 274–275 (1966).

124. *United States v. Falstaff Brewing Corp.*, 410 U.S. 526, 540–543 (1973), Justice Douglas concurring in part.

125. Phillip Areeda and Donald F. Turner, *Antitrust Law: An Analysis of Antitrust Principles and Their Application*, vol. 1 (Boston: Little, Brown, 1978), pp. 8–12.

126. Ibid., pp. 24–29.

127. Bork, *The Antitrust Paradox*, pp. 51, 7, 54, 203–204. See also Richard A. Posner, *Antitrust Law: An Economic Perspective* (Chicago: University of Chicago Press, 1976).

128. Ralph Nader, "Introduction," in Mark J. Green, ed., *The Monopoly Makers: Ralph Nader's Study Group Report on Regulation and Competition* (New York: Grossman, 1973), p. x; Nader, "Introduction," in Green, *The Closed Enterprise System: Ralph Nader's Study Group Report on Antitrust Enforcement* (New York: Grossman, 1972), p. xi; Green quotations, ibid., pp. 5, 21.

129. Bork, *The Antitrust Paradox*, p. 91; see also ibid., pp. 110–111.

130. William Baxter in *Wall Street Journal*, March 4, 1982, p. 28, quoted in Robert H. Lande, "The Rise and (Coming) Fall of Efficiency as the Ruler of Antitrust," *Antitrust Bulletin*, Fall 1988, p. 439; Charles F. Rule and David L. Meyer, "An Antitrust Enforcement Policy to Maximize the Economic Wealth of All Consumers," ibid., Winter 1988, pp. 684–686.

131. See Robert H. Lande, "Wealth Transfers as the Original and Primary Concern of Antitrust: The Efficiency Interpretation Challenged," *Hastings Law Journal*, 34 (1982), 68–69; idem, "The Rise and (Coming) Fall"; and Peter W. Rodino, Jr., "The Future of Antitrust: Ideology vs. Legislative Intent," *Antitrust Bulletin*, Fall 1990, pp. 575–600.

132. Nader, "Introduction," in Green, *The Monopoly Makers*, pp. xi–xii.

133. Green, *The Closed Enterprise System*, pp. 14–15.

134. The law repealing the fair trade acts was called the Consumer Goods Pricing Act of 1975. See Kintner, *Legislative History of Federal Antitrust Laws*, Part I, vol. 1, pp. 939–982.

135. Jack Brooks, quoted in *Congressional Quarterly Almanac*, 47 (1991), 292. On the general issue, see ibid., pp. 291–292; ibid., 46 (1990), 539–540; ibid., 44 (1988), 131–132; and ibid., 43 (1987), 280–281.

8. Liberalism and the Keynesian Revolution

1. An excellent study of the contending reform traditions that informed the New Deal is Ellis W. Hawley, *The New Deal and the Problem of Monopoly* (Princeton: Princeton University Press, 1966).

2. Arthur M. Schlesinger, Jr., *The Coming of the New Deal* (Boston: Houghton Mifflin, 1958), pp. 179, 55–67; William E. Leuchtenburg, *Franklin D. Roosevelt and the New Deal, 1932–1940* (New York: Harper & Row, 1963), pp. 72–73; Frank Freidel and Alan Brinkley, *America in the Twentieth Century*, 5th ed. (New York: Alfred A. Knopf, 1982), pp. 225–228; Hawley, *The New Deal and Monopoly*, pp. 191–194.

3. Schlesinger, *The Coming of the New Deal*, pp. 87–102.

4. Ibid., pp. 100–112.

5. Ibid., pp. 112–115; Freidel and Brinkley, *America in the Twentieth Century*, pp. 228–229; Johnson quoted in Schlesinger, p. 115.

6. Schlesinger, *The Coming of the New Deal*, pp. 115–116.

7. Arthur M. Schlesinger, Jr., *The Politics of Upheaval* (Boston: Houghton Mifflin, 1960), pp. 263–290, Roosevelt quoted on p. 289; idem, *The Coming of the New Deal*, pp. 119–176; Freidel and Brinkley, *America in the Twentieth Century*, pp. 229–232; Leuchtenburg, *Roosevelt and the New Deal*, pp. 66–70, 145–146; Hawley, *The New Deal and Monopoly*, pp. 35–146. The case was *Schechter Poultry Corp. v. United States*, 295 U.S. (1935).

8. Schlesinger, *The Politics of Upheaval*, p. 385 and, generally, pp. 385–398; Tugwell quoted in idem, *The Coming of the New Deal*, p. 183.

9. Leuchtenburg, *Roosevelt and the New Deal*, p. 149; Hawley, *The New Deal and Monopoly*, pp. 306–311, 328–329.

10. Hawley, *The New Deal and Monopoly*, p. 284 and, generally, pp. 283–303; Leuchtenburg, *Roosevelt and the New Deal*, pp. 149–150.

11. Franklin D. Roosevelt, "Recommendation for Regulation of Public Utility Holding Companies," March 12, 1935, in *The Public Papers and Addresses of Franklin D. Roosevelt*, ed. Samuel I. Rosenman, 13 vols. (New York: Random House, 1938–1950), vol. 4, p. 101; Hawley, *The New Deal and Monopoly*, pp. 325–337; Schlesinger, *The Politics of Upheaval*, pp. 302–324; Leuchtenburg, *Roosevelt and the New Deal*, pp. 154–157.

12. Roosevelt, "Message to Congress on Tax Revision," June 19, 1935, in *Public Papers and Addresses*, vol. 4, pp. 270–276; Hawley, *The New Deal and Monopoly*, pp. 344–349; Schlesinger, *The Politics of Upheaval*, pp. 325–333; Leuchtenburg, *Roosevelt and the New Deal*, pp. 152–154.

13. Schlesinger, *The Politics of Upheaval*, pp. 334, 505–509; Hawley, *The New Deal and Monopoly*, pp. 350–359.

14. Roosevelt, "Acceptance of Renomination," June 27, 1936, in *Public Papers and Addresses*, vol. 5, pp. 231–232.

15. Ibid., p. 233. Roosevelt sounded similar themes in his "Annual Message to Congress," January 3, 1936, ibid., pp. 8–18; and in a campaign speech at Madison Square Garden, October 31, 1936, ibid., pp. 566–573.

16. Hawley, *The New Deal and Monopoly*, p. 404 and, generally, pp. 383–403; Herbert Stein, *The Fiscal Revolution in America* (Chicago: University of Chicago Press, 1969), pp. 100–104.

17. Alan Brinkley, "The New Deal and the Idea of the State," in Steve Fraser and Gary Gerstle, eds., *The Rise and Fall of the New Deal Order, 1930–1980* (Princeton: Princeton University Press, 1989), p. 89. See also Stein, *The Fiscal Revolution in America*, p. 102.

18. Roosevelt, "Recommendations to Congress to Curb Monopolies," April 29, 1938, in *Public Papers and Addresses*, vol. 7, p. 305; Brinkley, "New Deal and Idea of State," p. 89.

19. Brinkley, "New Deal and Idea of State," p. 91; Hawley, *The New Deal and Monopoly*, pp. 453–454.

20. Brinkley, "New Deal and Idea of State," pp. 91–92.
21. Stein, *The Fiscal Revolution in America,* pp. 50–54.
22. Roosevelt, "Campaign Address at Sioux City, Iowa," September 29, 1932, in *Public Papers and Addresses,* vol. 1, p. 761; "Campaign Address at Pittsburgh," October 19, 1932, ibid., pp. 808–809. See also Leuchtenburg, *Roosevelt and the New Deal,* pp. 10–11.
23. Stein, *The Fiscal Revolution in America,* p. 43; Schlesinger, *The Politics of Upheaval,* pp. 263–264, 406–408.
24. Roosevelt, "Fireside Chat on Present Economic Conditions," April 14, 1938, in *Public Papers and Addresses,* vol. 7, pp. 240–241, 244; Stein, *The Fiscal Revolution in America,* pp. 60, 108–113; Schlesinger, *The Politics of Upheaval,* p. 407; Brinkley, "New Deal and Idea of State," pp. 94–97.
25. Brinkley, "New Deal and Idea of State," pp. 96–97; Stein, *The Fiscal Revolution in America,* pp. 102–120; Robert Lekachman, *The Age of Keynes* (New York: Random House, 1966), pp. 112–143; Leuchtenburg, *Roosevelt and the New Deal,* p. 264.
26. Richard V. Gilbert et al., *An Economic Program for American Democracy* (New York: Vanguard Press, 1938), pp. 25, 40, 45–93; Stein, *The Fiscal Revolution in America,* pp. 162–168; Lekachman, *The Age of Keynes,* pp. 152–156.
27. Thomas Dewey, quoted in Stein, *The Fiscal Revolution in America,* pp. 173–174; Employment Act of 1946, reprinted in Stephen Kemp Bailey, *Congress Makes a Law* (New York: Columbia University Press, 1950), pp. 228–232; see generally Stein, *The Fiscal Revolution in America,* pp. 197–204, and Lekachman, *The Age of Keynes,* pp. 165–175.
28. Stein, *The Fiscal Revolution in America,* pp. 381–382.
29. Hawley, *The New Deal and Monopoly,* pp. 407, 459, and, generally, pp. 454–460.
30. Ibid., pp. 470–471.
31. Brinkley, "New Deal and Idea of State," pp. 106–109, 94.
32. Ibid., pp. 109–110. Brinkley develops these themes more fully in Alan Brinkley, *The End of Reform* (New York: Alfred A. Knopf, 1995).
33. Stein, *The Fiscal Revolution in America,* pp. 172–173.
34. Ibid., pp. 372–422; Lekachman, *The Age of Keynes,* pp. 270–285.
35. Lekachman, *The Age of Keynes,* p. 285; see also Stein, *The Fiscal Revolution in America,* pp. 460–463.
36. John F. Kennedy, "Remarks to White House Conference on National Economic Issues," May 21, 1962, in *Public Papers of the Presidents of the United States: John F. Kennedy, 1962* (Washington, D.C.: U.S. Government Printing Office, 1963), p. 422; see also Arthur M. Schlesinger, Jr., *A Thousand Days: John F. Kennedy in the White House* (New York: Fawcett Premier, 1965), pp. 592–594.
37. Kennedy, "Commencement Address at Yale University," June 11, 1962, in *Public Papers,* pp. 470–471, 473.
38. Among the most insightful critiques of economic growth is Fred Hirsch, *The Social Limits to Growth* (Cambridge, Mass.: Harvard University Press, 1976).
39. John Maynard Keynes, *The General Theory of Employment, Interest, and Money*

(1936; reprint, London: Macmillan, St. Martin's Press, 1973), p. 104; Harold L. Ickes, *The New Democracy* (New York: W. W. Norton, 1934), pp. 142–143; Thurman W. Arnold, *The Bottlenecks of Business* (New York: Reynal & Hitchcock, 1940).

40. Alvin H. Hansen, "Wanted: Ten Million Jobs," *Atlantic Monthly,* 172 (September 1943), 68–69; see also Brinkley, "New Deal and Idea of State," pp. 97–98, 108.

41. Hansen, "Wanted: Ten Million Jobs," pp. 68–69.

42. John Kenneth Galbraith, *The Affluent Society* (Boston: Houghton Mifflin, 1958), pp. 144, 147.

43. Edgar Kemler, *The Deflation of American Ideals* (Washington, D.C.: American Council of Public Affairs, 1941), pp. 129, 63, 44.

44. Ibid., pp. 109, 130.

45. Rexford G. Tugwell, "Relief and Reconstruction," May 21, 1934, in Tugwell, *The Battle for Democracy* (New York: Columbia University Press, 1935), p. 318.

46. Herbert Croly, *The Promise of American Life* (1909; reprint, Indianapolis: Bobbs-Merrill, 1965), p. 454; Louis D. Brandeis, "Letter to Robert W. Bruere," February 25, 1922, in Osmond K. Fraenkel, ed., *The Curse of Bigness* (New York: Viking Press, 1935), p. 271; Tugwell, *The Battle for Democracy*, p. 319.

47. For an account of the debate between laissez-faire and reformist liberals, see Chapter 6, above.

48. Hirsch, *The Social Limits to Growth,* pp. 119, 121.

49. John Maynard Keynes, letter to *The Times*, April 10, 1940, quoted in Robert Skidelsky, "Keynes and the Reconstruction of Liberalism," *Encounter,* 52 (April 1979), 34; Keynes, *The General Theory,* pp. 379–380.

50. David E. Lilienthal, *TVA: Democracy on the March* (New York: Harper & Brothers, 1944), pp. 75, 88, 139.

51. Idem, *Big Business: A New Era* (New York: Harper & Brothers, 1953), pp. 7, 200.

52. Ibid., p. 40.

53. Ibid., p. 204.

9. The Triumph and Travail of the Procedural Republic

1. Harry S Truman, "Radio Address after the Unconditional Surrender by Japan," September 1, 1945, in *Public Papers of the Presidents of the United States: Harry S Truman, 1945* (Washington, D.C.: U.S. Government Printing Office, 1961), p. 257; see generally Godfrey Hodgson, *In Our Time: America from World War II to Nixon* (London: Macmillan, 1976), pp. 3–52.

2. Michael Barone, *Our Country: The Shaping of America from Roosevelt to Reagan* (New York: Free Press, 1990), pp. 197–199, 388.

3. Theodore H. White, *In Search of History* (New York: Harper & Row, 1978), p. 493.

4. John F. Kennedy, quoted in Allen J. Matusow, *The Unraveling of America* (New York: Harper & Row, 1984), p. 18; Kennedy, Acceptance Speech, Los Angeles, July 15, 1960, in Gregory Bush, ed., *Campaign Speeches of American Presidential Candidates, 1948–1984* (New York: Frederick Ungar, 1985), p. 100. On the anxieties of

the late 1950s as background to the election of 1960, see Matusow, pp. 3–29; Barone, *Our Country*, pp. 294–327; and Henry Fairlie, *The Kennedy Promise: The Politics of Expectation* (Garden City, N.Y.: Doubleday, 1973), pp. 17–35.

5. Kennedy, "Inaugural Address," January 20, 1961, in *Public Papers of the Presidents of the United States: John F. Kennedy, 1961* (Washington, D.C.: U.S. Government Printing Office, 1962), pp. 1–3.

6. Kennedy, "Special Message to Congress on Urgent National Needs," May 25, 1961, ibid., pp. 404–405.

7. Kennedy, "Remarks to White House Conference on National Economic Issues," May 21, 1962, in *Public Papers of the Presidents: John F. Kennedy, 1962* (Washington, D.C.: U.S. Government Printing Office, 1963), pp. 422–423.

8. *Minersville School District v. Gobitis*, 310 U.S. 586 (1940); *West Virginia State Board of Education v. Barnette*, 319 U.S. 624 (1943).

9. *Everson v. Board of Education of Ewing Township*, 330 U.S. 1 (1947); *Wallace v. Jaffree*, 472 U.S. 38, 52–53 (1985).

10. C. Edwin Baker, "Scope of the First Amendment Freedom of Speech," *U.C.L.A. Law Review*, 25 (1978), 993.

11. The communal case for the welfare state is offered, for example, by Michael Walzer, *Spheres of Justice* (New York: Basic Books, 1983), pp. 64–91, who writes (p. 64): "Membership is important because of what the members of a political community owe to one another and to no one else, or to no one else in the same degree. And the first thing they owe is the communal provision of security and welfare . . . communal provision is important because it teaches us the value of membership."

12. Samuel H. Beer, *British Politics in the Collectivist Age* (New York: Alfred A. Knopf, 1967), pp. 69–71.

13. Franklin D. Roosevelt, "The Golden Rule in Government: An Extemporaneous Address at Vassar College," August 26, 1933, in *The Public Papers and Addresses of Franklin D. Roosevelt*, ed. Samuel I. Rosenman, 13 vols. (New York: Random House, 1938–1950), vol. 2, pp. 340, 342; "Radio Address to Young Democratic Clubs of America," August 24, 1935, ibid., vol. 4, p. 339.

14. Roosevelt quoted in Arthur M. Schlesinger, *The Coming of the New Deal* (Boston: Houghton Mifflin, 1958), pp. 308–309; on the general point, see James Holt, "The New Deal and the American Anti-Statist Tradition," in John Braeman, Robert H. Bremner, and David Brody, eds., *The New Deal: The National Level* (Columbus: Ohio State University Press, 1975), pp. 27–49; and Theda Skocpol, "Legacies of New Deal Liberalism," *Dissent*, Winter 1983, pp. 33–44.

15. Roosevelt, "Message to Congress on the State of the Union," January 11, 1944, in *Public Papers and Addresses*, vol. 13, pp. 40–42.

16. See William A. Schambra, "Progressive Liberalism and American 'Community,'" *The Public Interest*, Summer 1985, pp. 31–48; idem, "The Decline of National Community and the Renaissance of the Small Republic" (manuscript, n.d.); idem, "Is New Federalism the Wave of the Future?" in Marshall Kaplan and Peggy L. Cuciti, eds., *The Great Society and Its Legacy* (Durham, N.C.: Duke University Press, 1986), pp. 24–31.

17. Lyndon B. Johnson, "Annual Message to the Congress on the State of the Union," January 8, 1964, in *Public Papers of the Presidents of the United States: Lyndon B. Johnson, 1963–64* (Washington, D.C.: U.S. Government Printing Office, 1965), vol. 1, p. 113; "Remarks in Raleigh at North Carolina State College," October 6, 1964, ibid., vol. 2, p. 1225; "Remarks in Los Angeles," June 20, 1964, ibid., vol. 1, p. 797; "Remarks in Dayton, Ohio," October 16, 1964, ibid., vol. 2, p. 1372.

18. The phrase is that of Samuel H. Beer, who offers an important statement and defense of the nationalizing tradition in Beer, "Liberalism and the National Idea," *The Public Interest,* Fall 1966, pp. 70–82.

19. Johnson, "Remarks to the Faculty and Students of Johns Hopkins University," October 1, 1964, in *Public Papers, 1963–64,* vol. 2, p. 1178; "Remarks at a Luncheon for Businessmen," August 10, 1964, ibid., p. 943; "Inaugural Address," January 20, 1965, in *Public Papers of the Presidents of the United States: Lyndon B. Johnson, 1965* (Washington, D.C.: U.S. Government Printing Office, 1966), vol. 1, p. 73.

20. On race and national community, see Johnson's memorable address on voting rights, "Special Message to the Congress: The American Promise," March 15, 1965, in *Public Papers, 1965,* vol. 1, pp. 281–287. On the implications of the communal ethic for poverty policy, see Alvin L. Schorr, *Explorations in Social Policy* (New York: Basic Books, 1968), p. 274: "If we are to be one nation, those who have money and power must devote the resources required to produce housing for poor people."

21. Johnson, "Remarks at the University of Michigan," May 22, 1964, in *Public Papers, 1963–64,* vol. 1, p. 704.

22. See Daniel P. Moynihan, *Maximum Feasible Misunderstanding: Community Action in the War on Poverty* (New York: Free Press, 1970); and Matusow, *The Unraveling of America,* pp. 243–271.

23. Johnson, "Remarks before the National Convention," August 27, 1964, in *Public Papers, 1963–64,* vol. 2, p. 1013; "Remarks in Dayton, Ohio," ibid., p. 1371; "Remarks to the Faculty and Students of Johns Hopkins University," October 1, 1964, ibid., p. 1177.

24. Johnson, "Address at Swarthmore College," June 8, 1964, in *Public Papers, 1963–64,* vol. 1, p. 757; "Remarks at Fundraising Dinner in Minneapolis," June 27, 1964, ibid., p. 828.

25. Johnson, "Remarks before the National Convention," August 27, 1964, ibid., vol. 2, pp. 1012–13.

26. During the 1964 campaign Goldwater qualified his earlier opposition to Social Security but continued to oppose Medicare, federal antipoverty programs, and the Tennessee Valley Authority. See Matusow, *The Unraveling of America,* pp. 144–148.

27. Barry Goldwater, *The Conscience of a Conservative* (1960; Washington, D.C.: Regnery Gateway, 1990), pp. 6–7, 11, 52–53, 66–68.

28. Milton Friedman, *Capitalism and Freedom* (Chicago: University of Chicago Press, 1962), pp. 5–6, 174, 188.

29. Ibid., pp. 34–36, 200.

30. On the development of AFDC and the agenda of reform, see R. Shep Melnick,

Between the Lines: Interpreting Welfare Rights (Washington, D.C.: Brookings Institution, 1994), pp. 65–82; and James T. Patterson, *America's Struggle against Poverty, 1900–1980* (Cambridge, Mass.: Harvard University Press, 1981), pp. 85–91, 157–184.

31. Charles A. Reich, "The New Property," *Yale Law Journal,* 73 (1964), 785–786; idem, "Individual Rights and Social Welfare: The Emerging Legal Issues," ibid., 74 (1965), 1247.

32. Edward V. Sparer, "The Role of the Welfare Client's Lawyer," *U.C.L.A. Law Review,* 12 (1965), 367, 369; see also Melnick, *Between the Lines,* pp. 75–80.

33. *King v. Smith,* 392 U.S. 309, 320 (1968).

34. Ibid. at 320–326.

35. *Shapiro v. Thompson,* 394 U.S. 618, 627 (1969). See Frank Michelman, "Welfare Rights in a Constitutional Democracy," *Washington University Law Quarterly,* 1979, p. 659; idem, "The Supreme Court, 1968 Term—Foreword: On Protecting the Poor through the Fourteenth Amendment," *Harvard Law Review,* 83 (1969), 7; idem, "In Pursuit of Constitutional Rights: One View of Rawls' Theory of Justice," *University of Pennsylvanioa Law Review,* 121 (1973), 962; and Laurence H. Tribe, *American Constitutional Law* (Mineola, N.Y.: Foundation Press, 1978), pp. 1116–18.

36. *Goldberg v. Kelly,* 397 U.S. 254, 264, 262, 265 (1970).

37. *Dandridge v. Williams,* 397 U.S. 471, 484 (1970).

38. Melnick, *Between the Lines,* pp. 42–43, 66–67.

39. Even Milton Friedman, despite his general opposition to redistributive policies, favored a negative income tax as the most efficient and least intrusive way of helping the poor; see Friedman, *Capitalism and Freedom,* pp. 191–195.

40. Robert Theobald, *Free Men and Free Markets* (New York: Clarkson N. Potter, 1963), pp. 15, 149–151; idem, ed., *The Guaranteed Income: Next Step in Economic Evolution?* (Garden City, N.Y.: Doubleday, 1966), pp. 229, 94. See also Patterson, *America's Struggle against Poverty,* pp. 187–188.

41. U.S. Congress, 91st Cong., 2nd sess.,William Ryan, House debate, *Congressional Record - House,* 91st Cong., 2nd sess., 116, part 9 (April 16, 1970), 12048–49; statement by Dr. Inabel B. Lindsay, Episcopal Action Group on Poverty, U.S. Congress, Senate, Committee on Finance, *Social Security Amendments of 1967, Hearings before the Committee on Finance,* 90th Cong., 1st sess., *Congressional Record,* September 1967, p. 1735; statement of the National Presbyterian Health and Welfare Association of the United Presbyterian Church, ibid., p. 1739. See Lawrence M. Mead, *Beyond Entitlement: The Social Obligations of Citizenship* (New York: Free Press, 1986), pp. 200–215.

42. See Daniel P. Moynihan, *The Politics of a Guaranteed Income* (New York: Random House, 1973); Vincent J. and Vee Burke, *Nixon's Good Deed: Welfare Reform* (New York: Columbia University Press, 1974); Mead, *Beyond Entitlement,* pp. 95–119; idem, *The New Politics of Poverty* (New York: Basic Books, 1992); Melnick, *Between the Lines,* pp. 112–132.

43. John Rawls, *A Theory of Justice* (Cambridge, Mass.: Harvard University Press,

1971), p. 28. See also Ronald Dworkin, *Taking Rights Seriously* (London: Duckworth, 1977), pp. 184–205.

44. Ibid., pp. 30–32, 446–451, 560. A similar view is advanced by Ronald Dworkin, who writes that "government must be neutral on what might be called the question of the good life . . . political decisions must be, so far as is possible, independent of any particular conception of the good life, or of what gives values to life." See Dworkin, "Liberalism," in Stuart Hampshire, ed., *Public and Private Morality* (Cambridge: Cambridge University Press, 1978), p. 127.

45. Rawls, *A Theory of Justice*, pp. 561, 560. Rawls revised his view somewhat in the 1990s. See John Rawls, *Political Liberalism* (New York: Columbia University Press, 1993).

46. Ibid., pp. 72–75, 100–108.

47. Robert Nozick, *Anarchy, State, and Utopia* (New York: Basic Books, 1974), pp. 160, ix, 26–45; see generally pp. 147–231.

48. Wayne W. Dyer, *Your Erroneous Zones* (New York: Funk & Wagnalls, 1976), pp. 4, 10–11, 36–37, 59. See also Gail Sheehy, *Passages: Predictable Crises of Adult Life* (New York: E. P. Dutton, 1976), p. 251: "You can't take everything with you when you leave on the midlife journey. You are moving away. Away from institutional claims and other people's agenda. Away from external valuations and accreditations, in search of an inner validation. You are moving out of roles and into the self."

49. Ibid., pp. 29, 225, 61.

50. Ibid., pp. 225–226.

51. Ibid., pp. 225, 230–231, 233.

52. Ibid., p. 233.

53. Wayne W. Dyer, *The Sky's the Limit* (New York: Simon and Schuster, 1980), pp. 36–38; idem, *Pulling Your Own Strings* (New York: Thomas Y. Crowell, 1978), pp. xv–xvii, 4–5.

54. Theodore H. White, The Making of the President, 1968 (New York: Atheneum, 1969), pp. 3–4.

55. Ibid., pp. 4–5; Barone, *Our Country*, p. 431; Matusow, *The Unraveling of America*, p. 391; Alan Brinkley, *The Unfinished Nation* (New York: Alfred A. Knopf, 1993), p. 829.

56. Barone, *Our Country*, pp. 431–434; Matusow, *The Unraveling of America*, pp. 390–394; Brinkley, *The Unfinished Nation*, pp. 829–830.

57. Barone, *Our Country*, pp. 436–453; Matusow, *The Unraveling of America*, pp. 395–439; Brinkley, *The Unfinished Nation*, pp. 830–833; see generally White, *The Making of the President, 1968*.

58. White, *The Making of the President, 1968*, pp. 29–30. White notes that the expression, widely used in 1968, derives from Ralph Waldo Emerson.

59. James Reston, quoted in ibid., p. 95.

60. Survey research on trust in government is presented in Seymour Martin Lipset and William Schneider, *The Confidence Gap*, rev. ed. (Baltimore: Johns Hopkins University Press, 1987); Warren E. Miller, Arthur H. Miller, and Edward J. Schneider,

American Election Studies Data Sourcebook, 1952–78 (Cambridge, Mass.: Harvard University Press, 1980); and Alan F. Kay et al., "Steps for Democracy: The Many versus the Few," *Americans Talk Issues,* March 25, 1994.

61. *Gallup Poll Monthly,* February 1994, p. 12.

62. Kay et al., "Steps for Democracy," pp. 4, 8, 9.

63. In 1960, 25 percent agreed with the statement "I don't think public officials care much what people like me think"; in 1990, 64 percent agreed. Miller, Miller, and Schneider, *Election Studies Data Sourcebook,* pp. 259–261; Warren E. Miller, Donald R. Kinder, and Stephen J. Rosenstone, "American National Election Study: 1990 Post-Election Survey" (Computer file, Inter-University Consortium for Political and Social Research, Ann Arbor, Mich.).

64. George Wallace, quoted in Stephan Lesher, *George Wallace: American Populist* (Reading, Mass.: Addison-Wesley, 1994), pp. 160, 174; also in Jody Carlson, *George C. Wallace and the Politics of Powerlessness* (New Brunswick, N.J.: Transaction Books, 1981), p. 24.

65. Wallace on "Meet the Press," NBC, April 23, 1967, quoted in Lesher, *George Wallace,* p. 390; and in Lewis Chester, Godfrey Hodgson, and Bruce Page, *An American Melodrama: The Presidential Campaign of 1968* (New York: Viking Press, 1969), pp. 280–281.

66. See Carlson, *Wallace and the Politics of Powerlessness,* pp. 5–18, 85–126; and the platform of the American Independent party, quoted in ibid., pp. 127–128; also Lesher, *George Wallace,* pp. 502–503.

67. Wallace quoted in Chester, Hodgson, and Page, *An American Melodrama,* p. 283; in Lesher, *George Wallace,* p. 475; and in Carlson, *Wallace and the Politics of Powerlessness,* pp. 6, 131. A characteristic Wallace campaign speech is reprinted in Bush, *Campaign Speeches,* pp. 185–193.

68. Lesher, *George Wallace,* pp. 313, 474.

69. Wallace, New York City, October 24, 1968, in Bush, *Campaign Speeches,* p. 191; Chester, Hodgson, and Page, *An American Melodrama,* p. 283; Carlson, *Wallace and the Politics of Powerlessness,* p. 129.

70. Wallace quoted in Lesher, *George Wallace,* p. 420; in Matusow, *The Unraveling of America,* p. 425; in Chester, Hodgson, and Page, *An American Melodrama,* p. 280; and in Bush, *Campaign Speeches,* p. 187.

71. From 1968 onward every successful candidate for president managed somehow to identify himself with the frustrations that Wallace identified. Richard Nixon ran on a platform of "law and order" and appealed to a "silent majority" fed up with crime and social unrest. Jimmy Carter and Ronald Reagan, in their different ways, ran as outsiders to Washington and critics of the federal government. On the contest for the Wallace constituency, see Lesher, *George Wallace,* pp. 312–313, 483, 491.

72. Carlson, *Wallace and the Politics of Powerlessness,* pp. 5, 148.

73. The best account of Kennedy in the tradition of New Deal liberalism is Arthur M. Schlesinger, Jr., *Robert Kennedy and His Times* (New York: Ballantine Books, 1978). For accounts stressing Kennedy's departure from conventional liberalism, see Jack Newfield, *Robert Kennedy: A Memoir* (New York: E. P. Dutton, 1969); and

Maxwell Rabson Rovner, "Jeffersonianism vs. the National Idea: Community Revitalization and the Rethinking of American Liberalism" (Senior honors thesis, Department of Government, Harvard University, Widener Library, 1990).

74. Kennedy at Utica, N.Y., February 7, 1966, in Edwin O. Guthman and C. Richard Allen, eds., *RFK: Collected Speeches* (New York: Viking, 1993), pp. 208–209.

75. See Beer, "Liberalism and the National Idea."

76. Kennedy at Worthington, Minn., September 17, 1966, in Guthman and Allen, *RFK: Collected Speeches,* pp. 211–212.

77. Robert F. Kennedy, testimony before the Subcommittee on Executive Reorganization, U.S. Senate Committee on Government Operations, Washington, D.C., August 15, 1966, ibid., p. 178.

78. See Schambra, "Progressive Liberalism and American 'Community.'"

79. Kennedy, testimony before the Subcommittee on Executive Reorganization, in Guthman and Allen, *RFK: Collected Speeches,* p. 179.

80. Kennedy at Indianapolis, April 26, 1968, ibid., p. 381; Press Release, Los Angeles, May 19, 1968, ibid., p. 385. See also Robert F. Kennedy, *To Seek a Newer World* (Garden City, N.Y.: Doubleday, 1967), pp. 28, 33–36.

81. Kennedy, Press Release, Los Angeles, May 19, 1968, in Guthman and Allen, *RFK: Collected Speeches,* pp. 385–386.

82. Kennedy, testimony before the Subcommittee on Executive Reorganization, in ibid., p. 183.

83. Kennedy, *To Seek a Newer World,* pp. 55–62; San Francisco, May 21, 1968, in Guthman and Allen, *RFK: Collected Speeches,* p. 389. See also Newfield, *Robert Kennedy,* pp. 87–109.

84. Newfield, *Robert Kennedy,* pp. 81, 83; Guthman and Allen, *RFK: Collected Speeches,* pp. 371–372, 379–383.

85. On these two themes, see Jimmy Carter, *Why Not the Best?* (Nashville: Broadman Press, 1975), pp. 9–11, 145–154.

86. Jimmy Carter, Acceptance Speech, Democratic National Convention, New York City, July 15, 1976, in *The Presidential Campaign, 1976* (Washington, D.C.: U.S. Government Printing Office, 1978), vol. 1, part 1, p. 350; Charleston, W.Va., August 14, 1976, ibid., pp. 501, 502. See also Acceptance Speech, p. 349; and idem, *Why Not the Best?* pp. 145–147. Another expression of Carter's penchant for immediacy was his impatience with the notion that intermediate forms of government reflect distinctive constituencies: "I see no reason for our nation to be divided. And I want to see federal, state, and local levels of government working together because we represent the same people exactly"; Evansville, Ind., September 27, 1976, in *The Presidential Campaign, 1976,* vol. 1, part 2, p. 822.

87. Carter, Portland, Ore., September 27, 1976, in *The Presidential Campaign, 1976,* vol. 1, part 2, p. 833; idem, *Why Not the Best?* p. 147.

88. Carter's preoccupation with detail was described by his former speechwriter James Fallows, in Fallows, "The Passionless Presidency," *Atlantic Monthly,* May 1979, p. 38.

89. Carter, Los Angeles, August 23, 1976, in *The Presidential Campaign, 1976,* vol. 1,

part 1, pp. 506, 504; see also "Meet the Press," NBC, July 11, 1976, ibid., p. 292: "I think that the differences among our ideological categories of people (sic) have been removed. . . . I think those sharp differences that used to exist between the liberal and conservative elements of our society have pretty well been removed."

90. See Fallows, "The Passionless Presidency."

91. Barone, *Our Country,* pp. 580–583.

92. Carter, *Economic Report of the President,* January 25, 1979, in *Public Papers of the Presidents of the United States: Jimmy Carter, 1979* (Washington, D.C.: U.S. Government Printing Office, 1980), vol. 1, p. 113.

93. Theodore H. White, *America in Search of Itself* (New York: Harper & Row, 1982), pp. 152–153.

94. Carter, "Energy and National Goals," July 15, 1979, in *Public Papers, 1979,* vol. 2, pp. 1237–38.

95. See Brinkley, *The Unfinished Nation,* p. 876.

96. White, *America in Search of Itself,* pp. 16–21; Barone, *Our Country,* pp. 587–592.

97. On the temporary rebounding of confidence in government during the early Reagan years, see Lipset and Schneider, *The Confidence Gap,* pp. 17, 415–425; Kay et al., "Steps for Democracy," pp. 9–10; Arthur Miller, "Is Confidence Rebounding?" *Public Opinion,* June/July 1983, pp. 16–20; Barone, *Our Country,* pp. 629, 643–644, 759–760.

98. Ronald Reagan at American Conservative Union Banquet, Washington, D.C., February 6, 1977, in Alfred Balitzer, ed., *A Time for Choosing: The Speeches of Ronald Reagan, 1961–1982* (Chicago: Regnery Gateway, 1983), p. 192.

99. Jerry Falwell, *Listen, America!* (Garden City, N.Y.: Doubleday, 1980), pp. 20–21, 251–252.

100. George F. Will, *Statecraft as Soulcraft: What Government Does* (New York: Simon and Schuster, 1983), pp. 19, 24, 134.

101. Ibid., pp. 19–22, 45, 125–131.

102. Ronald Reagan, Nationwide Television Address, March 31, 1976, in Eckhard Breitinger, ed., *The Presidential Campaign 1976* (Frankfurt am Main: Peter Lang, 1978), p. 67; Richard B. Wirthlin, "Reagan for President: Campaign Action Plan," campaign document, June 29, 1980, quoted in John Kenneth White, *The New Politics of Old Values* (Hanover, N.H.: University Press of New England, 1988), p. 54.

103. Ronald Reagan, Acceptance Speech, Detroit, July 17, 1980, in Bush, *Campaign Speeches,* pp. 264, 268, 271, 273.

104. Ronald Reagan, "Let the People Rule," speech to the Executive Club of Chicago, September 26, 1975, manuscript, Ronald Reagan Library, Simi Valley, Calif.

105. Republican platform, in Donald Bruce Johnson, ed., *National Party Platforms of 1980* (Urbana: University of Illinois Press, 1982), pp. 177, 187; Reagan, "Remarks at the Conservative Political Action Conference," Washington, D.C., March 20, 1981, in Reagan, *Speaking My Mind: Selected Speeches* (New York: Simon and Schuster, 1989), p. 100; see also "Remarks at the Annual Convention of the National Association of Evangelicals," Orlando, Fla., March 8, 1983, ibid., p. 171; "Address

to the Nation Announcing the Reagan-Bush Candidacies for Reelection," January 29, 1984, in *Public Papers of the Presidents of the United States: Ronald Reagan, 1984* (Washington, D.C.: U.S. Government Printing Office, 1986), vol. 1, p. 110.

106. Reagan, "State of the Union Address," January 26, 1982, in *Public Papers of the Presidents of the United States: Ronald Reagan, 1982* (Washington, D.C.: U.S. Government Printing Office, 1983), vol. 1, p. 75; "Remarks in New Orleans, Annual Meeting of the International Association of Chiefs of Police," September 28, 1981, in *Public Papers of the Presidents of the United States: Ronald Reagan, 1981* (Washington, D.C.: U.S. Government Printing Office, 1982), p. 845. Reagan's reference to institutions that "shaped the character of our people" was a quotation of Supreme Court justice Lewis Powell.

107. Reagan, "State of the Union Address," in *Public Papers, 1982,* vol. 1, pp. 72–77; "Remarks to International Association of Chiefs of Police," September 28, 1981, in *Public Papers, 1981,* pp. 844–845; "Remarks at Annual Meeting of the National Alliance of Business," October 5, 1981, ibid., pp. 881–887.

108. Christopher Lasch, *The True and Only Heaven: Progress and Its Critics* (New York: W. W. Norton, 1991), pp. 516, 39.

109. Michael S. Dukakis, Acceptance Speech, Democratic National Convention, Atlanta, Georgia, July 21, 1988, in *Congressional Digest,* 67, (October 1988), 234; Walter F. Mondale, Acceptance Speech, Democratic National Convention, San Francisco, California, July 19, 1984, in Bush, *Campaign Speeches,* p. 334. Fairness and distributive justice were also the themes of Mario Cuomo's keynote address to that convention, "A Tale of Two Cities," July 16, 1984, reprinted in Cuomo, *More than Words* (New York: St. Martin's Press, 1993), pp. 21–31.

110. Mondale quoted in Paul Taylor, "Mondale Rises to Peak Form," *Washington Post,* October 26, 1984, p. 1; Cuomo, "A Tale of Two Cities," p. 29. Other Democratic invocations of the idea of national community include Dukakis, Acceptance Speech, p. 236; and Barbara Jordan, Keynote Address, Democratic National Convention, New York, July 12, 1976, in Breitinger, *The Presidential Campaign, 1976,* pp. 103–106.

111. Alexis de Tocqueville, *Democracy in America* (1835), trans. Henry Reeve, ed. Phillips Bradley, vol. 1, chap. 5 (New York: Alfred A. Knopf, 1945), p. 68.

112. See, for example, William A. Schambra, "By the People: The Old Values of the New Citizenship," *Policy Review,* vol. 69 (Summer 1994), 32–38. Schambra, an advocate of civic conservatism, writes of the Reagan administration (p. 4): "A genuine return to local citizen democracy was never on the agenda." See also Lasch, *The True and Only Heaven,* pp. 22, 38–39, 515–517; Harry C. Boyte, "Ronald Reagan and America's Neighborhoods: Undermining Community Initiative," in Alan Gartner, Colin Greer, and Frank Riessman, eds., *What Reagan Is Doing to Us* (New York: Harper & Row, 1982), pp. 109–124.

113. The $826 billion figure is in constant 1993 dollars. From 1950 to 1978, real family income growth by quintile, from the lowest to the highest, was 138 percent, 98 percent, 106 percent, 111 percent, and 99 percent respectively. Comparable figures for 1979 to 1993 were –17 percent, –8 percent, –3 percent, 5 percent, and 18 percent.

Department of Labor figures presented with remarks by Labor Secretary Robert B. Reich, National Press Club, Washington, D.C., January 5, 1995.

114. Survey findings on political disenchantment in the 1990s are presented in Kay et al., "Steps for Democracy." See also *Gallup Poll Monthly*, February 1994, p. 12.

Conclusion

1. On republican arguments for and against freehold suffrage, see the debates in the Virginia Convention of 1829–30, in Merrill D. Peterson, ed., *Democracy, Liberty, and Property* (Indianapolis: Bobbs-Merrill, 1966), pp. 377–408; also Chilton Williamson, *American Suffrage: From Property to Democracy, 1760–1860* (Princeton: Princeton University Press, 1960). On defenders of slavery, see James Henry Hammond, "'Mud-Sill' Speech" (1858), and Josiah Nott, "Types of Mankind" (1854), in Eric L. McKitrick, ed., *Slavery Defended: The Views of the Old South* (Englewood Cliffs, N.J.: Prentice-Hall, 1963), pp. 121–138; also Kenneth S. Greenberg, *Masters and Statesmen: The Political Culture of American Slavery* (Baltimore: Johns Hopkins University Press, 1985), pp. 3–22, 85–106. On opposition to citizenship for immigrants, see Tyler Anbinder, *Nativism and Slavery: The Northern Know Nothings and the Politics of the 1850s* (New York: Oxford University Press, 1992), pp. 118–126.

2. Jean-Jacques Rousseau, *On the Social Contract* (1762), trans. and ed. Donald A. Cress, book 2, chap. 7 (Indianapolis: Hackett, 1983), p. 39.

3. Benjamin Rush, *A Plan for the Establishment of Public Schools and the Diffusion of Knowledge in Pennsylvania* (1786), in Frederick Rudolph, ed., *Essays on Education in the Early Republic* (Cambridge, Mass.: Harvard University Press, 1965), pp. 9, 17, 14.

4. Alexis de Tocqueville, *Democracy in America* (1835), trans. Henry Reeve, ed. Phillips Bradley (New York: Alfred A. Knopf, 1945), vol. 1, p. 416.

5. Rousseau, *On the Social Contract*, book 4, chaps. 1–2, pp. 79–81. See also book 2, chap. 3, p. 32: "If, when a sufficiently informed populace deliberates, the citizens were to have no communication among themselves, the general will would always result."

6. Hannah Arendt's account of the public realm also emphasizes this feature: "What makes mass society so difficult to bear is not the number of people involved, or at least not primarily, but the fact that the world between them has lost its power to gather them together, to relate and to separate them"; *The Human Condition* (Chicago: University of Chicago Press, 1958), pp. 52–53.

7. Tocqueville, *Democracy in America*, vol. 1, chap. 17, p. 299; see generally chap. 5, pp. 66–68, and chap. 17, pp. 299–325. The idea that freedom requires a common life that is nonetheless differentiated or articulated by particular, identity-forming agencies of civil society is central to G. W. F. Hegel, *Philosophy of Right* (1821), trans. T. M. Knox (London: Oxford University Press, 1952).

8. Immanuel Kant, "Perpetual Peace" (1795), in *Kant's Political Writings*, ed. Hans Reiss (Cambridge: Cambridge University Press, 1970), pp. 112–113.

9. James Q. Wilson, "The Rediscovery of Character: Private Virtue and Public Policy," *The Public Interest,* Fall 1985, p. 3. See also idem, *On Character* (Washington, D.C.: American Enterprise Institute Press, 1995).

10. This new line of argument is recounted and defended in Lawrence M. Mead, *Beyond Entitlement: The Social Obligations of Citizenship* (New York: Free Press, 1986); and idem, *The New Politics of Poverty* (New York: Basic Books, 1992).

11. Daniel P. Moynihan, *The Negro Family: The Case for National Action* (Washington, D.C.: Office of Policy Planning and Research, U.S. Department of Labor, March 1965), reprinted in Lee Rainwater and William L. Yancy, eds., *The Moynihan Report and the Politics of Controversy* (Cambridge, Mass.: MIT Press, 1967), pp. 39–124; quotation on p. 94.

12. Moynihan emphasized that the national interest in family structure extended to the civic consequences of family life, not to its moral character as such: "The object should be to strengthen the Negro family so as to enable it to raise and support its members as other families do. After that, how this group of Americans chooses to run its affairs, take advantage of its opportunities, or fail to do so, is none of the nation's business"; ibid., pp. 93–94.

13. Floyd McKissick, quoted in ibid., p. 200; the sympathetic commentators are Rainwater and Yancey, p. 162. See also William J. Bennett, "Reflections on the Moynihan Report Thirty Years Later," *American Enterprise,* 6 (January/February 1995), 30.

14. Nathan Glazer, "The Social Policy of the Reagan Administration: A Review," *The Public Interest,* Spring 1984, pp. 87–88; Robert D. Reischauer, "Welfare Reform: Will Consensus Be Enough?" *Brookings Review,* 5 (Summer 1987), 6; Mead, *The New Politics of Poverty,* pp. 22–23.

15. Mead, *Beyond Entitlement,* pp. 13–14.

16. Moynihan quoted in "Daniel Patrick Moynihan: Making Welfare Work," *Congressional Quarterly Weekly Report,* 45 (March 21, 1987), 507.

17. Bennett, "Reflections on the Moynihan Report," p. 32; idem, "Revolt against God," *Policy Review,* no. 67 (Winter 1994), 23.

18. Idem, *The De-Valuing of America* (New York: Simon & Schuster, 1992), p. 37; idem, "What to Do about the Children," *Commentary,* March 1995, pp. 24–25.

19. See Richard John Neuhaus, *The Naked Public Square: Religion and Democracy in America* (Grand Rapids: William B. Eerdmans, 1984).

20. Bennett, *The De-Valuing of America,* pp. 58, 121.

21. Glenn C. Loury, "Beyond Victimhood," *Times Literary Supplement,* June 10, 1994.

22. Idem, "God and the Ghetto," *Wall Street Journal,* February 25, 1993.

23. President William J. Clinton, "Remarks to the Convocation of the Church of God in Christ in Memphis," November 13, 1993, *Weekly Compilation of Presidential Documents,* vol. 29, November 22, 1993 (Washington, D.C.: Government Printing Office, 1993), pp. 2360–62.

24. Clinton, "Address before a Joint Session of the Congress on the State of the Union," January 25, 1994, ibid., vol. 30.

25. Joe Klein, "The Out-of-Wedlock Question," *Newsweek,* December 13, 1993, p. 37.

26. Joycelyn Elders and Donna Shalala, quoted ibid. See also Gertrude Himmelfarb, *The De-Moralization of Society* (New York: Alfred A. Knopf, 1995), pp. 240–241.

27. Senator Bill Bradley, National Press Club, Washington, D.C., February 9, 1995.

28. See Chapter 9, note 113.

29. David R. Francis, "New Figures Show Wider Gap between Rich and Poor," *Christian Science Monitor*, April 21, 1995, p. 1, citing a study by economist Edward N. Wolff; and Keith Bradsher, "Gap in Wealth in U.S. Called Widest in West," *New York Times*, April 17, 1995, pp. A1, D4, also citing Wolff. See also Edward N. Wolff, *Top Heavy* (New York: Twentieth Century Fund Press, 1995); and Kevin Phillips, *Boiling Point: Republicans, Democrats, and the Decline of Middle-Class Prosperity* (New York: Random House, 1993), p. xix, citing economic historian Claudia Goldin.

30. These and other factors are discussed in Robert B. Reich, *The Work of Nations* (New York: Alfred A. Knopf, 1991), pp. 202–224; Phillips, *Boiling Point*, pp. 32–57, 85–128; and idem, *The Politics of Rich and Poor* (New York: Random House, 1990), pp. 52–153.

31. Aristotle, *The Politics*, trans. and ed. Ernest Barker, book 4, chap. 11 (1295b) (London: Oxford University Press, 1946), pp. 180–182; Rousseau, *On the Social Contract*, book 2, chap. 11, pp. 46–47.

32. Robert B. Reich, "The Revolt of the Anxious Class," Democratic Leadership Council, Washington, D.C., November 22, 1994; idem, "The Choice Ahead," National Press Club, Washington, D.C., January 5, 1995.

33. Idem, *The Work of Nations*, pp. 249–315.

34. Ibid., pp. 268–277.

35. On the formative role of parks and playgrounds in the Progressive era, see Paul Boyer, *Urban Masses and Moral Order in America, 1820–1920* (Cambridge, Mass.: Harvard University Press, 1978), pp. 233–251.

36. Reich, *The Work of Nations*, p. 269.

37. Louis Uchitelle, "Sharp Rise of Private Guard Jobs," *New York Times*, October 14, 1989, p. 33.

38. Elizabeth Rudolph, *Time*, November 4, 1991, p. 86. See also Mickey Kaus, *The End of Equality* (New York: Basic Books, 1992), p. 56.

39. Kaus, *The End of Equality*, pp. 18, 21–22, 96–100. A political theory based on restricting the sphere in which money matters is advanced by Michael Walzer, *Spheres of Justice* (New York: Basic Books, 1983). On class-mixing places, see Ray Oldenburg, *The Great Good Place* (New York: Paragon House, 1989).

40. See Neal R. Peirce and Carol F. Steinbach, *Corrective Capitalism: The Rise of America's Community Development Corporations* (New York: Ford Foundation, 1987); Mitchell Sviridoff, "The Seeds of Urban Revival," *The Public Interest*, Winter 1994, pp. 82–103; Robert Zdenek, "Community Development Corporations," in Severyn T. Bruyn and James Meehan, eds., *Beyond the Market and the State* (Philadelphia: Temple University Press, 1987), pp. 112–130.

41. Those who relate CDCs to democratic political economy include James Meehan, "Working toward Local Self-Reliance," in Bruyn and Meehan, *Beyond the Market*

and the State, pp. 131–151; Richard Schramm, "Local, Regional, and National Strategies," ibid., pp. 152–170; and Charles Derber, "Coming Glued: Communitarianism to the Rescue," *Tikkun*, 8 (July–August 1993), 95–99.

42. David Clark Scott, "Ready or Not, Here Comes Wal-Mart," *Christian Science Monitor*, September 29, 1994, p. 8.

43. Hugh Sidey, "The Two Sides of the Sam Walton Legacy," *Time*, April 20, 1992, pp. 50–52.

44. See Constance E. Beaumont, *How Superstore Sprawl Can Harm Communities* (Washington, D.C.: National Trust for Historic Preservation, 1994); Jon Bowermaster, "When Wal-Mart Comes to Town," *New York Times Magazine*, April 2, 1989; Alan Ehrenhalt, "Up Against the Wal-Mart," *Governing*, September 1992, pp. 6–7.

45. Alex Achimore, "Putting the Community Back into Community Retail," *Urban Land*, August 1993, p. 34, quoted in Beaumont, *Superstore Sprawl*, p. 11.

46. See Steve Bishop, "Death of a Town," *Dallas Morning News*, January 26, 1992, p. 4J; Lisa Belkin, "Wal-Mart Is Closing, and Texas Town Reels," *New York Times*, December 14, 1990; Peter T. Kilborn, "When Wal-Mart Pulls Out, What's Left?" *New York Times*, March 5, 1995, pp. F1, F6.

47. Caroline L. Cole, "Greenfield Rejects Offer by Wal-Mart," *Boston Globe*, October 20, 1993, p. 45; "In Two Towns, Main Street Fights Off Wal-Mart," *New York Times*, October 21, 1993, p. A16; Sophronia Scott Gregory, "They're Up Against the Wal," *Time*, November 1, 1993, p. 56.

48. Al Norman, quoted in Andrew Friedman, "Citizens Fight Wal-Mart Sprawl," *Neighborhood Works*, October/November 1994, p. 10. See Chris Reidy, "Crusade of the 'Sprawl-buster,'" *Boston Globe*, July 7, 1994, p. 37; Joseph Pereira and Bob Ortega, "Once Easily Turned Away by Local Foes, Wal-Mart Gets Tough in New England," *Wall Street Journal*, September 7, 1994, p. B1; Jonathan Walters, "National 'Sprawl Busters' Coalition Emerges," *Historic Preservation News*, December 1994/January 1995, pp. 10–12; Jonathan Walters, "Taming the Mega-Store Monster," *Governing*, January 1995, pp. 27–33.

49. The primary texts of the New Urbanism are Peter Katz, ed., *The New Urbanism: Toward an Architecture of Community* (New York: McGraw-Hill, 1994); and Peter Calthorpe, *The Next American Metropolis: Ecology, Community, and the American Dream* (New York: Princeton Architectural Press, 1993). I am grateful to Gerald Frug for bringing these works to my attention. The movement is also described in "The New Urbanism Takes Hold," *Utne Reader*, May/June 1994, pp. 28–30.

50. Todd W. Bressi, "Planning the American Dream," in Katz, *The New Urbanism*, p. xxx; Peter Calthorpe, "The Region," ibid., p. xi. On gated communities, see Calthorpe, *The Next American Metropolis*, p. 37; and Timothy Egan, "Many Seek Security in Private Communities," *New York Times*, September 3, 1995, pp. 1, 22.

51. Quotations are from Calthorpe, *The Next American Metropolis*, pp. 17, 23; see also Bressi, "Planning the American Dream," p. xxxii; and Andres Duany and Elizabeth Plater-Zyberk, "The Neighborhood, the District and the Corridor," in Katz, *The New Urbanism*, pp. xvii–xx. For descriptions and photographs of Seaside and Laguna West, see ibid., pp. 2–29.

52. Harry C. Boyte, *Common Wealth: A Return to Citizen Politics* (New York: Free Press, 1989), pp. 49–61, 81–86; Ernesto Cortes, Jr., "Reweaving the Fabric: The Iron Rule and the IAF Strategy for Power and Politics," in Henry G. Cisneros, ed., *Interwoven Destinies: Cities and the Nation* (New York: W. W. Norton, 1993), p. 303.

53. Boyte, *Common Wealth*, pp. 87–99; Mark R. Warren, "Social Capital and Community Empowerment: Religion and Political Organization in the Texas Industrial Areas Foundation" (Ph.D. diss., Harvard University, 1995), chap. 2; Geoffrey Rips, "A Democratic Conversation," *Texas Observer*, November 22, 1990, pp. 4–5; Mary Beth Rogers, "Gospel Values and Secular Politics," ibid., pp. 6–8.

54. COPS organizer Christine Stephens, quoted in Boyte, *Common Wealth*, p. 90.

55. Peter Applebome, "Changing Texas Politics at Its Roots," *New York Times*, May 31, 1988; Laurie Goodstein, "Harnessing the Force of Faith," *Washington Post*, February 6, 1994, pp. B1, B4; Boyte, *Common Wealth*, pp. 90–94, 191.

56. Shirley Williams, "Sovereignty and Accountability in the European Community," in Robert O. Keohane and Stanley Hoffman, eds., *The New European Community* (Boulder: Westview Press, 1991), pp. 155–176; Vaclav Havel, Address to the General Assembly of the Council on Europe, Vienna, October 9, 1993, trans. Paul Wilson, *New York Review of Books*, 40 (November 18, 1993), p. 3.

57. Jane Addams, *Democracy and Social Ethics* (New York: Macmillan, 1907), pp. 210–211.

58. Herbert Croly, *The Promise of American Life* (1909; reprint, Indianapolis: Bobbs-Merrill, 1965), pp. 271–273.

59. *Our Global Neighborhood: The Report of the Commission on Global Governance* (New York: Oxford University Press, 1995), pp. 154, 257, 303–304, 5, 46–49, 336.

60. Richard Falk, "The Making of Global Citizenship," in Jeremy Brecher, John Brown Childs, and Jill Cutler, eds., *Global Visions: Beyond the New World Order* (Boston: South End Press, 1993), pp. 39–50; Martha Nussbaum, "Patriotism and Cosmopolitanism," *Boston Review*, October/November 1994, p. 3.

61. Montesquieu, *Mes pensées*, in *Oeuvres complètes*, ed. Roger Chaillois (Paris: Gallimard, 1949), nos. 10, 11, pp. 980–981.

62. Ibid., no. 604, pp. 1129–30.

63. Johann Gottfried Herder, *Ideas for a Philosophy of the History of Mankind* (1791), in *J. G. Herder on Social and Political Culture*, trans. and ed. F. M. Bernard (Cambridge: Cambridge University Press, 1969), p. 309; Charles Dickens, *Bleak House* (1853) (Oxford: Oxford University Press, 1987), chap. 4, p. 36.

64. Tocqueville, *Democracy in America*, vol. 1, chap. 5, p. 68.

65. Thomas Jefferson to Samuel Kercheval, July 12, 1816, in *Jefferson Writings*, ed. Merrill D. Peterson (New York: Library of America, 1984), pp. 1399–1400.

66. See Richard H. King, *Civil Rights and the Idea of Freedom* (New York: Oxford University Press, 1992).

67. Martin Luther King Jr., *Where Do We Go from Here: Chaos or Community?* (1967), reprinted in *A Testament of Hope: The Essential Writings and Speeches of Martin Luther King Jr.*, ed. James M. Washington (New York: HarperCollins, 1986), pp. 566–567.

68. See Aldon D. Morris, *The Origins of the Civil Rights Movement* (New York: Free Press, 1984).
69. King, *Where Do We Go from Here?* p. 611.
70. The quoted phrases are from Patrick J. Buchanan, Speech to Republican National Convention, August 12, 1992, and from Buchanan as quoted in Richard L. Berke, "A Conservative Sure His Time Has Come," *New York Times,* May 30, 1995, p. A1.

Index